"Fascinating and deeply disturbing. This amusing and colorful tour.... uses the predicament of the homosexual minority to demonstrate what is very wrong with the social health of this country."

—CHRISTOPHER ISHERWOOD

"Commands attention and respect.... Mr. White doesn't so much evoke the people he talks to as he dismantles them down to their cogs and springs."

—JOHN LEONARD, *New York Times*

"Consistently entertaining and often funny.... His novelistic gifts—curiosity about character, an alert ear and eye for revelatory detail—make this book absorbing."

—WALTER CLEMONS, *Newsweek*

"Acute writing from the finest stylist working in candidly gay prose.... It can be read, much as Christopher Isherwood's *Berlin Stories,* for its fidelity to history, to experience, to craft."

—RICHARD GOLDSTEIN, *Village Voice*

STATES OF DESIRE

STATES OF DESIRE

Travels in Gay America

Edmund White

A Dutton **Obelisk** Paperback

E.P. DUTTON, INC. · NEW YORK

This paperback edition first published by E.P. Dutton in 1983.

Four chapters of this book have appeared in a different form in
Christopher Street.

Published in the United States by E.P. Dutton, Inc.,
2 Park Avenue, New York, N.Y. 10016

Library of Congress Catalog Card Number: 83-70881

ISBN: 0-525-48223-7

Published simultaneously in Canada by
Clarke, Irwin & Company
Limited, Toronto and Vancouver

10 9 8 7 6 5 4 3 2

To Patrick Merla

Contents

Contents

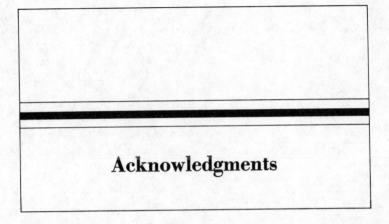

Acknowledgments

Charles Ortleb, Publisher and Editor-in-Chief of *Christopher Street,* originally suggested the idea of this book to me and guided four chapters of the manuscript through publication in his magazine. I am grateful to him for his advice and encouragement as well as the inspiration to do the book.

Bill Whitehead, my editor at Dutton, has also lavished his intelligence and careful attention on this book; he has been of especial help in preparing the final manuscript.

Christopher Cox provided endless hours of moral support and critical acuity during the writing of this book. He has been over every word of the text several times. David Kalstone has also given me the benefit of his thoughtful reactions and friendship.

Old friends in New York and new friends in the cities I visited shared their lives with me and put me in touch with still other people. Their openness and generosity helped me all along the way. Without that help this book would never have been written.

I quickly learned how hospitable gays everywhere are to each other; the warmth and candor with which I was received bear witness to that kindness.

INTRODUCTION
to the Obelisk Edition

by Edmund White

Just four years have gone by since I finished this book, but an indication of how fast gay life changes in America is that these pages have already resolved themselves into a picture of another era—the seventies. A few of the places and many of the prices mentioned here have changed, but because this is a portrait of that era, I have made no attempt to update the information or observations that follow.

The beaming, bearded self-confidence of the gay men I write about, their insularity and hedonism and materialism, already seem quaint. Given our taste for instant nostalgia, surely there should be some takers even for the seventies, that humiliated decade. Remember Ford? Vitamins? The Shah? *A Chorus Line*?

Remember gay liberation? Well, yes, since it's still with us, though in new, unexpected, sometimes attenuated forms.

The other night I had dinner with a seventeen-year-old printmaker from Brooklyn who was sporting a Mohawk haircut, a big silver bracelet on his hairless, muscular arm (high school wrestler), a few dyed feathers pierced through an earlobe, a not quite convincing Native American pedigree, a regional accent but

an outlook that was at least national in scope. He reminded me
that he had been three years old at the time of the Stonewall
Uprising. And all evening long he kept referring to "gays" with
particular contempt. I finally figured out he didn't object to gay
sex but to gay identity, though he disdained its sartorial more than
its political consequences.

He could afford the luxury of such disdain, I suppose, since
he had grown up always knowing that there are lesbians and gay
men—he had seen them on the "Donahue Show" and as characters in Hollywood movies. When he'd come out to his violent,
beer-swilling, unemployed and resentful father, they'd gotten
into a fistfight, terrible curses were exchanged—and then things
had settled down: "I tell you, Howie, youse not bringin' none of
dem fruits here—"

"Dad . . ."

"Okay, but none of dem *gays* is prancing in here and don't you
go axing dem neither."

The word *gay*, the simple word, chosen by homosexuals as a
name for themselves, has already created an ecological niche in
which we can feed and mate relatively free of predators. My
young friend at dinner could dismiss gay liberation precisely
because he was so indebted to it.

Curiously enough, gay identity, once secured, is now endan-
gered by two perils, one tragic, the other theoretical, and possibly
benign.

The tragic peril is AIDS (Acquired Immune Deficiency Syn-
drome), which first became a recognized problem in 1981 and
which had stricken 1,300 Americans by the middle of 1983. A
breakdown in the body's ability to fight off diseases, AIDS has
affected homosexual men more than any other segment of the
population (some 72 percent of all cases as of mid-1983). A large
proportion of AIDS victims die from such opportunistic diseases
as Kaposi's sarcoma and *Pneumocystis carinii* pneumonia. No one
knows what causes AIDS, but the prevailing theory is that it can be
transmitted through intimate sexual contact.

Sexual promiscuity, or at least the possibility of sexual adventure, has for a long time now been the essential glue holding the
urban gay ghetto together. The bars, the baths, the discos are all
sites for cruising. Whereas lesbians have united over feminist

issues—economic, legal, and sociological—gay men have had few ideological banners everyone was willing to march under other than the oriflamme of sexual freedom.

Now, suddenly, sexual freedom is threatened not so much from without (by Christian fundamentalists or the cops or local politicians) as from within. A mysterious plague has taken the gaiety out of gay sex and turned gay New York and San Francisco into wards for the terminally ill. People joke grimly and say our first gay senator should be a mortician. At every dinner with friends I wonder how long it will be before "the Subject" will come up—will we make it to the salad? The sale of pornography has soared; attendance at the baths has sunk. Guys at my gym tell me they've become chaste (why are they still working out so maniacally, I wonder). Like the narrators who trade stories in the *Decameron*, we are all sitting out the plague and remembering the amorous adventures of the past. Three of my friends have died and two more are in mortal danger.

Those guys who are still sleeping around have one prophylactic theory or another: stick with straight men at the dirty movie shows; stick with hustlers, since they save it for older men, their johns, a low-risk group; sleep with older men; pounce on anyone from the sticks the second he hits town; use a rubber; just get sucked off; get married; move to Australia.

Perhaps the new sexual abstinence will lead to new forms of gay life. Now time is available (indeed is required) to elaborate the arts of courtship. The tension that has been lacking in gay love—the very lack that, according to such writers as C. A. Tripp and the great French thinker Michel Foucault, has led to the formation of agonistic pleasures such as gay S & M—may now be replaced by the more traditional anxieties and frustrations of courtship.

In a recent interview Foucault has observed that until now gay men have not developed courtship since sex has been so readily available. As he put it, "The homosexual imagination is for the most part concerned with reminiscing about the act rather than anticipating it." Instead of Casanova's "The best moment of love is when one is climbing the stairs," the homosexual lover might say, "The best moment of love is when the beloved leaves in the taxi." Of course it is always debatable whether anticipation—the great moment of heterosexual desire—is superior to recollection.

In the last chapter of this book I proposed that there are two styles of gay politics: the moderate, pragmatic Washington style, which is turning lesbians and gay men into a powerful coalition that delivers a bloc vote in urban campaigns and backs a lobbyist in Congress and that seeks to bring gays into the mainstream of American life; and the more theoretical Boston style, which questions the value of American life itself and casts gays into the role of radical reformers. The advent of the AIDS epidemic, so practical a problem by its very nature—and so in need of all the resources of the established system—has favored the development across the country of the Washington style. For instance, the National Gay Men's Health Crisis has staged many impressive benefits to raise funds to finance medical research, to subsidize the health care costs of indigent gay men, and to disseminate health information in free booklets. Every step in this process has involved volunteers in the workaday machinery of fund raising, of forming medical review boards for evaluating research projects competing for funding, and of writing, publishing, and distributing AIDS literature.

This emphasis upon organization has come at the very moment when it was most needed to lend cohesion to a community robbed of its confidence and deprived of its great principle of integration: cruising. The infamous "irresponsibility" of gay life (its devotion to youth, pleasure, and beauty and its corresponding neglect of social continuity—its personal rather than its public values) may at last be giving way to a more conventional ethos. For instance, in the last year SAGE (Senior Action in a Gay Environment) has grown quickly. Its volunteers, many of them young men and women, are providing services (and society) to home-bound older people; the organization also holds monthly dinner dances and more frequent discussion groups for older lesbians and gay men. Here at last the age taboo, so terrifying to Americans, is being lifted by means of an equally American institution, the self-help group.

But if the Washington style of gay politics is prevailing, the so-called Boston style is still influencing gay theory. To be sure, some of the most influential voices have been accented—I'm referring to the Englishman Jeffrey Weeks, the Australian Dennis Altman and Michel Foucault. But American writers and academics have been quick to develop their ideas, and in John Boswell the United States has found a magisterial gay historian.

At the beginning of this introduction I mentioned that gay identity is imperiled not only by AIDS but also by possibly benign theoretical developments. In the first ten years of gay liberation the best political strategy was to assume that lesbians and gay men constitute something very much like an ethnic minority; the model of black culture—with its suppressed history, its new pride, its distinctive modes of organization, its fight against the denigrating status conferred on it by the majority culture—was always in the background, although the women's movement also served as an inspiration, especially in its conviction that intimate experience is political, not psychological. But now, in the second decade of the gay movement, all of these notions are being revised.

Jeffrey Weeks has argued that any concept of sexuality is determined by the surrounding culture and that the homosexual today is entirely different from the homosexual of ancient Greece, for instance. Weeks has elaborated this point by stating that homosexuality has played an entirely different role in every culture in which it has appeared. Foucault has modified Weeks's position by insisting that we not assume that the role homosexuality plays is ever easily explained. Indeed, every form of sexuality, according to Foucault, is produced by the collision of contradictory forces rather than by the expression of any simple function.

In the New York chapter of this book I argued that I thought that gay men, who now seem to be immersed in eroticism, will eventually lead us to a proper sense of sex as a pleasure or a kind of communication, as opposed to the current doctrine of sex as transcendence, of sex as the ultimate meaning of experience. Too late for me to use at that time was the nearly simultaneous English publication of *Power/Knowledge: Selected Interviews & Other Writings,* by Michel Foucault, in which he points out: "Now there is a trait which is fundamental to the economy of pleasures as it functions in the West, namely that sex acts as a principle of measure and intelligibility. For millennia the tendency has been to give us to believe that in sex, secretly at least, there was to be found the law of all pleasure. . . . " After tracing this tendency to Stoicism, Foucault concludes: "It is this that makes us believe that we are 'liberating' ourselves when we 'decode' all pleasure in terms of a sex shorn at last of disguise, whereas one should aim instead at a desexualization, at a general economy of pleasure not based on sexual norms."

The current health crisis has made gay men wary of anonymous sexual activity at the very moment that, in giving us a more sophisticated phrasing of the concept of pleasure, social philosophers such as Foucault have led us to question the primacy of sexuality. Moreover, revisionist gay theoreticians have prompted us to regard "the homosexual" as a false unity (or to use Boswell's distinction, a "nominalist" fantasy rather than a "realist" entity). What this line of thinking suggests is that to fight for the rights of "the homosexual" is to struggle on behalf of a creature defined precisely so that he might be controlled. The paradox is that the only terms by which we can struggle for freedom are terms of servitude; after all, Victorian doctors first coined the very word *homosexuality* as a medical category, a "humane" stigma.

And yet . . . . There are many of us who define ourselves as "gay," meaning something more by the word than our sexual habits. In the last two years I've been asked at least ten times to participate in discussions of "the gay sensibility." Surely not everyone could be interested in such an abstruse esthetic matter; I take the interest to be a symptom of a deeper question about gay identity. Where does it reside? Does it characterize works of art created by all gay men? All lesbians? If so, how could one describe it?

My views on this subject are expressed in *States of Desire*. I mention it here only because I want to suggest that a shared gay artistic personality or taste is being searched out only because people are seeking a mystical, unifying gay identity. I would contend that that identity, that intersubjectivity, must be traced to the objective conditions of contemporary gay life. How do we live? What are the forces—economic, legal, political, institutional, cultural—that shape us?

A question that returns us to sex. For as Jeffrey Weeks argued in a recent essay, "Yes, gay and lesbian identities are historical products; they do indeed narrow our definitions as sexual beings; but they are simultaneously inevitable and at this period of time necessary. It is our sexuality that is contested, not the color of our hair. To build a political identity around this is therefore no mean feat. It is not simply imposed, it is developed, out of personal struggle and sacrifice, both in homosexual men and lesbians."

That struggle and sacrifice—as well as the jokes, the fads, the aspirations, the crises of confidence, the cruelty and the kindness —were dimensions of American gay life I tried to capture in this book by simply describing the people I met. Or perhaps I should say by playing their tunes on the pianoforte of my own mind and heart. If some notes jar or go flat or are simply mute, I beg the reader to remember I was playing on the only instrument at my disposal.

My hope is that the current health crisis and the philosophical quandary about gay identity will somehow lead to a more profound vision of community, one that will fulfill the prophecy Walt Whitman made in *Democratic Vistas*:

> Many will say it is a dream, and will not follow my inferences; but I confidently expect a time when there will be seen, running like a half-hid warp through all the myriad audible and visible wordly interests of America, threads of a manly friendship, fond and loving, pure and sweet, strong and life-long, carried to degrees hitherto unknown—not only giving tone to individual character, and making it unprecedentedly emotional, muscular, heroic, and refined, but having the deepest relations to general politics. I say democracy infers such loving comradeship, as its most inevitable twin or counterpart, without which it will be incomplete, in vain, and incapable of perpetuating itself.

Edmund White
New York City, 1983

STATES OF DESIRE

LOS ANGELES

A Haven for Hedonists

The almost Oriental politeness of the West Coast is one of its distinctive regional features, in marked contrast to the contentiousness of the East Coast. One may grumble at a television performer out West but never at someone appearing "live." So few human contacts in Los Angeles go unmediated by glass (either a TV screen or an automobile windshield), that the direct confrontation renders the participants docile, stunned, sweet. I once attended a California picnic where I drank too much white wine and expressed quite a few silly opinions, but throughout the afternoon everyone nodded and smiled. Only later did I hear that I had struck the group as certifiably mad.

The polite friendliness of Californians is an ambiguous quality. Within the first ten minutes a visitor is showered with affection and familiarity, but that may be as close as one is ever likely to get to someone out West. This openhanded but superficial civility, linked to an obdurate and profound reticence, is precisely the granite wedge that all those hostile forms of California therapy are trying to dynamite. There is, however, a great public if not personal benefit to be derived from uni-

1

form good manners. People are able to cooperate. They can accomplish things.

My introduction to Los Angeles came through several New Yorkers, and it was fascinating to see how well or how poorly they had adapted to their new culture. One of these was an off-off-Broadway actor, a familiar type in the Village but exotic enough in Dreamland, where the dreams are peaceful and predictable. He had managed to hunt down something that closely approximated a SoHo loft, though it was located in the old Central Casting Building, a 1920s confection decorated with the figure of Mercury holding a camera and Venus a script. It had no hot water and a toilet down the hall, where all the urinals were out of order. Bob (let's call him that) had pieced together a life in New York out of patches of unemployment, brief engagements as a zany at La Mama and a secretarial gig for a Famous Silent Star. But he had tired of his frantic existence, that special Manhattan bohemian confusion compounded from equal parts of poverty and delusions of grandeur, the joint dreams (or pipe dreams, if the drug of choice is hashish) of popular fame and esoteric prestige that materialize after dusk as the roaches swarm over the bed ticking and one throws aside *Back Stage* to don a moulting feather headdress and listen to a favorite old 78. "It was too much," Bob exclaimed, pushing back his long, blond hair, "I was going crazy, I had this whole crowd of friends under my spell, they thought I knew everything—*I* thought I knew everything—but it was all terribly superficial. I came to L.A. to cool off."

His tenement pallor is giving way to a tan. His monologue pauses occasionally now for reflection or even for listening, and he has discovered in California that politeness I have mentioned, which he mistakes for acceptance. "They're very eager to learn out here," he announces confidently. Learn *what*? About the fool Florence Foster Jenkins made of herself two decades ago? About the exquisite niceties Charles Ludlam has brought to the role of Camille? Or the perverse banalities of Andy Warhol, the man whose heart is as warm as a hanky soaked in ethyl chloride? The sad truth is that Los Angeles is not interested in the faded chic of the East Village.

Bob hasn't noticed. He's getting laid in L.A. more than

he ever did in New York. He doesn't own a car, so he hitchhikes everywhere and often meets interesting young men that way. One ride led to a two-day session in a remote and featureless suburb with someone who'd composed lots of pop songs—"all brilliant," as Bob declares. He promised to find the composer an agent and hinted mysteriously at his New York "connections." Like Becky Sharp, Bob has learned to live on nothing a year. People rent his loft for projects, friends supply him with wine and dope, an actress who works as a waitress in the coffee shop downstairs keeps him fed and she also calls his friends for him when he doesn't have a dime to put in the pay phone that hangs on a wall of his loft. Next door to him is a recording studio where aspiring musicians caterwaul and pluck electric guitars all night long and wander into Bob's for a chat or another glance at the bibelots and bits of drag that litter the large room.

From the window can be seen the brutal sun, like a 200-watt bulb frosted by the smog, and the ten-story-tall palms that line the avenues and that end in bottom-heavy, microcephalic fronds that resemble a poodle's head with its clipped forehead and shaggy jowls. Bob proudly asserts that within his loft the "energy" is as high as it ever was in New York, though once he hits the streets he "mellows out." He idolizes Kim Novak and is spending long hours coaching a Southern actress to speak like her. He says (preposterously), "I'm bisexual," and speaks to his puppy in the dowager accents of Ruth Draper. Or he sings recent hits in the thin-voiced, pseudo-operatic tones of Jeanette MacDonald. Though he wears a T-shirt saying, "I Miss New York," he doesn't.

Another New Yorker, an actor I'll call Kevin, was having a hard time in Los Angeles. The agents, scriptwriters and producers don't quite get him. He played a major role in a Broadway hit, one that moreover had intellectual pretensions, but this success doesn't translate into cinemese. "Do you have any *film* on you?" the casting directors want to know. Shy, reserved and a bit scholarly, Kevin has trouble radiating "personality" during an interview (no one in Hollywood gets a chance to audition, that is, to *act*; one must already *be* the part during a face-to-face meeting in an office). Worse, the personality he is (rather than the one he might but can't assume) somehow doesn't go with his looks. For he is the Perfect Golden Youth, the boy next door—if the neighborhood were paradise. Athletic, blond, blue-eyed, smily, he should be giving William Katt a run for his money—but then he starts speaking out of his incongruous New York sophistication, mentioning his friend, the avant-garde stage director, or describing his paintings, which are derived from those of Agnes Martin (in a town where the only Agnes was surnamed Moorehead). And he wears unironed, baggy clothes while other young actors are still sculpting their hair under blow-driers and pressing their jeans. In a city that calls filmmaking the "Business" or the "Industry," Kevin talks disconcertingly about "Art." He is a hard "type" to absorb, much less to hire. In Hollywood the typology is almost as rigid as the hierarchy, and the hierarchy is so clear that a few years ago, when Streisand became nervous after the Manson murders, an agent was able to tell her, "Don't worry, Barbra, they're not after Stars. They're only killing Featured Players."

Tennessee Williams has mentioned somewhere that actors have the hardest time coming out and are the most penalized when they do because a straight audience does not like to see homosexuals embodying its own fantasies; who wants to watch a fag kiss the girl? Hollywood remains' tightly closeted, though in many cases the closet is roomy enough to hold dozens of people. When Kevin arrived in Los Angeles two years ago his first agent told him flatly, "No bars, no baths, and always appear in public with a woman." As it happened, the last command was easy enough to obey, since Kevin was living with an old friend, an actress who resembles the young Elizabeth Taylor. But the other orders struck him as unrealistic, or at least insufferable. He's switched agents and lives as he likes, not wildly but also not hypocritically; only time will tell (or rather not tell, since oppression in the entertainment business is always silent) whether his candor has hurt his career.

No one in Hollywood quite knows what stance to take toward gays and gay life. The head of one major studio has nailed the door to his closet shut, turning it into a coffin. An article in *New West* highlighted the baby moguls of the business, a group of directors, producers and agents who were members of

SDS during college and who are now—how does the old, sardonic line go?—working from within the system. The article promised that these radicals would give a break to women and gays, yet an entertainment writer I interviewed told me that several of the people in the piece are in fact notorious homophobes, no surprise to anyone familiar with the leftists of the last decade. As for the filmmakers who've made it in this decade, most of them are either explicitly or tacitly anti-gay, unless we're to think that bar full of renegade rodents and seedy insects in *Star Wars* was a gay bar. If it was, as some people like to think, then we must ask whether parody is the same thing as acceptance.

So much for the younger leaders of the industry. The older ones, especially those who are gay, are intolerable. Two movie executives who've lived together for three decades still arrive at parties in separate cars, each with a date. And they still pretend that one is just renting the coach house on the other's estate, a source of great humor to their friends. An agent who's homosexual flips idly through the hundreds of pictures submitted to him by hopeful male actors and rejects dozens at a time, shouting, "Too faggy." In production conferences the coded way of saying an actor is gay is to murmur, "I'm afraid he won't bring enough masculinity to this role." For a gay writer the formula is, "He's good on character but weak on plot." Whereas the casting couch may still be an aid to some starlets' careers, for young gay actors it is more often a launching pad to oblivion. After a handsome man is bedded by every gay big-wig in town, he is rejected for jobs in favor of someone unquestionably straight.

Neither of Hollywood's two leading gay film projects of the last few years, *The Front Runner* and *Good Times/Bad Times*, has gotten off the ground. *The Front Runner* has been through several treatments, some by gay writers, others by straights, and in one version the coach and the athlete are seen soul-kissing in close-up (a gay version) and in the next they're seen in the distance woodenly clapping each other on the back (straight). At one point someone wanted to solve this ticklish problem by turning it into a heterosexual film. Paul Newman, who held the original option, has let it drop. And *Good Times/Bad Times*, though it's signed up an impressive roster of stars, has not yet found its financing, which is a little odd since the author, James Kirkwood, also wrote the eminently bankable *A Chorus Line*.

The issue is a serious one, for most Americans still absorb their values, and certainly their images of romance, from the movies. Yet the best Hollywood can do is to mate a lesbian and a gay man, or to sneak a few Sensitives—those Troubled Youths with inclinations toward ballet or suicide—into otherwise dreary features. A full-length portrait of homosexual characters would probably be just as unpleasantly Sensitive and would certainly be equally suicidal at the box office.

Given Hollywood's way of ignoring homosexuality, it came as a shock to discover that *Cruising* was being made as a major feature. When this film was being shot in Greenwich Village in the summer of 1979, thousands of gays protested a script in which violence and S&M are studied while more normal scenes of gay life are reputedly not represented.

What's needed are scripts that play gay couples off against straights, as in Harold Pinter's one-act play, *The Collection*, or as in that sophisticated Hellenic novelette, written at the time of Christ, in which the members of a straight couple and a gay are separated. Only after surviving shipwreck, kidnapping, slavery, hard labor and attempts on their lives and chastity, are all four reunited for a happy double wedding.

If I mention the film industry at such length I do so because it dominates the life of Los Angeles; every day you hear a movie or a movie star talked about. Presumably engineers at Boeing do not invariably read the trades or mail out their résumés, but everyone else in the city does. Los Angeles itself also offers constant reminders of movies. I recall one house with a picture window that automatically retracted into the ground and became a doorway to a balcony overlooking the city, approximately the same view that James Mason offers to Judy Garland when he tells her in *A Star is Born*, "All this is yours." To a New Yorker, the "this" seems unsatisfyingly squat and peaceful, as though a lover were offering one Riverdale rather than Manhattan.

I met only one person who did not talk about the movies.

He is an old friend and a happily assimilated New Yorker (I'll call him Fred). He's not really a New Yorker, but rather a very rich Oklahoman who was educated in Boston, then lived in New York, later San Francisco, finally Los Angeles. Because he is very rich he can live anywhere, and I wanted to know why he had chosen Los Angeles. "The weather, I suppose," he said, indicating a sky so bright I was glad I didn't have to endure it every day, especially on days when I might be depressed. "And the garden." His hand swept through half a circle, taking in the hilly acre planted with camellias, azaleas, an avocado tree and a peach tree, the birds of paradise, the lemon tree and a patch of carnations frilled with white petals over red, can-can skirts kicked high to reveal naughty panties. "It's helped me unwind," he said, as generations of businessmen have said at the Moulin Rouge.

The one-story house was built in the 1940s as a sort of resistance to the sun, the *scuro* in the chiaroscuro of dramatic contrasts that Fred has recently bought but intends to neutralize. The solid walls will be replaced with glass, affording his spacious bedroom light and a view of the garden, which is sans pool. "That, too, will be remedied." His lane is too narrow and steep for the equipment needed to dig out a true pool; as a result, he'll flatten one hillock and float across it a six-foot-deep tank for paddling and an adjacent hot tub. While I sunned in a lawn chair Fred chatted with a salesman about hot tubs. The strapping young salesman—typically L.A. with his tan, burnished hair and diamond ring—proudly told us that he was "terribly aggressive." Only in America. When American firms run ads in Scandinavian newspapers seeking "aggressive" sales representatives, everyone laughs, since aggression there is regarded as bestial at best. This ambitious youth had brought along his girlfriend, presumably to protect his masculinity against Fred's blandishments, but when he caught the scent of Fred's millions (and a possible real estate project that made even my eyes bulge), he ignored her. After a bit, curiosity overcame languor and I, too, flipped through the colored brochure, astonished by the picture of two naked and bearded men grinning at two equally naked women, all four adults standing in swirling water up to their necks and crowded so close together in the cedar chamber they could effortlessly have exhaled marijuana smoke into each other's open mouths.

After the salesman, who promised to return soon, had gone, Fred told me that pools play a big part in Los Angeles gay life. "There's a party circuit here. You have to get on a list, and then you go to about three or four pool parties a weekend. There's always an orgy room; they'd *die* without an orgy room. The main criterion for being invited seems to be good looks and a modicum of money, or no money and fabulous looks. Some people spend days on end by the ·pool; there's a guy down the road who invented amyl nitrite or something and you can always find him lounging at poolside with six or seven marines. Staying on the lists for invitations is crucial; I've actually heard an irate queen threaten to excommunicate someone from her list. It's fun to use this campy talk with you. People out here don't go for it. They're terribly *real*. They're not the least bit witty, but then again they're not bitchy, either. No one talks about anything that might be troubling or sequential. No politics, no religion, nothing except drugs, tricks, cars. Drugs? Oh yes, but nothing like New York. People don't trip every weekend as they do on Fire Island."

The mention of New York brought up other comparisons. There's not the same urge in Los Angeles to go out every night for sex or dancing. During the week people stay home and watch TV or work on their houses. Their home improvement skills are often remarkable. Gay men do their own building, masonry, electrical wiring, plumbing. Nothing daunts them. "But mostly we just relax," Fred added. "We're very laid-back."

Everyone in Los Angeles will tell you he's laid-back. At first I took it as a rueful confession, an admission of regret, possibly an apology for tropical listlessness in the presence of the reputed dynamism of New York. It's true, Angeleans do complain about how hard it is to accomplish anything in their city. A host will say, "I just spent a typical L.A. day—I drove 150 miles assembling the twelve ingredients for supper." Or a long-time resident will exclaim, "So you want to write about L.A.? Just call it the *Mañana Mentality*." When I phoned a friend in L.A. from New York one morning, he said, "You sound wired. Have you already had six cups of coffee and a hundred cigarettes?" I said I had and asked if he was in a similar state. "No. Out here there's no reason to gear up. We're all laid-back."

Only after a few days in Los Angeles did I discover I'd been taken in by false advertising. Angeleans are as frantic as anyone. They work long hours for money and status, the twin gods of the city, and both gods smile with favor on the efforts of their devotees. Unlike San Francisco, with its dead-end economy and high rate of unemployment, Los Angeles is a boom town. Anyone who is reasonably talented, presentable and disciplined can make out in Los Angeles. Gay men there hold a wide range of jobs. They are technicians for the film industry, they are teachers, designers, waiters, hairdressers, lawyers, writers, and they are especially real estate brokers. People develop ulcers, suffer from hypertension, drug themselves into sleep, shake with job anxiety—and assure you they're laid-back. Whereas in New York you're obliged to tell friends you're overbooked even when you're idle, in Los Angeles you tell them you're relaxing by the pool even when you're huddled in your study over four phones and a desk loaded with contracts. Insouciance is a West Coast pose.

Many gay Angeleans leave town on weekends. A round-trip ticket to San Francisco is less than sixty dollars. Or they're off to Laguna, that hill town by the sea that looks like Positano but acts like the Pines. Or they go to Palm Springs in the desert. The wealthy travel to Santa Barbara, with its million-dollar estates (and gay hippie caretakers raising pet geese and overseeing things from the vantage of gardeners' lodges larger than most middle-class houses). In the winter skiers head north to Mammoth with its high mountains and excellent runs.

Since the week is devoted to work, Los Angeles does not have afternoon bars in the manner of San Francisco. The cruising that does get done is executed en route—which leads to the erotics of automobiles, the semiology of makes. The coupe, suggesting the intimacy of the couple, is naturally favored over the family nightmare implied by four doors. Since the car is experienced as an exact statement of personality, a clear projection of image, it must be clean, new, costly, ideal—or an impossible old wreck, which is read as no comment at all, a jammed signal, appropriate to kids who have just hit town (though even wrecks can emit faint messages, the hint of bravado in an ancient black Studebaker, say, if it is lined in red). The newest Mercedes 450-SL, though paradoxically as common in Los Angeles as the Ford in Waco, nevertheless stands for "exclusivity." Hicks (like me) at first assume that everyone driving this car must be rich. Only after a few days does one discover that most of the Mercedes are leased for $400 a month; a single man earning $20,000 a year can just afford it. Why not, since he spends most of his free time behind the wheel? The Seville is a cheaper version of the Mercedes, just as the $12,000 Corvette is the poor man's answer to the $25,000 Porsche. Whereas the Mercedes suggests what Oriental rugs, antiques, a Hampton summer share and an East Side address mean to New Yorkers, a Porsche might be twinned with spotlights trained on industrial carpet, a signed Mao poster, a ski house in Killington and a SoHo loft—the Porsche, that is, announces in conventional, even formulaic terms, "I am butch, an individualist and I like excitement (and I'm rich, of course)." The butchness is inferred from the difficulty of handling this powerful car; you must drive it, it won't drive you. The Alfa Romeo and the Datsun 280-Z are bright, snappy cars for gays, equivalent to a "cute" Greenwich Village walk-up outfitted with decorator pillows, plants on crates and a professional tape deck.

Convertibles of any sort are valued since they are so hard to come by (although there is one shop that will pry off the lid of your hardtop), and since they reveal to other drivers a few more inches of the owner's head and torso. The Volkswagen convertible is popular with those members of the pretty people set who wear Lacoste shirts and stand around demurely swaying (but not dancing) to the deafening disco music at Rascals on Santa Monica Boulevard and Robertson. The Fiat convertible suggests, "I am sporty, unpretentious and, above all, *relaxed*" (whenever people in L.A. describe themselves, nervously, in that fashion I'm reminded of Joe Brainard's title, "People of the World, Relax!").

The leather set drives pickup trucks and vans, which can be either big or little, old or new, without inflecting the basic signification. These vehicles recall blue-collar jobs and the male men who perform them; you can also have curbside sex in them and not need to walk more than forty paces away from the bar to do so. Jeeps—elaborately painted, crested by a golden eagle and lined with coordinated seats and wheel covers—also spell M-A-C-H-O, a condition that only gay men and a few suburban straights in Akron still aspire to.

The main gay neighborhoods are West Hollywood ("Boystown") and the Hollywood Hills ("the Swish Alps"), where even little houses are in such demand they're selling for $80,000. The "Sycamore Sissies" live in Spanish revival mansions along Sycamore Street—large cool chambers with tile floors and wrought-iron balconies overlooking tinkling fountains in shaded. patios; the rents there vary between $500 and $900. Silver Lake, where the rents are lower, is the leather and Western neighborhood. Las Feliz, with its 1920s mansions, is becoming the Beverly Hills for gays. The nearby gay beach community is Venice. But Angeleans can live anywhere; the car and the freeway made the idea of the neighborhood obsolete.

For cruising, gays go to Robertson Boulevard between Third Street and Beverly, especially the little park where bare-chested men sun or work out. The leather bars are all on Melrose as is Hardware, the boutique that carries not only the usual slave bracelets and athletic socks but also windbreakers and boxer swimsuits in semi-transparent, bruise-colored sleaze. The owners of Hardware invented the Guard douche ("Be prepared for anything . . . anywhere"). Griffith Park is cruisy, especially the footpaths near the Greek Theater. Hilldale Street is always busy. But Santa Monica Boulevard remains the Great Tan Way of cruising.

Let me take you on a tour of the city. First we'll have dinner at the Academy. The food is wretched but the decor is amusing, since all the waiters are dressed as cops and the *maître d'* as a police lieutenant. The menu gives the unspeakable dishes names such as the Plebe and the Cadet and in the john can be heard, as you placidly tinkle, a tape of a maniacal drill sergeant bawling out orders to hoarse, univocal troops. In the dim light over the tables you notice that a few of the customers are also dressed up as officers of the law. Although Angeleans do go in for leather, they much prefer the uniform scene. It was Bruno Bettelheim, I believe, who first described those concentration camp prisoners who avidly appropriated scraps of Nazi insignia and shouted commands at their fellow Jews. This strategy for survival, called identifying with the oppressor, perhaps explains how Patty Hearst became Tanya and later married her security guard. It may also account for the number of gays impersonating cops in a city with the most homophobic police force in the nation. The new police chief, I understand, is attempting to reeducate himself and his men; if the cops do shape up the fetish may wane. But for now, at least, groups of gay men continue to whisper about Florsheim Imperials in tones of awe. Or they tell you excitedly of the two dreamy cops who had been invited to give a slide lecture at their apartment building last night about ways of avoiding being raped; it was called "Lady, Beware" and the rapt audience was entirely male.

When Angeleans discuss the police I'm reminded of Jean Genet's coverage of the 1968 Democratic Convention in Chicago for *Esquire*. As a Leftist, Genet felt obliged to denounce the skull-cracking riot squads, but he couldn't help, at the same time, noticing the sadistic charm of those phallic billy clubs and powerful thighs straining against blue wool. . . . In the same vein, every gay man in Los Angeles has a horror story to tell about his run-in with the cops ("I was walking home late one night on Hollywood when these cops stopped me. They said, 'Hey, faggot, where are you going?' and I said, 'C'mon, man, don't call me names,' and they're out of that car and have me up against the wall, roughing me up and they book me on charges of lewd vagrancy or something"), but sometimes the story is followed by an unexpected, amorous sigh. ("I was in the clink a week and really fell for Officer Jones and I still send him notes on his birthday and Christmas. Oh, you should *see* him, these long lashes and a neck thicker than my waist.") Certainly the police do everything they can to harass gays. Everywhere in California people must by law carry identification papers, but only in Los Angeles do the cops insist that gay men produce them. Jaywalking is a five-dollar fine; parking beside

a red line is another offense, and both laws are rigorously up-
held, especially if the offender is in a gay neighborhood.

One policeman I know about *is* gay, and he and his lover
(not on the force) wear uniforms while having sex with each
other at home. More than elsewhere, in Los Angeles gay men
are entering occupations they consider hot, translating stoned
fantasies into sober realities. Some are telephone repairmen,
others install cable TV, still others work for Pacific Gas or drive
trucks. If you chat up that man with the tools dangling from
his utility belt, you may discover he has a doctorate in art history (though even in *that* field his imagination was already fertile, since he did his dissertation on Piero's *Flagellation*).

The ultimate cop trip I heard about happened sometime
before I arrived in Los Angeles, if indeed it happened at all.
It seems this young man deliberately sped down the freeway,
was pulled over by a handsome officer—and then suddenly took
off again. The cop pursued him, ordering him through a megaphone to stop. The runaway refused to slow down, and the cop
opened fire. The bullet found its mark and the car crashed.
When the wreckage was examined, it turned out the driver
had come a moment before the bullet entered his head. As the
person who told me this story said, "I don't see how anyone
still gets off on *civilian* sex."

Let's leave the Academy. If you want decent food, try
Lucy's El Adobe for Mexican food, or Ports or, if you want
haute cuisine, Ma Maison (which everyone in L.A. pronounces
"Mommy's Own").

Let's move on to a tour of the bars. Though it's only ten,
don't worry, we won't be too early. The bars close at two and
L.A. is an early-to-bed, early-to-rise sort of city.

Among the leather bars, the One Way is druggy, Griff's is
for older numbers, the Stud is good on Sunday afternoons. At
Larry's there is a ball and chain cast down on the bar, but it
seems no more authentic than a spinning wheel in a Williams-
burg eatery. In the back is a pool table where I chatted with a
painter who's teaching at a nearby junior college. Up front,
right beside the ball and chain, I met the young heir to a
pasta fortune who tells me he's toured Europe often but never

traveled in the States east of the Mississippi. Under a dim spot stands a tall, handsome blond in full leather; he's obviously aware of the exact nuances of his lighting. After a bit I overhear him say to a friend, "I met this tall, handsome blond in full leather. . . ."

My favorite tavern was the Detour, the easiest pickup place right now. It's a long, narrow room, the bar making it still narrower, and as you squeeze to the back you jostle past stoned smiles under ten-gallon hats that cast beguiling arcs of shadow over friendly eyes. Boots in pairs are suspended by their laces from the slats over the bar. In one corner hangs a glass ball in which the silhouette of a stagecoach slowly revolves. In the very back is a pool table. There is no room for playing a game since shirtless, sweating men, standing four deep, are boogying in place and sniffing poppers to the disco music.

Back on Santa Monica, across the street and two blocks down from Rascals, is the Blue Parrot. Here you can pick up the same beauties who snubbed you at Rascals earlier. But snubbing isn't all that fashionable in Los Angeles. People are friendly, and I doubt if the New York stare that says, "I despise you but I might condescend to fuck you," would go over very big out West. In L.A. there are no back rooms, the last resort in New York for those who spend all evening being overly fastidious but end up by being prodigally indiscriminate. And then, once you've driven forty miles to your suburban bungalow in L.A., you're quite definitively *alone* for the night as you listen to the dog barking down the street and look at the blue gloom emanating from your neighbor's tube. Better to have someone, anyone, by your side.

The great baths—and they are as great for the beauty of the clientele as for that of the setting—are the 8709 Club Baths. To get in you need I.D. (a driver's license or a passport) and the name and membership number of someone who has referred you. The first visit costs six dollars for a locker, four dollars afterward. The place is huge and seems still larger because it is mined with mirrors. L.A. has the most beautiful men in the world, and it is only appropriate that it should celebrate them with their multiplied images. I can still see one young man combing his hair under a blower and then shaking his head minutely from side to side so that the duck feathers might lie flat and overlap as *L'Uomo*—if not nature—intended. In his eyes were pinpoints of anxiety and across his brow one furrow of concentration, the fold in the taut silk.

These bodies are silken, tan, hairless. In each city we might say there is one body type, the Platonic form for that locality. In New York the body might be burly, Neapolitan hairy, bulbously muscular and less interesting from behind than in front. In San Francisco the body is trim, five-foot-ten, and the face wears a dark beard and mustache below warm brown eyes radiating good will. In L.A. the body is slender, the buttocks pneumatic with youth, a trail of gold dust shading the hollow just above the coccyx and between the pecs. Something fragile about the clavicle and tender about the nape causes the figure to oscillate between boyhood and maturity. The eyes are blue.

In one dark cul-de-sac I encountered someone who applied to my body hands and lips of such curious alertness that I led him by the hand back into the light and asked him why he was so feeling, so sensitive.

My question found a ready response. He told me about himself. "I'm from Genoa," he said, "by way of Buffalo. Now I'm out here, where I'm not very happy. You meet someone, you exchange numbers, but he never calls. And there are such distances here and no friendly little squares where people bump into their friends. I lived for a year just three blocks away from an old buddy I didn't know was out here—and I never saw him once. You don't bump into people in L.A. very easily."

So he's an Italian, I thought. That's why he's lonely for a piazza. Yet wasn't there something else about him he wasn't mentioning?

At last he explained. "I'm Catholic. See that man over there? He's a friend, a Dominican. I was very religious; I still am, but I can't stomach the Church as it is. So I just wander around. I'm a member of Dignity, the Catholic gay group. You'll think this is weird, but my way of worshiping God (I know this sounds heavy) is to come here and make love to as many men as possible. You see, I think God is in people."

Over the years how many intimate talks like this have I had at the baths? Straight people—and even gay men who should know better—shake their heads and make pronouncements about "anonymous sex," as though knowing a name promoted rather than defeated intimacy. As the Catholic confessor knows, anonymity is essential to telling the truth. To be stripped of your clothes (and, worse, in L.A., of your *car*) and to be sent out into a warm steamy room where no natural light ever enters, nothing but the regular heartbeat of disco—that is to return to a timeless, neutral but comforting infancy. There you have stepped out of your obligations to other people and the constraining fidelity to the person you have decided to be. There you can speak irresponsibly—that is, honestly—about things like God.

The nature of gay life is that it is philosophical. Like Nietzsche, though in a different sense, we could speak of the "gay science," that obligatory existentialism forced on people who must invent themselves. Most people's parents are heterosexual (so much for the role-model theory of sexual orientation), and everyone is raised to be straight. Once one discovers one is gay, one must choose everything, from how to walk, dress and talk to where to live, with whom and on what terms. The baths return us to that point of choice, "To the morning of starting out, that day so long ago," as a line by John Ashbery has it. There we curl up on a couch with a stranger and tell him everything.

Next door to the baths is the gymnasium where some of these slender but articulated bodies are created, for in gay life the body as well as the soul is elected. It is called The Bodyworks and bills itself as the "Nautilus Fitness Center." On the main floor are the Nautilus machines, as gleaming and forbidding as the blades of the Cuisinart. "We call this the assembly line," my guide informs me without a suggestion he's aware of the Chaplinesque overtones. "The client starts out at one end and works his way methodically to the other. He does only one exercise on each machine. At each position his card is checked and marked by one of the five instructors on the floor. He is then passed on to the next position. Never is a client left alone. We've learned that gay people hate to be alone, even for a moment. And they are willing to pay for service. We are very service-oriented. Another advantage is that the instructors keep everything moving; there is never a slow-down on the assembly line. A workout requires just twenty-five minutes, far shorter than the time needed for a session with conventional weights. When a client signs up with us, we measure his heartbeat, weight, dimensions and fat folds."

"His what?"

"The number of fat folds at his waist. We then set realistic goals for him, and if they're not achieved we guarantee him his money back. But there's no way the system can fail. If he's not making progress, we check his card and find out he hasn't come three times a week or hasn't increased his weights or reps. It's very scientific. After twenty-five minutes he leaves the assembly line and goes into the wet area."

I toured the wet area, where I observed two men lolling about in a huge Jacuzzi, looking as incongruous as if they had a passion flower behind each ear and were sipping pure alcohol out of a camellia—the embarrassed look of businessmen at Trader Vic's. I glanced at the spotless showers and cruisy locker room before returning to the assembly line, which was less ominous than it sounded. With the supergraphics on the wall, the five instructors just waiting to be discovered by a talent scout and the over-amplified disco, the Bodyworks joins science and art, an unexpected but happy marriage of C. P. Snow's two cultures. No wonder it costs $375 a year. To it can be attributed many of those trim physiques seen everywhere in L.A. As with cars, Angeleans have traded in the fuel-guzzling, overly massive bodies of yesteryear for the more practical, modern compact.

Gay men in Los Angeles have to be well built; they expect good mileage out of themselves and easy handling, and they usually get it. Never have I seen so many hustlers, both on the streets and off. All up and down Santa Monica Boulevard are bare-chested hitchhikers. I've been told you stop for them, arrange a price and conditions and swoop home with your rented booty, though *my* friends (as inept as I) ask them where they're headed and end up ferrying them all the way in silence to the hypothetical destination. Teenage male streetwalkers can be found on Main Street between Fourth and Sixth Streets; I saw quite a few all along Hollywood Boulevard. These are the tough blonds from Oklahoma, the kids with a few teeth knocked out and tattoos on their skinny but dangerous arms, the raisins —if not the grapes—of wrath.

For a glimpse of the kept boys, go to a restaurant, Numbers, on Sunset and Laurel Canyon Boulevards. There you see the big, rangy football players with beautiful manners nodding at their dinner partners, those purveyors of the latest gossip about digital computers or the petroleum industry. What's amazing is not that money can buy flesh but that it can purchase such angelic patience, since it must be less painful to score with these johns than listen to them. As the businessmen unroll their monologues (why do I think of player pianos?), waiters in numbered athletic jerseys float forward with ordinary if expensive dishes. At the door I overheard a fatherly man assure the delicate, dazed boy by his side that the boy was *not* too stoned to enter such a "fancy" place.

Keeping a young man is a more popular and less covert pastime in Los Angeles than anywhere else I've been, except perhaps Paris. A young man of twenty who had arrived in L.A. only a month before has already been offered a dozen situations. Wealthy men compete with one another for the privilege, no matter how short-lived, of supporting an attractive newcomer. I spoke to someone who moved out to Los Angeles in the mid-1960s before he had recognized his homosexuality. He must have been very handsome, for he was immediately placed under contract to a television production company and was deluged with more personal proposals from producers. This attention frightened him off; he dropped out of the entertainment business and became a CPA. With money from his GI Bill he bought a house, fixed it up and sold it for twice the purchase price.

He's now left accountancy and is working on his fifth house and installing and maintaining plants in clients' houses for decorators, one of those deluxe domestic services this city of rich homebodies thrives on. In the meanwhile he's become openly gay, but he never had a lover until last summer, when he met a Beautiful Boy in New York. The Boy returned to Los Angeles with him—and was instantly met by a big rush. At parties, right under his lover's nose, the Boy has received offers of everything from dinner or jewelry to plane trips to Egypt (accompanied, of course) or a ranch, deed and all. The Boy is susceptible to the very attentions that scared off his lover twelve years ago. Compared to the low-keyed pleasures of fixing up houses and puttering with plants, these offered splendors seem heady indeed. With the wisdom of a Colette, the older lover suggested the Beautiful Boy move out and experience things. The experiment has led to gratifying results; "We see more of each other than ever before," my informant told me. How much of a lark could that plane trip to Cairo be if it gives one time to hear four more tales of the petroleum industry?

I spent one evening and one long afternoon with a kept boy. In fact, he's no boy and I had trouble figuring out who was the kept and who the keeper, for there is little difference between the two in degree of desirability. The "boy," whom I'll call Eduardo, had been businesslike in setting his terms. He demanded weekly spending money, an additional drug allowance, a country place and a city place, and a revolving wardrobe. Right now Eduardo has adopted punk rock fashions and runs around in a black T-shirt on which "I Love Che" is written in what appears to be blood. At the country place there is no running water and every drop must be hauled in buckets up from a stream. Eduardo does not, mind you, help in the hauling, though he does take four showers a day. The lover, a successful cinematographer, suffers in silence. He puts up with Eduardo's moods and demands and sits wordlessly on the edge of the bed computing his quarterly taxes while Eduardo gets fisted by his latest find, a professor of homosexuality at a nearby university. "Now I have two daddies to buy me drugs," Eduardo exults, with the unbecoming greed of a Nana.

The custom of keeping boys may produce a spoiled sensualist but it more often launches a sturdy careerist. The keepers of today were the kept of yesteryear, and the gigolo of the Sixties has turned out to be the leading designer of the Seventies. I suppose buying a lover goes on everywhere, but only in Los Angeles is it so cheerfully and frankly acknowledged. In New York, for instance, Herbert the broker doesn't "keep" Tommy. No, he "helps" him get started as a jeweler in lucite—and we must all hear hours of how much they have in common, despite the forty-year difference in age. How salutory, by contrast, is the simple bartering in Los Angeles of youth for money, sex for status.

A less positive estimation of Los Angeles was delivered to me by a gay West Hollywood psychotherapist, who was kind enough to give me an hour of his time in his temporary office (the permanent one had just been blown away by a bomb hurled at a producer by a disappointed actor; one entire side of the building was demolished; I walked through rubble to reach the elevator). The therapist, serene despite this recent mishap, told me that cities can be seen at various stages of maturation. San Francisco, for instance, he judged to be in the early adulthood crisis, whereas Los Angeles is stuck in an adolescent phase. Gay men in Los Angeles, he said, run in teenage gangs of ten to twelve members, but these "friends" never share anything intimate with one another. Their true confidants are invariably outside the clique; within the circle everyone is too competitive to be open.

"The real problem here," he said, "is that smart people don't know each other. In a large nomadic population such as the gay group in this city, the rules must be kept very simple. In Los Angeles the one rule is sexual display and curiosity. Even the most brilliant man, once he is at a party, will succumb to the general vapidness. From nine to five these people are bright, clever, grownup, but after five they become emotional morons. At parties there are no serious conversations and little real warmth. People arrive an hour late (a sign of hostility) and leave saying it was a terrible bore. Of course they were disappointed; what they *needed* was companionship but what they thought they *wanted* was sexual adventure. I'm encouraging my clients to establish circles based on intelligence."

This smiling, quick-witted and well-read young therapist, who studied abroad but returned with genuine eagerness to Los Angeles, considers his charmed precinct of West Hollywood to be the most exciting place on earth. "There's an existentialist tang in the air here because we have so much freedom; the parameters are set by us alone. Gay men here are rich, powerful and intelligent, forming the most élite gay community in the United States. It's a city full of allure. The eyes! Everyone's a flirt! Of course it's all narcissism. Gay men seek in others what they lack themselves. Unlike heterosexual couples, gays share the same physical equipment and inevitably make comparisons. Even the most extraordinarily handsome men feel insecure—just part of the bottomless gay capacity for feeling rejected and unworthy. Narcissism is and will be the dominant problem here for years. I'm happy because I enjoy my work. Also because I recognize that I don't fit in, never will."

Pressed to characterize Los Angeles, the therapist told me he regarded it as a very middle-class city. ("Hygienic," one English writer concurred. "All those couples at Studio One arrive together and leave together. Sweet, really.") Cultural, racial, regional differences vanish here; there are no big parades for various nationalities. "Blacks in L.A. all want white lovers. So do Chicanos—I suppose it's just part of the desire to move up the ladder. The macho look (workshirts, workboots) took longer than elsewhere to catch on in L.A. Up till now people have wanted to be handsome in the classic mold—and of course they are. There's also a terrific pressure on people here to succeed, and to succeed early. In your twenties you're a maybe; in your thirties you're dismissed as a might-have-been. I have an unlisted number and take on patients only through referral. They're all in the professions."

He then returned to his pet theory of gay narcissism, and I lost interest. It is a word that baffles me. I never know what it means. The psychotherapist struck me as using the word to refer to a deep uncertainty about one's own physical appeal—precisely the opposite of the meaning of the myth, in which Narcissus tragically loved his own image (which, incidentally, he perceived as belonging to someone else since he did not understand the reflecting powers of water). Presumably *narcissism* could legitimately mean an unfulfilled longing for oneself (a condition I have never observed) or, metaphorically, it could mean a fatal attraction to someone who resembles oneself. But why fatal? I once met a pair of adolescent lovers who were identical twins. They appeared to enjoy perfect bodily and spiritual communication.

Perhaps the psychotherapist meant that today's gays belong to the "me" generation—but that generation also includes straights. *Narcissism* usually signifies little more than an "unhealthy" self-absorption. But then a disturbed gay (or straight, for that matter) who seeks out a therapist is bound to be more than usually self-absorbed. If that makes him narcissistic by definition, the word is tautological and a gratuitous insult. Unfortunately, it's an insult that has been hurled at gay men for decades because of our supposed fascination with our own looks. The desire to make a good appearance, of course, is typical of singles everywhere, whether straight or gay. Vanity, alas, is less characteristic of couples of either variety. Domestic bliss usually creates an eyesore.

The psychotherapist had his own complaints about L.A. gay couples. "Here people either trick or they get married. They know nothing about *romance*. I am teaching my clients how to be *romantic*; it's a great, if temporary, euphoria. Since Los Angeles is still in its adolescent phase these people are not ready for relationships. But *romance* is appropriate to adolescence, wouldn't you say?"

Kevin says most L.A.–New York conversations are dull because the people who have them would choose the same things in either city (drugs, baths, bars, discos, gyms). The styles of gay decor, he says, may be different but they are always comparable. In New York the stereo speakers are hidden behind ferns, in L.A. behind succulents. Sunlight in L.A. is a substitute for track lighting in New York. In New York everything is chromium and glass, in L.A. wicker and pottery. In New York the walls are gray with white woodwork and one sits on pillows; in L.A. the walls are pale green with salmon trim and the chairs are Mexican leather.

A few points of etiquette. When you're in L.A., don't gasp at the number of phones in a house ("Here's another one by the pool!"). Don't compare *anything* in Los Angeles to a David Hockney painting. Don't compare L.A. to New York, though you may compare it to San Francisco, so long as you prefer Los Angeles. Don't speculate on why there are so few legitimate theaters. Don't say, "Have a nice day," since the curse of Los Angeles is that everyone's always having one. Don't laugh at the absurd names and architecture of fast-food restaurants;

that's a form of East Coast wit that is at least fifty years old.

Angeleans are weary of such quips because they know their city is irretrievably ugly, yet they can do no more about the blight than the President about the economy. It is ugly. The streets seem to be on a Möbius strip that keeps returning you to the same sequence of dry cleaner, "adult" book store, dress shop, camera store and the shabby little buildings with grandiose names ("The Academy of Metaphysics" or "Dream Therapy Center—Don't waste one-third of your life asleep. Put those hours to work. Also Guided Daydreaming"). At first glance everything appears blandly and tragically new, though connoisseurs point out "historical" buildings, those revered landmarks of Zig-Zag Moderne, Hansel and Gretel ornament, Egyptian, Islamic or Mayan Revival, Regency, Streamline or WPA Moderne. Here and there are hints of poverty ("Dental Clinic—Credit Accepted—Pentathol [Sleep]"). And never have I seen so many furnished apartments for rent, usually by the week.

Only forty minutes from this urban squalor is a pristine world of sunstruck mountains and empty vistas—Topanga Canyon. At the community center there is a town bulletin board on which are posted notices. One notice offers the services of women willing to clean house, read poetry and make brownies. In another a woman, rather unpromisingly, invites seekers to her space for twenty dollars a day; "I give you nothing," she cheekily admits. "I give you yourselves." She does at least offer free juice and reminds us to bring along a "yoga mat." Yet another notice promises that several authorities, including Ashley Montagu and Karl Pribram, will discuss the "peak experiences" in their lives.

Kevin and I drove up winding roads past fields without crops or livestock until we climbed to the very top of a mountain and reached a 100-acre ranch. There we were greeted by our two hosts, handsome lovers, in their small house, which is decorated with an electric clock surrounded by neon swags and a nineteenth-century steam gauge uncovered in a basement back East; it glowed through its faceted red eye and blue eye. We were led down to the pool, which was as large as the house. There a cozy, sexy but somehow troubled—you could feel the trouble in his blurred social timing—Texan, swilling a beer, told us of good times during rodeos and the hunting season back home. In California he's also having fun. "I met this trucker at a rest stop. We got high together and just went up and down the freeway for days, stopping at honkytonks and a queer bar, the Starlight, where you see these big dumb ol' farm boys and sweet little sissies. That trucker and I just shouted over the tapes in his truck—I had a primal."

A big, friendly blowhard from Ohio, the sort of man in whom you can see the happily egotistical boy he must have been, seemed willing to discuss any subject. Each topic introduced by someone else presses a button for him and slides one of his tunes under the needle.

Kevin and I escape to a waterbed lying out on top of a pinnacle. There we gently slurp from side to side and free-associate. Soon the Texan and the blowhard and a nineteen-year-old school janitor join us. Someone mentions travel and the blowhard says, "I was on this plane flying from the Amazon with an exotic monkey I was sneaking out, and Paul Newman was right there beside me. His daughter fell in love with the monkey so I sold it to him for five hundred bucks." A joint is passed and our hosts join us. One of them tells me, casually, that he experienced rebirth in a hot tub with his straight brother. "We just kept leaping up and shouting, over and over."

From the waterbed, if propped up on a wobbly elbow, one can look down over fields of sage, buckwheat and goldenrod at the valley below. In the indecisiveness of this endlessly delayed evening, a few houselights flicker on—or are they windows catching the sunset? The thinnest voile of mist draws a scrim over the valley bottom. The sea, like God, is invisible, but the mist is its insubstantial, earthly envoy, its Ghost. Beyond everything the mountain ridges rise and fall behind each other, comprehensive medical charts, a blue EEG played off against a rose metabolic rate and a gray pulse. "One night," the blond host says, "we saw a *moon* rainbow. The mist had rolled in and the moonlight projected through it a faint arc on that hill over there. And there's a path we followed last week to a valley we never knew even existed. We found the remains of a hermit there."

While the light stays fluid, before it jells into darkness, we take a walk. Live oaks. Laurels. A tiger lily, wild orchids. Kevin recites James Merrill's "Days of 1964" through a megaphone. We step around three cars wrapped in muslin shrouds to keep the mice from chewing through the insulation on the wires. At the end of our path is a rope hung from the mythically distant top of a tree. Kevin swings out over a wide gulley and its thread-thick stream, shouting and twirling in the failing light.

After dark a producer of porno films leads us into the house and shows us one of his latest hits. The hero struts about wearing a hard hat (the only thing in the movie that is hard). Halfway through the film he mounts someone, performs pushups, then crawls down to his thighs, shakes the penis he finds there and frowns at it, at first as though it were a dangerous eel, then as though it were an unbreakable piggy bank. The suspicion dawns on me, then rises in full clarity, that the owner of this reluctant bank is sitting right beside me—none other than the nineteen-year-old school janitor. I hope his movie career prospers, since he was laid off at the school as a result of Proposition 13 budget cuts.

The film has its *longeurs* and I drift out to the lawn and chat with the sexy Texan. He tells me his lover just left him to return to a previous partner. "Tom was really broke, and his old lover came in one day while he was asleep and just *sifted* $15,000 in cash over him. No problem. I'll make some money and get him back—because" (here he stressed each word equally) "*I want it all*. Tom's bald with a tuft of hair here in front and a foot-long dick. He's from a rich family that disinherited him for being gay and he won't be happy till he's made his first million."

I think to myself, here's another voice moving on beside me, alternating between the smooth waters of ready-made phrases and the rapids of originality, a warm, masculine voice confiding its story to another stranger. We've rehearsed our stories with so many tricks, over drinks, on beaches, at home or on vacation.

Hedonism is the governing philosophy of gay Los Angeles. With the collapse of traditional values, hedonism seems as workable as any other available code. And, since Angeleans are so career-minded, their aspirations structure their love of pleasure into long-range hedonism, always more satisfying than the melancholy search for instant sensations. It is perhaps a New York trick of mind to *suspect* hedonism, to find the life of the body fatuous and materialism vapid. But what else is there worth working for? If we lived in a decent society, we might put off buying another Porsche until the multitudes were fed. Our energies would serve desperate needs and our resources would advance communal ambitions. In return we would be rewarded with an exhilarating sense of solidarity, the only state in which our ancient sentence of guilt would lighten. The family has died, and people such as Anita Bryant obstinately try to revive it by shouting themselves hoarse. The radiant community has not yet been born. In the meanwhile we make do. I see nothing inherently preferable—morally preferable—in wearing conservative tweeds to flapping about in a muu-muu from Ah Men. Nor is there anything better about writing books or attending concerts than lounging on waterbeds and splashing in pools. It's all dirty work in an economy built to be unfair. Paradoxically, the brewing storm of Eurocommunism is driving a new wave of immigrants, this time rich, to our shores. We are becoming the last Valhalla of greed, and until *Gotterdämmerung* we can expect this tiresome party to go on (I give it twenty years).

Hedonism embarrasses Americans. They feel they must transcend money and comfort and Help the Arts or Spread Knowledge or Do Good Works (given the rotten alternatives, good works may be the least reprehensible if still contaminated choice). At least the gay men of Los Angeles are looking after their own. The Gay Community Service Center has facilities for handling employment, health, psychotherapy, alcoholism, prison probation and parole, and so on. The center itself is a real, permanent *place*, an organization that owns its own facilities and building, a location politicians must visit if they are to solicit gay votes.

L.A. has the most active and civic-minded gay movement in the country. As the national center of glamour, it holds a benefit every few weeks, including star-studded banquets at the

Beverly Wilshire and $100-fashion shows in private houses. In New York rich gays chuckle at the whole dull, daffy, headache-making notion of gay politics (puh-*leeze* . . .) and respond only to class loyalties ("I'm sure Bryce and Beth *know*, but I'd sooner die than bring it out in the open; their parents lived next door to Mummy in Short Hills, did you know that?; I think you people make too much a fuss about sex; who *cares*, really, when you think about it, if you see what I mean; no need to be explicit, is there?"). In Los Angeles the rich, mostly self-made, have no such loyalties and bestow their wealth and prestige on the gay community. The rich are, of course, the only ones who can command respect from politicians, police chiefs, business leaders.

In L.A. many gay groups, supported by leading gay citizens, flourish, including the Municipal Election Committee of Los Angeles (which backs gay candidates), the gay rights chapter of the ACLU (which held a banquet for 1,200 at the Palladium, where Senator Alan Cranston spoke), Christopher Street West, gay athletic clubs (the gay baseball team has invited the cops to a game), gay student groups at the University of Southern California and the University of California in Los Angeles. The most charismatic gay leader is the Reverend Troy Perry, the one man who can reach all factions. He is the founder of the gay Metropolitan Community Church, one of the fastest growing denominations in the country.

Though most of the rich gays are active in the community, a few are not. For these men, the very atmosphere of fantasy that hangs over the city seems to permit them to indulge every caprice—and to justify the squandering of millions as a "camp." a "hoot," a hilarious "money trip." The alibi of unreality allows people to express their very real desires for conspicuous consumption, but whimsically; greed is passed off as a lark. Moreover, the consumer is in clover, since there is no Savonarola around to make him take stock, reconsider or regret, no one eager to burn his vanities.

One day Kevin and I called on a famous producer. He didn't answer the intercom beside the gates, those manifestations of paranoia I call "Manson Gates." Kevin, however, knew the secret of opening them and we drove up half a mile of newly

tarred drive past stockades restraining flowers and came upon
an English Tudor mansion that looked pure 1910 but was in
fact built recently. The doors were open. No one was around.
First we peeked into the new game room wing, where we saw
two pinball machines, human-sized fabric pencils, dolls, a stuffed
bird, a clown whose erect penis was the target for tossed rings
and, over the fireplace, a Pegasus in neon.

In the main house we moved through the tiled entrance
hall hung with Chinese brocades from the Ch'ing and entered
the dining room. The walls were padded with foam under
watered salmon silk; ten bucket chairs circled the table. In the
kitchen were two electric ovens and a refrigerator with an external tap for water and a chute for chipped ice. Next we came
upon a breakfast room where the table was a brass assayer's
scales (in this mode everything is really something else, a per-
version of function). A distorting globe of glass on the wall
held turbid ornamental fish and coral reefs; as a whiskered fish
swam toward us, it became as full-faced as an apoplectic. In the
"cathedral" living room stood a lustrous yellow and black art
deco lamp. There were colored pillows ("accents") arranged
acutely over the polysyllabic couches. Orchids and immense trees
rose out of woven Indian baskets. The sitting room was filled
with photographs of celebrities ranked on every table top. More
couches. More pillows.

Upstairs in the master bedroom the headboard was two
soaring church doors. On the night table were a stale popper
and a pocket mirror, one line of cocaine still uninhaled on the
silvered glass. From the bathroom built to resemble a green-
house could be seen the entire sweating, laboring city below.
Beside the Jacuzzi was a steam room for two. The walk-in closet
was a garden planted with row upon row of flowering shirts,
blooming slacks—oh, there was a system behind the horticulture.
He had simply bought ten of each item, one of every color.

But perhaps I've got it all wrong. Perhaps what I call
hedonism is in reality a covert spirituality, a luxury that paradoxically confirms a deeper austerity. In *A Single Man* one of
Isherwood's characters, a transplanted Englishman, speaks for
Americans when he declares, "We've reduced the things of the
material plane to mere symbolic conveniences. And why? Be-

cause that's the essential first step. Until the material plane has been defined and relegated to its proper place, the mind can't ever be truly free. . . . The Europeans hate us because we've retired to live inside our advertisements, like hermits going into caves to contemplate. We sleep in symbolic bedrooms, eat symbolic meals, are symbolically entertained—and that terrifies them, that fills them with fury and loathing because they can never understand it."

I suspect Isherwood's character may be right, all the more so about the rich gays of Southern California. Their houses—the lawn, the decor, the pool, the style of architecture, even the paintings of ancestors—have been ordered up on the phone from the Yellow Pages. Once installed, the "unit" is maintained in the desert by irrigation and air conditioning. Nothing is indigenous to the locale. This sudden, violent importation is the exact opposite of the European's patient *hoarding* of accumulated, inherited treasure. An Angelean will pay more for a copy of an antique than the antique itself because the act of replication is essential to his vision of life as transient, artificial and a bit droll. A Buddhist vision, really.

SAN FRANCISCO

Our Town

San Francisco is where gay fantasies come true, and the problem the city presents is whether, after all, we wanted these particular dreams to be fulfilled—or would we have preferred others? Did we know what price these dreams would exact? Did we anticipate the ways in which, vivid and continuous, they would unsuit us for the business of daily life? Or should our notion of daily life itself be transformed?

I lived in San Francisco for the last six months of 1972 in a jewel-box of a house on Russian Hill. It was, in fact, a tiny house behind a larger one, separated from it by a garden pendulous with fuchsia blossoms and resonant day and night with the sound of falling water. The living room, beige and gold, had for one wall a Chinese handscroll—or, to be more exact, a picture window looking out on the Bay and Alcatraz and up to Mount Tamalpais. San Francisco—or maybe it was the unhappy love affair that had begun in New York and was now unraveling in this new city—seemed melancholy to me, and every evening I found myself sitting before the huge window, watching the Bay fill up with fog, as I read Sung landscape poetry: "Don't ask who I am; the hill, the trees, the empty boat." Or these lines: "Great peace, though formless, here finds its form; solitary smoke curls upward; men live there."

I certainly wasn't happy. Although I was an editor of a magazine and had managed to bring along from New York as co-workers several friends and former lovers, I was drinking too much and smoking too much and the hills got harder and harder to climb. I abandoned my jewel-box and moved in for a few weeks with an ex who to this day looks like an English schoolboy and is now, as he was then, much given to Jungian ruminations on his own dreams. We would sleep, heavily if fitfully sedated on vodka stingers, on his Japanese *fou-ton*; I merely slept while he performed his serious dream-work. In the morning we'd open the curtain, look out at the mist and hear the foghorns. "Oh, no," we'd say and close the curtains. Then I moved out to an appealing hobbit-house in the Berkeley hills, the home of a professor at the University of California. I'd listen to his records of chamber music and read his collection of Renaissance mythographies and look at his engraving of Queen Victoria presiding over the opening of the Crystal Palace exhibition. A beautiful young heterosexual couple were courting me, but I was too depressed to respond even to this extraordinary chance; I felt more at ease with the hobbit-house and solitude and the Princess flower by the gate. My phone bills to New York were scandalous.

As for the famous gay life of the city, I sensed it rippling all around me, just beyond my reach. When my best friend flew out from New York to see for himself what was up with me, we took a leisurely drive down the coast to Carmel. On the way we stopped at a gay nude beach. The turnoff was unmarked, the road nothing but deeply rutted ground. An attendant showed us where to park, took our money and directed us to a narrow dirt path winding steeply down the cliff. When we had finally descended to the beach we strolled up and down, past naked men baking under the sun in airless moon craters hollowed out of the sand to escape the cool, constant traffic of the wind. We followed one naked pair over slippery rocks toward a cave; they kept looking back and smiling—but the tide was quickly rising and made pursuit impossible. That was an emblem for my stay in San Francisco: water boiling up to separate me from laughing, desirable men. I've almost never been able to get laid in the capital of gay life.

Of course I went about it all wrong, childishly longing for New York and its crowded, dirty streets, the theatricality of Sheridan Square, the sense that everything and everyone is about to break into headlines. Conversation, New York's biggest cottage industry, doesn't exist in San Francisco in the sense of sustained discourse and friendly contentiousness. Nor do San Franciscans approve of New Yorkers' obsession with career. Just before I left San Francisco someone drew me aside and said, "You know, you have a habit that's considered rude out here: you always ask people what they do. When they realize you don't mean what do they do in bed, or which drugs, they're offended."

"Why?" I asked. "Is it because they are all on welfare? Or overqualified for their jobs? It seems those people who are employed have a Ph.D. in Art History but work as stockboys in the supermarket."

"You *see!*" he exclaimed, offended himself by now. "We don't want to think in those clawing, grasping terms. Back East you have nothing but your careers to sustain you. And what do they get you? Debts, heart attacks, ulcers. We're engaged in something new: a true spiritual adventure, an expanding consciousness."

For the last fifteen years I've tried again and again to acknowledge the validity, or rather the superiority, of alternate kinds of culture—feminist, drug, drag, Esalen, estian—and the punishment for not bowing to these claims is to be labeled virilist, square, up-tight, homophobic, rational, or just foolish and blind. Since I like to think of myself as progressive politically and am, moreover, the first to admit the elitism and the arbitrariness behind the strictures of "high art" and "traditional values," I am susceptible to these charges. But I am still waiting for convincing art to be made by these factions. Until then I remain culturally conservative and socially radical—an excruciating position, I might add, and one quite opposed to the California impulse, which is for the most part politically confused though fascinated with every cultural innovation, especially if it can serve as a vehicle for "self-realization."

When I returned to San Francisco recently I rented a car and drove out to see David Goodstein, the publisher of *The Advocate*. His estate in Atherton is guarded by a high fence and an imposing gate. I rang the bell but received no response through the intercom. After I'd returned to my car to wait, I heard the distant crunch of wheels on gravel and observed the gate part—electronically activated by Goodstein in his approaching vehicle. I was waved into the compound toward automatically opening garage doors. As he later explained to me, 80 percent of the people on a list of planned assassinations drawn up by a California "liberation army" live in Atherton. "That's why we're all paranoid and live behind gates. I've also received a few death threats from liberation fairies."

Goodstein was not what I had expected: someone brash, large, egotistical, hyperventilating, a *Playboy* leveret on either arm, fiercely preaching lust and greed as he passed the bhang and expatiated on what's happening, baby, world-wise. I had heard rumors about his attempts to clean up the gay image by suppressing drag queens, leather queens, and other "freaks"; I knew he also was a disciple of Werner Erhard and had created a version of est for gays, the Advocate Experience.

But here before me was someone small, dark, quizzical, middle-aged, his body communicating pain in some way, an appealing, almost timorous boyishness in his eyes. If he was brash, it was only because he was so direct, a successful businessman used to making decisions and proceeding toward goals that seemed to him innately desirable. That this temperament is not suited to something as thorny, composite and mobile as gay politics (picture a traveling tumbleweed) should not expose him to scorn; perhaps only someone as idealistic as Dag Hammarskjöld and as passive as Freud could be a gay leader.

He asked me to swim with him in the nude in his large pool, heated to a sybaritic 75 degrees. The whole estate was empty except for us (a housekeeper had left a supper of several courses in the kitchen). In the lingering, late-evening light we dog-paddled about. David Goodstein told me I was a "fine figure of a man," and I was grateful for the compliment. Being back in San Francisco had made me feel undesirable and I needed a bit of admiration. No one surveyed us, for even the Greek statues on the lawn were housed in weatherproof sacks, like Christo-wrapped stiffs. I suppose they were under repair.

"I made a killing on Wall Street," Goodstein told me after the swim as we ate supper, "and then ran a gallery in New York. But one day Norton Simon came in and bought twelve paintings in one blow, leaving me with only a Manet, which is now in a museum. I had to close shop; I had nothing else to peddle. I came to San Francisco as the district manager of a firm. Though I was discreet, I did attend the opera with my lover of that time—and I was fired. That's when I decided to do something for gays and soon after bought *The Advocate*. Coming out—well, it's not a closet but a tunnel."

We were interrupted by a call from a trainer reporting that Goodstein's injured horse was suffering from bursitis and nothing more serious. As my host talked on the phone I inspected his riding trophies and his coat of arms with the motto *"Bono Vince Malum"*; that did seem to be his resolve—conquering evil with good.

After supper we sat in a formal living room under a huge canvas of tumbled Roman structures, Goodstein in jeans and a David Bowie T-shirt. Though he seemed perfectly content to remain where he was for hours, his body was by no means motionless. His hands described ideas in the air. His eyes flickered with bright fireworks of pride that then trailed off into dimming sparks of self-questioning. Goodstein is a man who, though small, suggests someone larger.

I asked him how he managed to live in such splendor. Though his paintings are old, the house is brand new. "Not by *The Advocate*, surely," he said. "Actually, I have the est attitude toward money: do what you really want to do and the money will come your way. I have an investment organization that I worked for last year only three days. I made two brilliant decisions, which funded all my other activities."

On the page such a remark smacks of braggadocio, but Goodstein has the successful executive's trick of making "funding" sound trivial, a mere matter of "implementation." This est casualness about money, I couldn't help thinking, works best for those already rich or soon to be so—or at least white, educated, male and well-connected. Corporate life trains its employees to be fearful and meek but rewards those who are, at strategic moments, frightening and strong. One function of est is to reinstate in the overly deferential some of the bluster of early capitalist inner-directness. Of course est insists its efficacy is not class-bound; it will be interesting to see how its current program of rehabilitating prisoners works. What sense will black prisoners, say, make of the injunction to take "responsibility" for their experience and to remember that they alone have created it? Est, like most self-help programs, regards the status quo as more or less immutable and the only change required (or possible) as individual; the only exception is the questionable est program to end hunger around the world. And yet, this "individual" approach in est is programmatic; whole groups are led through the same basic process, thereby losing the advantage of good therapy in matching particular insights to particular problems. Est, of course, maintains that all people are essentially alike, even mechanistic in their conformity—and indeed on the molar level of intimidation and submission people are, alas, all too similar, though on the molecular level of inner experience each is unique.

Gay liberation is struggling to understand homophobia as a political reality that serves a political function; analysis and action can, one hopes, modify both the reality and the function. Should we gays "take responsibility" for our oppression? Est would have us confront our fears, abandon our preconceived notions, "experience" rather than "understand" our degradation. ("Remember," Werner Erhard has said, "understanding is the booby prize.") But we *need* understanding that promotes political action as much as we need programming for personal success. Indeed, both should serve as aspects of the same process. What is uncovered in consciousness-raising sessions should lead to a political program, and the results of that program, ideally, would liberate homosexuals and heterosexuals alike. Feminists and gay liberationists are forging new links between public and private life intended to modify both. Businessmen like Goodstein (or Erhard) have been so triumphant within the system that they believe their successes can be emulated by everyone. Both these men are exceptionally intelligent and aggressive; a decent society should accommodate everyone, not just the exceptional. What's more, there are some of us who believe that a success within the system as it now stands can only be sterile.

None of my objections would mean much to Goodstein. He is retiring from direct editorial control of *The Advocate* and from gay politics, he told me, and devoting himself wholeheartedly to the Advocate Experience. In fact, when I saw him he was intending to give thirty hours of the upcoming weekend to a session. "First, a facilitator presents data. Then we stage some heavy confronts that blow the trainee away, then—" But I tuned out; as soon as such a program comes on my mental television, the screen turns to snow. "The best thing about the Advocate Experience for me," he said (suddenly the image is sharp with the return to the personal note), "is that I meet hundreds of people. I have found people don't know me well enough; otherwise I wouldn't have this fascist image." To intensify his own est training, Goodstein was about to attend a high-level six-day session with Erhard himself, who has become one of Goodstein's best friends. "It will be very rigorous, sometimes lasting twenty hours a day. I had to go through a complete physical and get a doctor's permission to attend. In this session, each of us must face the ultimate confront: our *act*."

"Oh?" I remarked, searching for something to say, "I've always felt the deepest thing is the surface—didn't Oscar Wilde say that in a witty way? Once when I was tripping I saw the most personal thing about me was my mannerisms, my ways of doing things."

Goodstein laughed pleasantly at the absurd suggestion. "No," he said, emphasizing his words as though they were about to be engraved in stone, "behind the act is the you that you fear, and behind *that* is the you that you are: pure love."

"Eh?"

"Absolutely. The inmost you is pure love. I'm really frightened and excited by this meeting."

I felt we were on the level of rhetoric where anything at

all could be said. Perhaps the inmost you is a banana. Or tolerance. Or hatred. Or a banana.

I asked Goodstein to give me his views on San Francisco.

"First of all, it's the city that works. New York no longer works; the social contract there has been broken. There are two large groups of gay men in San Francisco. One is composed primarily of men over thirty who have been here at least a decade. They serve on opera committees, work in the professions, show an interest and concern for the community. They're not so different from gays everywhere, though more of them here are out of the closet and they're better organized than in most places. We have some excellent gay business federations.

"Then, there's the other group, the Castro Street culture. It's essentially a refugee culture made up of gay men who, in a sense, are convalescing in the ghetto from all those damaging years in Podunk. If one's fortunate, after a while he emerges out of this group into the first one, though the leaders of the Castro group have been at it for eight to ten years—far too long.

"The Castro Street group is a really *rough* culture. Their relationships are brief, they don't work but live off welfare, they hang out like teenagers, they drink too much, they take too many drugs, they fuck day and night, they are scattered—and of course radical politically. They act like kids in a candy store. San Francisco has an unusually large educated white male population on relief. I oppose the gay obsession with sex. Most gay men have their lives led for them by their cocks. In return for ten minutes of pleasure they design the rest of the day."

The irony of the publisher of *The Advocate* (surely one of the nation's largest emporia for gay sex through its advertisements) denouncing promiscuity to a co-author of *The Joy of Gay Sex*—that irony was not wasted on me. "Hot, horny, hung stud . . ."—the words spelled themselves out before my imagination as on a ticker tape. I am, I must confess, suspicious of those who denounce others for having "too much" sex. At what point does a "healthy" amount become "too much"? There are, of course, those who suffer because their desire for sex has become compulsive; in their cases the drive (loneliness, guilt) is at fault, not the activity as such. Almost everyone is willing to draw the line somewhere—that is, will draw it for others. But why? When "morality" is discussed I invariably discover, half-way into the conversation, that what is meant are not the great ethical questions (how should we, say, adjudicate among the conflicting claims of family and friends, individuals and society, lust and love, art and politics) but rather the dreary business of sexual habit, which to my mind is an aesthetic rather than an ethical issue, a matter (so long as no one is hurt) of what gives pleasure rather than what is good or right. Few people today acknowledge that the sex drive varies from one individual to another and that what's too much for me may be too little for you. This biological variation we would ascribe to the psyche alone (which does, of course, play a part, though not necessarily the decisive one). Psychologists see sexual appetite as all mental, moralists see it as all moral, but it is, I believe, at least in part an inherited drive. The emotions that accompany sex are psychological, to be sure, but the drive may be biological.

"Now, I support the Castro group as refugees," Goodstein added, "though I do think able-bodied men should work. If a guy needs a year or two to become gay, to live out his fantasies, I'm all for it. After that I draw the line. But there are many things wrong with the Castro Street culture. Drugs and alcohol are huge problems for gays, yet Castro Street intensifies the problem. These men are also inconsiderate of one another; they don't blanch at knowingly infecting their partners with VD. And then they have a *shtetl* consciousness—you know, like the Jewish ghetto. They patronize Castro Street businesses; in fact, they seldom leave the area. It's like the man who went to the local Jewish tailor and later reported, 'You get a bad suit but lots of conversation.' "

Warming to his favorite theme, Goodstein spoke again about the Advocate Experience. "What I want to provide is a place where gays can meet each other in a nonsexual, non-competitive way. All we have now are bars for drinking, baths for sex, agencies for the poor, period. Gay experience is . . . scanty? I want to enrich it. I want to provide enlightenment, which means to make light of, to treat lightly. Werner speaks of the 'children of endarkenment,' the 'dark twins and their cousins: Grim, Careful, Significant and Serious.' " When Wer-

ner's name is mentioned, Goodstein goes all reverential. "Seriousness is a trap. Don't you agree? I'm trying to reach the gays
we don't ordinarily see. I'm convinced that 85 percent of the
gays in the United States lead very private lives, don't care
about the gay scene and go to bars no more than four times
a year. They're just like other suburban couples. *The Advocate*
is for middle-class readers—radicals don't read, they don't have
the time." I pictured all those suburbanites thumbing through
the ads for hustlers, lounging over the classifieds rather than the
comics on a long Sunday afternoon in Peoria. The fantasy of
the gay liberals (as opposed to the radicals) is that all homosexuals are basically the same as everyone else.

"I'm also trying to help gays free themselves of the damage
done by the four religions most oppressive to us: Jews, Catholics,
fundamentalists and Mormons. There is so much gay self-hatred.
I want to stage five or six happenings just to celebrate our own
aliveness and magnificence."

When I was with David Goodstein I liked him. I still remember our visit warmly. Part of the attraction, undoubtedly,
was our nude swim. That was a nice way to meet someone, to
shed the regalia of "casual" clothes (no clothes, of course, are
casual; they are so densely superscribed with messages it's a wonder the ink doesn't run when it rains). And part of the feeling
of friendliness was undoubtedly aroused by the wealth and good
taste his house so copiously displayed—like all socialists I overvalue the rich.

What's more, two of my friends have greatly benefited from
the Advocate Experience. One, a virtual recluse deeply unsure
of his physical and social appeal and inclined toward depression,
has made many friends through the sessions and has come to
take a much more charitable view of himself. Another, who previously could not grapple with his self-oppression as a gay, has
learned to accept and even to affirm his homosexuality. Less
personal or more openly political groups would not have reached
either of these men.

In retrospect, however, especially in the oddly lucid retrospection of writing, I find I question Goodstein's clinging to slogans, categories and lists. For language to stay honest it must
start from the beginning each time. Nothing can ever be fixed

in words—when it is, the fixative kills the butterfly and stills its
most distinctive characteristic, motion. As a writer I've cultivated an acute distrust of all words, not just catch phrases. I see
them as slender lianas that must be thrown across the chasm
between us again and again; they can bear the weight of meaning but not for long. They rot or they give way, for they are
living filaments. When someone resorts to ready-made expressions (and what does any cult consist of beside such expressions?)
I can hear the lines snapping and I'm seized by vertigo.

I spent the next day roaming about San Francisco with a
companion I'll call Buddy—precisely the sort of Castro Street
drifter Goodstein had denounced. It was a bright summer day;
if you touched a brass rail you were aware how hot the sun had
become, how much molten energy was stored up in the metal,
though the cool salt breeze disguised the heat and convinced
you that you were at sea, sailing. The whole city seemed excited,
astir, leaning into the wind and, if you closed your eyes, you
could almost hear the flapping of sails. That day it seemed
trumpets were always sounding just a block away—various beg-
gars and hippies tooting songs for their suppers. Or, in one
case, the toy trumpet was wielded by an amusing eccentric who
rose up out of the guts of a big box and tweeted a tune from
a stage no larger than a puppet theater: the automatic human
jukebox, a quarter a throw. As we hurried down steep streets
we passed minute gardens crowded with primroses and orange
California poppies before narrow, tall Victorian houses bristling
with gaily painted details—false gables, plaster or tin scrolls,
wrought-iron fences, rounded or squared-off bays, white trim on
gray, terra cotta on cream, blue on beige.

On the bus we sit next to a pack of loudmouthed nine-year-
old boys, one of whom shouts, "Bet you guys give each other
nice blow-jobs." Buddy, feeling no pain after the first two joints
of the morning, smiles sleepily and asks, "Where'd you learn to
talk like that?" The child instantly jabs a sharp little finger at a
laid-back young black man, his hair meticulously corn-rowed,
and pipes forth, "Our teacher taught us." The teacher scowls.
The whole giggling bratty troupe shouts and stomps off at the

next stop, still making indecent sounds with slurping fingers sliding into and out of dark red, rounded lips. "I'm not sure I'd raise my children in San Francisco," my friend murmurs. "They seem kind of precocious."

In New York and San Francisco, where gays are perceived as more a threat than in places where homosexuality is less visible, city kids and teens are often hostile to gays. Straight teens want many of the same things many gay adult men already have—glamorous cars, sporty clothes, memberships in the best discos, sexual license, lots of spending money, access to drugs. It's not that the kids want to be gay, far from it. Indeed, the kids are disturbed precisely because the gay way of life is too close to the one they'd like to lead. Heterosexual adults—married, a bit staid, not up on the latest fads—seem less attractive as models. Gay men are attractive in every area except the crucial one of sexual orientation; the conjunction of so many admirable attributes with a despised sexuality turns gays into natural targets for adolescent fag-baiting.

Three gay male tourists behind us start arguing: "Then *why*, Bobby, did you spend all your money the first day? I still have a hundred dollars left and I plan to have a very nice time." A smartly dressed lesbian, with telltale trimmed fingernails, balances from a strap with one hand and with the other holds a neatly folded gay newspaper. Two businessmen in dark suits, summerweight vests and rep ties, peer past over her shoulder to cruise us. But Buddy fancies the man in front of us—late thirties, hunky, in jeans, Italian T-shirt and carrying a Gucci briefcase. Buddy moves beside him, chats him up and returns with a phone number. "He's an accountant for some dirty magazine. We're going to get together this afternoon."

Next we're darting up and down the crowded smelly streets of Chinatown, past open-air greengrocers, the Chinese names of each vegetable boldly written on white cards in flowing black characters halfway between tidy seal script and elegantly illegible grass script. I glance into a basement through an open sidewalk door and see baby pigs hanging upside down from their trotters. We scurry up some dubious steps into a high, narrow room, a restaurant lit by buzzing neon tubes coldly reflected in the yellow formica tabletops. The waiter howls our order down a chute; within seconds the delicious, steaming dishes are cranked up from a subterranean kitchen I prefer not to imagine. My bill: $2.50; my friend's: $1.75. In a sidestreet shop a woman gently places before us blackened, glowing ginseng roots brought forth from a sandalwood box. She handles them as though they're jewels; indeed they are as expensive as some.

We catch a streetcar down to Fisherman's Wharf where crabs and loaves of sourdough bread are being hawked and overhear a conversation held by two passing gay men: "I'm dropping acid and seeing *Fantasia* on Saturday afternoon." "Oh, acid's all wrong; you see the flaws in the animation. Grass is much better"—this said with a connoisseur's firmness, as one might say, "But the Valpolicella will *swamp* the prosciutto."

At Ghiradelli Square more wildcat trumpets are on the loose, blaring faintly, violently in some other stone enclosure. Boutiques alternate with boutiques—sometimes, on my travels, I felt all America was nothing but shabby family neighborhoods surrounding nineteenth-century trolley depots, warehouses, canal-barge offices, all of which had been tarted up and relentlessly boutiqueified. If so, then San Francisco's Cannery and Ghiradelli Square provided the models for what is always termed the "urban renaissance." We wander into boutiques offering such items as beaded Victorian lampshades, needlepoint patterns showing the Porsche emblem, mylar balloons, the *Complete Jockstrap Book* (the "Disc Jockey" is an athletic supporter wearing headphones), flash cards to be held up in car-to-car cruising. Down the brick corridor could be heard an eagle-topped espresso machine hissing like an enraged goose. We stroll through the sideshows: a woman in a long dimity dress fiddling bluegrass tunes; another woman offering a long-stemmed white hash pipe ("Good for parties," she murmurs soothingly, "because it feels like a peace pipe"); a college-kid juggler tossing apples in the normal way—but then maniacally catching one apple in his teeth and eating it, bite by bite, toss by toss, until it's just a sopping core and his mouth is streaming with juice; a one-man jug band who, without aid, simultaneously pedals a cymbal, scrubs a washboard, beats a drum and blows through a harmonica held on a metal brace attached to his shoulders. Nearby a less ambitious girl liquidly trills on a water-filled blue plastic whistle shaped like a bird. Someone holds up crystals that fracture the sunlight into a million rainbow points.

We perch precariously on the side of a cable car teetering its way up a hill. The brakeman rings his bell, throws his weight onto the keel that sinks and freezes us in place, then he releases it and engages the humming cable coursing through its metal channel. Up, up we go. This rhythm—sliding stop, lurching start, gliding progress—soon becomes comfortable. We creep to the top of the hill, half of the passengers sober citizens going somewhere, the rest of us holiday makers who regard the city as an amusement park.

We hop off the car and after an endless walk find ourselves somehow at Cliff House, a complex of shops and restaurants overlooking rocks writhing with seals too distant to appear as the whiskered, frisky Edwardian rakes they in fact are; no, from here they look like the rock itself, flowing with a sort of queasy-making motion. From our window we look out at gulls in full flight and one blackbird huddling, ruffled, on the adjacent eave. We stare down at the waves and I think that if waves are horses, then the Pacific Coast is the finish line of God's Preakness. The afternoon fog is airbrushing out the line between the sea and the mountains.

Buddy tells me about all the jobs he's had. He is from a farm in Ohio, where his parents belong to the Church of Christ. He never mixed with other adolescents but just played with his five brothers and sisters. After college he worked for Vista in Arkansas as an arts-and-crafts counselor to poor rural people, many of them quite old; he was supposed to teach them how to make marketable handicrafts. Always moving around the country, he worked at different times as: a photographer; a jewelrymaker; a chef *au froid* in a French restaurant (he was confined to an icy, air-conditioned cistern in the basement where he prepared composed salads and cold fish courses); and an interpreter for the deaf in their dealings with doctors, lawyers and real estate agents (Buddy had learned sign language while in Arkansas). Through most of this period he was anxious and depressed, unable to come out. He had to eat six small meals a day, stick to a bland diet and consume quantities of Valium and antacid pills.

Now that he has overcome this anguish his stomach is good and he's designed an active, footloose life for himself. He spends the winter in Key West, the spring and summer in San Francisco, the fall in Dallas. He has a different lover and a different job in each city. In Key West he works as a gardener and houseboy, in San Francisco he's a laborer who restores old houses, and in Dallas he deals drugs. He is a slneder young man with a cap of black hair so shiny you can see the reflections of moving clouds in it. His teeth and complexion are faultless, and his eyes, black and sharp, suggest he harbors a secret that satisfies not only him immensely but might amuse you, too, if he were to confide it in you—if indeed he could articulate it. Someone later told me that I was making it all too complicated; the "secret" I detected was in fact an enormous penis, which indeed did amuse others and in which he did take an inordinate pride.

I watched a trick of his reproach him and attempt to make him feel guilty. It was all very professionally done, but Buddy didn't respond as intended. He grew silent, shrugged and left, still smiling, unperturbed. In sex, he tells me, he is a sadist; like most sadists he is gentle in his dealings with the world. Gentle and confident.

That night he took me to Coco Vega's Disco Birthday Party in the Haight-Ashbury neighborhood. It was held in a dilapidated store that now serves as a dance studio. In the window were two dolls, clever and accurate replicas of Tutankhamen and Bette Midler. ("To make the Bette doll," someone explains, "I just got high and played around with paste, paper, dirt and cigarettes.") The entire dismal room inside was lit by only one naked bulb in the ceiling. Many of the men were in drag, though the fashions were so bedraggled one would be reluctant to use such a glamorous word as *drag* to describe them. One male guest was done up as a 1960s "doll"—a mohair turtleneck sweater, long teased bubble-dome blond hair with a fringe of bangs in front, a black straight skirt over black slacks and black boots trimmed in dirty white fur. He was chewing gum and doing the Twist. The star of the party was Ambisextrous (listed in the phone book as Ambi). He was wearing a red bathing suit and a black bra over red tights, gold lamé spike heels, a diamond question-mark over the crotch, and butterfly glasses studded with rhinestones. His beard was outlined with a magic marker for emphasis. On me the effect was not one of sexual ambiguity but of conceal-ment—I wondered what he looked like under all that, just as I used to wonder what the clowns looked like under those melan-choly false noses and makeup. I suppose I was hypersensitive to the least hint of poverty and I imagined clowns could not be paid very much. A frail, malnourished, middle-aged man in baby clothes was not an appetizing picture. Ambi, running about in this dumpy "studio" and inviting people to admire his getup, seemed equally vulnerable.

Bums kept wandering in off the street; there was no one on the door. One bum was offering a few dresses for sale. Another one fell into a somnolent two-step with a compliant Ambi, who tried to imitate precisely his shuffle, empathy in the manner of the best psychiatric nurses. Coco Vega herself wore a body stock-ing and a long skirt and twirled by herself in bare feet, jingling her finger cymbals. A number of male and female belly dancers, indifferent to everyone, eyes lowered in a trance, gyrated grace-fully while a boa constrictor looped its way from body to hard, practiced, ageless body. Coco was running around when we left, shrieking, "Anybody got spare change for some *alcohol*?" Two punks, one with a red crewcut, the other with a green, rushed into the room and hurled themselves with all their might against two other dancers. Everyone ended up on the floor in a puddle, sick with laughter.

If this is one part of gay San Francisco, the broken sequined remnant of the Sixties, then another, more evident part could be seen later that night at any of the many discos: the young men with clipped mustaches and hair, tight-fitting button Levis, flannel shirts, workboots. Anne Hollander, in *Seeing Through Clothes*, has argued that we perceive the naked body through the medium of garments; clothes emphasize, eroticize, fetishize the vague animal reality underneath and mold our way of seeing it. If so, then the celebrated look of the so-called Castro Street Clone has created: a strongly marked mouth and swimming, soulful eyes (the effect of the mustache); a V-shaped torso by metonymy from the open V of the half-unbuttoned shirt above the sweaty chest; rounded buttocks squeezed in jeans, swelling out from the cinched-in waist, further emphasized by the charged erotic insignia of colored handkerchiefs and keys; a crotch instantly accessible through the buttons (bottom one already undone) and enlarged by being pressed, along with the scrotum, to one side; legs molded in perfect, powerful detail; the feet simplified, brutalized and magnified by the boots.

For gay men there are three erotic zones—mouth, penis and anus—and all three are vividly dramatized by this costume, the ass the most insistently so, since its status as an object of desire is historically the newest and therefore the most in need of redefinition. More recently still, the nipples have also been sensitized, indicated by the gold ring sunk through them. The exposed nape, neck and hands and the expressive face are the boyish, sensitive half of the body, its lyrical passage; it rests like a young prince on the bloodstained, barbaric throne of the lower half, which is impersonal, interchangeable, cruel, encased in impermeable denim. If this dichotomy is carried to extremes as I saw it done by one San Francisco leather man, then the torso will be expensively garbed in silk, a gold filament about the neck (the eccentric, the feminine, the smooth half), and the legs will be dressed in black leather chaps, the feet in engineer boots (the saturnine half, the nocturnal beast). Since the hand belongs to the torso but dangles below the waist into the dangerous zone of the crotch, it will mediate between both halves, a gold seal ring on one finger but a studded leather cock ring around the wrist. For outerwear the reigning fashion is the collarless green nylon jacket, an updated version of (or rather allusion to) the old high school letter jacket but without the embarrassment of nostalgia. More important, it is simple enough not to distract attention away from the sex machine below the waist.

If I describe this look with anthropological coolness, I do so in full recognition that it is only a costume, the one that "natural selection" has favored for cruising. It is an image of homosexual desire potent enough to have crowded out all others. I was interested to read recently that a group of gay Trotskyites in San Francisco has singled out this look for particular ridicule; apparently radicals have taken to jeering at clones even on Castro

Street itself. The action may be ill-advised; it seems to me that
we are still in a period when gay unanimity should be our goal.
But I can understand the animus, since the butch look so often
goes along with a whole world of part-time jobs, disco hopping
and drugs; the energy that might be released into political protest is now being tranquilized by literal and figurative opiates.
No one, however, should imagine that the men under the uniforms are interchangeable. They are sharply diverse and in one
sense the uniform may constitute their chief, perhaps sole badge
of "gay identity."

Just talk to any one of them for a while and you'll see
what I mean. My host lives just off Castro Street in what San
Franciscans call a "flat," by which they mean a floor-through
apartment with a private ground-floor entrance. We sat at his
old-fashioned kitchen table on a glassed-in sundeck tacked on to
the back of the house. The electrostatic air purifier in the bedroom kept popping like an angry parrot yanking with its beak
at the tines of its cage. Denton, as I'll call him, is thirty, tall and
muscular. He is alternately generous to a fault (an acquired
characteristic) and wary lest a guest get an extra, undeserved
helping of peas (an inherited, or at least childhood fear of being
deprived).

As it turns out, his childhood was unusually harsh. As a
little boy he lived on a farm in Louisiana, then in a small town
in Mississippi where his father ran a service station. His father
has always been the problem; a member of the John Birch Society, a supporter of George Wallace, a convinced Methodist, a
redneck he-man. As a child Denton was whipped once for referring to "doodoo," though his father swaggered about the house
blowing ripe farts and heehawing. "Daddy could leave the tub
dirty," Denton tells me, "but I had to polish it till it shone. He
could lounge about in his underwear, but I had to be impeccable, shirttail in, and any time he spoke to me if I forgot to
say 'Yes, sir' he slapped me in the face. My father is devoted to
sports and hunting; I infuriated him by my reading and listening to music. One of the books I read at an early age—somehow
I found it at the library—was about Hinduism. I remember
thinking, 'I don't know why I chose this incarnation.'"

Denton still seems underloved—somber, suspicious, afraid

that any pleasantry might be at his expense. He's not someone you can tease, and that lighthearted but rough badinage my New York friends and I indulge in had to be eliminated in deference to his feelings. Though he belongs to a gay discussion group and has a few friends, a representative picture of him would show him alone, wire-rimmed glasses glittering in the lamplight, sitting at the kitchen table working his way through clients' astrological charts. He moves with a rural slowness about the house, as though testing each room for danger before he enters it. Everything I'm saying he knows as well as I do, and he is engaged, as so many people in San Francisco seem to be, in self-improvement. He reads self-help books and tracts at the Jung, Krishnamurti, Gurdjieff end of the spectrum. He consults the stars for guidance and is exploring the levels of his present personality and the strata of his past lives.

Denton attended a Baptist college in the South, where he received a B.A. in psychology. To finance his education he won a scholarship and borrowed heavily. He then headed for New York, where he intended to work on a Ph.D. in clinical psychology, but after a few months in school he withdrew and became a salesman for a cosmetics firm. Within a few months he moved over to an $18,000-a-year job as an account executive. For three summers he held a share in a Fire Island Pines beach house. But gradually he became more and more withdrawn. "I felt like a warrior in New York; the city pits you against people who could be your friends. Everything there is competition, both social and sexual. I belonged to a clique in New York that was terribly driven, everything Gucci and chi-chi and 'How many drugs can you do.' Suddenly, one day, we all just stopped seeing one another. We needed more space. I stopped going out; I became a hermit."

And San Francisco?

"I came here last June on vacation and fell in love with a guy, just as my psychic had predicted. I thought there were so many pretty men here, and the countryside is so wonderful, much as it was back in Mississippi. I returned to New York reluctantly and sent out résumés to San Francisco firms. I landed a job here for $21,000 as a sales promotion manager. But the office politics were fierce and I was fired after a few weeks. I

then worked selling space for several gay publications, but that
was frustrating and paid very little. Next I went to an advertising company for $13,000—and got fired from that job, too. Now
I'm doing charts for money and just squeaking by. The job situation here is highly unstable, partly because there are so many
qualified gay people dying to live in San Francisco on any terms
at all. If a job might pay $35,000 in New York it would go for
$25,000 here. But then again, the quality of life here is much
higher and on $25,000 you could afford to buy your own house
and rent out part of it for extra income."

Denton is reserved at the beginning of any conversation,
eyes fixing you in search of the least sign of scorn or disapproval.
His wariness seems bred out of the deprivations of his upbring-
ing. I picture him coming home in the evening, preparing a
nourishing, solitary supper out of health foods, downing ten
different kinds of vitamin pills, lifting weights in his bedroom,
working on his charts, going to bed with an improving tract on
the soul or the stars. Between the mattress and the box spring
he's placed his pants, so that they will receive a free press for
the morrow. He refers to his sexual liaisons as "carnal," as opposed to his quite separate "spiritual" appetite. He perceives
a slow but steady progress in the world toward increasing spirituality. For me, since I don't believe in the spiritual realm at
all, these distinctions are difficult to fathom, but I suspect my
own (unexamined and indefensible) conviction that "we" are
inching toward political equality and sexual liberation is derived
from the very same Christian model of Paradise Regained. He
has retained the evolving spirituality of Christianity, though he
rejects Christ; I've translated the ideal of redemption into social
salvation. I'm sure neither one of us is less naïve than the other.

Returning to the subject of San Francisco, Denton tells me
in his low, measured voice, "One thing I like about this city is
that homosexuality is more open here than anywhere else. Even
in New York I had to stay closeted on the job. The San Francisco straight community accepts us more readily than elsewhere." In the week following the announcement of the Dan
White verdict for the murders of Mayor George Moscone and
Supervisor Harvey Milk, straights and gays angrily debated the
justice of White's short sentence. Arguments would break out on

buses or on street corners between straights and gays. Most San Franciscans, however, seemed to be appalled by the decision. Herb Caen, the most influential columnist in the city and a reliable index to public opinion, found the sentence far too light. Although anti-gay sentiment may reign in the Avenues, the middle-class area west of Twin Peaks, most of San Francisco is sympathetic toward homosexuality. But sometimes I wonder. A straight woman friend of mine told me that she had never heard more appalling fag jokes than among her heterosexual friends in San Francisco.

Denton went on, "The Mafia is not as strong here; it doesn't dominate the life of gay bars. People here are proud of their city, they don't want it to decay." This public spirit is certainly everywhere—convincing proof, if any was needed, that Freud was wrong in writing, "In the light of psychoanalysis we are accustomed to regard social feeling as a sublimation of homosexual attitudes toward objects." No city practices less sublimation of homosexuality than San Francisco, and none is more imbued with social feeling.

Denton delights in the macho men who live in the Castro area but frequent the leather bars on Folsom Street; he perceives them as people with good educations and good jobs who nevertheless enjoy "trashing around" at night. What he deplores are the flamboyant and antisocial elements, who give gay life a bad name. "Drag queens, freaks, offensive militants—they don't help at all. Nor do I approve when two men get on top of a building on Castro and start giving each other blow-jobs. That happened the other day." My response to Denton's remark is divided. Certainly he's right that in San Francisco, as nowhere else, gays constitute such a numerous and well-organized minority that the life of the city is to a remarkable degree within their power to shape. Figures indicate that at least 20 percent of San Francisco's 335,000 registered voters are gay. In other places gays have rightly assumed that society is their enemy, and they have adopted a duplicitous attitude of external conformism and selective, private, anarchic moments of rebellion. But here the society against which one might rebel is itself largely homosexual. This very success requires a shift of attitudes. Yet when Denton singled out drag queens and offensive militants as those who bring gay life a "bad name," my heart sank. Gay life, of course, *is* a bad name in the eyes of most heterosexuals, who do not stop to make distinctions among one sort of gay and another. For centuries we have all been perverts, deviants, sinners, degenerates—well, the litany is long, and it is recited over all our heads. Liberal apologists attempt to convince us and the heterosexual majority that "most" gays are just like normal people. We, too, have our homes, our cats and poodles (instead of children), our debts, our televisions, our impossible jobs and hypocritical marriages. The only real culprits (or so the argument goes) are those trouble-making radicals and those vile drag queens.

The scorn directed against drags is especially virulent; they have become the outcasts of gay life, the "queers" of homosexuality. In fact, they are classic scapegoats. Our old fears about our sissiness, still with us though masked by the new macho fascism, are now located, isolated, quarantined through our persecution of the transvestite. Just as many of us are willing to draw the line short of our own activity and decide what for others is "too much sex," in the same way we are ready to brand others as "too gay." Fear of transvestism is fear of homosexuality, and until we accept drag queens we have not accepted ourselves. Moreover, drag queens remain a true test case for the acceptance of gays by straights. When the women's movement decided to stick behind its lesbian faction, it made an astute move; feminists recognized that the worst thing a hostile man can call a liberated woman is a "dyke." Very well. Sensing that this "worst" thing is a condensed version of chauvinist antagonism, the women's movement wisely chose to endorse radical lesbians, to push them forward as heroines of the cause.

In the same way, gay men would be well advised to recognize that antipathy toward drag queens is in reality an aversion to us all. We lull ourselves into imagining that straight society accepts gay men who are "professional" or "masculine" or "respectable," but it is precisely bourgeois gays whom straight men regard as too close for comfort. Straights are amused by drag performers, but they are alarmed by more "normal"-seeming gays. Gay unanimity is the only strong policy advisable. Otherwise David Goodstein will exclude leather "freaks"; Denton (who is into leather) will exclude drag queens and militants; the militants, in turn, are likely to exclude David Goodstein. In all these acts of exclusion gays are merely passing along the homophobia that straights feel for us all.

Denton informs me that San Francisco is the S&M capital of the country. It is. Indeed, as one man told me, he likes San Francisco because the cool weather allows him to wear his leathers year round. The hub of S&M is Folsom Street, a dimly lit warehouse district thick with leather bars, among them The Arena, The Brig and, best of all, The Black and Blue. "The guys down in the Folsom area," Denton says, "are into heavy-duty sex—bondage, fist-fucking, you know. There's an S&M baths, The Slot, where you can rent rooms with slings in them for fist-fucking. The shower is outfitted with a long tube for douching. The place is dingy, raunchy, the floors are on a slant. Then there's another baths, the Handball Express, also for fist-fucking, though not quite so extreme."

I visited the area many times. At the Black and Blue the customers are so butch they swill Perrier water right out of the bottle (the bartenders jam the lime down into it). In the largest room a motorcycle rampant is suspended above the pool table under a heaven of twinkling electric stars. A bootblack plies his brushes and snaps his cloth below an old-fashioned stand from which a capped and goggled sadist can survey his minions. Two fenced-in yards open up off this room; one is a corral for bikes, the other contains an al fresco bath tub in which a naked undinist can sit and gambol about in water jetting from human fountains. The serious tone of the bar, however, can be broken; the tough guys are quite capable of linking arms and singing along with a record of Jeanette MacDonald warbling "San Francisco." The Brig is a smaller place with Tom of Finland paintings on the wall behind the bar and a leather shop in one corner.

Visiting Folsom Street spooked me because only a year before one of my friends had been killed there. He was a quiet man who had been deaf until he was sixteen. At that time an operation had given him normal hearing, though it did not wipe away his air of detachment, his steady inwardness. When a remark was addressed to him he needed a moment to remember that these buzzes, clicks and hisses were speech and required a response. As a teenager he'd been skinny and shy to the point of invisibility, but in his early twenties he'd decided, with a Marilyn Monroe act of pure will, to turn himself into a deity. He succeeded. For several Fire Island summers he was the most striking man in sight—tall, blond, smooth-skinned, tan, densely and intricately muscled, his teeth capped, his clothes artfully torn. In his mid-twenties he returned to college in San Francisco, earned top grades and was admitted to law school. Last year he stepped out of a Folsom Street bar and was gunned down by someone in a passing car. The murderer has never been identified nor has any motive been uncovered. New York friends flew out to claim the body and to bury it in the Midwest beside distant relatives (he was an orphan). He was so big and proud and conspicuous that no doubt he made a fine target for free-floating homophobia.

This sort of thing—think of the zebra murders, for example —seems to happen in San Francisco more often than elsewhere. Is it that the city attracts so many oddballs who have failed everywhere else and expect that here, at last, they will find sanity or wealth or love or a quorum of like-minded kooks? When they fail to do so, do they then vent their spleen on passing strangers? San Francisco does have the highest rate of alcoholism and sui-cide in the nation—indications, perhaps, of frustrated expecta-tions. Another, more generous explanation springs to mind: the city may simply have the most fully evolved group of people living the new life, and they may be shiny rods to draw the lightning of bigots. Unlike Chicago or New York or London, San Francisco is a small city; its "eccentrics" cannot hide out in New Town or SoHo or Soho. They are all constantly in circu-lation, on display. Everyone sees them daily. The mad and the murderous can never *stop* seeing the people they loathe.

Take Dan White. When he campaigned for the post of Su-pervisor, he handed out literature that read, "You must realize there are thousands upon thousands of frustrated, angry people such as yourself waiting to unleash a fury that can and will eradicate the malignancies which blight our city. I am not going to be forced out of San Francisco by splinter groups of radicals, social deviates, incorrigibles." Once he was elected, White was the only Supervisor to vote against a measure designed to reduce further anti-gay discrimination in the city. He also harangued against the proclamation of Gay Freedom Day. Finally, on November 27, 1978, White shot and killed Mayor George Moscone and (gay) Supervisor Harvey Milk. A waterworks employee who had gone wild and shot two fellow workers was convicted of first-degree murder, but at the same time an all-heterosexual jury found White guilty of just two counts of voluntary manslaughter and the judge sentenced him to just seven years and eight months in prison, with a chance for parole in five years. The gay community erupted in fury. On the evening of May 21, 1979, hours after the verdict was announced, about 3,000 gay demonstrators marched on City Hall and did about a million dollars' worth of damage. A night of violence followed, during which the police retaliated by trashing the bars on Castro Street.

I would *certainly* reject the far-fetched notion (advanced in some quarters) that gay sado-masochism adds to the level of public violence. S&M is a fantasy of dominance and submission in no way linked to the reality of crime. Leather men, as one study has revealed (and my own observations have confirmed), tend to be educated whites from upper-middle-class families, usually of English or northern European extraction. They are unduly sensitive to the sight of pain and, oddly, have frequently been either pacifists or vegetarians at one time or another. If not always liberal they are at least fiercely libertarian in their politics, with a healthy distrust of governmental authority. Far from being the neo-Nazi goons people imagine them to be, they are mild and public-spirited (motorcycle gangs are always staging benefits for handicapped kids or playing Santa Claus to orphans). Their sex lives, one might say, so thoroughly drain off the normal human reservoir of nastiness that they emerge as relatively benign beings. Why they are attracted to S&M in the first place is as mysterious as are all forms of sexual behavior. Some critics would say they are working overtime to reject their sissiness and to identify themselves with the most masculine images available —all drawn, incidentally, from the working class (cop, hardhat, truck driver, cowboy) since the middle class, obviously, provides no such models. What would they be? Board chairman? Golf player?

This theory has the advantage of explaining why S&M emerged, paradoxically, after the advent of gay liberation, which was supposed to have banished all role-playing and to have promoted angelic androgyny. But if effeminacy was a form of internalized self-oppression (we learn to act nelly because that's how straights see us), then the subsequent masculinization of gay life heralded a rebellion against this stereotyping.

That explanation, however, does not fit all the facts of the case; S&M, after all, involves much more than just being butch. To my mind it is an example of what Freud would call the "repetition compulsion," that is, the reenactment of painful scenes from childhood with the purpose of demonstrating mastery over events that were originally beyond our control. The reenactment lowers anxiety whether one is playing the master or the slave; relief is afforded not by the particular role that is assumed but because the drama is something one has initiated and can end at any moment. (This freedom to start and stop a sex scene is part of almost every S&M contract—and the very existence of such a "contract" proves my point).

But here I part company with Freud. He would discover the origins of sado-masochism in an arrestment at a particular stage of an individual's psychosexual development. I would guess that the ultimate source lies neither in the individual nor in his family but in the society at large. The Protestant culture (and S&M is neither Catholic nor Mediterranean) functions by fostering guilt, intimidation, suppressed desire and the worship of might. These mechanisms are not institutionalized, externalized in courts or confessionals and in an explicit feudal hierarchy as they have been in the Latin world; there the agents of oppression are all outside the individual's mind and the dream of atonement or appeasement is formulaic, age-old and public. In Protestant countries, however, these mechanisms are internalized (self-hatred, fear, the elusive scramble after status in what falsely bills itself as a democracy). The Protestant family is merely a tidepool in which the high seas of authoritarianism collect and where the child takes his first scary dip into society.

The child who grows up to be a sado-masochist, I would contend, is not enamored of authority. Quite the contrary—it appalls him. He is, as I've mentioned, unduly sensitive to the issue of individual rights and to the sight of suffering. S&M is his futile (and therefore endlessly repeated) attempt to tame, to control, to drive out the demons of the *real* sadism that ravage our entire civilization. For that reason S&M sex may merely be a more frank expression of the dynamics underlying *all* sex; perhaps gay liberation has merely given the leather boys permission to make manifest what is latent in everyone. Dr. Robert J. Stoller, for instance, writing in the *Archives of General Psychiatry*, observes: "Hostility, overt or hidden, is what generates and enhances sexual excitement, and its absence leads to sexual indifference and boredom. This dominance of hostility in erotism attempts to undo childhood traumas and frustrations that threaten the development of masculinity and femininity (gender identity). The same sorts of dynamics, though in different mixes and degrees, are found in almost everyone, those labeled perverse and those not so labeled." Stoller reached this conclusion after studying the erotic daydreams of several patients, in particular a heterosexual woman he calls "Belle."

I called on a San Francisco therapist who deals largely with gays. He is a Catholic and a former clergyman who taught theology for several years and continues to treat quite a few disturbed priests and nuns. He pays $400 a month for a flat on Castro Street that has an office, a bedroom, a dining room, a living room and a full deck in back. The decor is in such good taste that the apartment is featured in a photo book of classic gay interiors. Chocolate brown walls, enough votive candles to supply Lourdes for a month, suede couches, hand-painted shutters, a white double bed floating above the floor on slender chromium supports, rack after rack of animal horns—this is the look we call "elegant and masculine." Sean, as I'll name him, is also both. He is dressed in a striped, short-sleeve polo shirt and high-waisted green pants, very full in the leg but tight around the buttocks, as though they were army fatigues tailored by YSL. He is so deeply tanned that one is surprised to hear an Irish surname; he's the sort of person who virtually switches races in the summer. He has a mild, intelligent face devoid of nervous smiles, of *extorted* expressivity, though he's quite capable of kindling to humor; he doesn't match smile for smile, giggle for giggle, assent for assent, and he makes one aware how much one usually depends upon the continuing conspiracy of surface agreement in dealing with strangers. There's a touch of gray in the sideburns. After he hears a question he pauses—a very long pause —and then delivers a rapid, articulate answer—a voice-over, of course, above a disco tape. Everything in Sean seemed *chosen* and I was impressed by the way he had composed an odd personal bouquet out of such disparate elements—a bit of Aquinas, a bit of Donna Summer, a lot of East Side chic, a fern spray of Freud, a nosegay of socialism. His own personality is so strong he lends the odd blend a sense of integrity. I picture him sniffing it thoughtfully, rearranging it.

He gave me his views on Castro Street. "Oh, the problem has been overplayed. People aren't desperate. There's little panhandling, no hustling, few people are kept. Not too many people are unhappy about their own styles. A whole way of life based on unemployment has arisen and for some who are in their twenties and early thirties it's all they've ever known as adults. Of course there are those who commit suicide; frankly, I attribute many of the suicides to the effects of angel dust and perhaps *some* frustration with the system. Castro Street has a friendly village atmosphere; when I go out shopping I see lots of people I know. The bars here are very social. People are quite laid-back. I suppose the young suffer a bit. San Francisco is not very good to its young gays—a man in his thirties or forties, if he's in good physical shape, does much better than someone in his teens or twenties." In superb shape, Sean speaks with authority.

I asked Sean how he regarded homosexuality from a theological point of view. "It's a pseudo-problem," he said. "We must not look to the Bible for answers to questions that had not yet been formulated when it was written. For instance, in Biblical times no one knew anything about DNA; we wouldn't ask of Scripture answers to complex questions about biology. In the same way, St. Paul never thought in terms of *constitutional* homosexuality, that is, homosexuality that constitutes the very self of certain individuals. In his day people imagined that homosexuality was a vice that some people chose to adopt and could just as easily abandon. Many so-called theological issues are really psychological. And most fundamentalists are very selective about which Biblical bans they choose to enforce. For instance, there are 47 million single people over eighteen in the United States. Fundamentalism is against masturbation, premarital sex and homosexuality—so we must conclude that 47 million Americans are living in a state of mortal sin. One seldom hears that claim made. Theoretically, I suppose it would be useful to talk to fundamentalists about the Scriptures, but I wouldn't care to trade passages with them. Nor do I want to deal with them one at a time or for short periods of time. I wouldn't mind teaching a group for a semester."

Sean believes that the United States is going through a period of crisis, indicated by its swing toward conservatism (the fights against abortion, against busing and especially against the Equal Rights Amendment and the rights of homosexuals). "Gays and women must be touching very deep unconscious fears in order to elicit such violent reactions. I think the gay movement and ERA challenge people's deep-seated fears about any change in the patriarchal system. American life runs on a sado-masochistic model. People are scared of the alternative that gay life represents."

His total agreement with my own beliefs took my breath away and I was silent for a moment. He went on. "Everything in our society favors the tyranny of the family and of marital sex. You can see it in our language. For instance, there are no *good* words for feeling responsible to one's self. You can say someone is 'selfish' or 'egotistical' or 'self-centered,' but try to find a word that puts self-involvement positively. In the same way there's no good word for promiscuity, and yet having sex with lots of different people can be positive. In the past sex was justified because it led to procreation. Now sex is justified because it strengthens relationships. In the future, I hope, sex will be justified because it encourages individuation through fantasy. Right now gay theologians sanction gay marriages and sex within those marriages, but I would argue that the true function of sex is to discover, through erotic fantasy, all the selves within you. There are parts of me—jealousy, violence, tenderness, a desire to be nurtured—that I would never have known about if they hadn't come out in sexual fantasies."

The next afternoon I had a cup of coffee with a young gay

Chicano whom I'll call Ronnie. He was tall, willowy, with a gold earbob in one lobe and a dogged air, though he was quite capable of casting this aside and assuming one more festive. He told me that he'd grown up in different towns in Southern California. Though he had his first gay sexual experience when he was fourteen, he did not come out publicly in high school. "If you go to a school that is half Chicano, a quarter black and a quarter white, you don't come out," he told me. "I grew up in a world of drugs and gangs—we never went to school. In college that changed. I came into contact for the first time with gay white men who were out. I was elected president of the student body (I ran on a Chicano ticket) and the next day I came out during a big meeting. In my acceptance speech I called for fair treatment to all minorities, including Chicanos and gays. That was in 1973. Two weeks of silence followed; no one spoke to me, not even members of the Chicano group that had put me in office. Then they tried to stop the validation of a gay student union I was trying to organize—so I went to the Chicano group and confronted them. They backed down.

"At the same time I came out with my parents. I'm from a family of six brothers and five sisters; the kids around my own age already knew I was gay (I'm still close to them). But my older brothers were freaked; one actually threatened me, and we still don't speak. He thought it was worse even than when my sister became pregnant out of wedlock. I thought my father was going to give me silence, but he surprised me. He's a very proud man and was very strict when we were growing up. He told me I must hold my head up, not let anyone ridicule me for being gay. At first he started crying; he was sure he had done something wrong. I hope I reassured him that it was no one's 'fault.' He was very concerned, very interested, wanted to know more about homosexuality. As for my mother, she was . . . disappointed. She'll never be comfortable with homosexuality since she's extremely religious. But she's also the most feeling person in the family. *I* feel her sympathy, which isn't exactly what I want."

Ronnie told me about what he termed the "double oppression" directed against gay Chicanos. "On the one hand you have the gay whites. They discriminate against Chicanos. At some gay bars they ask Chicanos for three pieces of I.D.—and then they still won't let you in. There's a lot of racism among white gays in San Francisco, partly because so many come from places like Oklahoma or South Dakota where they're not used to dealing with Third World people. They have a built-in prejudice. Gay Chicanos get carded at the bars, they're turned away at the baths and even the gay party, the Alice B. Toklas Club, did not endorse a single Third World candidate in the last election. On official gay occasions Third World gays are never invited. But it's not fair for me to criticize; it's not as bad now as it was a year ago. So there's white oppression of Chicanos. Then there's the oppression of the straight Latinos against the gay Latinos. In the Latino culture, you see, there is so much pressure from the church, the family, and there are such rigid notions of honor and machismo."

I kept looking for signs of anger in Ronnie against this double oppression, but he seems to have been gifted with equanimity. He avoids rhetoric and the big political gesture. But he is, at the same time, not at all resigned. "I design counseling programs. I've been setting up a gay minority counseling service project to serve Third World gays, lesbians and gay youths. Two years ago I wanted a gay lifestyle course introduced into the public schools, but a Latino woman on the school board vigorously objected. So I went to her and told her what's happening. I mean, she didn't know *anything* about the problems of gay life, the realities. She was terrific. Once I clued her in she changed her mind. She voted in favor of the course; it passed and since then she's written letters supporting programs for gay youth. I think it helped that I'm Latino myself."

I could easily imagine the scene. The school board member opposes gays whom she thinks of as creepy white men in leather drag. Then a personable Latino spokesman talks to her about pregnant lesbian prostitutes, homeless, hungry gay teenage runaways, Latino youths driven to suicide—and the image of the "gay lifestyle" changes to include desperate children. Homosexuality is only an aspect of their problems; the three real issues, as Ronnie tells me, are alcoholism, drug abuse and suicide, and these problems afflict gays everywhere, of all ages, much more often than they trouble the straight population at large.

He told me that the Latino community perceives gay men as rich and decadent (though these attitudes can be gleaned only indirectly, since sex of any sort is seldom discussed among Latins). This negative vision of gays has arisen because in the Mission district Chicano families have been moved out of their homes, block after block, by new gay landlords. This same process of the so-called "urban renaissance" is now occurring in Haight-Ashbury, where poor blacks are being pushed out. The houses are being restored, split up into apartments and rented to white singles. "Of course," Ronnie remarked, "*all* real estate speculators, not just gays, are driving the families away."

The "urban renaissance," which is occurring in big cities all over the country, is a complex, painful phenomenon. Recently I read an article in the *New York Times* that jubilantly (and naïvely) celebrated the flight of blacks from the city and the influx of young, single professionals, the new mandarinate. The article was blatantly racist. One can foresee in the near future an era when the big old American cities (especially those such as New York, San Francisco, Chicago, Boston, Philadelphia and Washington that are financial centers and of historic interest) will be populated by an élite made up of the affluent young, the wealthy retired, rich foreigners and middle-class, childless couples—and gays. Only these groups will have the "disposable income" needed to afford the high rents and to patronize the chic boutiques. Living in the slums on the outskirts of these "restored" cities will be a deeply, structurally poor army of workers to maintain and service these urban centers; they are already with us, and they comprise illegal immigrants, blacks, Chicanos, Puerto Ricans and young whites unable to find better employment. As the United States moves into a "post-industrial" age and becomes the bookkeeper and technician of the world, the old, skilled, unionized labor force will be crowded out. Much of the money financing the new cities will come from European investors who regard the United States as the last bastion of capitalism.

Gays, of course, belong to every racial group and every social class. Gay women, in fact, probably constitute one of the poorest elements in the population. But middle-class gay white men are the most *visible* American homosexuals, since they wear a distinctive costume and frequent their own highly conspicuous bars, discos and shops, and they can be seen noisily roaming the streets in flamboyant wolf-packs. As a result, oppressed families (of whatever race) perceive gays as the enemy—those irresponsible, greedy young men, free of obligations to dependents, who buy up decayed neighborhoods, restore them with fiendish cleverness and industry and then resell them at staggering prices.

Without a doubt many gay men are the worker ants of our reviving cities. They deserve credit for having made our inner cities safe and attractive centers once again. Since gays are usually childless and yet nonetheless must pay city taxes to support the schools (and since the restoration of neighborhoods is raising the assessed property taxes), gays can even be seen as model citizens who make large contributions to the community and express few demands for city services. One could predict that the revival of the cities will eventually lead to improved schools, and the children of those few families left downtown will enjoy the benefits of these improved facilities.

So much for the positive outlook. The negative side remains depressing. Gay liberation was founded on the principle that women and gays of both sexes form an oppressed segment of the population that has much in common with other minorities (racial, ethnic and religious). The goal has always been a change in our society that would bring equality of opportunity and restored dignity and autonomy to us all. To effect such a change, progressive gays have attempted to forge links between personal experience and public life, between consciousness and politics. The only shortcoming in this approach, however, has been a steadfast denial of the real source of power in our society, i.e., money. Rich and middle-class gays are not likely to identify with the poor; they retain a loyalty to members of their own class, whether straight or gay. True, *within* gay life itself there are countless cases of well-to-do older gays helping out younger, poorer gays, but this system of patronage, entwined as it is with erotic interests, can benefit only fortunate individuals, not whole groups—and especially not oppressed groups of straight people. In San Francisco gay real estate speculators are in the position of actively oppressing minorities—and for some of us this spectacle is heartbreaking.

By no means do I want to single out San Francisco as the only or worst example of this phenomenon. As with most aspects of gay life, we have no statistics to document the degree and extent of this oppression, but one senses that it is happening in all major American cities. In the early years of gay liberation, most homosexual demonstrators and spokesmen were young, militant and unemployed. Partly because of their courage, an older, richer and more conservative group of homosexuals has now identified itself as gay. For this reason the popular, heterosexual image of gays has shifted. Minorities, who may have once been attracted to the outspokenness and the feistiness of street gays, now see us, as Ronnie put it, as "rich and decadent."

This image, of course, is false. One gay reporter I talked to found my point of view very odd. He said, "San Francisco considers itself the 'city that knows how,' and its know-how is all the savviness of its gays. We think that San Francisco has been spared the terrible fate of other American cities precisely because gays have stayed in the center city and fixed it up. Besides, there *is* a lot of friendliness between gays and minorities. For instance, in the Haight there's a straight black bar, Hank's 500, which is right across the street from a gay bar, and there are no hassles. We all get along."

Even in San Francisco, my informant feels, gays are still ignored and oppressed by the white majority. He pointed out that, symptomatically, the free tourist magazine handed out in hotels doesn't list gay bars and fails to mention that Polk Street is a gay thoroughfare. In the local media reporters still play up stories about "homosexual murders" but do not cover upbeat gay news. There's no gay columnist in either newspaper save for Armisted Maupin, who has gained a wide readership through his amusing "Tales of the City." According to my friend, the best thing about San Francisco is the general support from other gays and the relaxing atmosphere; the worst thing is the city's self-image as a gay mecca, which leads people to feel they must fall into an existence of cruising and going to bars. He had other criticisms. The shortage of good jobs causes gays to be unemployed or underemployed; at one hospital, for instance, all the clerks are gay—and most have M.A. degrees. There is, of course, a large community of gay professionals (lawyers, doctors, therapists), but they have a special problem—finding suitable partners. Since so many gays hold low or part-time positions (or none at all), a gay professional has trouble finding a lover on his own level, especially if his taste is for younger men.

A second problem is that the artistic life of the city is fairly feeble. "In fact," he said, "the city supports itself mainly on tourism. Nothing is going on here—no creativity, unless you consider all this 'human potential' crap creative. There are a lot of frustrated people here. When they come to California they experience a sudden *explosion* of expectations. They want life to be fulfilling, intensely sexual and exciting—and of course it isn't. They sought a gay nirvana and true love in a supportive milieu." He grinned sardonically. "Too bad; tough luck. This leads to crazy searches for magic cures—and a lot of political factions. For instance, San Francisco has both a gay Nazi group *and* a gay Jewish group."

One Saturday afternoon I went with a group of gay men to the Golden Gate Park for a picnic. We kept searching for a spot where the fog had burned off, and we finally found it; on a nearby hill, however, a cloud of fog—with more body, more substance than I'd expected—crept toward us, cold kitten on the prowl.

There must have been twelve of us, at least four gallons of wine and a delicious assortment of dishes. We got giddy, played frisbee, romped and talked all at once—but it dawned on me that almost every person at the picnic was restless and between jobs or discontent with his present one. One man in his forties arrived late on his Moped. He wore an orange crash helmet that, when he took it off, revealed close-cropped graying hair. He was bedizened with Indian silver rings and a bracelet studded with a large veined stone the color of a Negroni. After he parked his bike he embraced his friends with long, therapeutic hugs, silently searching their faces, one after the other, for the latest weather report of their subtlest, innermost feelings.

The sweetness of San Francisco life is certainly irresistible. One of my friends, a genuine native of San Francisco now studying in the East, tells me that what he misses most is the physical beauty of the city. "On the East Coast the weather is so rotten, you're inside all the time, talking, endlessly talking—sometimes I think I'll scream. In Berkeley I had a little apartment high up and I could just look up from my desk out the window and see miles and miles of wonderful nature. You can go hiking or skiing or swimming—it's all just a car ride away. Nature is so impressive that it dwarfs human things; it makes you modest, and San Franciscans sense that. The impact of Buddhism isn't just a fad. It's quite genuine."

This young man, now twenty-five, came out four years ago while he was an undergraduate at the University of California in Berkeley. Having grown up in the Bay area had done nothing to make him especially aware of homosexuality as an option; at his high school it was never discussed nor did he know any homosexuals. He's a tall, athletic, wonderfully handsome man and had always been popular among his straight friends. Then, in college, he found himself gravitating toward one particular friend, haunting his street in the hopes of seeing him, signing up for classes his friend was likely to take. For months this attraction was something he categorized under the cloudy rubric of "friendship," but one day it occurred to him it was a sexual attraction, *homosexual*—and the word eased him, arranged the puzzle pieces into a picture. He slept with a few men and enjoyed the experience. At the school gymnasium there was a deck for nude sunbathing (ah! California), and there he became friendly with the man who is now his lover. My friend had had gay sex but had not participated in gay life; his lover-to-be had many gay friends, had gone with them dancing to gay discos, knew all about gay life—but had never experienced gay sex. They quickly filled in the gaps for each other. The transition into gay life was as painless as any I've heard of, though both have been consistently active in gay liberation since the beginning of their romance, and that participation may be the reason they've been so little plagued by the guilt and depression gay life often engenders. San Francisco is probably the best place in the world in which to come out, for it presents to the newcomer a large, thriving and varied panorama of gay life—a sense of choices, quite a few of them attractive. Many of the gay men I met in the West had in fact spent a few years in San Francisco during their early twenties. The city can serve as a sort of gay finishing school, a place where neophytes can confirm their gay identity. For older gays, especially those coming from larger, more cosmopolitan cities, moving to San Francisco may be less beneficial, more akin to escapism.

"Gerry" is now forty-two, though he looks no more than thirty. He's been in San Francisco for ten years. He studied painting at the Art Institute in Chicago, then stayed on as a museum employee for five years. The pressures of the job, however, caused him to develop an ulcer; he decided the institute was an unhealthy environment for an artist and he moved to Florida, where he worked as a lifeguard. "But that's an awful place for gays; the straights are oppressive there, so I came out to San Francisco. I also served a brief stint in New York, but I couldn't take it—too hard-ass, everything's status, competition. It's not very loving. San Francisco is much more open and relaxed. Here you can get out of the city in twenty minutes. I go running around Strawberry Canyon or through Muir Woods. In New York you're cut off from nature, you're surrounded by constant noise. The art in New York is a poor substitute for the natural beauty of San Francisco."

Gerry is a twentieth-century phenomenon. In the past, as George Orwell has reminded us, the bulk of humanity passed almost instantly from being adolescents (amorous, high-spirited, open to experience) into being toothless, downtrodden, self-sacrificing Mum and Dad. Only the aristocratic few escaped this sudden transition and prolonged the period of introspection, dalliance, egocentricity, physical beauty. Even so, this grace period ended in one's early thirties (after all, the Marschallin in *Der Rosenkavalier* is just thirty when she bids farewell to romance).

In the United States, and especially among gay men, this period of adolescence is being extended for the first time in history into the forties, fifties, even sixties. It has become a way of life. Let me hasten to say that by "adolescence" I mean nothing derogatory; I am not asserting, as psychoanalysts once did, that homosexuals are "arrested" in their development, that they "refuse to grow up." Our so-called "immaturity" can be viewed, just as easily, as a prolonged and admirable resolve to stay attractive and susceptible to influence. After all, to choose an analogy, the advances primates have made over less complex mammals can be attributed to *neoteny*, the retention of immature characteristics into adulthood. Since childhood is the period of play, of behavioral experimentation, a prolonged childhood lengthens the time for learning. Gerry's unlined face, his trim, muscular body, his gentle, impressionable nature are a brand new invention of our times, the cultural neoteny of gay life.

When he first arrived in San Francisco he became an artist's model at various schools. He even helped form a guild for models in the area; for seven years he served as an officer of the guild, which required that he audition candidates twice a year. He chose models for the guild on the basis of body type and imaginative skill in striking posés. The guild has managed to raise models' wages to $5.50 an hour.

Modeling, however, now bores Gerry. For the last few years he has been working as a furniture mover for a gay service. Every morning he rises at six, swallows his vitamins and his blender breakfast and is at work by seven-thirty. By one in the afternoon he is free. Most of the people he and his friends move are gay themselves. "Gay clients feel less tension around gay movers," Gerry tells me. "They don't have to hide their pornography or feel embarrassed about the Louis Quinze vanity table. We're all real campy with each other and—oh, we've got these names: Mighty Mouse, Toots, Sugar Plum . . . you know." As soon as he gets off work he buys a slice of quiche at the bakery and sits in the sun for an hour or two. Then he takes a nap. He lives on the edge of the Western Addition in a seven-room flat with three other people, a gay couple and a gay single. "We have fun, dishing and joking, though we don't eat together. Our schedules are too different and besides I eat only chicken and fish. My share of the rent is just ninety-five dollars, which is handy, since I make only about $8,000 a year." In the late afternoon or early evening he exercises two hours every day. He either goes to his gym or runs or jogs—up to seven miles, depending on who's with him. Three years ago he took a program in running at the Esalen Institute that involved yoga, stretching and discovering one's individual biological rhythms.

Therapy of one sort or another has occupied much of Gerry's free time over the years. He did est for three years, which he claims "started me on an ongoing process of getting away from stereotyped maleness. It was a process of expanding the self and developing the capacity to love. Now I'm going to a shrink who follows no particular theory but is West Coast Eclectic— a straight man who's quite warm and friendly and who has a large gay clientele. *Plus,*" here a sheepish, questioning smile, "I'm also involved in a dream class. My teacher has her own methods. She studied in Zurich. On my way to work in the morning, while I'm waiting at lights in my Volkswagen, I make notes on my dreams. Then I write out my associations in my dream log and we look for underlying structures. There are five of us in the seminar. For instance, I had a dream of rocks falling at Yosemite, and we decided that stood for the calcified emotions I'm shedding. Then I dreamed of a bear—my own id-like qualities. Now that I understand them, they're less threatening. *Plus* I keep a regular diary in which I record the things that were wins and the things that were upsetting. But my greatest interest is photography. I started taking pictures when I was twelve, studied photography in college, and now I shoot wildflowers on weekends. Not now. I'm not content, and I can't work when I'm turbulent emotionally. I'd like to have shows, but I can't quite get it together. It's very important to me but. . . ."

In the evenings he often has dinner with a friend and attends a movie or the symphony. Several nights a week he dances at a disco from about eleven-thirty to one or two. One of his favorite companions is, as Gerry wryly puts it, "A slumlord and a hooker. He owns a few houses. As a hustler he runs ads in *The Advocate.* We work out together, go dancing together, go to the opera together (he's also a singer). He's perfect. He's very estian oriented. We might have been lovers, but he's into S&M, *so-o-o.* . . . But we have an emotional closeness. We kiss and sleep together sometimes, that's all. Once a week I visit my friend Anne in Marin. She's married and has a lover and two kids. We sit in the sun and dish and talk about men. I'm more monogamous than she. See, she used to be fat but she lost weight on that shot diet and once she became gorgeous she took a job as a hooker in a massage parlor. Her husband encouraged her; I think it excited him. But then she did est and decided to quit.

Now she has a jealous lover. I know all her relatives and her gay sister. I'm part of her family unit. It's really very nice."

In this book I am trying to describe styles of life that are unique to a city, not those that could be lived in any city equally well. Gerry's life—with its emphasis on communing with nature, expanding his consciousness, engaging in agreeable part-time work, participating in the cultural attractions of a true metropolis (the opera, the symphony, the excellent restaurants, the many discos), gathering together a sophisticated band of understanding friends—this life seems to me one that could be lived only in San Francisco.

PORTLAND AND SEATTLE

Clear Heads and Cloudy Skies in the Pacific Northwest

Once there were two brothers. The older was dark, overweight, a bit slovenly, his nails ragged and his shoes scuffed. The younger was blond, slim, immaculate. Everyone was drawn to the blond; he had a worldly manner, or so it seemed, though after an evening with him one would have been hard pressed to identify even a single trait that had revealed this sophistication. Perhaps his silences allowed one to attribute any virtue at all to him without fear of contradiction or hope of proof.

Because of the extraordinary looks nature had conferred on him, the blond was taken up by a dashing crowd, but this very popularity made him somewhat uneasy. He kept paying visits to his dark brother who, because he was less sought after, remained more natural, more spontaneous. To be sure, in the fast circle the blond had a reputation for being sincere and unaffected (this circle ignored the dowdy dark brother altogether). The blond was half-ashamed of his brother's lack of style—but he also envied it, as one might envy innocence.

In this parable the dark brother is Portland and the fair is

Seattle. I hope the reader will forgive this flight, but I could find no other way to suggest the comparison. Portland is the essence of the old Northwest—the strong individualism, the affectionate manners, the solid virtues, the somber stylelessness, whereas Seattle (richer, larger, flashier) is a conspicuous participant in the national culture. But people in Seattle keep looking back over a shoulder at Portland, convinced they are more progressive and elegant than their neighbors to the south, but worried about the discrepancy. Has something been lost? No one speaks ill of Portland, though mentioning it may draw a smile.

When I arrived in Portland I phoned a young gay timber-baron, whom I did not know but whose number had been given to me. "Come at once," he said. "You can stay here as long as you like. This is wonderful."

My taxi carried me over the Willamette River and past the Union Depot, a low, rambling building erected in 1890, the sort of station the Lionel Company might have designed long, long ago for rich children. Through dull city streets, clean if characterless, we went, and then we climbed up steep hills where the trees were so thick and tall they closed out the evening sky. Up and up we wound on curving lanes past large, comfortable houses set back from the road, the neighborhood I had dreamed of while I pored over my first-grade reader: safe, suburban, sheltered. At any moment I expected Dick and Jane to race by with Spot, as Father stepped out of his Hudson, a smile on his young face and the evening paper under his arm.

Portland is a quiet city of mild winters and cool summers, of overcast skies and sudden showers—perfect weather for growing roses (they bloom even at Christmas) and ideal for bringing rosiness to the cheeks of long-stemmed American Beauty boys—those six-foot-two men with glass-blue eyes that the rest of the world dreams about, their golden hair so radiant it must have been intended to compensate the gloomy Northwest for its lack of sunshine.

Gloom isn't quite the word, unless that signifies solid, Edwardian frame houses of many rooms and porches as ample as a matron's bosom (here the sexless singular applies, as does the sexist designation). Portland is a city of secure wealth, a place where the response to "Thank you" is "Why, you bet," of big steak dinners served to dignified families at five-thirty in the afternoon, the meal complete with baked potatoes and onion rings soaked in milk for a week. This is a city many people leave after adolescence and miss for the rest of their lives.

At last the taxi sputtered to the very top of the pinnacle and to a house that from the street looked misleadingly small. As I soon discovered, it staggered down the hillside beyond in several stages until it had become really quite large.

My host was flame-cheeked, smooth-skinned, his blue eyes protuberant and his upper teeth slightly bucked, as though his features were racing forward to see deeper, bite off more. He was wearing boots, jeans, a lumberjack's shirt—his uniform on the job, not the latest disco drag. His house was lit by the evening alone—*l'heure bleue*, sacred to Magritte, in which the thousand streetlamps and houselights in the valley below glowed more intensely than the darkening sky, that massive, sensitive cortex to the world, if the cortex is the part of the brain where consciousness occurs. The living room and the adjoining sun room at first seemed empty, prepared to receive as many of the sky's thoughts as possible, telepathy of dying light—but after a bit my eyes picked out Persian carpets on parquet, commodious couches and easy chairs pushed against the wall and into corners and, on a bookshelf, a photograph of a woman in a feathered hat, a picture from the Forties, her face so grownup it mitigated the frivolity of her headgear, and one would no more have questioned her style than have smiled at an African chief's painted torso.

Within seconds my bag had been wafted into the guest room and I was sitting in stocking feet on the floor beside my host, sipping a drink, staring into the gathering night and listening to his life. He was at once confident and insecure. The confidence, I suspect, came from his wealth (most of which he'd made on his own) and from his sense of preeminence in the community. Wherever we went over the next three days, people knew him and, within the terms of the democratic manners of the Northwest, deferred to him. With waiters, filling-station attendants, the neighbors, he had a knack at joshing, lightheartedly and inoffensively, and at generating weightless small-talk.

He was at ease inside his skin, and its outermost layer was Portland.

In a restaurant he struck up a winningly impertinent conversation with strangers at the next table. Any topic would do (taxes, the weather); Helmut (so I'll call him) even felt free to chime in on intimate talk. "Are you going to take that from her?" he'd ask a middle-aged husband under attack. "Come on," the wife would say good-naturedly to Helmut, "why don't you get on my side? I'm the one who needs an ally." Such instant contact may seem unusual only to a New Yorker, who regards the membrane between strangers as almost always impermeable. But even the most easygoing Westerner would be impressed by Helmut's aplomb; he acted as if he owned the city and as if its citizens all recognized him—as indeed many did.

Such confidence, which he exhibited in ordinary social encounters, deserted him as soon as he was with other gay men or even when he merely thought of himself as a sexual being. Then this man who had salvaged his family fortune, who had logged off whole forests, who had built or rebuilt scores of houses, who raised thoroughbred horses and who never doubted his judgment of people, his taste in decor or his instinct for profit, who harbored an unassuming pride in his heritage and his own achievements—then this man, as soon as he had to be gay, turned into a neurotic, frightened child. He was reluctant to enter a bar, he feared (with some reason) he had alienated most of his gay friends through unwarranted suspicions or pestering erotic demands, he stood before the mirror detesting his own face and body—and he had never had a lover, much as he insisted he wanted one.

"I'm so glad you're here," he said with reckless urgency. "I've become terribly withdrawn. I never go out of the house. I don't see anyone. Part of it's business; I haven't decided what to do next. But part of it's—" and he broke off.

With only the slightest urging he unfolded his history. The last child of seven and the only boy, he was born twenty-five years ago. His parents owned a farm, where his mother also raised thoroughbreds. Their life was hard, if baronial. His father not only tended his herds but also worked as a lumberman, and Helmut himself rose at three in the morning to do chores. His paternal grandfather had been a socialist and a friend to prominent men in the party. "But my father," Helmut said, "didn't participate in, uh, life. Both of my parents are well read, much better than I am—I'm too hyper to read. This is my mother's mother," and he picked up the photograph of the woman in the feathered hat. "When you write," Helmut asked suddenly, "how will you describe me?" He had told me he wanted to be "written up."

"As mad Ludwig of Bavaria," I said, teasing him.

He blanched. "Ludwig was a relative."

Helmut's parents were land poor. No income could be derived from the farm, and the furniture was shabby, the rugs threadbare. This state of affairs had mortified little Helmut; children are the greatest snobs. Helmut had wanted to go to a boarding school, but his mother, while vaguely promising him that she would send him, compulsively spent every cent she could find on her horses. Tyrannized by their holdings, his parents fought constantly.

Suddenly Helmut was up, racing about, snapping on lights. The glare on the windows cancelled out the vision of the city below and returned to us our own reflections and revealed an interior—massive, old-fashioned, mahogany—that I fancied he had assembled to provide himself with the inelegant security he had lacked but dreamed of as a child.

"Since I was a kid," he said, rejoining me, "I have been fascinated by sex. But I grew up alone, my sisters were so much older. We were really very isolated. And I feared women—they meant responsibility: pregnancy, marriage. As for homosexuality, I didn't know it existed. I had never even heard the word."

Baffled by sex, he plunged into work. The family's anxiety about money troubled him and he was determined to make a fortune. When just sixteen he borrowed $3,000 from a sister and invested it in a piece of timber. The returns on this speculation were rapid and gratifying; with this newly acquired capital he bought up a chunk of Disney stock the day after Walt Disney died; the price had gone down dramatically but Helmut knew that with the opening of Disney World it would rise, as rise and rise it did.

Through his business deals, most of them in timber, Helmut

earned money in seven figures, enough to buy his parents' farm
from them and to maintain them there in considerable luxury.
He rebuilt the country house and outfitted it with oriental
rugs, Chinese porcelains and hardwood floors. He also bought
a house for a sister, sent one nephew to college and another to
trade school. In the midst of this hard work he managed to
finance his own education. He received a degree in business. "But
I was a C+ student," he confesses. "Restless, unable to concen-
trate."

"I came out when I was twenty-two," he goes on. "I had a
girl friend who, like me, was interested in horses, porcelain,
furniture. We knew another girl whose brother was gay, so we
went along with him one night to a gay bar—it seemed terribly
exciting. A few seconds after I was in the door I knew I was gay,
which disturbed me. I had to be—I still have to be—very cau-
tious; I'm the last bearer of my family's name, and it's a name
everyone knows. Still, I'm grateful to gay life. I've met famous
people through it, one governor, two senators, an opera diva.
You have to remember, I had had no big-city sophistication; gay
life gave me that."

As Helmut talked he descended into a serious mood, held
there by the stories he was relating, his face weary with the
recollection of responsibilities. But this adult gravity lightened
the moment he returned his attention to me, and suddenly he
became a playful, skitterish lad, voice piping, eyes beseeching
or sly.

Helmut's virtues and faults derive from his unchallenged
position in his world. If he were to live in another, larger city—
San Francisco, Boston, Washington—he would be compelled to
turn himself into a standardized, more marketable commodity.
He would have to court new friends, make an impression, strike
a recognizable figure. But in Portland he can stay as he is. His
friends are all childhood friends, those dear creatures who fortify
our sense of self and weaken our character by treating our faults
as though they were inevitable—or invisible, since to find fault
one must first stand apart. A braying voice, paraded depressions,
a waspish tongue—one no more criticizes these in a childhood
friend than flaws in one's own housekeeping; they seem as in-
eradicable as the rust stain in the porcelain under the tap.

Helmut could be called "the boy who stayed home." If he has not turned out as streamlined as another city might have made him, neither has he become as interchangeable. He is certainly memorable—I, at least, shall never forget his demands and generosity. For he was generous. When he wasn't bossing me around, he was showing me the sights. We drove through Forest Park, 5,000 densely wooded acres within the city limits. We visited Pittock House, a mansion (now a museum) far above the city constructed in 1914 during a wave of local pride by Oregon craftsmen out of Oregon materials (save for the Italian marble). Despite its age the house has its original indirect lighting and a centralized vacuum system (plug in the sweeper in any room and let the mechanical lungs below inhale the dust). Or he was lining up new "types" for me to interview—a therapist, a concert pianist, the druggist. "Come on," Helmut bellowed at the dark man in the white synthetic smock, "talk to him. I've been telling him all about my life for *hours*." "What?" the druggist said, smiling, "you mean you haven't gotten your story down any better than that? Mine takes just an hour." This sort of homely wit suits Helmut fine; he himself is given to phrases such as "You can't win for losing" and "We were either high on the hog or low on the bone."

Through Helmut I met someone I'll call Tom, a six-foot-two, angular redhead with a hooked nose, a mustache shaped to resemble an upright horseshoe, tight skin, and squint lines earned on the glittering slopes; he is a champion skier. He is exactly Helmut's age and has known him since infancy. Their shared past leads Tom to submit to Helmut's ceaseless whirrings and proddings; I pictured a patient hibiscus feeding a humming-bird. In some hypothetical elsewhere they would not have been friends. A man as correct as Tom would have rejected Helmut's eccentricities ("Tom has a *very* large basket," Helmut announced, describing Tom to me in front of Tom). In Portland Tom simply grins and bears it, or rather shrugs and studies the floor as the color rises to his cheeks. If Helmut's family can claim mad Ludwig, Tom descends from a Swedish princess of the last century who ran away from home (castle?) with a sea captain, then jumped ship in Astoria, the port at the mouth of the Columbia

River, where she resourcefully set up shop as a prostitute. (As the 1940 WPA guide to Oregon could still say, "All glitter and brittle air in summer, all hush or foggy mystery in autumn, and all bluster and fury during winter storms, Astoria never lacks the characteristics of the sea that has drawn Finns, Norwegians, and Swedes in such numbers that shop signs in the various languages are commonplace.")

Tom hasn't worked a regular job in the last three years. He keeps busy tending bar in a hangout for young straights (where gays also visit and dance from time to time) and by landscaping the lawns of the big houses on the Clackamas River, but no two days are alike. His boss at the tavern knows Tom is gay and couldn't be less concerned. "Nobody cares about people's sexuality here," Tom told me. "Oregon's had a consenting adults law for five years; we even have a gay lobbyist in Salem. The straight community accepts gays. The police are liberal. No problems. There are about five dirty bookstores in Portland where people carry on. Not much car cruising. Of course the gay bars have to be discreet and conservative, because the owners don't want to run afoul of the Oregon Liquor Control Commission, which is powerful and puritanical. Back rooms? Oh, the Commission would be sure to revoke a license for that."

A lot of gay life in the Northwest gets lived out of doors. In the summer Portland gay men ride horses, camp and climb in the Cascades, or sunbathe and frolic in the nude on Sauvie Island, thirteen miles east of Portland, where the Willamette flows into the Columbia. The island is a small farming community and also an animal shelter for wild turkeys, geese, deer and elk. The other nude beach is still farther along the Columbia: Rooster Rock, or "Cock Rock," as it's known. "For a while," Tom says, "the cops were harassing gays at Rooster Rock, but now everyone knows we're there, and they leave us alone." In the winter skiing on Mt. Hood, fifty-five miles east of Portland, is the big sport. The season begins in mid-November, when the Timberlane Lodge opens, though some runs are good all year round (Mt. Hood is 11,245 feet high and always snow-capped). "There are a tremendous number of gay men and women who ski. A lot of the instructors are gay, too. Sometimes fifty gay

guys will rent a bus together and take off for the weekend."
Tom's dream is to own a tavern in Sun Valley and make it the
first gay hangout in that area.

Tom and Helmut sometimes act like overgrown teens, *i
vitelloni*. When the three of us walked through the downtown
streets, past bus kiosks cryptically coded with stylized beavers,
snowflakes and maple leaves, Tom ran up to a bronze statue of
a nude woman, placed along the curb by the city council in a
questionable attempt to beautify the mall—and tweaked her hard
breasts, doubling up with giggles. Another howler was to call
the J. C. Penney store "Jacques Penée." In their company I felt
a resurgence of that old, silly adolescent flush of running in a
pack, sniffing the air for any lame witticism, laughter in our
mouths and, in our hearts, an imperiled because doomed-to-end
sense of belonging to other men, joined to them by an eager
if insubstantial lust for . . . well, anything would do. Even a
shift in the light.

Tom wants to leave Portland because he is fed up with
what's happened to the city. "About sixty or seventy of my old
friends have moved out of town," he says. "Most of the natives
leave. Five years ago Portland was a great place, open and
friendly. But now it's cliquish; you can't meet someone except
through a member of his clique. The out-of-towners are mostly
from the Midwest or West—a lot from Salt Lake City. They come
here because it's beautiful, comfortable, laid-back. And they
come for jobs. There are lots of jobs—six whole pages listing
them in the paper, about a third for unskilled labor. There are
two new aluminum plants which are always hiring folks. But it's
all gotten up-tight."

I couldn't help taking him with a whole shaker of salt; as
a citizen of the Mysterious East, I felt like saying: "Up-tight?
Have I got up-tight for you, *bubbela*." Never have I been in a
warmer, more agreeable town. A visit to the popular gay bar,
the Family Zoo, is enough to reveal how friendly the animals
can be. No one is so "got up" as they might be in a larger city
(Portland has 378,000 people). The instant you walk into this
big, *gemütlich* bar, you feel the difference; it could be a ski
lodge—all it lacks are the fire, the buttered rum and the dozing

St. Bernard. Here's a man with a ponytail held back with a rubber band, there's one with a full dark beard and a shiny cloche
of blond hair (the colors of the Western meadowlark—the beard,
in fact, is shaped like the bird's black necklace against its gold
breast). This guy has the mild, blinking, benign eyes of a big
cat dozing by day; that guy the small, intent face and long arms
of a spider monkey. These are not the studied, exercised bodies
of big cities, those *first* impressions so ruthlessly achieved before
full-length mirrors. A lot of the guys here are wearing glasses;
a few gay women are laughing in the corner; everyone seems to
know everyone else. Nothing is tense, expectant, guarded—the
three adjectives that assuredly must apply to any ordinary make-
out bar. Perhaps people don't make out here (Helmut lodges
that complaint). Nearby at the disco, The Rafters, the same
friendly atmosphere reigns. Helmut and I dance with two stylish
lesbians.

North of West Burnside is a heavily gay neighborhood
("Vaseline Heights"), but most gay men in Portland live scattered all over the city, and this dispersal has led to an unusual
degree of integration with the straight community. A gay single
or couple must deal with the family next door and the widow
across the street; the proximity promotes a mixed gay-straight
social life—parties, dinners, bridge games, a shared cup of coffee.
Although the Northwest is an extraordinarily openminded place,
it does not offer anywhere the concentration of homosexuals
that, say, San Francisco does. Many men in the Northwest, in
fact, have gone to San Francisco for a few years in their twenties
to learn how to be gay (and how to accept it). San Francisco
provides the chrysalis for the metamorphosis from confused caterpillar to lustrous Monarch (or Queen, if you insist).

When I visited "Hank" in Portland he was about to get married. He spent hours telling me that what he was doing was
right. Though he liked me, I think (I certainly liked him), he
found my whole project of writing gay travel notes wrong-
headed. Hank considers homosexuality a trap. He is not interested in "relating" to men alone. The gay world, he insists, is
unhealthily obsessed with sex, and this is especially true of the
gay press. Hank has seen it all, he's been to bars and baths (and

he is so handsome he must have been welcomed wherever he went), but he dislikes the frenetic pace of gay life—and the promiscuity. He believes in fidelity above all else, whether one's partner is of the same or opposite sex. But to be a part of gay life, irretrievably? "Oh, it's too damn limiting. I resist categories. Sex is a disease. The gay community has prioritized sex as the most—but it's not. No, it's *not*—the most important thing." He uses words such as *prioritized* because he's been to business school.

Hank doesn't look you in the eye when he talks. He's scattered, his sentences trail off, he sighs frequently, as though he's so intelligent he's always frustrated by the formulaic nature of speech (each sentence a ride you can't get off once the attendant buckles you into the car). Or perhaps he is simply anxious about his impending marriage—and the reactions of his friends, especially his lover. For he has a lover, someone who because of his work must live on the East Coast, though the two men meet for ski weekends in Colorado, hiking dates in Arizona, a mid-winter break in Acapulco, Christmas in Portland. It is one of those high-strung affairs that require distance to cool off or heat up or perhaps just to iron out the wrinkles that get creased into their nerves whenever they're together. I know the East Coast lover as well, and I get the impression that their affair is as potent, as hostile and as magic as Oberon's and Titania's, an alliance that demands separate retinues, separate lives and squabbles of almost supernatural intensity in order to produce, at the odd moments when they finally come together, a molten intensity. Domestic love—the day-in, day-out routine of intimacy—answers our needs for a companion, for a witness to our lives, for a helpmeet, but it betrays the needs of the imagination, and anyone who lives with a lover chooses the comforts of repetition over the dangers of adventure. I know, I know: I'm crazy and no one will agree with my "bleak" view of love (to me it seems not bleak but tragic). Hank and his lover have institutionalized danger into their lives by always fighting, always reconciling, always toying with other loves—and now by Hank's announcing his engagement.

He is blond with a dark beard, and teeth that look as

though a German fashioned them one by one out of Meissen.
His blue eyes go violet with thought but brighten with sudden
sunshowers of giggling. He has delicate fingers, thick thighs, an
athlete's pigeon-toed walk, no ass at all and forearms furry
enough to suggest embraces in a cold winter bed.

Hank grew up isolated and horny on a farm sixteen miles
out of Portland. He came to town and church three times a
week. His social life, such as it was, revolved entirely around
the church. He was overly zealous in his faith in the manner of
the intelligent misfit who doesn't quite believe—never complacent, always dogmatic and edgily eager. Now he is a vice-presi-
dent of his family business (which, as Henry James would say,
makes "a small domestic item"), plays tennis with friends, paints
small abstractions on weekends, serves on two committees, one
promoting ecological balance and the other cleanliness in a
state that already seems unhealthily hygienic. He lives in a conservative straight neighborhood in a tidy two-story house with
a lawn clipped to putting-green perfection. He keeps a vegetable
patch and a small rose garden and fights the slugs that love the
moist soil of Oregon. He is proud of his house.

Having drifted away from the family faith and joined another church, today he is liberal to the point of atheism. He
condemns the Baptists for their stand on gays. "From my community work I've come to the conclusion that most of the violence in our society stems from sexual repression. If the Baptists
could be made to look at that—and a lot of other things, including some good theological arguments and their own lousy morals
—I think they'd shape up. Baptists aren't very introspective
people. But up here, at least, most people believe in individual
rights. They're libertarians, if not always liberals. Of course we
need more legislation to define privacy. Even my dad, when he
heard about Anita Bryant, said, 'I don't know why she's making
such a big deal out of it.' But I must tell you, I think gays are
part of a particular lifestyle, not a minority. I'm sick of hearing
gays compare themselves to blacks and Jews—that's ridiculous.
They should be compared to swingers or nudists or playboys—
that's all it is, a lifestyle."

I asked Hank if he had a personal reason for condemning

the way gay men live. He answered by telling me that when he was in his twenties, he lived in Los Angeles and would spend weekends at Laguna Beach. "Lots of partying," he mumbles. "Breakfasts for twenty guys. Pool parties. Orgies. Drugs. I had one—" his eyes graze mine—"one bad acid trip. It all seemed so awful. I fled back to Portland."

Hank's present "normality"—his house, his solid position in the community, his will to be a family man—could this be what happens *later* to those nervous, guilty roisterers we see on Fire Island or at Laguna for two or three seasons; those beauties who nurse their tans by day and stagger around the meat rack by night, eyes spiraling with drugs; those men who go too far, prolonging the party till dawn and blasting out the neighbors with their tapes, but who wince when someone makes a casual, lewd reference to sex (Hank cringed when I said "Suck cock" in reference to something or other); who don't sleep well, have nightmares, yet tell you with eerie emphasis that they need their rest, that they prize nothing so much as nine hours' rest? I've always wondered where those guys land after they bail out. Perhaps they return to Portland.

Zen Buddhists sometimes seem to be saying that the man who has reached Satori goes home, drinks a beer, mows the lawn. Is this what has happened to Hank? He thinks so. After Los Angeles, after his transcontinental affair, after so many and such contrasting episodes that range from his boyhood on the farm, raising Sedan grass for wild ducks, to weekends of sex and sun at a melting montage of resorts, Hank feels he has returned to the external form of bourgeois life—a life, however, that is illuminated from within by experience. I confess I have misgivings about the future he's chosen (as I do about my own), but what seems characteristic of the Northwest is this unexpected blend of conservative style and liberal content, of conventional decorum and progressive thinking. Few people in the Northwest *appear* to be individuals, but many do think for themselves. Elsewhere the reverse is true; the originality is all on the level of manners, not morals, of costume, not content.

The train ride from Portland to Seattle took me through

dense forests of firs, their boughs sway-backed with luxuriance, and stands of cottonwood (trees, unlike blonds, are lighter when their hair is blown back). During strong gusts the ruffled leaves appeared to be foaming white blossoms. For a second the forest primeval split open to reveal a six-lane superhighway below. Unpainted farmhouses and corrugated tin warehouses were conveyed past me; over there, an unwheeled, twenty-year-old trailer was quietly rusting to death on someone's lawn. And here, in this tiny logging community, is an old hotel of fifty rooms, deserted, paper blinds drawn. The poverty of the farmhouses is overshadowed by the richness of the forests: the Chinese ideal of a rustic hut confronting the liquid, calligraphic landscape. These country people (like the woman beside me) do not despise nature as they once did. No, like city-dwellers, they discover views and praise the clarity of streams or the purity of the air; so far has the nature cult of Romanticism spread that what was once the prerogative of the urban élite is now a nearly universal taste for scenic beauty.

The primary human colors are maroon and a weathered green, shades of the clocked socks of a small-town businessman: pale green houses, forest-green cars, the maroon and black yang and yin of the Northern Pacific Railroad. On board the train are older men dressed up for the trip in maroon sports jackets, open shirts, checked pants, and women in pants suits they have sewn themselves out of an unspeakable synthetic; the sewing machines of America have been disastrously busy. Instead of the two or three good ensembles an ordinary European might have, too many Americans have a closet overflowing with dozens of these "cute" ill-fitting outfits.

The trees on one side suddenly run out and reveal Puget Sound; bits of scrap wood, even whole logs, litter the waters. On my right rise the Cascades; to the left, across the Sound, the faint blue line of the Olympic Mountains hovers over the dark coast. The hills are irradiated by the sunset; they are well named, since they should be the abode of the Immortals. We slide past a storage installation right on the water: two layers of aluminum cylinders topped by a rectangular platform on which brood tall, hooded lampposts like gulls hunched up to snooze.

I believe Gore Vidal has called the Northwest the Scandinavia of America and wondered why it doesn't secede. Seattle
is certainly progressive. If a freeway pounds through the downtown, the city caps it over with a many-tiered park thunderous
not with hurtling cars but with a plunging waterfall. Since the
business district used to be clogged with traffic, the city solved
the problem by providing frequent buses, free to ride anywhere
downtown. When Pike Place, the farmer's market along Elliot
Bay became dilapidated, it was ingeniously restored (and the
old brick streets were re-cobbled). If too many wild cats are
going hungry, then the city opens a free spaying service.

If further proof of its rationality were needed, one could
point out that Seattle has the lowest church attendance in the
country. But too much may have been made of that statistic;
perhaps the cause may simply be everyone's urge to rusticate.
On Friday an exodus takes place to the country and the mountains. Twenty minutes out of Seattle there are mountains to
climb, and skiing goes on nine months out of the year. Since
Seattle is built on water, people arrive at work by boat—and
make a speedy getaway to island retreats. On Opening Day, the
first Sunday in May, some 15,000 pleasure crafts crowd the harbor. The outdoor life is certainly appealing, and gay Seattleites
look at exhibitions of new gear—snowshoes, tents, crampons—
with the erotic awe other gay men reserve for stag films of stags.

Here are a few snapshots from my mental album of Seattle:

• Dinner at a restaurant on the water. A sailboat, powered
by its motor, ripples up to the dock twenty feet away. This is the
hour when white people are most golden, and the young men
and women on board the craft give a literal sense to *jeunesse
dorée*. Slowly but too fast they pull white trousers and shirts
over their swimsuits, run fingers through their hair and stroll
with stylish nonchalance into the restaurant for food.

• An elderly straight woman stands up during a Seattle
church discussion and remarks, "I have nothing against homosexuals, but a girlfriend of mine in San Francisco complains
about the tromping outside her house by gay men cruising all

night long. And even during the day, whenever she opens her door, there it is: sex. Boots, boots, boots, as Kipling would say. I do hope that won't happen here."

• A long, wonderful evening with three new friends. First stop, a drink on the deck at Ray's for the nine-thirty sunset (the twilight lingers on another hour). Salmon leap above the water with muscular thrashing to catch mosquitoes. We are looking across the place where Salmon Bay debouches and down the articulated length of the Olympic Mountains—massive, rigid, aspiring, as though the earth had thrown out a challenge to God and then frozen in fright. To the left, just across an inlet, a forested hill juts up abruptly; half-concealed houses are lighted from within. Second stop, Hiram's-at-the-Locks, where we sit in a plush booth and regard the last of the day. A train passing over the locks (which divide the salt-water sound from the fresh-water lake) is carrying stacked automobiles; their windows, depthless silhouettes, press patterns into the tender sky. Next stop, a lookout spot on Queen Anne Hill. Below us is the city as brilliant as a brooch on black velvet. On to the bars.

• A visit to a professor at the University of Washington. We sit, bare-chested, on the grass, squinting into the early-afternoon light. Students with books slouch past. "I'd say that Seattle and Houston are the hippest gay cities after New York and San Francisco. It takes about fifteen months for a new kink (fistfucking, say) to travel from San Francisco to Seattle. There may not be as much sex on the hoof here as in San Francisco, but I make out at the bars any night of the week I go. The city itself is as homogeneously middle-class as any place in the country."

• A young man of twenty-two tells me his coming-out story: "I had a spastic colon. After it didn't get better, the family doctor said, 'I know what's wrong with you, and so do you. I won't say the word—it would embarrass us both. But why don't you visit this place?' And he wrote down for me the address of the city's office for sexual minorities' counseling center. I went twice, the therapist got me to say I was gay. That night I was listening to a record that says, 'Don't wait, don't hesitate, your youth is a mask, it won't last'—and I decided to tell my friends and family. My twin took it well. I didn't think he would, but he told me he loved me—the first and only time. 'If that makes you happy, then fine.' He and my dad and my younger brother are all in the construction business. Very macho. My girlfriend, who was already fed up with me because I wouldn't sleep with her, cried when I told her. I cried, too. She's a very feeling person. We're still best friends. She shows up whenever I'm down. I sometimes think she must be psychic.''

• Someone asks me: "Are people *really* into leather in New York? I mean, is it a *popular* scene?"

• I attend a benefit for gay politics at Jack McGovern's Music Hall, a vaudeville palace erected in 1929. Gays have bought out the house, but the floor show was obviously created for straight conventioneers. A man in white tails rises out of the floor playing some Barry Manilow treacle on a mirrored piano while chorus girls in pasties and scanties kick vigorously. No one except me seems dismayed by the low consciousness of the event. When I mention to someone it seems odd for gay men to patronize a tits-and-ass display that could be viewed as exploitative of women, he says, "Oh, there's so little to do in Seattle"—which, strictly speaking, isn't true, since the Seattle Opera presents Wagner's entire Ring Cycle in July both in German and English and the Seattle Repertory Company performs six nights out of seven from October to May. The Joffrey Ballet, on summer tour, is a Seattle favorite, and the Pacific Northwest Dance Ballet Company has a long spring season.

The leading lady of the Music Hall, who really is a talented singer, appears dumbstruck by the ovation. "Who *are* you guys, anyway?" she exclaims. "You're great!" When she introduces the chorus boys, one by one, the applause varies according to the Peter Meter. The master of ceremonies, an old hand at conventions, reels off the names of the sponsoring gay groups without consulting a list or placing inverted commas into his tone and then throws the spotlight on the reigning drag Empress of

Seattle—and on me, the "famous sexual authority." Nods and smiles all around, and on stage the finale, an energetic, brainless "salute to Broadway."

• Drinks halfway up the Space Needle in a cocktail lounge slowly revolving five hundred feet above ground. A child nearby is served a smoking blue potion in a goblet larger than his head. He bends over the steam, like someone in Macbeth (a line, "Cool it with a baboon's blood," darts through my brain). The bay inches into view as imperceptibly as dawn and we watch a stray Tall Ship pull into harbor; Seattle is still small enough for *everyone* to be excited about this event. As tipsy in the middle of the day as corporate-executives, we call a taxi; our driver tells us about his son, who's just now adding a few grace notes to his dissertation on the reticular activating mechanism.

For me the most representative gay man in Seattle was "Ned." He is six-foot-five (how happy Frederick the Great's father would have been in the Northwest, he who paid bounties for—and even kidnapped—soldiers over six feet tall). Ned's eyes are gray, his hair dark blond, shading into an auburn beard. His voice makes good gold fillings resonate on the harmonics and his personality is so candid that through sympathetic magic it could evince the truth out of a career diplomat. He lives just off Broadway, the gay strip, on Capitol Hill, the gay ghetto.

He grew up in a small town in Washington across the border from Portland. Though he messed around with the neighbor boys during puberty, those experiments fell off—until he was sixteen and attended his first meeting of the Gay Liberation Front (that was in 1969) with a gay buddy he'd known since junior high. "I told my parents I was going to a 'coffee house,' that's all I said, but they were so worried I'd become a hippie they grounded me. That made me mad enough to run away for a week and drift around town. Finally I came home so my mother wouldn't worry. Actually, I was so introverted that the gay meetings had little effect on me (I can hardly remember all this stuff, it happened so long ago). Well, in my senior year I told my friends I was gay. Everybody was hip back then, remember, and they just said, 'Dig it.' Now, of course, my old high school has sunk back into the 1950s. I tried very hard to go straight, but I couldn't; somewhere in me is a fierce individualist who won't conform, no matter how hard *I* might try."

Ned clearly is his own man. In a city where weightlifting hasn't caught on yet among gay men, he punctually pumps up three times a week. Though he is about as self-conscious as a mountain waterfall, he is fascinated by the arts. In New York we are studiously underplayed with potential tricks and wildly expressive with old friends; I always know someone fancies me when he's grimly monosyllabic—and has lost interest when he starts gushing over Baryshnikov. I could find none of this guile in Ned. Though I was a potential (and soon actual) conquest, he rattled merrily on about "loving" this and "adoring" that while he trudged hugely about his living room or laboriously unlaced his hiking boots.

"I came to Seattle for college and went underground. I was too broke and too young to go to the bars and too shy to attend gay meetings. Besides, the only *visible* gay men were too outrageous to appeal to me. But in acting class I made a friend and we went to Shelly's Leg, the most fabulous disco ever, which I'm afraid has closed now. Shelly was a radical lesbian whose real leg was shattered in an accident; with the insurance money she opened her place. That was in 1972 and it was Seattle's first disco: beautiful paintings, deco decor, lines outside every night. But Seattle isn't as friendly as Portland and I was afraid to approach anyone. Now the big disco is the Brass Door, I guess. People here are so conservative that one night when I appeared there in full leather (a Seattle first), I overheard someone say, 'Looks hot on him but I couldn't be seen with him—what would my friends think?!' "

Ned has had one year-long affair with another youthful giant, something that ended unhappily because his friend was *too* flirtatious. ("Promiscuity doesn't bother me. I certainly don't believe in fidelity. But all those *dates* with other men?")

Ned is a true booster of Seattle, despite a few reservations. He's come out of his shell (picture the shell for such a big turtle) and has made a host of friends. His bar technique now is im-

peccably assured (he goes four times a week), and he also meets
many men at the gay beach on Lake Washington beside the
university arboretum or during the gay volleyball games in the
park on Sunday afternoons or Wednesday evenings or during
the gay *bowling* period on Sunday mornings at the Palladium
Bowl. ("All twenty lanes are packed!")

Like most Seattleites he can also list the city's more general
advantages. Its numerous art galleries in Pioneer Square. The
three miles of paths for jogging around Green Lake. The
world's largest salmon, halibut and crab fleet. The new King-
dome stadium where the Seahawks play football, the Super-
sonics basketball and the Mariners baseball. The port's $50 mil-
lion revenue a year, which makes it one of the busiest in the
country. The seventy-four acres of the Seattle Center, the 1962
World's Fair grounds. . . . I pleaded total devotion to Seattle.
Ned grinned approval and said, "But don't tell anyone how
great it is. We already have too many people and too much
good publicity (*New West* said Seattle is the most liveable city
in the country). But you can tell gays; we need more of them."
Several times I heard citizens give the pitch and resist the sale,
caught in the ambivalence between civic pride and innate iso-
lationism. Both drives are strong in Seattle and leave the out-
sider confused.

Ned was active in the fight against Initiative 13, the measure
worked up by two Seattle policemen to revoke the city's fair
employment and open-housing ordinances (in effect almost ten
years). These ordinances protect homosexuals against discrimination. The cops, David Estes and Dennis Falk, were interesting
characters. Estes, a Mormon, made his anti-gay crusade a bit
fuzzy by dragging in larger "philosophical" issues. As he said,
"Homosexuality is not the problem in America. Humanism is
the problem in America. This humanism has crept into the
churches. What we're fighting is to get this back out of the
churches. There have to be some absolute moral values." A creep-
ing sign of "humanism" (which doesn't sound all bad to me,
whatever it means, but what do I know?) is, according to Estes,
a growing "toleration" of "suicide, euthanasia and abortion."
His crony, Falk, used to serve on what he called the "queer

detail" and remarks, "We worked on queers, prostitution and narcotics. And the three are interrelated many times." Before that Falk tried, back during the university upheavals of the late Sixties, to slap some sense into Leftist students. Quite literally. He still relishes the memory of the leather gloves he wore with the lead linings, which he attests were very "effective" in gaining "respect." The mayor had to remove the overly eager Falk from that assignment. Two years ago Falk was in trouble again with his superiors, this time for carrying "hot-load" or supercharged bullets, which travel faster than regulations allow. He was sent off to a psychologist for treatment. But no amount of discouragement can cause Falk to give up the force, despite the fact that he is independently wealthy (he and his brother are rich land developers).

Following the revocation of pro-gay ordinances in Dade County, St. Paul, Wichita and Eugene, the two cops could have justifiably expected an easy victory. But they made several mistakes. Estes, in his battle against the scourge of humanism, took a swipe at women as well. Initiative 13 would also have removed the enforcement and investigative powers of the city's Office of Women's Rights and turned them over to another agency, thereby destroying a major bulwark of Seattle feminism. As a result, the president of the League óf Women Voters came out against the measure.

Whereas shrewder bigots have focused on the sensitive issue of homosexual teachers, Estes and Falk chose to attack fair housing and employment standards. Though few heterosexuals might want to *endorse* homosexuality, still fewer want to *deny* anyone's right to rent an apartment or get a job. Worse, when Estes and Falk published the sources of their campaign funds, much of the money turned out to be from outside the city and even out-of-state (Anita Bryant was a major contributor)—something that riled the xenophobic Seattleites.

But the most disastrous moment for the anti-gay and anti-humanism crusade occurred when Falk found himself killing an unarmed black robbery suspect. Though Falk was acquitted of wrongdoing in the shooting, he lost the support of a black leader, Wayne Perryman. SOME (Save Our Moral Ethics), the Estes-Falk campaign, was beginning to smell bad.

On the gay side, the leaders of Citizens to Retain Fair Employment hatched a simple, well-rounded strategy. As Charles Brydon (now cochairperson of the National Task Force) explained to the *Seattle Weekly*, "One of the things we found in looking at campaigns in other cities was that the issue was not articulated in a way that people could feel comfortable supporting it." They realized that few ordinary citizens would stand up and say, "Sure, I'm for homosexuality." As a result, the committee made privacy the central issue and drew up a poster of a keyhole with an eye peering through it. "YOUR PRIVACY IS AT STAKE! WHO'S NEXT?" was the slogan. Privacy is something that the people of the Northwest can easily get worked up over. Throughout the campaign pro-gay speakers invoked the days of the McCarthy witch trials. Sexual morality and lifestyle were not brought up.

The best thing that happened for the Citizens was the strong, early pro-gay stand that the Seattle Church Council took. At a forum on the measure a Catholic priest said that Initiative 13 was "a confused, stupid law . . . that would enshrine prejudice." Protestant ministers and rabbis also condemned the Initiative. Another priest, somewhat less clearly, explained, "The church's teaching can be summed up in this way: homosexuality is evil; homosexual acts are evil; and the homosexual 'alternate lifestyle' is a deviant lifestyle. But homosexual people, who are not responsible for their homosexuality because they did not cause it, should be treated with love and respect." Don't you love theology? A rabbi pointed out that a quarter of a million homosexuals were killed in Nazi concentration camps. The leader of Women Against Thirteen said, "This is a dangerous initiative. It opens us up to mass discrimination, and I wonder who's next." The mayor, his wife and their children all took a stand against SOME. One newspaper columnist dismissed Falk and Estes as belonging to the "fright wing," and another consulted the Bible and decided Jesus intended us to love and forgive one another (Estes seems to be more impressed by Moses than Jesus). The debates left some voters confused. One said, "Of course I'm not going to vote for it—I don't think homosexuals should have lower property taxes."

On November 7, 1978, Initiative 13 was defeated by an overwhelming 65 percent. Once again the Northwest demonstrated its unpredictable individualism. At the same time this progressive move was made, voters eased restrictions on police gun use and said no to mandatory busing. No matter how I might feel about these particular issues, I could only be impressed by this independence of mind. We are sometimes told that democracy doesn't work. But it's flourishing in the Northwest.

SANTA FE, SALT LAKE CITY AND DENVER

Sex and Temperament in the Rockies

Santa Fe was a benign stopover on my way to Salt Lake City. I couldn't get any closer by plane to Santa Fe than Albuquerque; from there I rode overland an hour and a half in a shuttle van beside two elderly lesbians of the sort one keeps snapping mental shots of along the arcades of shops or through the window of a passing station wagon or at the opera. One was robust, jolly, cheeks as healthy as a farmgirl's; she was faintly deferential to her companion, a Xerox copy of Gertrude Stein (Roman nose, hooded eyes, hair *en brosse*), except this woman also had earlobes as stretched out as a bodhisattva's and never spoke above a murmur. She had an aristocratic limp and (too good to be fictive) a malacca cane. Now she was in denims and a silk blouse whose pattern showed two women in Empire gowns outside a gazebo (perhaps Austen's Emma and the pliant Harriet Smith, who "certainly was not clever, but she had a sweet, docile, grateful disposition, was totally free from conceit and only desired to be guided by anyone she looked up to"). I saw the bodhisattva at night during the intermission of *Tosca* in black linen slacks and a lace *rebozo* glinting with brilliants. A cool breeze had blown up. Retired gay men in jackets the colors of Italian ices melted around her. In the distance the lights of Los Alamos glittered provocatively. She looked very rich and very remote.

New Mexico has been since the Twenties a desert retreat for wealthy, older lesbians and homosexuals, those heirs to fortunes whose origins are shadowy, those dilettantes who paint or sculpt or write poetry in their expensive, simple adobe houses and who emerge on the streets at brief intervals in much-laundered sneakers, elaborate turquoise-and-silver jewelry, a mane of white hair streaming away from a bronzed face. The story of their lives—their straightlaced childhoods, their failed society marriages, their self-imposed exiles in the desert, summoned there by the call of such prophets as D. H. Lawrence, Witter Bynner, Willa Cather, Mabel Dodge Luhan, or Georgia O'Keeffe—this story will never be written, for privacy is something they equate with individuality, which by definition (they think) cannot be explained by resorting to such "crude" terms as money, artistic vogues, or sexuality. My own sketch is just a vague impression compiled over the years from glimpses and hearsay.

The only notion that occurs to me is that when sexual deviation was still the province of the visionary bohemians of the past, there was approval within that tiny group of strange, even bizarre patterns, and quite varied physical, spiritual and artistic destinies were expected and even hailed. A man might construct for himself, say, an elaborate erotic existence with a homosexual man his own age *and* a younger married couple *and* an older bisexual woman. Systems of occult thought gave permission to such a constellation ("Doris is my anima, Fred my solar twin, the darling Murrays reenact for me the Hopi ritual of rebirth"). But with the politicization of sex in the Seventies, people are pressured into more narrowly prescribed ways of rebelling. Chastity, for instance, is now suspect, and bisexuality (despite evidence to the contrary) has been declared a form of rank hypocrisy. I want to contrast the individualism of the past with the liberation movement of the present. The sort of individualists one sees in Santa Fe are the remnants of a wealthy bohemian clan that sponsored Isadora Duncan, Imagism, and native crafts; in their own lives people of the clan justified their behavior by invoking the pleasure principle and their privileges as superior (that is, artistic) people. The new liberationists, as Octavio Paz has pointed out, have yet to mention "pleasure" at all. For them the new sexual morality is a matter of science (homosexuality is natural) and justice (homosexuals should have equal rights). That an argument about nature should be cited as the basis for a social policy is peculiarly American, according to Paz, for only in the United States has science been so enshrined. In other cultures, what is legal is based on what is good for society (and the natural is seldom seen as socially beneficial).

As we approached Santa Fe the earth became redder and the terrain hillier, each gentle hummock covered with small dark bushes (the hills looked like poppy-seed rolls). The town itself has no public transportation, no taxis and only about 60,000 people, who fall into two classes: rich and poor. Three cultures meet here: Anglo, Native American, and Chicano. The rich Anglos live outside town along dirt roads in adobe houses that sell for at least $100,000. The Indians and Chicanos live everywhere else; some of the Indians continue to dwell in their pueblos, where many of them practice crafts. On weekdays in the summer Indian women sell turquoise jewelry and blankets under the arcade in front of the Governor's Palace, a block-long, one-story building first erected in the seventeenth century. They display their merchants' licenses and signs that declare, "Genuine Indian Jewelry" (the Anglo hippie jewelrymakers sell here illegally and are periodically driven away by the police). The Indian women sit impassively in folding metal chairs with blankets over their knees, their calm silence interrupted only by a sudden flurry of anger when a tourist tries to take their picture.

Santa Fe is so high that the air is thin and with my deeply smoked lungs I found it hard to walk more than a few paces without feeling faint. As a result I saw the town through a veil—sparkling, separated from me, dreamlike. I stayed with my oldest friend outside town in the dormitory of a small liberal arts college, where every teacher is expected to teach every subject and the students work their way through several yards of Great Books. In this rarefied atmosphere (literally and figuratively) I sat through a three-hour-long seminar on Aristotle's Prime Mover, during which the professor refused to give his own opinion and confined himself to asking questions of the students. This is the education I theoretically approve of—anti-authoritarian, idea-oriented, stripped of facile opinion-mongering—but when confronted with it I had to deal with the impatient Hitler within, that internal dictator who wanted to shout, "But it's pointless to continue—you're making a category mistake!" There was something humbling and patience-inducing about sitting still, not speaking and listening to ten people of all ages and backgrounds (the summer scholars) grope toward a rather good consensus.

I spent an evening with a gay undergraduate, whom I'll call Phil. He was slender, small-boned, delicate but with a powerful forehead pulsing with a single vein, lightning striking twice, thrice, repeatedly in the same place—the kind of young man who defers to someone else's silly views but then hesitantly and methodically corrects them. He seemed as nervous and natural as a wild animal and as little concerned with his appearance (which, despite disregard, remained beguiling). "Santa Fe is a good place to come out," he said. "My straight friends here at school were either neutral or supportive." (*Supportive*, incidentally, is the one new word that all Americans are saying these days—a word, drawn from psychotherapy, that suggests endorsement but leaves room for some divergence of opinion. More importantly, whether one is "supportive" or not is more a question of sympathy than of policy, of emotional range rather than intellectual accord). "In this town," Phil added, "people expect men to be gay. Of course there are no active gay groups here—it's too small. But you can be openly gay anywhere on jobs downtown. I'm openly gay at the shop where I work. My boss is gay and his partner, a straight woman from Texas (she's fabulous, she calls everyone 'Tiggy Two-shoes')—she gave him an orgy on his birthday."

Phil threw in "orgy" with a quick, testing glance and a half-suppressed grin. He told me he knew little of the world beyond Santa Fe and was uncertain about what shocks or bores big-city gays. Sophistication, or at least madcap behavior, held a fascination for him I would not have anticipated, given the fact he himself was as straightforward as a Quaker. He folded both feet under him in his chair and assumed the Lotus pose—apparently his normal position. The thunderbolt vein down his forehead continued to shazzam, lending an odd emphasis to his understated words. "Here at school I came out with another student. At first I was paranoid and afraid I'd lose friends. But people here are very detached; soon I was staying in his room in the dorm or he in mine. Guys fast-dance with other guys at school dances, and no one assumes they're gay unless they say they are."

Phil told me that in most Chicano families he knows about there are usually five or six children, and one of these is invariably gay. "Some of the gay Chicanos are so disciplined and so devoted to work that they think an affair with a guy would be too messy. I met this one Chicano, but he was so loaded down with Catholic guilt that he couldn't come. He lived at home with six brothers and sisters; when we'd have sex we'd have to drive to the ski basin and find a place off the road. I wanted to go with him, but he didn't like the idea."

As Phil talked in my dormitory room (as cool and stark as a monk's cell) I realized he was completely devoid of manner; the room and his personal style seemed equivalently undecorated. In my own students at Johns Hopkins I've seen a similar directness —no feminine wiles in the girls, no masculine bravado in the boys. When we read *A Streetcar Named Desire* in one class they found no pathos or faded charm in Blanche DuBois; they were merely irritated by her deviousness. ("Why doesn't she say what she means?") Privately I felt a bit assaulted by their lack of comprehension, but as I looked out at their open faces (the girls in pants and wearing no makeup, the boys unpompous in their dealings with girls) I flashed on the thought that this is the future. To be nostalgic for the male-female role-playing of the past (imaginative and artificial and tragic as it might have been) is as irresponsible as being nostalgic for the neurotic games of gay oppression (imaginative and artificial and tragic as they might have been). A generation is growing up that takes the tenets of feminism for granted; lack of sympathy for Blanche DuBois seems a small price to pay for their health.

In the winter Santa Fe is a small town where the local gays

flock to the gallery openings and linger in the bookstores hoping
to find someone to talk to. Blizzards sweep down from the mountains and confine people to their houses. The few gay men who
venture forth to the bar called the Senate sit around, gossip with
friends, and speculate about the beautiful numbers next summer will bring. Hippies in sheepskin coats come down from the
mountains to warm up. The gay Indians stick together. In the
back straight Chicano men shoot pool. At closing time someone
announces an impromptu party that attracts four or five in-
somniacs and rattles on into the night like a pickup truck down
a deserted road.

In the summer the Plaza (the square in the middle of town)
is crowded with tourists and the possibility of adventure is always just around the corner—or even now strolling toward you
down the arcade. "But I prefer the winter," a gay man who
works in a bookstore told me. "The prices go down, people
become homebodies, and the art world and the gay world overlap—it's really very nice. At Christmas time people put candles
in those gutters that protrude from houses and the buildings
shine like giant Christmas trees."

In July a cat's tail might be dangling from such a gutter,
twitching lethargically in the heat, a rhumba in danger of extinction. The adobe shades from faded brown to burnt siena to
geranium pink. Everything is low and horizontal and few
masonry corners are sharp—the adobe, like an Italian soldier,
resists a crisp right-angle turn. Because the clay is so easily
molded it assumes the shapes of fantasy: oval, even round doors;
archer's slits for windows; tilted, asymetrical halls; a cascade
of outdoor terraces—big, little, potbellied, or pressed up to the
wall like a shadow at noon. In San Miguel, the oldest church
in the United States, grass sprouts out of the walls in an effort
to remind us that adobe is clay from the earth. I wandered under
dark wood beams beside crudely turned wood pillars along the
Plaza and into a chapel where a rehearsal of contemporary
music was in full bleep, crash, honk, and screeching tape-rewind
(the bearded composer in short sleeves perspiring over his own
score, like a new cook approaching the tenth step of Julia
Child's Veal Prince Orloff recipe). Angels in nineteenth-century

paintings looked down on the stylish cacophony with hyper-
trophic eyes and rounded lips.

"It's hard to explore your sexual fantasies in a small town,"
a young professor told me. "I've been living here for five years
—virtually the entire time I've been out. There's a large art
colony here, but it's cliquish and the college forms my entire
society. I'm openly gay at school but I won't have sex with the
students; if I'm fired I want it to be clear it's because I'm gay
in the abstract, not because I've fucked up some student's head.
As it turns out, my homosexuality is no big deal here."

We sat in the college coffee shop while children of all colors
played beside us under the supervision of a student. This place
seemed the fulfillment of all the liberal dreams of the Sixties:
the races, religions and ages integrated, differing sexual orienta-
tions respected, luxury banished and decent comfort insured—
though of course such peace to think, such open, uncontaminated
mountain vistas to contemplate, such a sweet scent of wet grass
and piñon pines to inhale—these are the luxuries that now are
beyond the means of us all. I envied these students reading
Homer and hearing the roar of Zeus in the thunder rolling
across the hills and *arroyos*.

The professor told me about a Native American friend who
lives nearby in a pueblo. This man, whom I'll call Arnie, is
in his sixties and holds a respectable position in the community.
When he was just six years old his parents told him he would
not become an ordinary male but would be a "substitute
woman." This prediction was offered simply and matter-of-factly
to the child, who accepted it in the same spirit. Though he does
not strike others as effeminate, he has always played the "female
role" in sex (French active, Greek passive, as the ads say; will
archaeologists in the future speculate about our obsessive interest in foreign verbs?). His sexual partners have always been the
straight men of his village, those whose wives are absent or ill
or ill-disposed toward them; they knock at night on Arnie's
door. He likes men who have at least four or five children, a
proof of their virility. He lives in a large rambling house, surrounded by books, and sleeps in an old four-poster bed. He is
short, thin, smooth-skinned, wonderfully pacific.

Two Anglo gays of his age who've known Arnie for years have tried to convince him he should sleep with gay men, but he regards the idea as laughable. He does not frown on gay men; in fact, he is intrigued by them and is eager to meet more. But homosexuals he thinks of indulgently as "sisters," nothing more or less. (Or as "birdlovers," since the word in his language for penis is bird.) His own approach to sex (and his place in the pueblo) is so secure he senses no need to question it.

Younger gay tribesmen, however, do not enjoy this tranquillity. They have absorbed Chicano ideas about machismo and Anglo ideas about gay liberation—and the result is total confusion. Some of them are drinking themselves to an early death. When I visited the Senate I saw one Indian staggering about begging money for drinks. As he stood in the flashing disco lights I studied him. He was tall and slender, his clothes ragged. Long, coarse, shiny black hair fell away from a ravaged young face: deepset eyes alternately anxious and swooning, chipped teeth, a small black goatee curling back over his chin toward an Adam's apple as prominent as his great aquiline nose. His presence seemed to annoy a table of three sleek, plump Indians nearby, their long hair pulled back into ponytails secured by red bandanas.

Arnie stands above these crosscurrents. He is part of the dying traditional culture. For instance, he is important in the Clown Clan, which participates in the annual harvest dance. The clowns are often homosexual. They cover their legs in white chalk on which they paint black stripes. Their hair is caked with white mud and twisted into two knots that look like horns. Each clown wears around his neck a crucifix on which Christ is also dressed and painted as a clown. Many of the clowns wear bits of drag (a woman's blouse or jewelry). The job of the clowns during the ceremony is to provoke laughter and cause the other dancers to stumble. References to homosexuality are guaranteed to elicit good-natured mirth—as when Arnie suddenly performed a mock wedding ceremony between two unsuspecting men known to be gay. The humor is not malicious or nervous; homosexuality lies comfortably within the system of this culture. Now, however, everything is deteriorating. The young men are either indifferent to the old rituals or too drugged or drunk to participate in them.

I flew into Salt Lake City beside a six-foot-five, twenty-year-old missionary who was returning to Utah after two years in Kansas City amongst the "Gentiles" (as Mormons call all non-believers). He was a dull, torpid fellow; I doubt if he was effective in proselytizing. Like all young Mormon men he had been expected to serve as a missionary for two years (there are about 26,000 in the field now). Like the others he had paid his own expenses out of his savings. Besides the few things in his bag all he owned was the shiny black suit and skinny black tie he was wearing. He kept craning his neck trying to catch a glimpse of Salt Lake beyond the bald, forbidding Wasatch Mountains; looking down on this dramatically corrugated wasteland I shuddered, imagining the agonies of the first Mormon pioneers crossing the Rockies on their way to Zion in the spring and summer of 1847.

The state symbol of Utah is the beehive. A black beehive on a white shield decorates every highway sign and is frequently an insignia for Mormon activities. When the Mormon pioneers first settled the West they owned a true empire (comprised of present-day Utah, most of Nevada and Arizona, Southern California, much of Wyoming, Colorado and New Mexico and parts of Oregon and Idaho), which they dubbed "Deseret," the word for honey bee in the *Book of Mormon*. In the Tabernacle itself a beehive is sketched on the ceiling above the organ. The hive is an emblem of industry, and one is reminded of the hair-raising original Fourteenth Article of Faith (now substantially toned down), which concluded, "An idle or lazy person cannot be a Christian, neither have salvation. He is a drone, and destined to be stung to death, and tumbled out of the hive."

A first impression of Salt Lake City presents an image of industry, solemnity, conformism and remarkable organization. Every street in the city is numbered on a grid outward from the Temple which, its six spires illuminated at night, can be seen from miles away. A gold statue of the Angel Moroni (the son of Mormon) dominates every vista. As one drives through this immaculate city one sees row after row of solid, homely houses, organized into "wards" that, in turn, make up larger units known as "stakes." In Salt Lake a ward comprises only three or four blocks, though in rural areas it may cover many square miles. Each ward characteristically has its own chapel, recreation hall and classrooms for religious instruction.

Mormons do not believe in smoking or drinking (though in fact many do both and the rate of alcoholism in Utah, where 70 percent of the people are Mormons, is alarmingly high). These prohibitions have affected life in the state, where the distinction between religious and civil authority is more theoretical than actual and where most officials are church members. Smoking is forbidden in public places, except in specially designated areas, and restaurants do not serve drinks. There were once several heterosexual pornographic movie houses in town, but all except one have been driven out of business, and Mormons continue to picket the last holdout.

A full summary of the tenets of the Church of Latter-Day Saints (as the Mormon faith is properly called) would be beyond the scope of these notes, but a few must be mentioned if the church's attitude toward homosexuality is to be understood. Every man and boy over the age of twelve may hold the priesthood in this religion without clergy (and indeed must if he is a member in good standing). The priesthood is divided into two branches, one concerned with temporal affairs, the other with spiritual. Women cannot be priests; in fact, an unmarried woman cannot rise to the highest rank in heaven. Only through her husband's intervention can she "obtain a fullness of glory." The body shall be literally resurrected (though without the blood).

Mormonism is the only true faith. As a consequence, the Mormons pay no attention to the usual distinction between Protestants and Catholics; to a Mormon they seem equally misguided. The end of the world is coming soon, during which a mighty battle will be fought between the forces of good and evil. Armageddon is so imminent that most Mormon houses have a "fully furnished basement" as the realty ads put it: a storeroom stocked with a two-year supply of food and other necessities and considerable ammunition. That the specter of

the end of the world happens to coincide with the passé craze
for bomb shelters is merely a neat overlay of two millennial fantasies. A person can be saved only if he or she is baptized, but
ancestors can be posthumously baptized if their names are
known. As a result, the Mormons maintain huge, computerized
genealogical files. These files contain literally billions of names.

There are four million Mormons (including one million
who live overseas). Church income—from tithing and many
church-owned businesses—is rumored to exceed $1 billion a year.

Since its founding in 1830, Mormonism has forbidden black
men to enter the priesthood. Their skin color is taken as evidence that they are of the cursed descendants of Cain mentioned
in the *Book of Abraham* (1:26). But the Mormons believe in
continuing revelations from God, and on June 9, 1978, President
Spencer W. Kimball announced that a new revelation had rescinded the previous injunctions against blacks. This decision
—in response to embarrassing lawsuits from black organizations
and the moral outrage of many young, liberal Mormons—has not
pleased older conservatives; the "Concerned Latter-Day Saints"
published a full-page advertisement in the *Salt Lake Tribune*
on July 23 denouncing the revelation.

One evening, stoned on grass, I walked with a Mormon
friend through the city. Though it was late, past dinner, the
summer light persisted. There was a sense that the city had in-
haled a sharp intake of breath and refused to release it. There
were no clouds in the sky except a few amateur finger paintings
against the horizon. Everything had a glow and purity about it.
Light seemed to well up from within objects; the lawns burned
with green fire. Mountains rimmed the valley all the way around.
The broad streets, laid out by Brigham Young, are 132 feet
wide, the sidewalks twenty feet wide—thoroughfares for giants.
A mauve peak in the distance was as sharply detailed as the individual rails on the porch of the house beside me. No one was
out and no sound could be heard. We crept along through this
entranced place and for a moment I could believe it was the
City of Saints. Then the distant dome of the Utah State Capitol
transformed itself into a beehive and I pictured myself being
stung to death.

The status of marriage holds a special significance for Mormons. Those marriages that are "Temple-consecrated" seal the partners together for eternity. Their children shall also abide with them forever. Anyone who is excommunicated from the church (as avowed and unrepentant homosexuals must be) is therefore divided from his or her family not only in this life but in the next.

Feminism has made few inroads; President Kimball, in his book *Marriage*, is able to describe a conventional patriarchal union with a confidence unthinkable in most other American sects. "You wouldn't want to work away from home anyway, Mary," he tells the hypothetical bride, "for women are expected to earn the living only in emergencies, and you must know that many are the broken homes resulting when women leave their posts at home. You see, if both husband and wife are working away from home and come home tired, it is very easy for unpleasantness and misunderstandings to arise. And so, Mary, you will remain at home, making it attractive and heavenly, and when John comes home tired, you will be fresh and pleasant; the house will be orderly; the dinner will be tempting; and life will have real meaning." Throughout his writings Kimball betrays such a certainty about things-as-they-were that he begins to seem almost charming. Habituated as we are to trendy double-talk, Kimball's uncompromising position seems refreshing.

But he has caused great suffering to homosexuals. Years ago he became a self-appointed "expert" in homosexuality and he has been making pronouncements about it regularly ever since. In his writing he advances the idea that homosexuality is an "evil habit" that is initially "chosen" by the transgressor and that can be cured only by "repentance" and positive thinking—despite the fact that many people feel they are homosexual though they have never developed a "habit" of relations with members of the same sex, despite the fact that no homosexual feels he or she has "chosen" to be gay and despite the fact that no amount of "repentance" can silence this particular need for affection in those who feel it.

One of the most clearheaded and sincere and touching documents I have ever read is a pamphlet titled *Prologue: An Examination of the Mormon Attitude Toward Homosexuality* by

an anonymous undergraduate at Brigham Young University.*
The author was prompted to write this fifty-eight-page essay in
response to a bigoted, moralistic lecture on homosexuality he
heard in a beginning psychology class at BYU. The essay not
only reviews all the leading psychological theories about the
etiology and treatment of homosexuality, it also specifically addresses itself to the church's position. We learn that, aside from
the repentance approach, the Mormons have instituted a program of aversion therapy. A case history of a young gay man
undergoing such therapy is cited:

> *He was given a battery of tests and interviews, then
> was set up on a conditioning therapy program coupled with
> hypnosis and supportive counseling. He was sent to Salt
> Lake to magazine stores to find pictures of naked men that
> excited him. These were made into slides and flashed on a
> screen while he sat in a chair with electrodes strapped to his
> arms. As the pictures were shown, he was given a shock; the
> purpose being to couple the pain of the shock with the
> stimulating picture in order to condition him so that he not
> only disliked the shock but also the picture. This was the
> first time he had ever looked at pictures of naked men. He
> was given a dial to determine the strength of the shock, and
> was soon keeping it on full strength, as he was determined
> to be cured as quickly as possible. He came out of these
> sessions nauseated, shaking and with mild burns on his
> arms. He was hypnotized and told he would no longer think
> homosexual thoughts but would instead have heterosexual
> ones. The therapy sessions progressed well, and he was sent
> again to Salt Lake to find pictures of nude girls which were
> shown to him without the shock. He was counseled to let
> his imagination have free play on these pictures and was to
> let them be the basis of his sexual fantasies. He understood
> what they meant.*

---

* *Mormons interested in reading this essay or in contributing their
own accounts to a second publication about church attitudes toward
homosexuality are invited to write* Prologue, *P.O. Box 8666, Salt Lake
City, Utah 84108.*

For two years this therapy lasted, during which time he felt confident that he was changing and that homosexuality was behind him. His therapist was extremely pleased and had him write a letter, stating that he was now cured through these reconditioning techniques.

He was not cured.

Elsewhere in the essay we learn that the Mormons seem to spawn an unusually high number of homosexuals, that few of these men and women are able to leave their religion or family, that most of them marry and that they suffer and create suffering in their spouses. There is also a high rate of suicide among gay Mormons. A therapist specializing in homosexuality is quoted in *Prologue* as saying, "Oh! Those Mormons! What are they doing to their children? They seem to produce more homosexuals and yet they treat them so cruelly!" Similarly, another therapist, this one in the Los Angeles area, has said, "I work with more Mormon homosexuals than from any other religion, and I simply cannot understand how a church professing Christian ideals can do such dastardly things as that church does to its homosexual members. It is shameful. I have one coming with his parents to see me this evening. He is to meet with his bishop tomorrow. I am very concerned about what will happen in that interview."

The Open Door, a gay newspaper for Utah Mormons,* in one issue ran a reprint of a document, "Homosexuality, Welfare Services Packet," a brochure designed for officials of the Church of Latter-Day Saints in their dealings with homosexuals. It reveals that "a homosexual relationship is viewed by the Church of Latter-Day Saints as sin in the same degree as adultery and fornication"—that is, no better nor worse than heterosexual relations that occur outside marriage. The origin of homosexuality is again attributed to habit, often initiated in a child molested by an adult: "Some young children are molested by strangers, acquaintances or even relatives. This is usually deeply shocking and may cause feelings of unworthiness in the innocent victim.

---

* *The Open Door, P.O. Box 6186, Salt Lake City, Utah 84106. A year's subscription (twelve issues) is six dollars.*

Believing himself to be unclean, he is easy prey in later experiences. However, not all who are molested become homosexual. Self-control, free agency and help from others are very important in avoiding homosexuality."

The great fault of homosexuality is that it stands in the way of marriage and the fulfillment of God's plan for men and women: "Exaltation or enthronement and patriarchal leadership for eternity is a father's greatest reward. It is only possible when one is married. A woman is both wife and mother. A man is both husband and father. None of these roles can be performed through homosexual relationships. Any behavior that prevents one from receiving these eternal blessings is evil." Therefore, a single heterosexual would theoretically be considered as reprehensible as an unrepentant homosexual. If the real animus against homosexuality stems from a more general opposition to single life, then homosexuals are simply the most seemingly committed singles, emblematic of the others, and thus especially reprehensible. Whereas a heterosexual single can be perceived as someone who has failed to marry *yet*, this consoling notion will not accommodate homosexuals.

I spent one long day with "Norm," a balding blond in his thirties with a handsome face and a manner that shimmers between the winning charm of a child and the anxiety of an adult. He would like to be taken care of, seated on your lap and soothed, but a bristling fear of other people and an entrenched self-hatred cause him to freeze at some distance from you, where he stands grinning and crying and hurting. I've seldom seen anyone in such pain. He worries about his age, his looks, his sex appeal, his lack of money, though he is still young, handsome, appealing and far from destitute. Typically, he has thrown away his hairpiece because he's decided to be bald and proud, but now he wears a baseball cap to conceal his thinning hair.

Norm was born the son of a Roman Catholic father and a Mormon mother. His father left his mother when Norm was seven and went off to Colorado to become a sheriff and a hunter. Norm's mother remarried, this time to a staunch Mormon. They had two more sons. As he was growing up, Norm was told every day by his stepfather that he was ugly, weak, a sissy and "as useless as tits on a razorback hog." When he was nineteen he went to Los Angeles for a year, where he came out. But he couldn't find a job and limped home. When he was twenty-one he attempted suicide, survived and left for Los Angeles again. This time he found a quiet corporation exec who became his lover. They lived together for eight years. The exec bowled, never spoke ill of anyone, attended football games, avoided gay life (which mystified him); in his pachydermatous way he loved Norm—but Norm couldn't bear to have sex with him. He could become excited over the odd trick but not over his lover; a psychologist, more ready to interpret than I, would surely point out that guilt-ridden homosexuals prefer the instant, disposable trick to the permanent fixture of a lover, that built-in reminder of the continuing crime of same-sex love. During this period Norm kept visiting Salt Lake, seeking parental approval and never receiving it.

His relationship with the pachyderm ended. Norm returned to Salt Lake, then headed off for San Francisco, where he lived on Castro Street, grew his mustache, stayed high and horny—and reached the depths of poverty and despair. Once again he came home. He decided to work up an affair with a high school friend, another Mormon. "We've tried everything else and lost," they told each other. "Why not try each other?" This wise-sounding project, of course, ended in disaster.

In his attempt to win his stepfather's approval, Norm took a job in his firm. Though he did well, his parents continued to spurn him. One night he got drunk with a woman friend ("She gets off on the fact I'm into men, since she is, too"). This woman, who also worked for the firm, had recently had her favorite older brother die. With the bottoms of martini glasses for spectacles, Norm and his friend saw a vision: they decided to get married in order to placate his parents and to receive some lucrative presents from them (Norm has been disinherited three times). They called Norm's mother and announced the news. She wept and said it was the happiest day of her life. Though she is normally close-mouthed, she told everyone instantly about the impending wedding. But when Norm sobered up the next morning, he realized the marriage would be cruel to his woman friend and a sham for him. He never went back to work and stopped answering his phone. He has not spoken to his parents for three months. Now he is self-employed and living hand-to-mouth. Norm hops around jauntily and downs beer after beer, talking in a hopped-up doomsday voice. Just watching him made a skullcap of pain tighten around my head.

When he was a child he hated his genitals and if he could have urinated without touching his penis he would have done so. Despising the sexual organs appears to be something many Mormons feel. When a young person is brought into the church, he or she is given "garments" (a kind of long underwear) to protect him or her against the sins of lust. People wear their garments to bed, even bathe in them, and women have pelvic examinations without taking them off. Norm has had sex with Mormon boys who have refused to shed their garments. On the street one can detect the outline of garments under ordinary sports clothes.

A friend of Norm's dropped in to tell me his story. He had big ears, a boy's wild laughter, a sweep of blond hair worn Dennis-the-Menace fashion over his eyes, small, pointy features —and what came through this rather hectic appearance was a severe sense of purpose, an absolutely calm, adult idealism. He had, until recently, worked as the head of a rehabilitation program for convicts, focusing on those who need drug and alcohol counseling and psychotherapy. Les (as I'll call him) created a model program for the whole West and traveled from city to city setting up new facilities and advising already established units on how to improve their treatment plans.

But the charity for which he worked depended upon a sizable yearly contract from the federal government, money awarded to pay for the psychological preparation of federal prisoners about to reenter the world. When Les's boss asked one of his co-workers if Les was gay, she refused to speak and began to cry —which confirmed the boss's worst suspicions. The boss felt a moral issue was at stake; since Les can recommend early release and weekend passes and has access to prisoners' files, he could theoretically pressure a prisoner into having sex with him in exchange for favors. When the issue was presented in this light to a new federal judge (who also happens to be a bishop in the Mormon church), the judge said he would have to cancel the

government's contract. Although no one demanded Les's resig-
nation, he did not want the program he had built to collapse,
so he quit voluntarily. He has passed through the usual stages:
hurt, anger, weariness. Now he is considering starting a gay
disco with two other friends. When people complain about the
energy and ingenuity gays devote to silly pursuits, they should
be reminded that so many serious ones are closed to us.

A lesbian friend—Lana, as I'll call her—sat around with us
through the long afternoon. There was a kind of trench-buddy
excitement in the air; Norm confessed that other cities and non-
Mormon homosexuals seem dull after the tension of Salt Lake.
I recognized that they were all familiar with each other's sagas,
but they were eager to hear every word again. They couldn't
get enough of this talk about the Latter-Day Saints. Nor were
they willing to dismiss the church. Though none was still active
in it, all respected its achievements—its excellent medical care
for members, its famous charity system, its iron resolve in ad-
versity, especially during the pioneer days. As Lana said, "Now
those people you could respect. It's just their descendants I hate;
they've gone soft but are still living off the prestige of their
ancestors."

Lana was born and brought up in Northern Ireland as a
member of the Church of England. But she converted to the
Latter-Day Saints and brought her parents and brother and sister
into the faith as well. The whole family emigrated to Utah. Lana,
very much under the romantic spell of the United States, married
a GI, had a son and daughter—and got divorced after four years.
She had recognized that she is a lesbian. She has had many jobs
and trouble keeping them due to Mormon prejudice against
homosexuals. Her brother and sister, each of whom has spawned
a large family, will not permit her to be near their children lest
she molest them. When Lana first started going with her present
friend, the girl's parents, powerful people in Salt Lake, had Lana
fired from her job and evicted from her apartment; they also
attempted to get her deported by telling the immigration authorities of her lesbianism. None of these efforts stopped the
affair, which has been going on for fourteen years now. But Lana
and her friend were treated so coldly by their neighbors in Salt
Lake that they moved to a small town not far away, where

they ride horses, go cross-country skiing and live in relative isolation close to nature.

Not all gay Mormons talk obsessively about their oppression. Thaddeus, as I'll call him, bears the last name of one of the most renowned pioneer families, but he refuses to discuss Mormons or gays—or virtually anything, for that matter. He's twenty-two, a part-time student, stoned day and night. The letters he writes are marijuana fantasias, which a Viennese psychiatrist would consider adequate grounds for commitment but which any American under thirty would find endearing or at least familiar: doodles, crayoned stick figures, little yelps and gurgles ornamenting the margins, the mood of any sentence fragment dictated by which band of David Bowie the author happened to be listening to at the moment of composition.

From time to time Thad lives with his parents in a small Utah town, but for the most part he's crashing with friends in Salt Lake (for instance, with a jive-talking, pigtailed gay Mormon dropout back from New York) or tooling around in his beat-up van, following small rodeos that tour the West. With his restless, gimlet eyes, faded denims, unshaved, scruffy face, his slouch for a walk and the slow, sexy wink that is the only expression his stoic features will condescend to make, he might well be an out-of-work cowhand himself. Except a real working man will eventually unbend, tell you his story, clue you in on his theories about cancer, UFO's and the Truth about Who's Running This Fuckin' Country. Not Thad. His silence was as scrupulously observed as a holy vow.

Once, when we were driving past the Temple, he did refer to it under his breath as "Cinderella's Palace" and to the Angel Moroni as "Tinkerbell." And he did show me his grandparents' mansion in Salt Lake, near a polygamist's house. "Sure, polygamists are still around. My granddad was a polygamist, by the way, but he's dead now. See that high fence? Those polygamists never let their kids play with us. They were really shut off." On the other side of town he pointed out another polygamist's house but only to admire the architecture: the large main house, shining white under spots in the trees, connected to three lesser houses in the same style for the minor wives and their broods, the whole as immaculate as a boiled shirt front. Topiary bushes and clipped conical pines gave the mirage that extra fillip of un-reality—emerald studs on the shirt.

If I asked Thad a question about his family, his background, his religion, he'd mumble, "I don't know." "What?" "I don't know." Once he asked me if I was a private eye (he seemed serious). He had, by the way, an excited sexual imagination. The Mormons—with their witch-hunts, Old Testament patri-archs, their fetishizing, shame-inducing garments and shock-treatment therapy—have succeeded in producing a generation of gays with tastes kinkier than anything adumbrated in the grisly pages of *Drummer*. In this silent, sacred city, where the streets are deserted by nightfall, gays (and possibly straights) are acting out in bed fantastic resolutions to the eerie problems proposed by their religion.

The Mormons might seem merely an aberrant variety in our national bestiary did they not make manifest some latent tendencies which are widespread in American culture. The farm-ers in upstate New York who first embraced this religion were largely refugees from the Massachusetts Bay Colony, those whom the Half-Way Covenant had disinherited, seventeenth-century remnants surviving anachronistically into the nineteenth cen-tury. By contrast, the bustling, prosperous merchants in the nineteenth-century cities were busily discarding the morally de-manding, austere, comfortless religion of the Puritans and re-placing it with a cheerful, sentimental cult of self-help and self-congratulation more in keeping with the business ethic. This was a movement, engineered by newly disestablished min-isters and female belletrists, that resulted in today's *schlock* mass culture, as Ann Douglas convincingly argues in *The Femin-ization of American Culture*. The Mormons chose to reject these bewildering ameliorations of their forefathers' stern ideals. They may have added doo-dads of pseudo-science, half-baked philos-ophy and absurd "revelations" of Christ's sojourn in the New World to the chaste outlines of the old religion, but basically Mormonism is a recuperation of patriarchal values. The one "gain" of the Latter-Day Saints over Puritanism was a loosening up of the old belief in predestination (no matter that this gain has merely muddied the waters of logic). With the introduction of pleasing ceremonies and choirs, a redistricting of heaven into not one but four stages and the added thrill of continuing revelation, the conversion of the old church into the new was complete and an edifice of beliefs was ready for occupation.

Today, when many Americans feel they have nothing to choose between except mass culture (instant, fattening and unnourishing) and the fundamentalist sects (meat and potatoes), no wonder so many are drawn toward the sects. They offer standards and, just as important, regimens. The Mormons, for instance, structure every day of the week for members. Every moment, in fact, is accounted for; the beehive hums.

But the Mormons do not live in their own century and country. The demands of blacks have already toppled part of church doctrine. Women are unlikely to accept much longer their inferior position in the hierarchy. And gays are literally crying for succor. Whereas those few black heterosexuals who do convert to the Latter-Day Saints may presumably be fitted into the existing mold, feminists and political gays represent a more disturbing challenge to the Mormon supremacy of the family. The obvious solution—that dissident Mormons simply leave the hive—isn't available. The Mormon way of life, which penetrates every waking moment, makes all other kinds of existence seem alien. Gay Mormons always find a reason for returning to their families. Those I met in Salt Lake City had all had their years in Los Angeles, San Francisco or New York, but they had all come back. They want into the system, though their admission would change it profoundly.

I have no idea whether becoming gay is a political act. How can it be, if it is involuntary, as I feel it is? Or must we revise our ideas about the will? As a child I knew I didn't want to be "ordinary"; homosexuality, when it came along, seemed a permanent pledge against the soul-destroying family. Did I feel myself to be different because I already had intimations that I was gay? Or did I become gay as an outward symbol of the inward state of difference? Would we gays have preferred fitting in? Or did we have early glimmerings of another life and did homosexuality become the vehicle for our eventually traveling there? Are we victims or dissidents? Psychiatrists say men become gay when their fathers are distant and their mothers overpossessive. But (assuming there's some truth to this questionable hypothesis) could it be that we pushed our fathers away? That we were the ones who elicited overprotection in mothers who sensed their children wanted to live in another place and in another way?

Whether becoming gay is a political act or not, homosexuality always carries some political impact. The *intention* may be personal, but the *function* of homosexuality is social. Because most Americans dismiss "politics" as something that happens at the polls in the sham contests between two virtually identical parties, because they have substituted for the few issues that emerged in the Sixties an inane cult of "personalities" in the Seventies (thus *New Times* dies as *People* thrives)—because of this shallowness, Americans are not prepared to analyze the political force of feminism and gay liberation. But both movements have been made possible by particular social and economic conditions (namely the growth of cities and the decline of the family as an economically useful institution). Now, however, that our fuel sources are drying up, inflation is soaring and jobs are becoming scarce, we can anticipate a clash between singles and families. This conflict, long building as a sharp difference in values and attitudes, needs only the spark of a depression to set it off. Nor will the ideological virulence of either side be reduced through the new poverty. Feminism and gay liberation may have required times of plenty as a necessary if not sufficient condition for their birth, but by now these movements have molded expectations, and they will not be starved into extinction. But a dip in our national fortunes will undoubtedly confirm middle-class heterosexuals in their homophobia. In competition over a job, a God-fearing family man will feel justified in eliminating all rivals, especially singles; and righteous indignation will find its true target in gay women and men and in feminists, all of whom are rightly perceived as hostile to things-as-they-were.

Most gay Mormons, I'm convinced, want no part of this struggle. The anonymous author of *Prologue* concludes his essay by writing, "You have no idea of the envy I experience as I see my brothers, sisters and close friends marry and have children. In spite of all I know and have experienced about curing the homosexual, I still cannot let go of the eventual possibility of it for myself. But it is an undeniable fact that I am homosexual, and complete honesty in relationships precludes my getting married."

The center of gay life in Salt Lake City is the Sun Tavern, just a few blocks away from the Temple. It is a thriving establishment. There is one bar in the front manned by shirtless bartenders. Next to it is the disco, with supergraphics on the wall; many people stand to one side on a raised viewing platform and stare at the dancers. In the back is a big Western bar, where a six-member "hat band" was playing when I visited the Sun. In warm weather people sit outside in a patio at little metal tables and listen to someone goofing around on an electric piano. In still another part of the bar is a game room filled with pinball machines, a pool table and an oversize TV screen. Everyone gay or just odd comes to the Sun; it has a delightful ambience, the camaraderie of outlaws. At points the bar might seem straight, since so many gay women and men dance together.

I asked a middle-aged redhead to dance. He had haunted eyes and became acutely uncomfortable when I touched his hand. We went to a corner of the Western bar and had a drink. He told me his remarkable story. Until seven years ago he had been "just an ordinary gay man." Then, one day at the office, he experienced a strange euphoria, a sense of rising. He wept— and when he looked around he saw that the two other workers in the office were weeping, too. They had felt the same divine presence. After about two hours the aura faded. The other workers did not want to discuss it; the woman was afraid and the other man said they had been visited by the devil.

But Harris (as I'll call him) determined to investigate the event. That night he was sitting in his third-floor condominium when he heard a voice. He went to the window, but he saw nothing. He returned to his chair, heard the voice again and felt a warm hand in his. He has never felt the hand again, but ever since he has been receiving constant revelations. He has learned that God first created woman in man (Adam before his rib was plucked out of him) and this creature is The Homosexual. Harris's great secret is that gays make up the lost tribe, the holy 144,000 who are superior to straights: the elect. God, who needed to hide his true people, put them under the yoke and has made them suffer over the centuries. But soon Armageddon will come and the gays will conquer the straights (among whom the Mormons are especially evil). After the battle has been won, gays will be quickened and will live here on earth in bliss—*all* the gays who have *ever* existed. A few of the gays will go to heaven. The straights will all be damned.

Before Harris was touched by the Angel Michael (for that is the presence who visits him) he was fired from three jobs for being gay, one after another. In one case a boss, expecting a check, thought his secretary might have thrown it away by mistake. He went through her wastebasket and found there the first draft of a love letter Harris had written to someone in California. The boss pieced the scraps together and fired Harris the next day. Soon afterward Harris got the job he still holds—and began hearing his voices.

In the coming cataclysm, Harris will lead the gays to victory. The only price he must pay for this position as leader is total chastity. There are a few straights masquerading as gays, and if Harris were to go to bed with one by mistake he would be infected by evil. "If I sleep with a son of Satan," he told me as the banjo players picked out their tunes, "I will defile the temple."

He instructed me in how to read the Bible properly. Christ and his disciples were all gay. In the Old Testament, Jacob was gay, Esau straight. Harris eventually wrote out all the key Biblical passages for me, but I will include only a few. When the Lord tells Rebekah that "Two nations are in your womb" (Genesis 25:23), he is referring to the straight and the gay. When Christ says in Matthew 19:5, "The two shall become one flesh," he is referring not to straight marriage but to the androgynous homosexual body. Perhaps the real giveaway comes in Luke 20:34, when Christ says, "The sons of this age marry and are given in marriage, but those who are considered worthy to attain to that age and the resurrection from the dead, neither marry, nor are given in marriage; for neither can they die any more, for they are like angels, and are sons of God, being sons of the resurrection."

Harris is a well-liked, accepted figure in Salt Lake, but his

ordeal of chastity has made him suffer terribly. "Chastity is painful because the body aches," he told me. "But there's no turning
back. I have to come here to be near my people; I'm at the bar
nearly every night. God, by the way, announces himself not only
in the Bible and through revelation but even in the lyrics of
popular songs: 'I Write the Songs' by Barry Manilow, 'Let It Be,'
'Bridge Over Troubled Water.' You see? Okay? I have lots of
other signs. A constant palpitation of the heart, which is the
'quaking' mentioned in the Old Testament as the presence of
God. Or my arm will fall asleep, which happens because the
spiritual arm is rising up to touch heaven. Or horrible stomach
cramps, which is an announcement sent by the Holy Ghost.
You see?"

After Salt Lake City, Denver seemed an abrupt reentry into
the twentieth century. Thousands of blacks had converged on
the city for a Church Ushers' Convention. Ladies in white
gloves were holding parasols against the vicious sun and ambling
through the downtown; two of them posed before a shop window, one on either side of a giant Chinese vase, pretending to
hold it up while an elderly man shot their picture. A jaunty gay
waiter rushed in late to work in a restaurant where I dined
alone; he stripped out of his shirt on his way to the kitchen
and emerged a second later in his uniform, sibilant and joking.
In the still hot and sunlit evening I sat on a doorstep in restored
Larimer Square and listened to a blues singer belt out "Boozin'
and Gamblin' and Stayin' Up Late" while hippies lounged
nearby. The typical Denver youth is permanently tan, has long,
dirty-blond hair, a black beard growing in and is slender though
he's beginning to show signs of a nascent beer belly. He is shirtless and in cut-offs and he's hitchhiking, dealing drugs or playing
frisbee. In Cheesman Park, a gay cruising spot, I watched the
Caucasian members of a Korean karate group exercise in white
pants and jackets in the brilliant evening light, so bright it hurt
my eyes. Korean numbers were barked out by the Korean instructor and then repeated by the diligent students in a soft,
Western drawl. As one student pushed another around like a
human wheelbarrow, holding his ankles as he staggered about
on his palms, an aged hippie sat down beside me with a gallon

of rosé to watch the tomfoolery. The Rockies, always visible, have that "noble" look of the unfinished portrait of George Washington. On the grass a boy and girl were entwined like yang and yin.

Denver is known as "Crystal City." Eighty percent of all the drugs in the United States flow through Colorado. People speed all day and drink themselves to sleep. "No high pressure here," as someone told me.

Denver gay life is much like that on the two coasts, only it's a bit smaller and a bit more conservative (I said a *bit*, not much). All the Western bike clubs come to Denver in June for a pow-wow. Leather, fist-fucking and S&M have become part of the scene, but only in the last two years. At the bars people still buy strangers a drink just as a way of saying hello, not necessarily as a way of facilitating a pickup. The gay men go to gyms and dance long and hard at the Broadway, the "dynamite" disco. An AWOL sailor (who'd run away from his base because he was about to be court-martialled for homosexuality) wandered into the Broadway with me; within a few moments he had a trick and a place to stay. ("This poor lost puppy's found a home," he murmured as he rushed past.)

One twenty-year-old I spent a day with told me that he had become very active in straight life starting in the eighth grade. He's had sex with hundreds of women, and is currently sleeping with the hostess at the restaurant where he works as a waiter. He was popular in high school and still keeps in touch with most of his straight friends. But in his senior year he began to branch out. A kid a year older who'd gone to his high school invited him on a camping expedition. Impulsively, Guy (as I'll call my friend) took two days off from school. The two campers did an eight-mile hike, some blotter and a case of beer. "That night it was cold, so we made a fire and slept together. That's how I came out. We're still friends. No big deal."

His straight friends failed to have a reaction when Guy told them he'd tried gay sex: "a big so-what." Some of them go with him now to gay discos; in fact, one straight friend insists he's more comfortable at gay discos since there he doesn't feel the pressure to make out with girls.

When I asked Guy whether he thought he'd "end up"

straight or gay, he replied, "It's hard to speculate about the future. I certainly don't plan to marry; I don't like kids. I could see spending the rest of my life with someone. Women have a slight edge over men for me right now. Women are more obliging—but I despise that at the same time; women let men manipulate them."

Guy and I took a day-long drive into the mountains. On the way we passed a small house being hauled somewhere on a truck; Guy explained that it's cheaper to convey a pre-fab house than to build one in the mountains. Idaho Springs, a true Old West town complete with Victorian houses and storefronts, floated past; hard on its heels were ugly mobile homes resting on concrete blocks. Up, up we went. At 10,000 feet we entered a pass; a silvery stream rushed by. Purple, white and yellow flowers were flung over the roadbeds. Cloud shadows engulfed us in gloom for a moment, as though a giant dirigible were hanging over us. Pebbles littered the road and a sign warned us of the danger of falling rocks.

Denver is a city of transients. In one fancy suburb a quarter of the houses are sold every year. The corporate shuffle is responsible for these comings and goings. Two women have opened a service to acquaint the distraught corporate wife with her new city before she must pack up and leave it. Texans own most of the private property in the state, and Coloradans resent the takeover. As the local expression goes, something (whatever) is as "common as rattlesnakes and Texans." Immigrants from the West Coast are also plentiful; natives display a bumper sticker: "Don't Californicate Colorado."

I spent a pleasant evening with a gay builder in his fifties. He met me at the door to his Victorian mansion wearing a buttonless Cardin shirt and matching cream, pocketless slacks, a purse under his arm—and then quickly told me that these clothes belong to a previous lover, now a designer in New York. "I got dressed up for you," he confessed, "but I feel more comfortable in jeans and a workshirt." His face was lean and hawk-like, his red hair bristling with energy, his forearms and hands permanently freckled. With his bushy eyebrows and intense eyes he resembled one of those scary guardians who stand outside Japanese temples—except he was quite a bit more cordial.

His house was charming: big, brown, sedate, with a small vegetable garden in the back. Inside, over the dinner table hung a nineteenth-century chandelier with a kerosene lamp in the center and twelve candles surrounding it. His current lover, whom he's been with for seven years, lives just down the street.

He showed me his scrapbook, made up mainly of photos taken at his ski house in Breckenridge. In one, an electrical engineer posed in the buff on his skis, his ass looking abnormally pink and vulnerable against the snow. In another picture my host could be seen standing beside his four gay sons (he also has two sons who are straight). "Sure, my straight sons accept the rest of us—we're all in the construction business together, except the youngest, who's still in college. Last year I had a birthday party for myself. I invited a hundred people, about half gay, half straight. My married son and his wife were there; so were the gay sons and their lovers. And of course my lover was on hand. It was very nice."

I felt far from Salt Lake.

TEXAS

Sissies, Cowboys and Good School Citizens

The day in July when I flew to Houston I was hung-over and exhausted. I had had too much stimulation and too little sleep the week before and was looking forward to hiring a car, heading toward some sedate Texas hotel or other, and curling up for the night; I thought vaguely of buying cool summer pajamas and ordering toast and tea from room service. I was a bit surprised to notice the plane was packed at one in the afternoon on a Tuesday, but I didn't become alarmed until the French engineer beside me said that a room might be hard to come by. "We're flying in from all over the world for a petrochemical conference. There are eighty of us. My assistant·has been on the phone for a week searching for rooms somewhere, anywhere, but as of now we still have three vice-presidents on cots in a single."

Fraternal and amusing as those arrangements sounded, they didn't augur well for me—I who have always, when traveling, counted on fate to play the resourceful concierge. "But Houston is like that," my engineer said. "Always overcrowded, the whole world standing, hat in hand, at the door, wanting in. We may laugh at it—it *is* frightfully vulgar—but we are its clients." He turned back to his copy of Voltaire's *Micromégas*; a bit later he explained that he was "really" a writer and, though he'd been working for thirty years as an engineer, that was just a curtain-raiser to the main piece, his upcoming career as an author and thinker. I who have been a teacher, truckdriver, editor and PR man, understood the delay.

In the airport I was cruised by two men and asked them where I should stay. One of them recommended a motel where he had lived for a few months upon first arriving in Houston. It was, he said, near the action, only somewhat "infested" and it was quite cheap. The other man expressed mild surprise that I was visiting Houston for "pleasure." None of the rental services had a car; the attendants smiled wearily at the naïve request. Nor could I find a taxi. At last I resorted to the bus—fortunately, since the airport is a costly distance from the city. (The optimistic Houstonians expect that one day the city will surround the airport. Certainly most of them are predicting that by the twenty-first century their city will outstrip all others in size, wealth and power.)

As I was driven in I observed through the tinted panes empty fields out of which erupted, here and there, not the expected house or store but an imposing bronze skyscraper, jutting up like a bold exclamation point following a bland, run-on sentence. Past me flew miles of mobile homes for sale, those shingled and windowed rectangles longing to lose their mobility and sink peacefully into a plot and join their pipes to those in the raw earth. Fields of weeds, dusty trees, the odd skyscraper and then a motel; its raised billboard proclaimed not "Welcome Engineers" but "Waitress Wanted—Top Pay—Bellboys, Too." We swept past an extensive development of what I believe are called "town houses" (terraces of row houses), all crunched under top-heavy mansard roofs. One ambitious design had even managed to pull the mansarding down nearly to the ground, turning the top three floors into stacked garrets peeking out at the weeds and skyscrapers through dormer windows; only the ground floor had a clapboard siding, painted the pale orange of an unlicked popsicle. The odd proportions reminded me of a little boy half-hidden by his father's giant sombrero. But all buildings in Texas give an overall sense of prefabricated units that have been *landed* on the terrain. They are pure expressions of will and bear no relationship to the surroundings. Even the most modern space capsule, however, is awarded a name out of history. If there is a restaurant in the building, it too will have a historical name, though not necessarily of the same period. Thus we will have Bluebeard's Dungeon in the Queen Victoria, or the Old West Saloon in the Sans Souci.

Finally the city itself materialized. My first glimpse of it was blurred by the sudden, cloacal collapse of a searing, five-minute rain. It was as though the devil had decided the infernal heat needed just a soupcon more of humidity to become the sort of torture he had had in mind. The buildings were indifferent to the miasma; with their spotless white mullions and smoked glass or blue, mirrored skins or long, tall, merlons flanking windows no wider than a medieval archer's crenel, they were as alien as space stations deposited on hostile Mars. One suspected they were self-sufficient, tenantless, fully computerized; if they retained windows at all, they did so only as a courtesy nod to the past.

Later, when I toured the business district, I discovered no one was visible because so many of the buildings are interconnected by air-conditioned second-story covered walkways or by tunnels underground. The major buildings are the headquarters of oil companies, and all but one of them have been erected since 1968. The latest development is the Houston Center, which comprises twelve buildings (including 5,000 apartments). The architecture is so advanced that it was used with no modification as the set of the sci-fi movie *Logan's Run*. The floors and walls here are pink Texas granite; on a balcony one sees a bent aluminum tube (sculpture? exhaust?); the escalators are outlined in cold white neon. One glimpses a restaurant filled with foliage and twinkling lights and sees flirtatious couples huddled over little tables—no, it's a bank, and those are officers and depositors conferring at desks. I kept thinking there's no reason Houston should have skyscrapers at all; land isn't *that* valuable yet. But of course for Houstonians the buildings are tinker toys. They contemplate the business district from a distance and say, pointing, "Now you need another black one over there—maybe a trapezoid. And then square that corner off with a nice silver one."

The bus deposited me at a terminal where a long row of brightly colored telephones promised to connect me instantly with a wide assortment of hostelries. Every place was full, including the motel the guys at the airport had recommended. In a panic I decided to apply in person to their motel. I ordered a taxi and after a long wait obtained one. At the motel office I was for some reason accepted; I was directed to the sixth and last building of the complex, a good half-mile down a blinding gravel service road. Behind the motel were parked several semis; hanging over the balcony railing were trim black women in micro-skirts, plastic boots and bouffant wigs. The rather dour whites I passed kept addressing one another as "Brother This" and "Sister That." Saudis in turbans were streaming into the restaurant. Dazed by the heat and feeble to begin with, I had difficulty in reconciling these elements. Was I feverish?

As it turned out, the motel was notorious as a hangout for hookers who serviced truckers. They and their stylish pimps occupied half the rooms; all night long men were tapping on my door and imploring Judy to "Open up." The rest of the place had been rented by Jehovah's Witnesses; there were 55,000 of them convening in Houston for a pow-wow at the Astrodome. Hookers and Witnesses rubbed shoulders all week in the coffee shop, which was also popular with Arab students who'd come to Houston to master the mysteries of petroleum technology. To add to the fun, Barnum and Bailey had also descended on Houston—elephants, like overheated tanks, had rumbled through the empty streets that afternoon, their massive bulks hosed down with cold water every block or so to keep their radiators from boiling over. Agitated by so much that was *mal assorti*, I left my room with its moderate infestation of roaches and water beetles and its *two* double beds, both their backs broken, and I sallied forth for a walk—only to discover the town fathers had neglected to provide this neighborhood with sidewalks. There I stood, far from a bus route and unable to walk or rent a car or hail a taxi, and watched the traffic hurtle merrily by. I contented myself with an overdone steerburger, a rather sweet little covered basket of biscuits and a large milk as I eavesdropped on Arabs, whores and the religious—those poor souls subscribing to no smoking and only light drinking in a city where Mexican grass sells for a third of the usual price and where more beer than water is consumed in the summer months, a place that has the third highest rate of alcoholism in the nation and a crime rate that rose 12 percent in the first six months of one year. Houston also has no zoning laws and as a consequence a church will be squeezed in between a shopping center and an adult bookstore and peep show. It is a city of unlikely company. Although one group is campaigning to keep the bookstores at least two thousand feet away from the churches and schools, the proposal for such a *cordon sanitaire* violates the Houston charter, which grants every microbe the run of the city.

Unsteady as I might have been (it was now ten in the evening), I telephoned for a taxi and headed to the best leather bar in town, The Locker. There I stood in the back patio, propping myself up against a corral fence and looking out at a withered, spotlit tree. Its small leaves weren't stirring. Along one wall was painted a large mural of cacti on the moonlit mesas, looking like disembodied rabbit ears out for a midnight stroll. At one end of the yard rose the false front of an Old West hotel, a Potemkin set where pairs of men nursed funny cigarettes. The air was sweating, dreamless, more in a faint than asleep. The men around me, conserving their energies, weren't talking; the only vital sign was an occasional shift from foot to foot, unless that was an illusion performed by the heat waves.

And then, interrupting this saurian torpor, entered someone very much in motion. He hovered up to me, engaged me in conversation and permitted me to buy him a beer. He was twenty-two and chubby and was experimenting with a mustache, which looked like a caterpillar paralyzed by stage fright halfway across a winter melon. All the little movements he produced (and he was as active, as rippled, as the draperies of an Ascending Virgin) arose from inner turmoil—the familiar conflict, for instance, between a desire to establish contact and a fear of being snubbed. As he talked on, I turned my lidless eyes toward him, unscrolled my sticky tongue in a trial run and watched my fly buzzing around another contradiction—his inclination to be flamboyant and his resolve to be butch (one imagined him wearing a gold anklet under his cowboy boot). And then it wasn't clear whether he wanted to seduce me or himself, for though half his talk was about sex and the possibility of having it, the rest was devoted to his Past, a plot by Dreiser written in the vivid style of Victoria Holt.

Apparently even his life, his novel, was tremulously ambiguous, as was his recital of it; he had a trick of saying something sad about himself, which elicited sympathy—and then he sprang on me, out of nowhere, a big, disconcerting, shit-eating grin. When he spoke he kept himself in modest profile but when he produced that grin he turned toward me with shocking intimacy. He seemed to be a writer who enjoyed torturing both his reader and his protagonist, despite the fact that the reader in this case was a potential pickup and the protagonist his own immortal soul. My only fear is that I make him sound sinister; have I made it clear he was, despite the boots and mustache, that perennially endearing figure, the Southern Sissy?

"My father," he said, "liked me, but my mother never did. She didn't want us kids, didn't want to cook for us—heck, didn't even want to talk to us. My dad liked me—" and then the grin is unleashed—"because he was gay. I found that out by going into his closet (no pun intended) and discovering all these dirty magazines. When I was eighteen he died from lung cancer, and he wasn't the smoker; my mother smokes and is still going strong. She threw me out of the house as soon as he was under the ground." Southern speech, no matter how casual, always lilts with little literary touches: the parallelism of "out of the house" and "under the ground," even the old-fashioned periphrasis of "under the ground."

"I got a job and some credit cards. And then I just charged and charged—" the "charged" is drawn out, sung first on a high note, then on a low—"until I'd run up a bill of $15,000. I didn't know what to do. So I fled town and came to Houston with nothing but a bag and a five-dollar bill."

"And *then?*" I asked anxiously; I am not one of those people who believes, as Rilke did, that the world will take care of you, that its hands are under you and will catch your fall.

"It's very easy to succeed in Houston," he said. "In one night at a bar you can make four or five friends and they will put you up one after another. Everyone's new here."

"And *then?*"

"I went into a beauty supply store and asked for a job. I lied and told them I had a degree in cosmetology. They put me to work that very day. Now it's a year and three months later and I was just named the store manager."

"How," I asked, already suspecting the answer, "did you fake a knowledge of cosmetics?"

He seemed caught in another crosscurrent of uncertainty. His hand flew up to pat an invisible but palpable chignon, the chic saleswoman's bun, pierced *ukiyo-ye*–style with several pencils at odd angles, while simultaneously his voice dropped into a lower register: "I know all about *that;* I had a lot of . . . uh . . . *friends* in drag." (The well-known "friend" strategy: "Doctor, I have this friend who's homosexual and needs advice.") "And what do you do?" he asked. It was his first acknowledgment that I, too, might have a life, might be more than a reader, though I suspect he was more eager to get away from the subject of drag than curious to explore my story.

"Write," I said.

"So do I!" he exclaimed, more delighted by the coincidence than I, since I had already been perusing his work. "I'm a writer, too. I loved English in school. My favorite period of poetry was the Romantic, and my favorite poet Percy Bysshe Shelley." Naturally. If Americans, as Gore Vidal says, are both Puritans and Romantics, then the Romance must begin in the South. Shelley is the South's favorite poet; Southerners name their sons Shelley.

Texas is at least partly Southern, and it can never be understood if it is totally seceded from the Confederacy. Take the racism. In small towns and among older people it persists unchanged. Among the Houston young, the racism may be disguised by lighthearted "nigger" jokes told on the understanding that, of course, we're both liberals, we all know better—and isn't it fun to say "nigger," to use the real down-home word, the very word *they* use?

And so it might be if integration were more secure, equality more fully achieved and the past more distant. As things stand, the jokes betray anxiety at best, bigotry at worst.

Or take the rural character of Texas life. Although four out of five Texans live in cities, they are mostly from farms and dream of returning to them. The big, raw countryside—the fly-blown Nehi sign, the glass of iced tea on the porch swing in the sweltering evening heat, the shriveled grapes in the arbor in the back yard, the "bauking" of chickens, the rust-speckled blades of the creaking windmill, the trail of dust behind the pickup truck—this desolate countryside is both literally and spiritually close to the booming metropolises.

"What are you doing here in Houston?" my friend asked. "Business?"

"No, just looking around."

"You came *here* for *fun*? To Houston?"

Texans may be chauvinists, but few of them are loyal to Houston (though some transplanted Northerners defend it). It is only a place to run away to, a town where you can make a fast buck and then get out without regret—a sort of cloverleaf in the American Road to Riches.

My friend, sensing I was more chatty than randy, and confident that I'd studied his text with care, hailed a waiter he knew and started giggling with him. Perhaps we'd understood each other too well to be attracted to one another. There were no occlusions in communication, those breaks in understanding that awaken desire. Sex with strangers is an alternative to conversation, the code that replaces chit-chat.

Inside the Locker things were picking up. It was midnight and the dance floor was crowded, as was the pool room. The prevailing "heavy" look for this malarial climate seems to be a black, sleeveless T-shirt, black or blue denims and cowboy boots. Here and there, however, were ensembles that seemed ill-sorted. A tall, lanky man ambled past decked out in a ten-gallon hat, a faded workshirt, patched jeans—and sneakers. Home on the range in sneakers? Or a forty-year-old stood beside me, wearing engineer boots, a black leather vest and chaps—and a cowboy hat. Yet another man had on an S&M top (chains, leather, tattoos)—and shorts.

These are expressions of individual tastes in a state where personal flair is still regarded with nostalgic approval. By day, as one walks through the air-conditioned corridors below the business district, one sees mostly fresh-faced executives in three-piece summer suits. But every once in a while one encounters an old, unbowed Buffalo Bill, his white locks flowing out from under his weathered Stetson, his $300-boots worn but polished and a string tie around his neck—he is the magnate who grumbles about how the Yankees have turned Houston into a damn dude ranch.

Despite its architectural splendors and its hospitality to the arts, its influx of Northerners and its go-go economy (in Houston a survey revealed that young executives regarded a 10 percent annual raise as the minimum they would accept), the city remains raw. One talks to a tall twenty-year-old with an Adam's apple that rises and falls obscenely along his taut neck. His voice is too loud given the social distance but it goes with the depthless eyes that seem focused on a distant figure. "My damn dad," he drawls rapidly—that is the trick of the Texas accent, a Southern intonation speeded up—"tried to stop me going with guys. Ha! I beat that son of a bitch up. I slugged my goddam brother, too, till he was a bloody pulp. My mom was screaming so I chased her around the house. See," here he lowers his voice a bit, "I'd gotten this damn bitch I knew in high school pregnant, so the old man was hollering about that, too. But I'm bigger than him, I'll knock out his fuckin' teeth. I told the bitch to get her cunt scraped—then I moved in with Joey." He told me more, of night rides in old cars with six buddies gulping down a carton of beer, of straight guys from high school he lured home—and then fucked—by using cooperative girls as bait, of parents howling around the house trying to shut down a late pot-and-disco party, but I withdrew from him. I didn't want to hear any more. Sure, I like tough guys, but only if the toughness is undermined by warmth and experience, only if I sense that in this man's head there is somewhere a court of higher appeal. I felt awed and overpowered—was this the gay liberation we had had in mind?—and headed home to my motel, at last to sleep.

This Houston rawness crops up everywhere. This is a city

where businessmen chew gum, wear long ginger sideburns, sport Baptist pins on their lapels, smoke cigars, dangle calculators from their belts, carry pens above their hearts in aqua plastic pocket inserts and choose beige summer suits with dark brown stitching to match the dark brown shirts beneath. It is the place where, during the fuel shortage in the North, a block-long Cadillac carried a bumper sticker that read, "Drive 70—Freeze a Yankee."

It is also the town where I met someone I'll call Harv. He approached me at the big disco, Numbers, with an opening line so contrived it was winning: "I'm doing a survey for the *New York Times*. Do you like blonds? How do you feel about blue eyes? And how would you like the best blow-job in Houston?" We never got to the blow-job stage, but we did have a couple of drinks together in the glassed-in booth upstairs. Downstairs lights strafed the crowded floor and illuminated from behind white silk curtains billowing inside tall, fancy scrollwork frames (I was reminded of the decor of a 1920s movie palace). Harv was a computer expert; he had been working late all week unscrambling a lousy program written by someone else. The pride he took in his work was all the greater because he was a self-made man. He had always fought with his parents, he told me —dark, murderous fights—and they fought with each other. When he was eight he begged them to send him away to boarding school. They complied but when he came home for holidays he found his folks even more intolerable. The old hostility flared up again. After a particularly tormented, tormenting session his parents kicked him out. He was fourteen and had only three dollars to his name. He worked in stores around his little Texas town until he finished high school. He then joined the Navy and was assigned a job in intelligence. At night he took more and more courses, determined to make something of himself.

After the Navy he obtained a position in Houston with a computer programming firm and rose rapidly. Now he was just twenty-four and owned a 1972 Oldsmobile and a two-bedroom suburban house. Harv's goal was to make $200 million. His taste in men was correspondingly ambitious; his first lover had won a major muscle-building contest. The only problem was the lover's laziness. He was thirty-one and refused to work. "I did everything for him. I moved his mother into my house and took care of her. I bought him a new car and kept the old one for myself. But he kept pushing me. He didn't come home for four days, so I went after him. I entered that bar and ordered him out. He said, 'I ain't going.' I cleared the bar right out, I hit him, I ripped his shirt off, I lifted him by the seat of his pants and hauled him out. Then I asked him, 'You wanna come home or you wanna go back in the bar?' He said, 'The bar, but I'm too bloody.' So I said, 'Well, I'll drive you home and you can change and drive your car back, 'cause I don't want to fool with you no more.' I got him and the old lady out of my house. Now I live alone."

I've omitted to say that Harv is a boxer and presses 300 pounds but is short and baby-faced and sprays his hair and drenches himself in cologne. We necked for a while and he was soft, yielding. I had the impression of being in the plush grip of a powerful androgyne; beneath the hairless skin lay lethal muscles. On the dance floor four guys were passing poppers, stomping fast and hard and ripping out rebel yells. Given the heat, the humidity and the darkness outside, the feeble porch-lights streaked with worrying mosquitoes, the disco seemed all the more improbable, an overnight, Klondike improvisation. If the electricity being piped in were to fail, the lights would dim and cease their arbitrary but assured revolutions, the air would warm and thicken, the tape would grumble into silence—and we would be left in a hot, tin shack somewhere in the middle of the bayous.

The gaudy stereotype of American machismo is the Texas cowboy, but a visit to a gay cowboy bar forces one to recut that worn old plate and to print from it in fainter, more somber inks. The Brazos River Bottom is on a quiet sidestreet but looks out toward the glowing spires of the business district. Inside are well-mannered couples sitting around the bar. A few people are playing pool. Most of the men are in their forties or fifties. A juke-box plays sad country and western tunes while cowboys dance cheek to cheek. They sway to the strains of "Waltzing Across Texas" or do the two-step, or they perform a brisk fox trot to an upbeat song such as "Big Ball's In Cowtown Tonight" (the title always draws a smile). Over the polished wood floor hangs a sign, "Get Hot or Get Out." That is the only modern note, though the redneck belligerence neutralizes the up-to-date vocabulary.

The etiquette is formal, almost severe. A brief nod of the head has taken the place of the dance-class bow from the waist. If both men are the same height, one of them (usually the one who leads) removes his 10V Ranch cowboy hat and holds it in his hand behind his partner's back. Since it is summer most of the hats are straw. The shirts, however, are long-sleeved; cowboys are frugal people who wear the same clothes year in and year out. As the men danced to the impassioned strains of Tammy Wynette singing Johnny Paycheck's "You Hurt the Love Right Out of Me," their faces were unsmiling. I was reminded of a story an Argentine once told me of a tango contest on the pampas; as the gauchos glided back and forth to heartbreaking lyrics about jealousy, great hot tears steamed down their stoic faces. It was the same here, except the words also covered divorce and the Pill.

When a city slicker has a jerk-off fantasy about cowboys, he usually forgets their true distinguishing marks—the air of detachment and the polite, old-fashioned decorum. He ignores the fact that cowboys are low in perceived status, suspicious of outsiders, grave, insecure, a bit touching—and quite conventional about sex (they would be appalled by rough stuff, for instance). At the Brazos River Bottom, smoking grass (so common in all the other Houston bars) is forbidden, as is pissing in the patio (a curt sign reads, "Rest Rooms Are Inside"). The spirit that reigns is respectable and cozy—a few old friends getting together for a beer.

Only about half of the customers are genuine cowboys or farm people; they are the ones most reluctant to discuss their origins and work, as though they are afraid you might laugh at them. But for all Texans the emergence of the Western look has come as a relief. Ten years ago most Texans were uncomfortable in their alligator shirts, chinos and Top-siders; now they have received permisson to slip back into the clothes they wore as teenagers.

For most Northerners, Texas is the home of real men. The

cowboys, the rednecks, the outspoken self-made right-wing millionaires strike us as either the best or worst examples of American manliness. The metal-drilling voice; the flashes of canniness and dry humor; the slow walk and the rangy gestures; the readiness to offer help and the reluctance to accept it; the unspoken code of personal honor; the physical courage and the unexpected grace in combat—all these are aspects of the Man, and for most of us He is a Texan.

This is, obviously, the movie version, but it is based on fact. The ideal is not an illusion nor is it contemptible, no matter what damage it may have done. Many people who scorn it in conversation want to submit to it in bed. Those who believe machismo reeks of violence alone choose to forget it once stood for honor as well. Until recently, as a Houston lawyer told me, Texas businessmen could conclude staggering transactions with just a handshake. Today, the invasion of Yankees has meant that all deals must be firmed up with written contracts. The gentleman might have been more tough than gentle, but he was at least honest.

Nor are courage, strength, a touchy price and a muted range of emotions without their usefulness. They are the traits of the pioneer, quick to defend what he has won and slow to complain about what he has lost. Nor is the frontier a mythical past in Texas. Both my parents are Texans and all my relatives still live in Texas. My paternal grandfather came to Texas from Louisiana in a covered wagon. My maternal grandmother's parents were homesteaders, and my mother remembers vividly her girlhood on that farm with its smokehouse, its cool dugout under the pump house, its pecan trees along the creek, its rooms tacked on to the original cabin, its tribe of twelve uncles and aunts ruled by a mother who presided from an oak rocker where she read the Bible, chewed tobacco and concocted herbal cures. Her husband was silent, hardworking and strong.

When my mother returned to her home town for a reunion a few years ago and stepped breezily out of her Cadillac, an ancient woman wearing a bonnet approached her and asked her name. The name was given and the woman said, "Then I am the first person who kissed you. I was the midwife. As soon as you were born, I said to your mother, 'I'm going to kiss her.'

Your mother said, 'Don't kiss that nasty old thing till you've washed her,' but I didn't wait. I was afraid someone would beat me to it." My mother is seventy-five, the midwife must be in her nineties. I mention all this only to remind the reader that the day of early settlers is within living memory for *some* Texans, and that the frontier ideal of manliness was until recently functional, needed. My own father worked as a cowboy when he was young, before he moved North and became a business-man. My childhood was a battlefield on which two opposing Texas forces fought it out—the strictures of manliness and the aspirations toward culture. My parents divorced when I was seven and I was shunted back and forth between them. What my mother wanted me to be was artistic, creative and someone who "contributed" to society; her father had been a math prof in a rural junior college and she herself had taught grade school. Texas has always spent large sums on education. The school-teacher remains the beacon of culture, and many a modest home has a good library of the classics, headed by the Harvard Five-foot Shelf. Even today a dedication to culture is maintained in Texas; after all, Houston is the only American city aside from New York to have a full complement of resident opera, ballet, theater and symphony. No matter that old oilmen snore through a Handel revival; they have at least done their bit toward up-lift.

My father subscribed to my mother's values in passing, though they struck him as more appropriate to a daughter than to a growing boy. What he wanted in a son was someone brave, quiet, hardworking, unemotional, modest. I can remember once traveling to Mexico with him after I'd spent a year with my mother; I embarrassed him by being a know-it-all and by ad-miring the cathedrals with too much enthusiasm. He drew me aside and said, "A man doesn't say I love that building, he says I like it. Don't talk with your hands. And you shouldn't correct older people, but if you must, say 'In my opinion' or 'I believe' or 'I may be wrong, but I've heard. . . .'" He also told me that I should never wear a wristwatch, smoke a cigarette, or put on cologne—those are all sissy things. Men have pocket watches, smoke cigars and use witch hazel. These are principles, alas, I have failed to observe.

I've talked with many Texas men about the way machismo was instilled in them, and they all agree it was done indirectly. I've never heard one male Texan say of another, "He's a real man," or "He's not very masculine" or anything of the sort, though I have heard a few women say of a child such things as "You'll like him. He's all boy." Usually the comment is repeated: "*All* boy." But manliness is never mentioned by men in Texas. I suppose the subject is too momentous and too tender to be voiced. What is talked about is sissiness. The shape of the unspoken province of manliness can easily be inferred from the explicit, exact and surrounding contours of sissiness, much as Canada might be partially deduced as a potent shadow from the glittering boundaries of Alaska and our northern border.

If there were only two choices, manliness and sissiness, facing Texas WASPS, then most of them would resemble the Chicanos, who are usually either fiercely butch or extravagantly nelly. But there is a third option availiable to white, middleclass men in Texas: the good school citizen. He cannot talk in a high voice or *love* the arts (though he may like them) lest he descend into sissiness. But he need not play contact sports or drink or brawl in order to ascend into manliness. The good school citizen can run for the student council, earn excellent grades, do charitable work and lead his church group. He may date an equally serious, upright girl and "respect" her virginity. This option is the one most of the gay men I met in Texas took as teenagers. They may have experienced themselves as sissies, but they were not taken as such by their friends and neighbors.

There's one last thing that should be said on this subject— the extraordinary naïveté among rural people about homosexuality, at least in years gone by. Today television talk shows and the antics of Anita Bryant have made the word *gay* part of everyone's vocabulary, but when I was a boy I never heard homosexuality mentioned once. And when I was twelve my mother, sister and I visited my grandparents in the village where they lived, formerly "the oil capital of the world" (as a tattered banner over the main street proclaimed) but by then virtually a ghost town (the wells had run dry). My grandmother let me bunk with my grandfather and he and I made passionate, unending love all night. So far so good, but in the morning

I heard him in the living room telling the others, "That Eddie is such a sweet boy, we just hugged and kissed all night long." My grandmother cooed with affection, "Well, isn't he the sweetest *thang*," but my mother and sister subsided into ominous silence. I slid out of bed and turned on the gas burner in the corner without lighting it; it was one of those free-standing grills, blue flames reddening bone-colored asbestos, fed by a hose out of the floor. Though I intended to kill myself I chickened out, turned off the tap and at last crept sheepishly into the living room. My mother was clearly alarmed, my sister derisive, but my grandparents beamed at me with all the charity of their innocent hearts. So gay love must have been in the nineteenth century. Other Texas boys have told me their own tales of gay idylls on farms and in small towns where general ignorance assured them personal immunity. I do not want to romanticize rural life, nor do I long for a return to Arcadia. I am simply suggesting that in the old Texas what could not be named was unknowingly tolerated—a far cry from the half-informed but well-indoctrinated Baptist bigotry of today.

"Bill," the young man who took me to the Brazos River Bottom, fell into the category of the good school citizen. He was not a cowboy, though he felt more comfortable there than in the other bars. He grew up in a small town as one of the three children out of six who eventually became gay (the others are a grown sister and a teenage brother—a whiz at macramé—still at home with his folks). An older, straight sister doesn't see Bill because she's "hurt" that he's homosexual. His parents know about their children's sexual orientation, but the gay kids dare not say too much to their mother because she easily becomes "hurt." The word reminded me of the way some Southern women control their families by displaying a conspicuous wound—the wound of pouting, of a long face and swollen eyes, of meals eaten in silence and dishes washed in martyred solitude, of unusual afternoon naps taken restlessly behind a half-closed door to the tune of resigned sighs. This is the mother who tells her gay son, "I don't care what folks say about me, but it breaks my heart that they should laugh at you."

As an adolescent Bill weighed a mirthful 230 pounds (he loved eating and didn't mind the consequences). He was proficient on several brass instruments and the organ; his parents even bought him an organ. As he explains without a trace of Freudian chagrin, "My older sister wanted an organ, too, but she was too skeered to ask for one. Me? I just upped and asked and got me a great big old organ."

True enough.

During grade school and high school Bill saved ten dollars a month for college. As an undergraduate he slimmed down to 160 pounds by eating nothing but tuna and swimming daily. He became so talented in the water that he was asked to join the swim team. He gained local renown by singing show tunes in a silvery falsetto voice. After graduation he moved to Houston and became—well, I don't want to reveal his identity, so I'll say a repairman of expensive European equipment. He likes his blue-collar work that brings him into contact with the carriage trade and earns him a handsome salary. His friends, however, regard him as "unsettled"—a polite way of saying "low-class."

I met Bill at an interesting moment in his life. He is just twenty-two, blond, handsome and naturally trusting, though newly skeptical about other men's interest in him ("I know I'm good-looking and don't want to be liked just for that. Everyone is after me"). His attachment to the cowboy bar and the repair shop keeps him within a safe, small-town milieu. Yet that familiar circle is evaporating around him, a mist burning off to reveal larger but more perilous vistas. He dreams of knowing educated and sophisticated people and hopes he may find them in Texas but suspects they all live in the Northeast. He has just abandoned his old apartment, two rooms in a frame house where he kept comfortable family furniture and surrounded himself with images of his totemic animal, the tiger—tigers painted on black velvet, photos of tigers, stuffed toy tigers. His new place is in the Heights, the only hilly residential district of Houston, an area of big trees and houses that have porches, back doors, even attics. Here someone gay might buy his first house before moving on to a more modern and costly neighborhood.

Bill has purchased his house with an older friend, Chuck, a native of Houston (that rare species). It is a nice, slightly run-down place built in 1915, which they are restoring and improving. They've already installed central air conditioning and assembled one of those kitchens that foreigners and New Yorkers first envy and then laugh at (a cause-and-effect relationship). Wood cabinets, reaching all the way up to the twelve-foot-high ceiling, fill in the spaces left vacant by the microwave oven, the electric range, the dishwasher, the washing machine and the garbage compressor. On one high shelf sit antique toy cars, a crude Dusenberg in painted balsa wood and a Hudson in gilded tin. Concealing the toaster in her skirts is an Aunt Jemima doll. In the window hangs an etched-glass reproduction of a Mucha poster of Bernhardt. No wonder Bill left his tigers on velvet behind; he is being inducted into the new art of Art Nouveau and camp memorabilia.

The living room is less resolutely up-to-date. Though an impressively thick *Houston House and Gardens* magazine lies open on a chair, the decor here has not yet emulated those co-ordinated pastels, those careless conversational islands stranded in a sea of beige carpet under an abstract, palette-knife daub. No, in this room the presence of the old Texas can still be detected in the facing, matched couches covered in brown gingham, each paired with its own symmetrically placed mahogany coffee table, a place for dull visits from company rather than animated little chats. Inside a covered-glass dish, tinted a delicate pink, rises a mound of miniature Tootsie Rolls and foil-wrapped candy kisses; one pictures relatives passing the dish around while discussing the route they took and the mileage they got. The curtains are drawn and the venetian blinds tilted to screen out the afternoon glare. Here devolves that tedious Southern ritual called "visiting" (as in "Don't do the dishes right now, sit down and we'll visit for an hour"). Visiting is a long, ambling account of the births, marriages and deaths of every person ever known by anyone, especially kin, no matter how remote.

Chuck tells me that he runs his own business, a pesticide service. For $100 a client's house is sprayed four times a year. He needs to work only five hours a day; the afternoons he devotes to soap operas on television. He is enthralled by one program and proudly tells me he once met two of its stars when they visited Houston to perform in a dinner theater. He longs to travel to New York in order to see the studio where the show is taped.

He explained to me the gay social life in Houston. "The men in the A group are well-to-do, over thirty-five and very exclusive. They have lots of parties. You have to remember that Houston is a big party town. We party long and hard. One year the A group had the Mother's Party—everyone who *dared* brought his mom, so there were just hundreds of gay men and these nice old ladies. It was supposedly a great success. I wasn't there. I'm not a socialite. They also had the Bicycle Party. About six hundred men rode from house to house on their bikes, and at each place they were given drinks and joints. It went on all Saturday until everyone fell off his bike. Or so I've heard tell. Now the other group—"

"The B group?"

"No, we've got A's but no B's. The other group, which is younger, puts on the Miss Camp America contest to coincide with the real pageant in Atlantic City. It's held in a hotel ballroom and more than a thousand guests attend. Each of the ten finalists displays his talent and presents himself in swimsuit and gown. I was Miss Hawaii, but they ruled me out for smoking my grass skirt." He pauses; only a second too late do I realize I've been told a joke. "When the contestants are presented they're introduced with a dish."

"A what?"

"A dish. You know, an embarrassing story about something they did during the last year. Like: on the big cook-out your steaks weren't rare; or on the freeway last October you got an attack of diarrhea all over yourself; or you're known to have sucked a nigger-dick—no, they wouldn't say that, since blacks are present. They'd refer to dark meat or something."

Lavish entertainments do comprise a large part of Houston gay life. Members of the A group throw patio parties for more than a hundred men and decorate the grounds with cabanas and parachutes stretched from the trees. One spring's big event was the "Mardi Gras Madness." During the holiday invitations were handed out in New Orleans to attractive strangers; as they passed back through Houston on their way home, about a thousand congregated for the party. Houstonians stand in friendly opposition to Dallas. Whereas Dallas is characterized as snobby, pissy, phony elegant, up-tight, Houston sees itself as down-to-earth, butch, rowdy and egalitarian. The rivalry is amiable and gay men from the one city are perpetually racing to the other to attend parties. In Houston jeans, crewcuts and S&M are in vogue; in Dallas designer slacks, styled coiffures and social climbing rather than lovemaking are preferred . . . or so the Houstonians would have it.

Chuck mentioned to me that he was interested in gay liberation but was unaware of anyone active in it. He was grateful when I passed on the phone number of someone I was planning to visit next. This young man, the perfect school citizen, was one of the organizers of the Houston Town Meeting held in the Astroarena. The meeting, an open forum at which all members of the homosexual community could vote on major resolutions, was one of the first grass-roots political events for gays in the country. Despite the fact that homosexuals in Houston tend to be socially conservative, the meeting attracted some 3,500 women and men. It provided Houston gays with a badly needed sense of community. There is no gay center. Until now the Wilde'n'Stein bookshop and the Unitarian Church have functioned as the only meeting places aside from bars.

The forum covered such topics as religion, mental health, the police and the military. Before the meeting the Houston papers and television stations had ignored gay rights altogether, but the forum generated two front-page stories and several talk-show discussions. One of the newspaper stories concerned the attempt of the Harris County Commissioners Court to refuse the use of the Astroarena to a gay organization. In the article, one commissioner expressed his fear that a "nudist colony" would be asking for the arena next; another official, a Methodist, said, "My religious beliefs don't go along with this." The remaining three commissioners who decided in favor of the gays were equally squeamish, but their libertarianism overcame their distaste. One of them said, "As a conservative and advocate of limited government, I feel the constitutional protection of free speech must always take precedence over personal opinions of government officials." The chairperson of the meeting was Ginny Apuzzo, a professor at Brooklyn College and leader of the Gay Rights National Lobby; the keynote speaker was Frances

(Sissie) Farenthold, a Texas feminist and political reformer. Forty-two Texas gay organizations were present. One of these was an engineers' group that has about a hundred members. As one of them told me, "You'd never believe those fellows are gay. They talk about nothing but oil drilling, offshore rigs and freight forwarding. I guess we're deliberate, rational, macho. But we want to be freer."

Perhaps the biggest problem facing Houston gays is violence in the streets. The gay ghetto is Montrose (once pronounced "Mont Rose" but now said, Yankee-style, "Mon Trose"). In a two-month period there were three stabbings and eight beatings in Montrose. The victims were gay men and the muggers teen-age Chicanos. The police ignore the danger; if they do respond to a call for help, they often arrest the gay victim on the charge of public intoxication, a vague measure that permits officers to harass anyone they choose to. The town meeting called for the formation of a citizens' police assistance group to patrol Montrose. It also asked for a civilian police review board.

Police brutality remains troublesome. Five policemen beat a Chicano named Joe Torres and drowned him in the Buffalo Bayou (two of the cops were convicted of a misdemeanor). Two years ago a gay bartender, Gary Wayne Stock, made an illegal left turn and was shot to death by a Houston policeman, who has been cleared. The cop claims that Stock refused to pull over and was gunned down during a high-speed chase. But only eight minutes elapsed between Stock's departure from work and the moment he was killed. Since he was shot only a few blocks away from the bar, he could scarcely have been speeding. The court failed to subpoena any gay witnesses.

Police raids on bars and adult bookstores are a familiar part of Houston gay life. Not long ago the cops raided the Locker and made sure TV cameras were there to publicize the identity of the arrested patrons. There used to be a back room at the Locker where customers had sex on a dark balcony; plain-clothesmen infiltrated the crowd and picked up one person after another by whispering "You're under arrest." On another occasion the police entered the bar with guns drawn, turned off the jukebox and ordered the customers to put their hands above their heads against the wall. A new mayor and a new police chief seem to be less hostile but gays have no legal assurance against further harassment.

The Town Meeting also called for the repeal of Section 21:06 of the Texas penal code, the sodomy law. Finally, the meeting censured discrimination within the gay community. The formation of a gay Chicano organization was especially welcomed—in recognition of the pressures exerted on gay Chicanos by their straight compatriots and by gay Anglos.

The next Town Meeting will undoubtedly discuss the problems of housing and employment. As things stand, two men or two women usually cannot rent a one-bedroom apartment in Houston, and if someone takes an apartment on his or her own and then moves a lover in, both of them can be (and usually are) evicted. Since houses sell for about $80,000 in Montrose, most gays are forced to rent and are clearly victimized by this form of legal discrimination. As for job discrimination, four of the men who organized the Town Meeting were fired from their jobs because of their activism. One of the co-chairs of the meeting wrote his name simply as X, explaining that his "lifetime career would be imperiled by openly signing this decree." When photos were taken at the Town Meeting, many of those attending panicked. The fuss was still going on a month later when I visited Houston. One gay group had gone so far as to steal the photos from the archives.

Oppressive as this situation sounds, Houston gays stand a real chance of gaining power within the Texas Democratic Party. In a city of newcomers, where there is no Italian vote or Jewish bloc or labor vote, where everyone is young, materialistic and indifferent to politics, a hardworking gay organization could become a force, especially since gays are so highly concentrated in the Montrose district. Similarly, gays in Dallas are sending delegates to the Democratic state convention, where they almost passed a resolution against the sodomy law. If only more gays would vote. . . .

The young man I met who is high up in the Town Meeting and the Houston Gay Political Caucus is in his twenties and from what Texans would call a "fine family." Prematurely balding, he has only a tuft of silky hair to indicate where his fore-

head once stopped. His dimples are so deep that in an overhead
light his mouth appears to be a slim dash between thick parentheses. His eyebrows grow together, suggesting not jealousy but
rather wistful earnestness. Yet when the phone rings this shy
man sounds jocular, backslapping—a good ole boy. It is a manner that works wonders with older Southern businessmen. Houston gays are lucky to have Tom (as I'll call him) as a spokesman.

The story of his coming out is a tribute to his tenacity. As
early as seventh grade he knew he was gay, but like many truly
queer boys he did not engage in the normal homosexual romps
of puberty. In high school in Louisiana he was the first-chair
flutist and became friendly with the first-chair oboist, notorious
as the school fag. Because of their friendship Tom was kept out
of the prestigious Junior Kiwanis Club, so he turned around
and started an American Field Service Club (the school citizen
strategy, but initiated dangerously late in the day). This office
catapulted him into the president's council. His reputation as
a homosexual, undeserved up to this point, continued to haunt
him; anonymous teenage boys called him and threatened to reveal his queerness to his parents, and two guys in the band asked
him outright for blow-jobs. When Tom demurred, they started
a whisper campaign against him.

The oboist had by this time discovered a gay bar. Tom went
along one night. When someone asked him how long he'd been
gay, he didn't answer—he didn't know what the word meant.
The oboist was dating an older man. When the affair cooled off,
the oboist hanged himself from a tree. The police grilled Tom
for hours about a possible motive. Tom kept silent, but he was
so upset he nailed the closet door shut. In college he majored
in marketing, became an officer of his fraternity and went to bed
with women. But the cure didn't take. One of his schoolfriends
was making gasoline money as a hustler. Tom went with him
to a gay bar and ran into a fraternity brother who said, "It's
about time you came out, Miss Thing."

Tom did come out—and immediately came down with hepatitis. When he returned to school his fraternity brothers began
to harass him; they hounded him out of the house. When he
told his parents he was gay, they were outraged. Rich and prominent in politics, his father said, "We don't want to consort with

your kind." His sister, an admirer of Anita Bryant, dropped him. Ridiculed and disowned, Tom could do nothing but leave town. Like so many other gay Southerners, he was attracted to Houston, the Ithaca of so many adventurers. College graduates such as Tom go there to find good jobs in industry; working-class teenage runaways become hustlers. Recently Houston TV ran a five-part program on hustlers that "embarrassed" the gay community. The program did ignore the efforts of gay organizations to help runaways. Nevertheless, I'm not convinced that embarrassment is appropriate. Houston is, after all, the site of the "Houston murders," those grisly slayings of homeless youths. There is no use pretending the gay community is free of psychopaths. This problem must be dealt with openly and interpreted lucidly to the public. Considering the way in which oppression deforms us, the miracle is that more of us aren't mad.

In Houston Tom has found independence and freedom. He has a good position with a corporation that knows about his activism and accepts it. He owns a small apartment building, a brick four-family structure on a pretty street, and he lives there himself. His participation in gay politics has turned him into a sane, steady man, the very sort of upstanding type his parents would embrace if they had sufficient wit to do so. Tom confirmed my belief that activism is not only valuable for the community but also essential for one's own mental health. Being gay in a straight world, even in a hypothetically permissive straight world, is so alienating that the only way to avoid depression is through the assertion of one's own gay identity. Anger can take three forms—self-hatred, uncontrollable rage and calm but constant self-assertion. The first solution is tiresome, the second useless, the third wise; Tom has chosen wisely.

Hank and Eddie, as I'll call them, invited me to dinner one night. They live in a Montrose apartment complex that is 70 percent gay and subject to the usual Houston rapid turnover of tenants. Hank has been there longer than anyone else—three years. He is twenty-nine, a handsome Floridian who is as smooth as a PR man; he knows how to project his considerable charms, but quietly, quietly. Eddie is twenty-five but looks seventeen, a small, perfect, exquisitely made animal so endearing that the

desire or envy he might awaken is instantly tranquilized into
friendship for him—the only recourse for an admirer since his
beauty is the kind that would otherwise inspire covetous lust
. . . and frustration. He is lapis-eyed and wears his black hair
slicked back in a d.a., a quaint "period" touch that lends poi-
gnancy to the slender neck and small head. His youthfulness
embarrasses him and on the job he smokes cigarettes, drinks
coffee and wears a tie to appear older. He grew up in a small
Texas town but is now quite the sophisticate. He works for a
shipping broker (Houston is one of the country's busiest ports).
Most of the two hundred fifty people in his office know he is
gay and accept it, even relish it. Women ask him to explain the
fine points of fellatio, which he does; recently they've moved on
to more serious questions about back rooms and fist-fucking.
They also feel free to pat him on the ass ("because I'm a man
and gay," he observes with a trace of irritation). He's called the
"token gay" to his face; that's a standing joke. When Hank
sends him flowers, Eddie can put them on his desk and everyone
beams. What they can't grasp, Eddie tells me, is that he's not
Hank's "wife." Any suggestion that their roles are reversible
puzzles, even vexes his straight co-workers. Just as the Saturnalia,
that grotesque mirror of society, confirmed the Romans in their
belief that the world is hierarchical and proved (through its
temporary elevation of slaves to freedom) that slavery and freedom must be enduring categories, in the same way the perpetuation of the male-female relationship by homosexual couples
serves to demonstrate the inevitability and "naturalness" of such
roles. The only threat of anarchy that homosexuality poses is in
those new relationships free of the ancient subjugation of
one partner by another. If Eddie is not the wife, then marriage
itself is challenged and heterosexuals are no longer able to find
in gay life fun-house distortions of their own unsatisfactory
arrangements. I am not, mind you, opposed to gay role-playing;
that would be impertinent and display an ignorance of our moment in history. I'm simply noticing that the new gay ethic,
which pairs equals and attempts to dismiss jealousy and posses-
siveness as leftovers from an era when marriage was primarily
an economic transaction rather than an affectional tie—that this

new ethic distresses many well-disposed heterosexuals though it delights pioneering feminists, straight and gay.

When I arrived in Dallas, it was suffering from its seventeenth straight day in the hundreds. It was, as Texans say, one of those days when chickens lay fried eggs. No rain had fallen for more than a month and the trees were turning brown. At night the temperature dropped only into the eighties. People were buying 400-pound blocks of ice and dumping them into their swimming pools, with no appreciable effect. Everyone was pale; it was too hot to take the sun. Six people had died in the last week from heat prostration. The incidence of crimes of passion had increased but the number of robberies had declined; it was too hot to go out to steal. The mood of the city was crazy with cabin fever.

The mood of Dallas also struck me as near the riot stage. Down the street from my hotel a crowd of Chicanos in the park was protesting the slaying of a twelve-year-old boy. The child had stolen eight dollars' worth of goods. When he was arrested a cop interrogated him while playing Russian roulette with a pistol aimed at the boy's head. This game resulted in the boy's death—and a very short sentence for the officer, who was convicted of involuntary manslaughter.

Dallas is more sure of itself than Houston, more rigid and smug. Whereas Houston is a young town, Dallas is the usual gerontocracy. Dallas is richer than Houston (it has 1,000 million-dollar companies, as opposed to Houston's 600). Houston has new oil money, Dallas old banking wealth. In Houston gay circles, money counts for little and family for nothing; Dallas, by contrast, is status conscious.

Dallas is the design center of the Southwest and I was pleased to spend an evening with a successful decorator. His high-rise apartment was in Turtle Creek, the most expensive gay neighborhood (Oaklawn is the less expensive ghetto). His apartment was decorated in taupes, browns and grays and commanded a full view of the city. On one wall hung an eventless Barbizon landscape, the thick gold frame alone certifying the significance of its pastoral inanities. There were bookcases, but

they were filled with untouched matching sets with gold bindings
—"book furniture" as they say in the trade, ordered by the yard.
The fur throws hurled everywhere would have seemed oppressive
had one remembered the temperature outside, but one does not
remember it in Texas. Just as Houston sells more sables in July
than New York does in December, in the same way Dallas decorators ignore the climate, the terrain and our century and concoct
their fantasies of a polar Paris of the *Belle Époque* and seal them
in air-conditioned cubes.

Steve (my invented name for him) wore a white, short-
sleeved Egyptian cotton shirt into which had been sewn blue
panels. Around his neck dangled a silver bauble. His slacks were
pocketless, revealing his trim figure; though he is in his mid-
forties he still weighs just 145 pounds, lean for his height (five-
foot-nine). Under his arm he carries a purse shaped like a dop
kit. He drove us in his Lincoln Continental to the Bronx, a restaurant for straights and gays with a friendly atmosphere. In
Texas coffee is served throughout the meal. Over our first cup
Steve told me, "I've been wanting to have plastic surgery for some
time now, but my daughter wouldn't let me. She said, 'People already think you're my brother or boyfriend.' We went on a Carib-
bean cruise together and folks did make that mistake. 'Wait till
I'm married,' she said. Well, I just gave her away to a nice boy
and now I'm going to have my eyes tightened, my nose thinned,
my chin made stronger. The whole thing will cost only $3,000.
I never get a chance to visit with my mother; she'll come to
Dallas and take care of me for two weeks while I recuperate.
The doctor's here in Dallas. I like his attitude. He considers a
facelift preventive and says the second and third operations are
always easier. Some of my friends, I fear, waited too long."

I ask him how he happens to have a daughter. "I'm from
a town in East Texas," he says. "My father was a deacon in
the Baptist church, my wife's father was a deacon and I became
a deacon. My wife and I met at a Baptist college, married young
and had a boy and a girl. Although I had fooled around with
guys, it never occurred to me that two men could love each
other. My wife and I were married happily for ten years and
then I met a handsome guy from Oregon and fell for him.

I told my wife the next day I wanted a divorce but I never confided in her that I was gay.

"Her parents were astounded; we were considered the ideal
couple. Her father hired a private eye to investigate me. The
detective found out everything. My father-in-law confronted me
with the dirt and invited me to pray for strength to overcome
this terrible sin. I refused the offer. A week later he tempted
me with a tremendous sum of money. When I rejected it, he
said, 'We're going to ruin you, take every penny you've got. Boy,
a year from now you'll be in the gutter.' In court my wife demanded a million dollars, half of my net worth, but she asked
for it in *cash*. I was given three years to come up with the money;
to do so I had to sell my holdings at a big loss. My ex-wife has
remarried, this time to a man whose first wife left him for another woman. Well, they have something in common.

"My lover and I bought an old Victorian house for the price
of the lot, $30,000. We spent twice that fixing it up, of course."

"You stayed in that same town?"

"Yes. For *two years* no one would speak to us, just whisper
behind our backs. But we hung in there. One day, I've heard,
four important ladies were playing bridge and one of them said,
'You *know* what they are,' and the *grande dame* of our town replied, 'I don't care. They're the only interesting men in town
and I'd sleep with either of them.' Everybody laughed and had
to agree. It was a very dull place. Eventually we joined a country club as a couple and were invited to all the parties."

"Did you live in an entirely straight world?"

"Lord, no," he said. "We'd have big weekend parties of
fifty men or so. They'd drive in from Dallas, Fort Worth, Houston, Austin. In the attic we'd set up an orgy room, twelve mat-
tresses on the floor, and show fuck films. On the second floor
people would get high and eat. On the ground floor they'd dance.
Our maid would prepare several big meals in advance, but even
so it kept us busy—people wouldn't drive all that way just for
one night.

"My children would visit and they loved my friend as much
as me. We never discussed our homosexuality with them. Then,
when my daughter was going to college, her mother wanted her
to attend a Baptist school. My daughter refused and I backed her

up. My wife was so furious she sent a letter to my daughter telling
her everything about me in the ugliest terms. When my daughter
phoned me, I said, 'Well, it's all true. I'm glad your mother wrote
that. Maybe she'll calm down now.' We had a good laugh."

"And are you still with your lover?" I asked.

"No," he said. "He wouldn't work. I set him up in several
businesses, but they all failed. Finally he blamed me for his
failures and left me. I've moved to Dallas and started a whole
new life. It's very exciting."

"Are you still a Baptist?"

"I no longer go to church, but I still worship God. I just
assume He will reward me for the good things I've done and
ignore the bad."

"The bad?"

"My homosexuality."

The Baptists in Dallas, as elsewhere, are the storm troopers
of the anti-gay offensive. A zealous if not overly scholarly Baptist
minister thundered against homosexuals regularly from his television pulpit. In interpreting a passage from the Scriptures about
who will not be admitted into heaven, the minister identified
"effeminates" as lesbians and the "philanderers" as gay men. The
rest of his sermon was on that level. As a teacher used to hand-
ing out grades, I couldn't help feeling this minister was himself
the big D in Dallas. I was pleased to learn that a Dallas station
cancelled the weekly show of an evangelist who condemned
homosexuality.

Across the street from the First Baptist Church one finds
the Baptist Book Store—the usual outlines for sermons, a section
for teenage missionaries and many tracts designed to prevent
Baptists from lapsing into astrology, the occult, Buddhism and
Mormonism. Quite a few volumes were devoted to the "Biblical
way to pray away pounds." One observed the folksy note (*Ain't
God Good?*), Colson's and Magruder's Watergate confessions,
the inspirational volume (the tale of a famous star's blue baby
told from the blue baby's point of view) and books for teens in
their own language ("I hear where you're coming from, Lord").
For those who find reading a nuisance, much of this literature
has been transferred onto cassettes; there is a whole battery of
tapes on how to save your marriage.

In a Baptist encyclopedia of psychiatric disorders I glanced through a long, confused entry on homosexuality. The genetic argument was rejected (you're not born gay); I suppose the doctrine of free will would insist on that. The causes of homosexuality that were cited included faulty glands (aren't they genetic?), a domineering mother and a shadowy father (such a mother and father have always struck me as sounding like Italians, and I wonder why so few Italian men turn out to be gay). Fear of women was listed as another possible cause, for which the cure is —no, not man-woman sex, but mixed group therapy. Lesbians were ignored altogether. The entry concluded by saying that many practicing heterosexual men have psychological scores that indicate they *should* be gay. The reason they're not is that they've heard the call to God. In repression lies salvation.

My cousin's son is studying at this very Baptist center to become a minister. Two years ago I visited his family in West Texas. At first I resisted discussing religion, but then I joined in the debates. For these people religion is the only form of intellectuality. They rise at six in the morning in order to spend an hour alone with their Bibles before breakfast. They have examined every aspect of the Scriptures and my cousin's son is learning Greek, Hebrew and Aramaic in order to plumb the Bible's depths. Not only is religion an exciting intellectual sport, it also establishes decency within the family. I think it might be hard for some of my readers to understand that many households are perilously close to alcoholism, shiftlessness and violence, and that religion represents an opposing urge toward sobriety, industry and order. Finally, I became aware that in order to raise their four children and send them to college, the parents had to make big sacrifices, never larger than now when inflation is squeezing out the middle class. Daily sacrifice requires a rigorous regime, and the Baptist church provides that discipline.

To understand the vehemence of Baptists one must recognize what they are fighting: the broken home; the drunk father; the philandering mother; the meals eaten alone standing in front of the refrigerator; the arbitrary beatings of wife and children; the straying of teenagers into truancy and drug addiction. What we must bear in mind is the strain on the family, especially in the United States—the only nation in the industrial world that has no guaranteed family income program. Since the U.S. is also one of the few advanced countries with no public health system and very little free higher education, these expenses must be borne by the parents. Having children in a city is economically useless, a drain rather than a benefit, and the advantages of raising a family today are only spiritual or conventional, rarely practical. Religion is a last attempt to keep the family afloat.

Southern Baptists dislike homosexuals because they perceive gay men (they seldom think about lesbians) as hedonistic, selfish, dissolute—the very qualities they observe in families that have gone to seed. Some of the animosity must also be envy. Self-sacrifice doesn't come easily to anyone, nor does fidelity. If gays are seen as both rich and promiscuous, as capable of indulging their every whim as consumers and Don Juans, then they represent a temptation, an affront, which must be condemned. Moreover, the very *perversity* of homosexuality must seem like a first step toward abandoning *all* moral strictures; if someone can face the ridicule of being branded queer, then he is "outside the flock" (which is what *egregious* means). He has broken the social contract, and is perceived as capable of anything.

Of course gay men and women don't really give up the harmonies of their youth; they simply transpose them into a new key. That was made clear to me on one evening I spent in Dallas with a group of young gay professionals—a lawyer, an executive and an architect. The lawyer, brought up in the Church of Christ, had come out in college with his "little brother" in the fraternity. The lover was a local rock star, and between them they dominated campus life. In college in the late Sixties he did not defend gays—he didn't know anyone gay—but in 1969 as a high officer in the student council he worked to integrate the school and ease blacks into fraternities. Today he is a bit closety on the job but busy in gay politics. He is an attractive, liberal, thoroughly decent man. The executive had been a Methodist minister before he came out. He is in an awkward position, since he is a feeling person sensitive to the slightest sign of pain or unhappiness in someone else—and also the leader of the most snobbish gay clique in Dallas. Proust once observed that snobbishness is a deep but narrow vice that cannot be extirpated but that need not infect the rest of the character. "Ted," the executive, nevertheless feels the strain between his universal compassion and his exclusive tastes. Naturally enough he denied that there were cliques in Dallas and would admit to nothing more definite than "overlapping circles." Once that distinction was established, he proceeded to tell me about last spring's Easter Bonnet Party (some men wore feathered hats larger than those seen at the Folies-Bergère), about camping weekends by a lake in Oklahoma where some people (not *our* circle, which is too butch and sensible) hung chandeliers in the trees above their tents and ate off silver service on damask and about the big Texas-OK (Oklahoma) football weekend in October when gays swarm in the streets as though it were Mardi Gras and Dallas hosts throw open their doors to five hundred guests at a time. Servants, stereos, drugs, open bars. . . .

It was easy to see how Ted had climbed to his social pinnacle. He had dark, almost Indian features, a solid white crescent for teeth worthy of a Wrigley's ad, an imposing build and the nervous attentiveness of the professional partygoer who nods and grins through one conversation while devising a plan to rescue a friend from the bore in the corner. When he left he kissed his host and murmured, "Well, good night, Sugar Booger." My mother would like him; wouldn't yours? The energy these men would have injected in another, heterosexual life into church clubs and country clubs is now diverted into gay social life and politics.

After Ted left we all discussed cliques and the difference between Northern and Southern manners. In the South a host introduces a newcomer to everyone and says the guest's name at least twice to make sure it has sunk in; in the North the host, sprawled and stoned on the couch, might confer a chilly nod on a new arrival. In the South people have a distinct party style quite different from their tête-à-tête manner. At a party people joke and clown, keep it light and seldom disagree. In the North people don't know how to behave in groups. They isolate one other person and argue with him. In the South, touching signifies friendliness, nothing more; in the North, it is invariably a sexual innuendo. Northerners consider Southerners to be "phony"; Southerners think of Yankees as "rude." These differences are so subtle and yet so divisive that a Texas university is offering a course to Yankees in how to get along with Texans.

What irritates Texans the most is Yankee condescension. It is surely a mistake to regard Texans as fun-loving braggarts or to expect them to rustle up grits or rope a bronco at the drop of a Stetson. They are proud people who do eat black-eyed peas on occasion but who also fuss over French wine; the rich ones do own ranches but they also buy villas on the Riviera. No state has been more satirized than Texas, and Texans, accordingly, have become wary of outsiders. Even their own accent troubles them. They remember bitterly how LBJ was made fun of by Yankees, long before he had done anything to merit their ridicule. In some contexts Texans think of their accent as the way people should talk; it is the sound of sociability and sincerity. But they also know it is considered comical, substandard. Many educated Texans speak like Yankees at work and like Southerners at home and with friends.

One night I went home with a big hunk of a Texan who had jug ears, meatpacking hands and slightly overlapping teeth. We got stoned in his "town house" and entered a fantasy in which—oh, I won't spell it out. Suffice it to say he was the handsome stud, I his twelve-year-old son and at one point he was in nothing but boots and hat.

His was the consummate Texas rap, complete with the expression, at the moment of climax, "I'm fixin' to come." Everything anyone could desire. And of course it was all learned in New York, where he had worked as a hustler. He'd gone to New York to act the part of a Texan in a play, but when the production didn't materialize, a New York madam packaged and sold him as a Texas oil driller. After six months of earning a lavish living, he returned to Texas. He still wants to be an actor. Of course he already is.

This young man has become an image broker. He has made himself into a sexual wish-fulfillment for other people, and in doing so he has presented, with great sophistication, his own real-life teenage naïveté. "I'm fixin' to come," which he once said with the panting urgency of youth, he now introduces in-

authentically at the critical moment of the well-rehearsed play.
Method actors may do well on opening night, but it is the tech-
nical performers who can sustain a role through a long run.

I would contend that most Texans experience themselves
from the same quizzical, difficult, uncomfortable angle. If Texas
had been poor it might never have lost its innocence. But since
many of its people are rich and travel everywhere, since hungry
Yankees are descending on them in daily hordes, a new, ever
more complex society is evolving. If you want to meet simple,
hospitable, relaxed people try the Northwest. Texas is a moiré
of old and new, Northern and Southern, pristine and jaded. For
that reason it interests me; I'm an aficionado of the provisional.

THE MIDWEST

Cities of the Plain

Kansas City is hot and muggy in July. Trapped in an airless river valley, it fills up with steam until one can almost hear the frantic jiggling of the safety valve on top of the pressure cooker —the jiggling of one's own nerves. If one bends over a page to write a letter, sweat stings the eyes, drips on the page, blurs the ink. On the street the buildings warp in the embrace of heat devils. The still, green foliage seems to grow, to bulge in front of your eyes: thick, murderous. Asphalt boils and stinks. Only mad dogs and New Yorkers go out in the midday sun.

The steward on my flight in told me to look up a trick of his in Kansas City, but when I got there the trick wasn't buying any. "No, I'm not interested in gays," he told me over the phone when I asked if I could interview him.

"I'm sorry," I said, "I thought you were gay."

"I am," he conceded, "but I hate gay people. Gay bars are boring. I don't care about gay lib. I just raise Arabians and show them at Class A shows and, if someone wants to buy one, occasionally I make a sale. Otherwise I just see my lover, who's a test pilot for the government."

In Kansas City I met more rejections and incomprehension than anywhere else on my travels. When I mentioned I was interested in gay life, in how gay men live, people assumed I was compiling a bar guide. Gay bars *are* gay life, they believe. In a bar or bed a man may be gay; otherwise he is straight—a person just like anyone else. The notion that affectional preference, sexual appetite, shared oppression might color all of one's experience eluded them.

Sometimes gay friends my age or older ask me if I ever miss the good-bad old days before gay liberation. Surely, they suggest, it was more *fun* in the Fifties when you had to sneak around and you felt you belonged to a secret fraternity. By day you'd wear your Brooks Brothers sack suit and "pass"; by night you'd haunt bus stations and suck off sailors. With your "sisters" you argued about who was better, Callas or Tebaldi, while you drank martinis and played Mabel Mercer records and made pious lists of famous homosexuals in history (*living* famous homosexuals, of course, were subjects of contempt). Sex was furtive and dirty and exciting.

We all romanticize our youths, but a visit to Kansas City reminded me of what my adolescence had really been like. Kansas City is the Fifties in deep freeze. I recalled that, back then, everyone was always pursuing chicken. In Kansas City, the manager of one bar, a handsome guy of thirty, lives with someone who is now twenty-four. They met when the younger man was just nineteen. The "boy" worked for his lover as a bartender and responded sweetly, submissively to his every desire. If someone would ask little Bobby to dinner he'd lower his eyes and murmur, "I'll have to check with Fred." Fred and Bobby, as I'll call them, exchanged rings. Their scrapbook is full of parties and happy vacations.

But recently Fred broke up with Bobby on the grounds that Bobby has become too old. Bobby still loves Fred and cries himself to sleep every night. Oddly enough, Fred also remains attached to Bobby, despite Bobby's advanced age. They still live together, though after they broke up they moved to a larger house, where they each have separate quarters and where they each bring home tricks. Fred makes out better than Bobby does. Bobby is in a romantic hiatus, since he's no longer young enough to be one of the adorable "kids" and is not yet old enough to have the money or confidence or inclination to pursue chicken on his own. For the moment he makes do with less attractive men who are beyond the fatal pale of thirty. Fred is dating, one after another, a string of teenyboppers.

Naturally there will always be older men who prefer younger ones and vice versa. But on the two coasts and in such sophisticated interior cities as Houston, Denver, Chicago and Minneapolis, the *beau idéal* is no longer the "beautiful boy" of eighteen but the "hot man" of thirty-five. Moreover, *two* hot men in their thirties or forties are now free to find each other attractive. In Kansas City such a union would seem weird, not to mention aesthetically displeasing. The compliant, slightly nelly boy and the dominant, quietly masculine man form the usual couple. The age difference between them and their different degrees of assertiveness approximate the dimorphism of the heterosexual husband and wife, a model that the gays also emulate through a lot of role-playing.

An important older businessman in Kansas City recently fell for a college student, whom he invited to move in. When the student, testing the strength of his own allure and the limits of his lover's patience, made a few clumsy passes at his lover's friends, he was quickly sealed off into hermetic seclusion. The businessman has dropped his gay friends and pulled the student out of bar life. No one is surprised or offended by this decision. "You can't trust fairies, honey," as someone pointed out. "Anyway, why should they be seeing other gays *now*? They already have each other." Gay friends are companions while you stride the widow's walk; once the ship comes in and hubby is home, no need to keep around those jealous, bitchy, treacherous queens. If you must have friends, why not see some nice straight folks, or your own relatives—that is, if they'll tolerate you and if you dare to let them in on the dirty little secret of your sick sex life.

I may have overdrawn the picture a bit, but it roughly represents the attitudes I grew up among and that still prevail in places untouched by gay liberation. In Kansas City gay life is seen primarily as a milieu in which one may bag a partner. Once one has paired off, one returns to the "real" world of heterosexuality. The self-hatred that underlies this attitude is poisonous. This is a game in which everyone loses. The beautiful boy can look forward only to outgrowing his looks and his beauty. The older man retains his attractiveness by virtue of his power and position in the world—a precarious perch. Since the man over thirty is regarded as having lost his youth, the essential ingredient of physical appeal, he sees no reason to exercise or to dress carefully. As a result, only a small segment of the gay world is perceived as possessing any attraction, and as soon as age dims this lustre the beautiful boy of last year is brutally dropped and dismissed as a superannuated wreck of twenty-four. Worse, such a system, encouraging pliancy and effeminacy in the young, in no way prepares them for the bullying forcefulness they will need as they grow older if they are to make conquests on their own. Traditional heterosexuality, at least, does not expect the *same* sex to play, serially, two quite opposite roles. Women are raised to be women, men to be men, whereas old-style queers are supposed to be first nelly and then butch. This extraordinary expectation is especially cruel to the shy, sexually passive lad who is prized for these very qualities when he is young and spurned for them when he is older.

In the heartland, such values have prevailed so long and changed so little that they seem immutable. This is the part of the country where the women's movement amounts to no more than a snicker on TV or a bit of larking over inane questions of protocol: Ms., Miss, or Mrs.? The Beats, the hippies, the New Left, the war protesters, the sexual liberationists have come and gone without leaving a mark on Missouri. For Kansas City gays, whose beliefs and values are the same as those of the dominant culture, whatever ennui or alienation or despair they experience they attribute to a personal rather than a political failure. All questions that elsewhere might be considered economic or social are here reduced to issues of personality—one's own or someone else's.

Kansas City has half a million citizens, many of them wealthy from the manufacture of paper and the sale of wheat and other farm goods. It is also a major railroad and transport nexus and a center for automobile assembly, though agriculture remains its economic mainstay. The city's cultural conservatism can be attributed to its rural character and to its religious sects. It is a Methodist stronghold; the church is very businesslike and organized to resemble a corporation, as its members are proud to tell you. It is also the international headquarters of the Church of the Nazarene, a fundamentalist sect to the right of the Southern Baptists (many Nazarenes regard Anita Bryant as too liberal). One of their by-laws states plainly that a member cannot be homosexual.

Even the local chapter of the gay Metropolitan Community Church reflects the prevailing religious tone. The church, with its two hundred members, is the seventh largest MCC chapter in the country. Its services begin with a "singspiration" in which the congregation works itself up into a frenzy of spiritual enthusiasm by bawling out hymns—much in the manner of the Pentecostal Church. Only after this fever pitch has been reached does the organ come in to introduce the serious part of worship. The MCC in Kansas City is resolutely nonpolitical; recently its members passed by only one vote a resolution to enter a float (Kleenex and chicken wire) into a gay parade. In the local Dignity (the gay Catholic organization), members do not use their last names.

Kansas City gay bars often refuse to post notices of gay-pride marches on the grounds that such demonstrations are too "controversial." The bars shun all publicity; when a local paper did a story on them a few years ago, they feared violent attacks from rednecks. The eighteen members of the local gay Democratic Club, called LIFE ("Liberation Is For Everyone"), recognize that "flamboyant" (i.e. activist) methods would be ineffectual in Missouri. The club's only tactic is to register gay voters by advancing the slogan, "The voting booth is the safest closet in the world."

One of the most prestigious gay social clubs is called "SIS," which stands for "Sisters in Sin"—which about says it all. When Leonard Matlovich and the Reverend Troy Perry visited Kansas City, 250 people attended a fundraising banquet in their honor. But SIS refused to participate; most of its members are married and some are extremely prominent in the community. In the eyes of the "Sisters," a really good social event is a "pasture party," a rip-roaring drunken orgy held on a blazing summer day in the middle of someone's remote farm. When one guest went to a recent pasture party, he was shunned because he had a bad reputation for being a gay activist. He had to be reintroduced to people he had known for years, even old friends who had been to his house many times. All day the party kept drifting away from him.

There are very few gay entrepreneurs in the city (fewer than twenty) who have the courage or the inclination to hire gay employees. One lesbian who appeared on television on behalf of gay rights was unable to find a job afterward, despite the fact that she had a doctorate in sociology. She now lives in New York, where she has landed a good job but is no longer active in gay politics. At the New Earth Bookstore, a lesbian-feminist oasis, I spoke to a woman from California who has been in Kansas City for eight years. She longs to return to California but stays on because she believes so much work remains to be done. "There's a huge gulf between lesbians and lesbian-feminists in Kansas City," she told me. "Though two hundred gay people protested Anita Bryant when she came here to address a conference of Southern Baptists, that was one of the two or three times a large number of lesbians or gay men has come out of the woodwork here. Most gay people, women and men, think that gay life and gay identity are synonymous with the bars, pure and simple."

One morning a gay activist had breakfast with me. He was a man with a low voice, clear skin, straight hair; he looked as though he had lived a virtuous life and his manner was simple, honest. His body was of more-than-ample proportions and he conducted himself with innate dignity. When he was sixteen, living in a small town in Indiana, his stepmother discovered that he was part of a circle of older gay men that included several cops and the mayor himself. She created a tremendous fuss and Evan, as I'll call him, was slated to be sent off to a state mental hospital. Somehow he escaped and ran away. "For a year I lived in a little town outside St. Louis under a fictitious name. Then I joined the Army. After I was discharged I enrolled in a bogus beauty school. When I graduated I didn't even know how to give a haircut. So I worked at a shit job for three more years to save up the money to attend a proper beauty school for one year. Finally I received my license from the State of Kansas; I earn my living now as a hair stylist. My being active in gay politics is risky, since the state could always jerk my license— there is a clause about immoral character that has been used to put several gay hairdressers out of business."

I asked Evan how he had become that *rara avis* in Kansas City, a gay activist. "Well," he said, "six years ago I was arrested for 'soliciting.' In fact, I was in a bar and I said no to a drunk vice officer in disguise. The cops send out handsome decoys into the bars, but we all know not to speak to strangers. In one bar if the owner sees a regular talking to a stranger, the owner eaves-drops so that he can serve later as a witness." Despite Evan's precautions, the officer arrested him when he came out of the bar. The case was tried in the municipal court, where thirty decisions are handed down every hour and where you are always guilty. The judge instructed Evan to see a psychiatrist; after four visits to a doctor chosen by Evan's lawyer, his record was stamped "Cured." Had he been convicted of sodomy as well as soliciting, he would have served six months in prison (until re-cently the sentence was two years to life).

"I got off lightly," Evan said, "but my lover didn't. He had rheumatic fever. He also drank too much; he had never been able to accept his homosexuality. When he heard I had been arrested, he went to bed and drank himself to death. He was just forty-one. His relatives descended and stripped our house bare. When I removed my own things, they accused me of steal-ing them. They still call me at work to harass me. I have no legal rights. Though we'd been together for years, we weren't married. It was an illegal relationship. That's when I became an activist."

Evan's chief goal is to end police harassment. A few years ago cops beat one of his friends with pool cues during a bar raid. During the last Republican convention, Kansas City, Missouri, cops (much tougher than those on the Kansas City, Kansas, side) threatened to arrest homosexuals if any pro-gay leaflets were handed out. The Missouri police force regularly practices entrapment of gays. On the previous Memorial Day, Missouri cops set up a roadblock at the exit from a gay event; everyone was questioned and thirty-one people were arrested.

When Evan talked to the Police Chief about such tactics and argued that the Constitution guarantees even homosexuals the right to assembly, the Police Chief replied that where there are so many homosexuals there is bound to be solicitation; since solicitation is illegal, any gathering of homosexuals must be equally illegal. Q.E.D.: "Queen, eat dirt."

In Kansas City the police stage raids on public restrooms and parks. The cops have installed a telescope on top of a hospital overlooking notorious Memorial Park; periodically they turn dogs loose on the bushes. One afternoon Evan was strolling through the park when a policeman stopped him. He said that a woman had accused Evan of "waving his penis" at her; the cop solemnly informed Evan that if he was ever seen in the park again the police would "ruin" him. When Evan asked to see the woman, he was refused.

One weekday afternoon I visited the baths next to a "Teen Mission," a religious center for rescuing adolescents. The baths were dim and under repair and there were only about six or seven souls padding about. No pool, no sundeck, just a dangerous-looking hot tub and one forlorn barbell on a pressing bench. A young man in his early twenties fluttered past in his towel. He was wearing a silver choker on which bits of green glass had been threaded. His teeth were stained and broken; his expression was at once sweet and nervous, like Jane Wyman's. He asked me, "Are you from up here in Kansas City?"

"No, New York."

"I hear that's chocolate city."

"Chocolate . . . oh. Don't you like black people?"

"I like to dance with black chicks, but these black men are so pushy. They think you're just dying for it. When my lisp starts coming out, they get so excited. One of them says to me, 'If you keep asking for it, you're going to get it.' Some of them are pretty nice, I have to admit."

One had the feeling he'd take up with anyone who bothered to court him. He was ready to be courted. When he saw I wasn't going to, he nimbly decided that I would be if not a suitor then a sister. He sat beside me on the pressing bench in this room where the air conditioner was losing its battle against the day outside. The heat stole over me like a lover, trailing fingertips of sweat down my body. My friend smiled conspiratorially; there was a gala glint in his eye. He was up in Kansas City, where they've gone about as fer as they can go.

"I grew up in a town of 2,500 people, where I thought I was the only gay, but I ran into a high-school classmate in a gay bar in Columbia and he told me half of our graduating class of eighty is gay. Now they're all married except me. My first old man was an officer in the Army. I answered an ad in a gay paper, but the soldier who had run it had decided in the meanwhile he was straight, so he gave my picture and phone number to his Army buddy. I went with that guy for a while, but he ditched me when I got too old."

"How old?"

"Twenty-one. Now I live with my grandmother and I'm a nurse in the hospital. Lord, if all the gay people on the hospital staff got together and screamed you'd hear us clear over in St. Louis. Of course, I think all men are really gay."

"All?"

"Maybe some are bisexual. My mother's second husband was gay. Before she married him, she was warned by his ex-girlfriend, but Mother just thought that woman was jealous. I never slept with him, though he tried plenty hard."

"Why not?"

"She'd liked to have died if I'd tried; we're very close. I've got a third cousin who's gay. I met her at a party and after we talked a long time we figured out we're kin. She works in a rest home—big fat beer-drinking dyke." After he imparted each unit of information he subsided into silence until a new happy thought sprang into his head.

"Right now," he said, brightening, "I'm excited over this man at the ice cream drive-in back home. He's very . . . what's that new word? Macho? Yeah, he's that. He's always eyeballing me. The other night he asked me to stick around till closing time. Then we went out in his car someplace and smoked some weed. He kept swearing and saying 'Faggot this' and 'Faggot that.' Finally I upped and said, 'Look, leave my sisters *be*.' He said, 'Thank god' and took off his pants. He may have looked . . . macho, but he was queer as a three and had me inside him in two seconds without Vaseline." He subsided. Sighed. "There's not much going on where I live. Did you hear the Ku Klux Klan has taken over Joplin? Now, they're dangerous. It was a nice town but it's gone red."

"Red?"

"Redneck. There's a bar here in Kansas City for reds called the Red Door." He inched closer. "Did you ever go in drag?"

"Not really. When I was thirteen I wore makeup on the streets—I was a flame queen."

He nodded. "I wear drag only at private parties, though once—this was the wildest moment of my life—I stood in the square in front of the courthouse in my hometown. I was wearing hot pants and hose. The pants were real cute: two rows of sequins above the cuffs and outlining the pockets and fine silver threads dangling down. No one was out; it was ten at night and everyone was in bed. If someone had rode by, honey, I'd of rushed to my car. But I stood there in the town square and I just screamed and screamed." He shrugged. "I don't know why. But I couldn't stop screaming—that's how gay I am."

As we talked a man in his fifties, his powerful body covered with white hair, kept finding excuses to walk by. We were, after all, among the very few people available for cruising. When my friend went off exploring, the older man engaged me in conversation. His earnestness almost embarrassed me, as though he had grown up in a world that demanded more complete honesty than mine did. He was a retired Army officer, and he possessed an admirable military directness. How else can I explain his ease in telling me so much so quickly? To be sure, he had a need to talk and must have welcomed someone willing to listen. He told me that he'd been in Kansas City for eight years, ever since his retirement; his wife was from Kansas and owned a house here. Until two months ago he'd been drinking so heavily that his liver was now shot. Recently he started attending a gay AA which as few as three, as many as twelve people go to.

"I think I drink because of my homosexuality. I attribute being gay to the fact that as a child I had a heart murmur, which made my mother overprotective. I've always been gay. I like to suck cock. I admire beautiful bodies."

"You have one yourself," I said.

"I'm working on it. I swim every day. But I'd like much bigger arms."

He paused. "I don't want to be gay," the man said unemphatically, as though he had just turned the page and read the first sentence he found there. "I like straight life. I'm used to it. I like playing bridge with other couples too. But I'm afraid things may fall apart with my wife. She's slim, she's a good dancer, she knows how to draw people out, she's an ideal companion. But sex with her. . . ." He looked away. "For years she thought I was just undersexed. Now she knows I'm gay; I told her. We read *The Homosexual Matrix* out loud to each other. We went to a marriage counselor for two months (he was a real fool). My wife wants me not to jack off or go to the baths; she thinks that will make me so horny I'll want sex with her. But it won't. I wish she had a lover. What do you think I should do?"

"I have no idea," I said, feeling that it would be presumptuous to offer advice to someone in a situation so foreign to my own experience. I did suggest they could move to a more liberal community where his wife might receive some support from understanding friends—but I wonder if such a place exists. I could have offered examples of other people's arrangements, but each depended on the couple's creativity, freedom from convention, emotional resources, money and so on. My favorite professor in college lived with his wife and children, his wife's admirers, his own leather boys and assorted strays in a great house on top of a hill—but this ménage was built on his wife's wanting a complex, fascinating husband and on the husband's tireless energy in inventing and sustaining new forms for love. It also depended on her considerable wealth.

What could *this* man do, however, he who truly loved his wife and felt uncomfortable among gays? Was he to abandon their bridge games for smoky discos? What saddened me the most was the thought that he and she might have been happy together had they found a form to accommodate their dilemma, a way of naming and imagining their relationship. Our society, with its single word *love* and its single institution of marriage, is pitifully impoverished.

That evening I hit the bars with a man who seemed to like

me though he did say, "You have a touch of larceny about you."
We went everywhere. Most Kansas City gays live in the Plaza
area and there can be found the best bars. The Dover Fox was
my favorite, a disco with a tiny but crowded floor. A remnant
of the past is a bar so *ancien régime* I won't name it. We had
to push a speakeasy button and wait to be rung in. The bar is
circular, dramatic red fabric draping the top and crystal drops
inside the canopy. On the walls are mirrors, sconces and murky
"Old Master" oil paintings—the "elegant" gay taste of the past.
The owner, of course, is heterosexual. Another popular disco is
the Sundance. These bars are all within walking distance (though
no one walks) of Country Club Plaza, a fifty-five acre Spanish
folly, the nation's oldest shopping center. A nearby restaurant,
Places, open twenty-four hours a day, is a hangout for gays after
the bars close.

Kansas City, in spite of (or perhaps because of) its conservatism, is a thriving center for hustlers, male and female. Black
hookers were all around my hotel, wearing blue cotton athletic
shorts trimmed in white and knee-high athletic socks, even
in the 103-degree weather. One woman drove past me in
her Thunderbird and called out, "Wanta date, honey?" The
boys—scruffy, loud, dangerous—hang out in and around a bar
with an Aztec motif. One black hustler, glamorous behind
white sunglasses, a purse under one arm and a *Vogue* under
the other, pranced three steps ahead of his weary, more
mundane "husband" with a tweezered mustache, a pleasant
round face and a Banlon shirt holding his belly as though it
were a baby asleep in a sling. The bartender, a fifty-five-year-old
redheaded woman, listened patiently to the hushed, nonstop rap
issuing, like hissing, gurgling spring water, from an obvious
glandular case. In the toilet one graffito read, "Wanted Hot
Young Dude 6″ Want Regular Blow-Job Whites Only Apply."
It was followed by the response, "You to Illiterate For Me You
Ofay Whore."

My companion, whom I'll call Hank, drove us to his "town
house" in a "village" twenty minutes out of town. The real estate
boom has not yet sent prices up in Kansas City. At the time of
this writing a modest house sells for $25,000; a two-bedroom

apartment in the fashionable Plaza area goes for less than $200. Hank's town house, which he owns, costs just $250 a month in mortgage payments; he pays an additional forty dollars to the community for the upkeep of the lawn, the pool, the recreation center.

I had never visited such a "village" before. We drove beyond the city limits and into lush farmland. A turnoff brought us into the community, masked by thick trees from the highway. The streets described graceful arcs. Frosted globes on slender poles lit the clipped lawns and the walkways to the identical houses. There are four "units" in each building; Hank is the second owner of his unit and accordingly the oldest resident in the village. Half the people here are single, and of these, five are gay men. "Last Saturday we took over one end of the pool," Hank said, laughing. "I'm sure the straights must *know*."

Since Hank was terrified I might describe him, I'll say nothing more beyond registering that he regards Kansas City as more congenial than the other cities where he's lived. He detested the coldness and competitiveness of New York and the drugginess of Los Angeles. Seattle came close to the mark but Kansas City hit the bull's-eye. Only in Kansas City has he found an unpretentious set of down-to-earth gay friends and a congenial way of living well without great expense. I suppose a city can't be all bad where FFA still stands for "Future Farmers of America."

When I arrived in Cincinnati, I was awash with feelings, currents, crosscurrents and turbulent eddies, the white water a cruiser generates as it throbs into a slip. I was born in this town and lived here until I was seven, when my parents divorced. Until I was graduated from boarding school I spent every summer in Cincinnati with my father. I had not been back since— some twenty years. I knew no one in town now except my father and stepmother, and I was reluctant to call them. When I was fourteen I had told my father I was homosexual so that he would pay for my psychoanalysis; I wanted, fervently, to be cured. My father had doubted my story, thinking I simply wanted to "get attention," and hired a private eye to check my story out. The detective confirmed that I was, indeed, homosexual. I was permitted to see an analyst three times a week for five years. When the analysis proved unsuccessful (the doctor went mad, among other things), I was sent to a Viennese Freudian for two more years. All to no avail.

After I was graduated from college I moved to New York City against my father's wishes; he felt I could never earn a living there as a writer. At times his prediction has seemed close to the truth, but somehow I squeak by. In his remote way my father became proud of me, though he was distressed when an early story of mine was published that had gay overtones and when a play of mine was produced Off-Broadway in which homosexuality figured. "I suppose it's about the *usual*," he said at the opening with a trace of disgust. I had always wanted to please him, though I felt an equally strong need to express my homosexuality (to displease him, or was the displeasure unintended if inevitable?). In college I had joined his fraternity, while insisting I considered such institutions ludicrous. In New York I worked for Time, Inc. for eight years partly because he thought it a blue-chip firm. Since then I've helped to send my sister through graduate school and for two years I brought my nephew to live with me in New York. These good deeds were calculated to impress my father as to what a fine family man I'd turned out to be, despite my "usual" vices, which in his world were most unusual indeed. But in my fourth and final go at therapy (this time, at last, with a gay psychologist), I'd finally come to some sort of terms with my homosexuality. In the aftermath I co-authored *The Joy of Gay Sex,* which was promoted widely enough that I supposed some rumor of it might have reached even the Republican Valhalla of Cincinnati.

My father had never mentioned the book to me. He had also stopped writing me. For that reason I was reluctant to face him. Thank God I did; he died a month later. At the funeral my stepmother told me he'd never known of the book. She had torn out the ads for it from the newspapers and no one in his circle could have begun to form the syllables making up its title.

The Cincinnati of my adolescence is indelibly mapped onto my cortex and I could still lead someone through that phantom city. It still exists—shabby, circumspect, as German as knockwurst—in my imagination, but nowhere else. When I returned I checked into the Netherland Hilton—the Netherland Plaza of my childhood. During World War II my mother and I would inch into town on rationed gas on a weekday afternoon and I'd lunch on a tidy little chicken pot pie and a single scoop of chocolate ice cream in a frosted silver goblet as we watched an ice show at the Netherland. Everything about the skating seemed fascinatingly "indecent"; the darkness of the room by day, the gently misting slab of ice, the band members lit from below by their hooded lamps, the fixed impersonal grins of the skaters, their thick makeup, the slash of blades and the sudden shower of ice dust through the gelled spotlights. . . . The hotel is still elegant and ornate, an art deco temple. When I looked out on Fountain Square, I saw the lovely old green fountain, but the square has been transformed altogether. Its oval shape has been turned into a rectangle, skyscrapers and glass skywalks now hem it in and the hustlers have flown away along with the thousands of starlings that once whitened everything. As I walked through the darkened, deserted streets by night, I could find none of the run-down places I used to frequent. The block where we once owned an office building has been razed to make way for a gleaming new hotel. Here and there I could detect familiar landmarks—the Enquirer Building, the Cincinnati Club—as one might discern a family resemblance in a friend's grandchild.

I headed for Badlands, which is the only gay bar of any significance in Cincinnati. I wanted just a taste of gay life before I saw my father. I set out on foot but I got lost and a passing taxi driver warned me I'd be safer riding with him. I paid a dollar to get into Badlands (which turned out to be just a block away from the hotel). The front room has a Western motif. I sat next to a handsome teenager who attends the same military academy I went to briefly so many years ago. "They'd kill me at school if they knew I was gay," he told me. "I'm on the football team, I take out a girl and everything—when I was a freshman two guys were kicked out because they were caught fooling around with each other." It's always amused me the way gays assume that boys' boarding schools are hotbeds of horniness; the only gay action I ever found or even heard of at the two schools

I attended I had to scare up myself after months of Machiavellian scheming.

In the back bar at Badlands I talked to a tall, skinny, blue-eyed, bearded masochist of thirty-two. With his keys on the right, his sleeveless black T-shirt and tight jeans, he seemed from another planet, or at least another decade amidst the "collegiate" Cincinnatians. "This town is very conservative," he told me. "I never realized how much so until I went to San Francisco last summer for vacation. I had never done drugs—no one here does, beyond a little grass. Out there I shot up speed—*me*, I shot up speed! I couldn't believe it. People here aren't into rough sex or fantasy sex—something of a drawback in my case, as you might suspect." He smiled wearily.

"Luckily I have a lover," he added. "We have a renovated brownstone right here in town. We're pioneers. Absolutely no one else has started the move back into the center city except us. My lover is a decorator. Through him I've learned so much. You see, Cincinnati is really two quite different cities. I grew up in East Cincinnati, which is ethnic and insular, mainly Irish and Italian Catholics. When I came out at nineteen and moved over to the classier half, West Cincinnati, I didn't know a single person, not even the name of a single restaurant. Quite literally I'd never been to West Cincinnati. You mustn't think that East Cincinnati is poor. Cincinnati, I believe, has the highest per capita rate of money in savings accounts of any city in the country. The people are just terribly frugal. Take my parents. They're well-off, but they had the same furniture they bought when they married—until last year when my lover did their house over. He mirrored one wall, put a Parsons table against it, painted the walls banana, installed chocolate-brown wall-to-wall carpet, hung black drapes with a thistle pattern in them. My mother was horrified at first, but then her friends all swooned and now she loves it. You see, Cincinnatians have no taste," he said complacently.

A new subject occurred to him. "If you're gay, the big problem is meeting gays in the professional class. They simply don't go to the bars. It's a very sedate, closety city. Even the men who do go to the bars don't make a move; they're afraid of being rejected. As for cruising, there's a bit on Fourth Street late at night and some action in Eden Park."

My friend and I danced in the small disco. On the floor I caught the eye of two chubbies who, in the most flattering way, did nothing to veil their interest in me. I went home with them in a pickup truck (aptly named), laughing and joking and smoking dope and drinking all the way. One of them had become fat while he worked as a chef at a country club and had settled into the domestic nightmare of marriage. Now he's divorced and is working for his dad—and is slimming down. His bulk was, in any event, smooth and healthy and he carried it with a hearty boyishness.

Not so his friend. He was yet another Catholic casualty. He was dressed in artfully torn jeans, a vaguely repellent fishnet T-shirt under a red-checked flannel shirt. His eyes were sunken and ringed in black, though he told me he was just twenty-two years old. His hair was cut in a tonsure, a style he'd invented so that he need never waste time combing it. His two-room apartment was the same combination of fantasy and practicality: canvas garden chairs, striped and faded; a lit and bubbling aquarium that contained no fish; curtains right out of the package, creased where they'd been folded; a morose, heavy china cabinet that he hoped to excavate with a handsaw and convert into a birdcage. "I keep trying to get this place together. I've been here a year. My sister is coming to stay with me tomorrow —that's why I bought the curtains. But I can never find the time or the energy. I should have been cleaning up all night, but. . . . The truth is," he confessed, "I'm an alcoholic. That's why I can never accomplish anything." He sighed, half in jest, half in earnest, showing his teeth, which were in braces. "I grew up Catholic. By the time I was three I knew I was gay and—this is weird—by age five I was hanging around the locker room just so I could see naked men. I didn't have fantasies about doing anything; I just wanted to see them, and that felt sexual, at least it's the same way sex feels to me now: dry throat, sinking sensation in the stomach of fear and fascination, shame and longing.

"In my block there were seventeen houses and about fifty kids. They all knew I was queer—me and another little kid. The others teased us. When I was twelve I had sex with three other boys in the block, but then I went underground and didn't come out again till I was nineteen. I became a Jesus freak in high school. I had always been tormented by pains in my knees that no doctor could diagnose. I went to a meeting of the charismatic Catholics and they cured me. But the other members detested gays. After my freshman year in college I wanted to enter a seminary, but I learned that there was a rigorous psychological test you had to pass to get in, so I got angry. I dropped out of school and went to California. There I got into glitter drag and took too many drugs. Now I'm back in Cincinnati. I work as a waiter at a restaurant. I drink on the job, bourbon and Coke. I make myself a big quart bottle of bourbon and Coke at the beginning of the evening, and as the night wears on I work my way through it and make another. When I get off work I go to Badlands. I get even drunker there. I know I'm going to die on the road. I can't see when I'm driving home. And my waist has blown up—it's a thirty-six! Can you believe that? But I'm not fat, am I?"

The next day my father and stepmother drove into town at noon to pick me up at the Netherland. We went to their house and sat up until very late discussing everything and everyone—relatives, friends, even my father's long-dead childhood friends. Although my own homosexuality was never mentioned as such, my father did tell several anecdotes about friends of his who had turned out to be gay. I sensed an unspoken acknowledgment of my sexuality.

Cincinnati is so small that everyone knows everyone else's business. My father had acquired a novelistic appetite for the patterns people's lives form; his imminent death (he knew he was dying) had awakened in him an interest in how these stories turn out. He filled in a grand Balzacian canvas of greed, corruption, competition and disappointment, a composition crowded with figures. He knew everyone's pedigree and pretensions, the scope of their infidelities and the true size of their bank accounts (so often popularly under- or overestimated). In the light of such absolute omniscience, how could anyone expect to look respectable? He was a generous man when it suited him, but when his

warm impulses came up against his cold standards of respectability, he was capable of unexamined cruelty. Without a trace
of retrospective guilt, he told me that he had once hired a man
who had at first seemed "all right." "But when his 'roommate'
was drafted into the Army," Dad confided, "Blair fainted at the
news. That got me suspicious. Then once when I visited him
I saw a known homosexual there—so I knew Blair was a queer
and I fired him on the spot."

Why was he telling *me* this ancient story, I wondered. Was
it a cautionary tale? I thought of protesting, but I had been
warned not to antagonize him, since the excitement might trig-
ger another heart attack. His queer-baiting, moreover, was of a
piece with his other attitudes: his scorn for blacks and his hatred
of Jews; his pro-Shah and anti-China stance; his economic theories (he traced inflation to an oversupply of paper dollars and
the unbalanced federal budget). The odd thing was that he was
accepted as something of an intellectual in his circle and would
be consulted by his friends on these various issues. As Mary
McCarthy once pointed out in a piece about an Army officer,
anti-Semitism in his case was a first step toward intellectuality,
toward abstraction, and to have taken his vile opinions away
from him would have been similar to stripping the ancient
Greeks of the syllogism.

To my mind, however, the malignant moral climate that
permitted my father to maintain his dismal views is polluted
because it never stirs. Nothing ever changes in that world, and
as a consequence no one imagines that personal or social change
is possible. In the seventeenth century no one, least of all the
"thinkers," doubted the existence of witches; the most humane
position anyone could take was to doubt whether *burning* witches
was efficacious. In the same way, in such Midwestern towns as
Kansas City and Cincinnati no one has stopped to ask if respectability is a valid standard; the most one might ask for is
compassion toward those never or no longer respectable. And
for whose benefit is this pose of respectability? There is no play-
fulness in this world, no sense of the frightening but exhilarating
high-wire act we are all performing.

The good side of Cincinnati stolidity is evident in the somber, noble mosaics that once decorated its train station and that now have been removed to the airlines terminal. As I waited to board my plane I studied one that had been executed in 1933. It showed a worker in a Prussian blue uniform and cap standing beside unscrolling rolls of paper passing through a cutter. The worker, and the supports of the paper machine beside him, cast long, columnar, gray shadows across the tan floor. In the foreground were stacked blocks of brick red and forest green sheets of paper, cut, trimmed and ready for shipping. In the background, silhouetted against sketchy cylinders of paper, stood a worker in blue coveralls lifting his arms to manipulate a pulley. His hands were undifferentiated mittens and his face a gleam of light on a dark skull. The atmosphere was one of intense, almost monastic concentration—the patient, humble, religious dignity of work.

No one leaves Chicago in the summer. There's no need to, since the weather is beautiful and the lakeshore is one of the nicest beaches in the country—and certainly the most accessible to city-dwellers. Mile after mile of highrise, luxury apartments line the Outer Drive and face Lake Michigan. This is the famous "Gold Coast," which might more accurately be called the "Gold Mask," since it has been fitted carefully and cosmetically over the decaying slums that hide behind it.

Because Mayor Daley and the Machine ruled Chicago for so long, there is virtually no grass-roots political activity in the city. Chicagoans have simply never acquired the habit of organizing—and this passivity is as true of gay Chicagoans as it is of any other constituency. To be sure, gays have formed a self-protection league in New Town, the gay ghetto, to defend themselves against the attacks of marauding teenagers. But gay liberation is a feeble affair in Chicago; few prominent gays have come out, and the best known gay personality in the area is Charles Renslow, the owner of Man's Country, the gay baths. Typically, when the American Psychiatric Association was planning a gay conference in Chicago in the spring of 1979, it could locate only two avowedly gay psychiatrists in the whole city.

After Cincinnati, however, Chicago comes as a relief to the

gay traveler. Chicago is a huge, sophisticated, wealthy city. The
main gay thoroughfare, Broadway, is busy night and day; its
boutiques and bars are always crowded. For the cultivated gay
woman or man Chicago is certainly the chief oasis between the
two coasts. The symphony is one of the three or four best in
the nation. The Lyric Opera season, though short, is innovative
and frequently presents new or neglected works and always hires
the greatest international stars. The Art Institute contains an
outstanding collection of French Impressionist paintings and
Japanese prints; it is also the home of Georges Seurat's *Sunday
Afternoon on the Island of the Grande Jatte,* Picasso's *The Old
Guitarist* and El Greco's *Assumption of the Virgin,* among other
treasures. Architecturally, the city is a showcase of every innovation of the last hundred years, beginning with the delicate
friezes of Louis Sullivan's 1899-1904 Carson, Pirie, & Scott building and continuing through Frank Lloyd Wright's prairie
houses, Mies van der Rohe's 1000 Lake Shore Drive apartments,
the John Hancock Building and the recklessly tall Sears Towers
—serious tourists can be seen, guidebooks in hand, working their
way through block after block of architectural masterpieces. The
Richard Daley Center is a massive new building intended to rust
gracefully, as indeed it is doing. In the plaza stands a Picasso
head that has, perhaps symbolically, two mouths to talk out of
and lyre strings for a brain. (A bum was asleep in front of it.)
Nearby, the eternal flame lit for war veterans looks incongru-
ously low and pedestrian, something like hell's version of a public drinking fountain.

   After my parents divorced my mother moved to Chicago,
and there I grew up, off and on (more off than on) for the next
eight or nine years, with time out for one year in Texas, one
back in Cincinnati, one in Rockford, Illinois. We lived in
Evanston, which styles itself "the city of churches" and prides
itself on being a good place to raise children. Indeed, the schools
are progressive—or were—and the population is racially integrated. It's a fairly safe town and it has no liquor stores; whether
it helps to raise children in such a sheltered environment is
another question.

   It sheltered me from nothing. By the time I was thirteen

I was riding downtown on the elevated train as soon as school let out in order to hang around a bookstore that was owned by a gay man. Weekday afternoons between three and six (when I was due home for supper) are not prime time for cruising, and a thirteen-year-old was few people's idea of a safe pleasure. The bookstore owner, a slim, campy, intelligent and warm Southerner, was in love with a cop; it was he who kept paying for the cop's wife's *accouchements*, baby after baby. Although I pleaded with the bookstore owner to go to bed with me, he obliged me only once, but he did introduce me to an astonishing band of characters, including a harpist whose bedroom was furnished with a massive four-poster, hung with curtains, a *prie-dieu* and hundreds of altar candles. His walls were lined with photographs of a Great Russian Dancer, formerly his lover. In a moment of despair the harpist decided to commit suicide, or so I was told; he dressed himself in a spotless toga, wove flowers into his hair, reclined on a bower of more flowers and turned on the gas. At the last moment he thought it would be an "effective" touch to light just one candle—which caused the room to explode and himself to end up, charred but alive, in a heap of smoldering, humiliating rubble.

One of my favorite hangouts was Bughouse Square, a city block frequented by soap-box orators and hustlers. I hired quite a few of those boys, many of whom were several years older than I. In those days they all pretended to be straight, spat frequently and permitted themselves to be done, nothing more. When I revisited the square, at the intersection of Delaware and Dearborn, I found about forty hustlers cruising at eight on a Sunday evening. All of them were parading along the periphery of the park, not in it; they wanted to be visible to johns passing by in their automobiles. I spoke to several of them, and they were all frankly gay, many of them rather nelly. One of them, "Rhonda," was as pretty as a girl—slight, Mediterranean, smooth-skinned. He told me that every winter he migrates to Florida, where he works in clubs as a drag performer. In the summer he hustles in Chicago. In the past he had hustled in drag, but recently another drag hustler was stabbed to death with an ice pick by a john, so now Rhonda is afraid to wear women's clothes when he "works the Park." His best friend, or "sister," is "Alex," a tall black from Grand Rapids, Rhonda's home town. When Rhonda drinks too much or does too many drugs, Alex scowls fiercely and, snapping his fingers loudly as he flings his hand out away from his chest, announces, "I'm cuttin' you *off*, Miss Rhonda." Alex, Rhonda and five other hustlers passed a joint as they lounged against a car and eyed the passing johns. When one john walked by, sneering, Alex observed, "Have you ever noticed how all these queens smell like cologne at a distance—Chanel and Canoe and Charlie—but up close they all smell like *Comet*? They're hausfraus, honey, not lovers."

One of the hustlers drifted off with me for a snack at a nearby diner. He told me that he didn't really hustle; he had a bit of money and was living in his parents' condominium on Lake Shore Drive. When he was eighteen he confessed to his parents he was gay; they were quite unexcited. A few days later they introduced him to a forty-one-year-old man whom they'd met on vacation in Florida and whom they considered quite "suitable." Their son disliked his suitor at first, primarily because the suitor wanted to have sex on the first date. Gradually, however, the younger man was won over, and they lived together for a year. The boy finally ended the romance because he felt the man was interfering with his schoolwork; he was always tempting the boy away from his studies.

One night I went to Man's Country, Chicago's most popular baths. On the ground floor are the showers, a steam room and a hot tub, all fitted into a stone grotto. On the second floor are rooms, lockers, the TV room and the orgy room—TV viewing and orgy viewing seemed comparably tranquil. Upstairs I found the disco. Lying on mats along the wall were sleeping bodies. A twirling mirrored ball cast scintillas of light over these dreamers. At one end of the room was a spotlit stage, bracketed by art deco caryatids framing a set: a painted skyline of skinny skyscrapers in black and white, stylized to look hundreds of stories tall. The polished dance floor was empty until a black man in red-striped, calf-length athletic socks, a jock strap, a red T-shirt and a baseball cap began to dance by himself. He was joined by an outrageous white fatty, who performed something "interpretive"—of what, I couldn't be sure. Coiled metal stairs led me up to the roof garden where, under a cool, blowy sky, I watched two couples fucking.

I left the baths with a sexy illustrator who was fed up with Chicago's lack of style, its failure to keep pace with the dynamism of New York and Los Angeles. "Chicago is the second city," he said. "Second to L.A., second to New York, second to Houston, second to San Francisco. If you want something second-rate, come to Chicago." I heard precisely the opposite opinion from a gay salesman the next day. "Chicago is *the* twentieth-century city. All the cities built in this century, from Los Angeles to Houston, have imitated Chicago. It's a city that functions beautifully—no teacher strikes, no garbage strikes, no fiscal crises. There are *lights* in the alleys; that may seem a small thing, but I find it heartening. Everyone criticizes the Daley machine, but it's what has made this city work. The 1968 Democratic Convention spoiled Daley's image, caused him to look like Mussolini—"

"—who was also effective in suppressing strikes," I pointed out.

"But that's all wrong. We live here, and we appreciate the orderliness of the city. New York is decrepit and clogged with traffic; that's because it's a nineteenth-century city. Chicago has as many ethnic elements as New York, but here they live peacefully together. No one talks about New York anymore. True, New York is the fashion center—"

"And the art center and music center and publishing center and media center and financial center," I might have added.

"But Europeans now ignore New York and talk of nothing but Chicago."

As Ronald Firbank used to say when he heard something absurd, "I wonder."

What Chicago does have, superlatively, are lifeguards. Across the street from my hotel, The Drake, stretch the wide sands of North Street Beach. Within five minutes one can move from the hushed elegance of the hotel—with its wide halls, its bedspreads covered with top sheets, its uniformed elevator at-

tendants, its seafood restaurant that receives Dover sole flown
in daily from England—and be on the beach. As I emerged from
the underpass—cool, dark, damp, its cement walls thick with
scrawled obscenities, as though the graffiti were exposed root
systems—I passed the lifeguards' locker room. Disco blared
through the half-open door and I overheard the joshing of
straight male teenagers, wariness posing as aggression ("Get out
of here! You assholes on the morning shift . . ."). I looked:
there they were, the bronzed demigods of my adolescence, the
minor deities of the beach who lorded it above us on their
white wooden towers, faces cryptic with white paint, muscled
legs bristling with gold hair, blowing imperiously on their
whistles at someone who'd gotten in too deep. I was always too
deeply fascinated by them, and I had to ration out the number
of guilty, hungry glances I dared to send in their direction.

The suburbs along the North Shore are the ideal breeding
ground for such young men, their families rich enough to give
them flawless white teeth, to nourish their slim, powerful bodies
on expensive proteins and to instill in them that fearless blue
gaze, that easy sovereignty over the yellow sands. At twilight
they can be seen wrapped in the romance of a downy gray wind-
breaker and pacing the shore, the fading light boosting the
brightness of their baggy orange trunks and deepening their
tans—"Your desires are so banal," one of my shrinks, exasperated, told me once. "What you want everyone else, classically,
wants." Desire, of course, *is* banal or, to use that more flattering
word, classic. No wonder that the liberationist, after preaching
against the ugliness of virilism and role-playing, either gives
sex up altogether or daydreams of living in a trailer and cooking meatloaf for a truckdriver.

The Belmont Rocks are the gay cruising spot. One strolls
past an *al fresco* chess pavilion and a lakeside rifle range and
comes upon broad cement steps descending into the water. Here
men in trunks or thongs mingle with those in full business regalia; this strange confluence of the undressed and the over-
dressed on rocks halfway between the water and eight lanes of
speeding traffic turns Chicago by summer into the Rio of North
America.

As though to confirm the impression, the first group I chatted with were three Latinos—two from Mexico and one from Cuba. Chicago has a large Mexican population, two gay Latin restaurants and a popular Latin gay bar, El Dorado. The Cuban found nothing to condemn and everything to praise about Chicago—except the terrible winters (as a child, I remember, I would pray God not to let me freeze to death as I walked home from school). "But even the weather is okay," the Cuban told me. "I was in Cuba until five years ago. I lived in constant fear of being detected as a homosexual. I'm not one of those crazy Cubans who hate Castro and say he took away my family's Cadillac. We didn't have a Cadillac; we were poor. I give Castro credit for helping the poor and improving education and health facilities. But he hates gay men and has sent them to work camps. I had a friend who spent several years in a camp for gay people. They were draining swamps and turning the place into farmland, I believe. Hot, muggy, mosquitoes, very little food. Things got better when a visiting Czech student group objected.

"It would probably help if Americans objected, but American liberals don't want to hear about Cuban concentration camps for gays; they treat you as some kind of nut. If they're straight they say, 'Maybe gays were decadent. Maybe they were exploiting poor Cuban boys. Havana was a fleshpot for rich foreigners.' True enough, but then again even poor Cubans can be gay. I'm poor and gay. Our greatest writer, José Lezama Lima, was gay. He was forced to marry. He wasn't allowed to publish his masterpiece, *Paradiso,* in Cuba. Anyway, after Cuba Chicago does seem like my idea of paradise. I realize that rights for gays are not a big deal for most people—not terribly important in reforming a country. Unless you happen to be gay."

Without a doubt Chicago is a good place in which to be gay. The city is sophisticated, rents are not as high as in other large cities, there are many bars and discos and an attractive gay ghetto. Gay life is concentrated in three areas. One is the Near North around Clark and Illinois, where the Bistro (the leading disco) can be found and many bars, including Flight (for hustlers), Marilyn's (for women), and the Gold Coast (leather) as well as the Machine Shop (adult bookstore).

The second gay area is New Town, near Clark and Diversey; this is the ghetto and here are such bars as the Broadway Limited (disco) and Cheeks (a cruise bar). The third area is the Northside, where one finds Little Jim's (the city's most popular cruise bar), the Bushes (for the cocktail crowd), El Dorado (Latins) and Man's Country (the baths).

Homosexual acts between consenting adults are legal in Illinois, and activists are hopeful that the new mayor may issue an executive order ending discrimination against gays in city employment (although in her first months in office the police have been stepping up harassment of gay bars). The governor has promised on television to issue such an order for the whole state. A gay rights bill is up before the legislature in Springfield, not for the first time; gay leaders are confident that eventually it will become a law, guaranteeing gays equality in housing and jobs.

Chicago is, however, definitely a conservative city. The most powerful gay organization is the Metropolitan Business Association, which has forty-eight members. Its chairman is Charles Renslow, who got his start in the 1950s as a beefcake photographer and later as the publisher of *Mars*, a physique magazine. Seventeen years ago he opened the Gold Coast (now the oldest leather bar in the country). More recently he became the owner of Man's Country. As Renslow told me, "Chicago is much more closety than New York or Los Angeles. The gays here are hardworking. Few of them are unemployed. Quite a few feel they *could* come out on the job, but they choose not to. Similarly, Illinois has had closeted gays elected to high office for many years; everyone knows they're gay, but it's never mentioned. That's the Chicago style. Activists here choose to work through the establishment, not through demonstrations. As long as you don't make a big deal out of things, you can get away with a lot in Chicago."

"Why is Chicago so conservative?" I asked.

"We've got the largest Catholic archdiocese in the country, for one thing. But it's probably more general, the Midwest work ethic. Everyone stays home during the week, preparing for work. Doing well on the job is the most important thing to Chicagoans. That's true everywhere in the Midwest; it's just distilled here."

I arrived in Minneapolis shortly before Christmas. Snow had been sitting on the ground for so long that it had grayed and cracked; new snow was now falling, fresh whipped cream over stale meringue. Winter is such a fact of life here that it neither daunts nor depresses Minnesotans. Even in the wake of a blizzard gays shovel their way out of garages and plow into town on intrepid snow tires, heading for the bars. On a night that in any other region would be declared a national emergency the bars are packed, business as usual.

I was met at the plane by a friend of an acquaintance. I'll call him Claude, for that name suggests his look of a World War II pilot, trimmed blond mustache above the white silk scarf and brown flight jacket. He was of an uncertain age (or "of a certain age," as the Victorians put it), and no subsequent conversation with him or his buddies cleared up the puzzle. When I asked one friend point-blank, he merely smiled and said, breathing out huskily, "Huh!" as though to suggest, "Wouldn't you *just* like to know." One might more easily ask Jackie to comment on Chappaquiddick. Naturally one assumed Claude's age was fabulous (sixty? seventy? more?), though perhaps he was no more than forty-five, a figure that jibed with other "internal evidence," as literary critics say when they're not certain. This prying interest in vital statistics is of a piece with Claude's clique, which keeps close tabs on all relevant data. They miss nothing. They are leaders of fashion in Minneapolis, aware of their status, half-humorous about it—but the other half is gravely serious.

As we putter into town in his appealing vintage foreign sports car, I look at his wonderful processed blond hair (he explains frankly that the color is "assisted" and, technically, not blond but "hamster"). His blue eyes stare out at the swooping and diving cut-offs and overpasses through lids that have been surgically tightened. His fingers on the wheel glitter with gold rings. He speaks with a tenor voice of a peculiarly sharp resonance and much too loudly; the loudness, I suspect, is meant to suggest honesty in someone who is a master of irony and calculated effects. When I met his friends I discovered they all spoke this way; the heightened volume served several purposes. It lent an air of vivacity, of cooped-up energy, to the millionth evening spent among the same six or eight people; the choice seemed to be between resigned, irritable silence and a willed gaiety. The bright, clear voices also functioned as steely pruning shears cutting through thickets of in-jokes, hostility, bitterness. This group is like a preservation of *The Boys in the Band*, except they are less bitchy, more teasing, and they'd *never* play the truth game—in fact, it's the suppression of the truth that keeps things perking along. They are cold, intelligent, taunting; they have discovered that frigid people make out, though their frigidity is spiritual, not sexual.

"There used to be only three cliques in the city," Claude explains, or rather announces in the clip-clip-clip of his metallic voice. "I was the head of one of them—the best, if I may say so. If you didn't belong to a clique you'd slit your throat. What would you do on these long winter nights? Now that's all changed. Drugs have mellowed everyone out. Now people just drift about. The bars—we have just two good bars—are always filled. There's no social ladder left to climb. Better this way."

He described his friends to me as we made our way to their house. The words "fabulous" and "fantastic" alternated, though they were affixed not to personal qualities (insight, loyalty, compassion) but to acquisitions, accomplishments, positions, possessions. A door was flung open at the top of stairs and we hurried through the painful cold into the rosy warmth. Literally rosy, since all the lights were pink. It was an art deco museum, the sort of milieu F. Scott Fitzgerald, that chronicler of Minneapolis wealth, might have passed through if not approved. Plants were heaped high in every corner, the lamps dripped with fringe, a chromium and faded leather sofa was pulled up close to a blazing fire, advanced art hung on the walls (gaudy pessimism), pink indirect lighting filtered down from the dropped ceiling. The two hosts, both synthetically blond and suavely coiffed, talked with hard, loud voices. One of them seemed to have been sewn into his jeans; I worried about the pressure on his vital organs (a doctor could have conducted a thorough physical without the patient ever undressing). Like a Bedouin wife he was encrusted with gold rings and gold chains. Something deep inside me winced—and marvelled—at the sight of these starved, remade bodies, the capped teeth, wasp waists, tucked-back faces, processed hair. Drinks, many drinks, were passed around, as were abundant joints. The laughter grew louder, the tone more fascistically frivolous ("Is the lecture over yet?").

Our group, stoned and drunk, sped off in three cars to a brand-new Chinese restaurant. Paper cups of liquor and more joints traveled back and forth from front seat to rear. In the restaurant greetings were called out to the familiar face of a Japanese waitress who had somehow ended up here. "'Doesn't she look fabulous? No, really, that haircut. Turn around, honey. Isn't that fabulous? It's perfect, it frames your face, does wonders for your bones. Look, Fred, isn't her look fabulous?"

She waited on us. By the riotous end of the meal and dozens of elaborate drinks later, we were all listening to the waitress's prim but honest account of her last affair. "It just last six month. Now over. Kaput. He walk out after six month." She smiled and bobbed her head forward, as though she'd just told us a joke. "Now I look for Capricorn woman."

"What!" the table roared.

More giggles. "Yes," she said. "Capricorn woman. I sick of men."

"Quite right," someone said, suddenly serious. "Stick with your own sex. You don't want to go messing around with people who aren't your own kind." Everyone nodded in agreement.

At one point the topic of conversation drifted toward suicide. The man on my left said, "I don't disapprove of suicide. I think we must revise our prejudices against it. One of my oldest friends just killed himself. I didn't feel guilty. We all have friends who are walking along the edge. *We* are; our lives are fast and dangerous. If we go over the edge, well, that's the game."

The group split up. One part of it, including me, went to the bars. First stop, the Gay Nineties, a restaurant, disco and bar all in one. Diners sat in red booths and looked up at chandeliers. Red flocked paper lined the walls. Above us a whole carriage from the last century had been hoisted aloft, and on the walls were pictures of antique cars ("The owner keeps a whole showroom full of old cars, just for his own amusement," someone told me). In the back was a small disco floor surrounded by tables and people of all ages, sizes and sexes. A door led to the oval-shaped bar; here an older, more relaxed crowd gathers, especially at cocktail hour. Men send drinks to those they admire. I received one from a baker in his mid-thirties who looked like me. He told me that he was from Northern Wisconsin, where he'd cooked at various resorts. He loved the woods and small-town life, but he almost never met other gay people in the area. "I'd work twelve hours and then fall in bed. Nothing else for me to do. Finally, in desperation, I moved to Minneapolis, though I prefer the country." It occurred to me that one aspect of oppression is that it tends to force gay singles to live in the city. No hardship on those of us who love urban life, but painful for those who hate it.

"A waitress I worked with in Wisconsin had just moved from Chicago. We became great friends, though she had campaigned against gays in Oak Park. Finally, after an unhappy marriage she got divorced, moved to Wisconsin—and met me. She liked me and I told her I'm gay. I also pointed out to her that her oldest son must be gay (he's lived with the same roommate for seven years and had a nervous breakdown when the roommate got sick). But I think what really made this waitress stop hating gays is that as a newly single woman she was being treated as a slut when she went to bars alone. Singles' rights became a new cause for her. She learned what it's like to be discriminated against. Before that, back in Chicago, her homophobia had been regarded as an 'interesting' hobby by her neighbors."

Claude rejoined me. He told me that years ago he had spent a few months in Los Angeles when he was a student and that he still considers himself an L.A. person. "I like the weather, I like pretty people, I like people who are into their bodies. But my business holds me here. One of these days I'll move to L.A."

He introduced me to a hustler—a six-foot-tall blond who had his hair slicked back in the style of a Fifties' greaser, very heavy, black eyebrows, a coarse nose and an impressive torso under a T-shirt from a bar ("Your Place") in Toledo. Although he was working a Christmas job these days, he had failed to show up at the shop this morning. "I met this really hot man and we did a lot of drugs and balled all night so I just called my boss and told him I wouldn't be in. I've always got my hustling to keep me going. I'm nineteen now and I've been hustling for six years—mostly married men who are looking for something *new*. My mother was a stripper; she's got tits out to here. My mom's had six husbands; I've slept with two. The first one, when my mother found out, she broke every dish in the house. She wants me to marry a guy with lots of money. Actually, last year I did get married—we both wore powder blue tuxes and pink carnations and my mother held a reception for seventy-five."

"Don't believe a word of it," Claude said, kissing the hustler on the cheek and steering me back to the dance floor. "Never stops lying. But he's hot. Good body. And *hung!*"

We walked down the street to the other bar, the Y'all Come Back, which is also a bar and disco, though in no other way does it resemble the Gay Nineties. Here the motif is Western. Blown-up porno photos adorn one wall. In a second bar neon wall plaques of cactus cast a faint glow on the drinkers. The small pool room is lined with unpeeled birch logs and spectators sit on an old wagon. In the back room there's yet another bar and a hamburger grill.

Claude's lover, by now quite drunk on black Russians, drew me aside. He was thirty-one and told me he'd come out when he was twenty-seven. His face was oval, his nose pert, upturned, and his hair curly ("It's a permanent—I have terrible hair"). He was wearing a striped, collarless shirt and had pushed sunglasses back into his hair. "I'm really mediocre," he said. "Or slightly better. I'm not a ten at anything, but I'm an eight across the board—face, body, personality—and I come across as a ten. Actually, I have a fabulous body. It's a real shame I have to wear clothes. Not a weightlifter's body, but a good figure. I'll never lose it, it's in the family—a good, slender body that makes up for my face. People may wonder why someone like Claude chose me, but I'm *there*, in his house, so I must be good enough, don't you think? Looks are where it's at—pretty people are very important. Or money. If I go to a party where everything's gold bracelets and rings and Gucci, I can't keep up, so I give them *body*. My body's as good as a twenty-three-year-old's. People wonder why Claude doesn't have a younger, prettier lover, but as someone with solid eights across the board I do just fine.

"Claude controls me about 75 percent of the time just by being so noncommittal. 'No hassle. Let's be mellow,' that's what he's always saying. I work a lot around the house (I want us to get a smaller town house, so we can think about other things), but I never get any appreciation. That's why I trick out, I think, in order to get some appreciation. Maybe not. But sometimes I get so tired of the gay rat-race—the emphasis on pretty people and money. Claude says he wants to live in L.A. but he'd have a breakdown there—he'd be a small fish in a big pond. But I don't want to talk about him; I want to talk about *me*. For once."

By chance I had fallen into a very distinct crowd of Minnesotans. When I mentioned their views to other gays I met in that city, they asked me where had I found them and insisted no such relics of the past existed. Of course they do, preserved intact in the arctic ice; in fact, they feel they are not only representative but dominant figures, the leaders of the gay community. They kept congratulating me on having discovered them and complimented my sure instinct in going to the heart of things.

My hotel, the Marquette Inn, was just a few blocks from the bars. It was in the IDS Tower, the highest building in Minneapolis, connected to most of the other buildings downtown through an intricate maze of skyways. These glass-enclosed passageways are one story above the street level and during the day they are crowded with shoppers and office workers, some in down jackets but most in suits and dresses, cozy in this giant terrarium. By day I would wander through this world under glass. In one of the malls (a flight of metal sculptures tacked to a brick wall), a group of old-timers was sitting in folding chairs and listening to the Hugo Busch band (a violinist, an accordionist, a drummer—and a woman playing the piano and singing with a Scandinavian lilt in her voice) as it performed the "Minnesota Polka" and "Edelweiss," as charming as a snowfall inside a glass ball. During the polka four couples danced while in the audience people sipped free cider from paper cups and swayed to the music.

In the IDS atrium (the Crystal Court) I heard an excellent high school orchestra play Sibelius and a medley of Christmas and Chanukah tunes. I also watched a runaway in shiny blue pants and high-heeled, square-toed black boots ingratiate himself to a tall man in a racoon coat—a "nice womanly man," as a character in *Valmouth* might put it.

Minneapolis, I'm told, becomes another city in the summer. Then people live outdoors, the streets are cruisy and gays frolic on the beach beside Lake Calhoun or on the nude beach on the banks of the Mississippi just below the bridge between St. Paul and Minneapolis. Lakes and flowers and trees insinuate themselves into the concrete grid of the city, reclaiming it for nature.

I paid a visit to the Gay Community Services center, a handsome brick building at 2855 Park Avenue "serving affectional preference minorities and their families," as the literature stated.

The center has several goals. It is primarily a mental health agency, providing counseling to gays and their families. It also undertakes to educate the general public about gays. And it functions as an advocate for gays. I interviewed a warm, well-spoken lesbian who was twenty-two years old, wore lavender pants tucked into boots, a colorful knit sweater, glasses and no makeup. "My best training for this job," she told me, "was being a street person. I hope I never lose touch with that experience. When I was sixteen I ran away from home and started living in the gay ghetto, Loring Park. I worked as a lesbian prostitute. A lesbian prostitute makes love to another woman while a man watches; a lot of men are willing to pay for that. I was also heavily into drugs."

I asked her if she is a therapist at the center.

"I'm not trained for that. No, I do several things, some in the advocacy area, some in the education area. Right now I'm working to get two gay men out of a mental hospital; they were committed years ago for being homosexual. I work with gay senior citizens; I'm trying to make sure they get fed properly.

We have a 'Meals on Wheels' program here in Minneapolis for the old and infirm, but these two old lovers freaked out the person who delivers the food when one of the lovers started feeding the other. I'm conducting a pilot program assessing attitudes of students in the public schools toward gays. I want to develop a model for investigating discrimination against gays. We're trying to get funding for the in-service training of hospital workers; we'd like to make hospital workers more sensitive to gays by having them work here at the center. We have a suicide intervention and crisis training program; volunteer social workers answer the suicide hotline. I talk to straight teachers and social workers from all over the state. Many of them are sophisticated, but many are quite ill-informed and ask me things like: If you could be straight, would you? Can people be cured of homosexuality? Is it a sin? What causes it? That sort of thing."

She told me that a pro-gay ordinance was passed in Minneapolis in 1974 by the city council. It guarantees freedom from discrimination in obtaining housing, employment, access to credit and education and such public services as hospital care and legal aid. There is now some underground challenge to this ordinance, and she is eager to make sure it is not rescinded, as a similar ordinance was in St. Paul.

She lives with a lover and is helping her raise her child. "Kids can handle lesbianism and homosexuality better than adults. When I told my younger brothers and sisters that I was going on TV to speak out for gay rights, I said that if I didn't live in Minneapolis I could lose my job or apartment. The kids were impressed. They said, 'That could really happen? That's dumb.'"

For a few minutes I chatted with the director of the center, a bearded, soft-spoken man slow on the uptake; he considered his answers carefully before dealing them out. He had recently moved to Minneapolis from Milwaukee, and he was very happy with his new town. "Milwaukee is nonpolitical, bar-oriented, whereas Minneapolis is progressive and there are more professionals in the gay community—of course that simply reflects the higher level of the community as a whole."

He runs several different group therapies, including a gay father's group and one for people in the process of coming out. I asked him to identify the biggest problem facing married gay men. "The loss of status," he answered. "Heterosexuality brings with it a lot of privileges. If you have a wife and children you have a position of respect. Furthermore, the family *nurtures* the father. When you become gay you lose respectability. And when you enter the gay world you plunge into a foreign environment. It takes two, three or four years to master the gay lifestyle. In the process you must break your dependency on straight relatives and friends."

"What about the children of gays?" I asked.

"I think they have a better chance to develop a broad view of the world than do the children of straights—of course things differ from one individual case to another. You see, in America we don't respect differences. Our country is made up of so many different ethnic groups; basically we have very little in common with each other. In order to form a nation we had to suppress these differences, we had to melt everything down. Now, of course, there's a reverse trend. People are trying to return to their roots, recover their national identity. In this climate I think gays will find more acceptance."

Later that afternoon a young woman came to lunch at my hotel. She has been active in the Minnesota Committee for Gay Rights, and before that she worked for the St. Paul Citizens for Human Rights—the group that lost the vote so disastrously. I asked her about that defeat for gay rights.

"It's odd," she said. "No one wants to discuss it. A lot of the gay leaders have left the city. For me it was a real shock. The polls had said we would win by 60 percent, though as it turned out the voters were against us, two to one. We had the mayor's support. We used his campaign headquarters. He made radio ads for us. We had most of the city council members on our side. The archbishop came out in favor of gay civil rights. The Lutherans were behind us. We got support from all of the unions except one. Then why did we lose? First, the gay community is not as visible in St. Paul as it is in Minneapolis. Many people had never met a gay—or so they thought. Second, the city is religious; people think homosexuality is a sin, no matter what religious leaders say. Third, there was a right-wing blitz right before the vote. Anita Bryant came to town and her husband spoke to a large group. Billboards were suddenly proclaiming, 'Preserve the Family.' Parents' rights were stressed, the right of every parent to have his or her child taught by a moral person. The wording was very confusing on the ballot; people were asked to vote 'Yes' to save the schools and parents' rights. Who wouldn't want to vote *for* parents' rights? And then I think Bob Kunst, the gay radical from Miami, did a lot of harm. St. Paul is a parochial town and doesn't like outsiders. A lot of people called our office telling us that they were against repeal until they saw Kunst on TV. And then St. Paul has lots of old folks' homes. People live longer here than elsewhere. We weren't allowed in to see them. Whereas a *candidate* must be allowed entrance, people advocating an *issue* are barred. I think that if we'd been backing a candidate, that person would have won; an issue is very different from a candidate."

She smiled. "Then there's the paranoid explanation of why we lost. Please bear with me. I feel that the right-wing doesn't really care about gays. They simply want to scare up voters to support their candidates. You see, the right-wing is made up of two very different groups: the working class, owners of small businesses and religious people; and those who run the country. There's nothing really uniting the two factions—they *need* phony 'moral' issues such as homosexuality, abortion, ERA, gun control laws, the Panama Canal to give them a semblance of unity. Their unity is built on ignorance and prejudice. Of course big business does have *some* stake in preserving the family and in defeating gay liberation. Housewives supply business with cheap labor; 50 percent of all married women work part-time, usually at low wages. They don't belong to unions, they keep losing their seniority when they drop out, they accumulate few benefits, they don't make trouble. And then the average father of a family can't afford to leave his job. He's forced to be compliant. Family life trains people to be good little workers. No wonder there's such hostility toward homosexuality."

I asked her what could be done to improve matters.

"Come out. Everyone should come out. The best way to educate the public is for all gay people to identify themselves—

if only to one other person, a friend or a relative. For lesbians in particular silence is the biggest problem. I didn't come out until four years ago. Before that I had no idea I was gay. I couldn't figure out what was wrong with me. Now I'm angry that I wasn't told it is possible to be gay and happy. I was shocked to discover how many people are gay. The number one problem for lesbians is visibility. Gay men are more visible—and receive more out-and-out oppression. You hear more faggot than dyke jokes. But to be ignored is also a problem. The news will report that 'homosexuals' demonstrated somewhere; later it turns out the demonstrators were lesbians. The work of lesbian writers has been suppressed, Sappho's work is in fragments, the history of the Amazons has been lost. Women are given the silent treatment because they're seen as passive, unimportant; when two women make love it's not seen as sex, not *real* sex, since sex depends on the penis."

Her activism, her strong sense of lesbian identity, her political ardor impressed me. For generations homosexuals and lesbians have led furtive, self-hating lives in the Midwest—static, dreary lives. In Minneapolis I sensed both a refinement of this old self-oppression ("I'm a solid eight across the board") as well as something new, fresh, pure. Since Minnesota is at the source of our greatest river, perhaps this new spirit will someday flood the entire region, wash clean an area that seems, more than anything else, complacent. No place else in America has lived with the status quo for so long. In the South industrialization and the end of segregation reoriented all values. In the West the frontier spirit, no matter how faint, can still be sensed. In the East, wave after wave of social change has made everything seem transient.

Only in the Midwest has so little changed over such a long period. Only here can people sneer at the antics of less stable populations. The rest of us know how foolish it is to plan ahead or regard anything as permanent. We know that the values we received as children are worthless now, and that those we presently entertain will have to be revised yet again.

The stability of the region, of course, has its advantages. The Midwest is not as faddish and rootless as the West Coast nor as class-conscious and pretentious as the East Coast. Depending on the individual, the stability of the Midwest can be felt as irredeemable despair—or as wholesomeness. Many gays, especially gay couples, are able to fit into the work-centered, down-to-earth, conservative Midwest with ease and satisfaction.

FLORIDA AND THE SOUTH

The Masked Cadre

Miami is a conservative town, its population composed of refugees from Castro's Cuba, retired Yankees and relatively poor black and white Floridians. Most residents are past fifty—which also makes for conservatism. The gay segment of the population reflects this political climate. As an article in *The Advocate* reported, the most successful gay element in south Florida is Closet Clusters, a fundraising chain of groups for prominent gays who do not want to be publicly identified. Although an estimated 150,000 gay people live in the Miami–Ft. Lauderdale area, the leading gay rights organization is lucky to lure fifteen participants to its meetings.

I visited Miami just before Christmas. Along Collins Avenue each lamp was decorated with a nonsectarian yellow tinsel ball suspended from an inverted treble clef mark. In the middle of the boulevard stood a red tinsel plastic tree, circle after circle of widely spaced hoops narrowing toward the top, from which emerged a small, pale flesh-colored cross, looking a bit like an anemic nightclub performer stepping out of her burdensome gown. The shopping centers were clogged with people seeking holiday gifts, but the event seemed perfunctory in this big, modern, hot city—a mere memory of a ritual, its significance lost somewhere along Arthur Godfrey Road, perhaps under the billboard of Telly Savalas lying prone and advertising Black Velvet.

The season, however, was attracting patrons to the nightclub in my motel on the beach, the Windward. Although the place is gay, most of the customers at the club were straights come to see the female impersonators. On a weekend night there are three shows—at nine, midnight and three. Fourteen impersonators do segments from *Annie* and *Mame* and take-offs on Marilyn Monroe, Donna Summer, Diana Ross, and Eartha Kitt. Members of the audience seem delighted and rush up to press tips on the drags. All of the performers lip sync to records.

I talked to one of the drags, a thin white boy whose chest was shaved down to his nipples and whose eyebrows had been plucked nearly clean. "People like it because it's an art," he said. "My goal is to write my own comedy material and do it live; that's a lot more impressive than this lip-sync stuff. Many of these show queens are saving up to have a sex change. We get paid $125 a week plus room and tips, which can be quite big. A lot of the kids have already had silicone injections for their tits and a few have had their beards removed through electrolysis. And some, as I said, want to have the nip and tuck."

I asked him whom he found to go to bed with. "Oh," he said, "a lot of straight guys want to go to bed with a man, and the pill goes down easier if the guy's a drag. After all, to have both tits and a cock is the best of both worlds. Lots of straights bring girls to the show, take them home and then come back later alone. These straight men like to hold onto tits while they're getting fucked."

Do you ever sleep with the other drags? I asked him. "No, that wouldn't be professional." And is there much rivalry among the various impersonators? "No, we all do something different."

I had a conversation with a charming former female impersonator. He told me he had given drag up because people have a bad opinion of transvestites. "People think you're a liar, you're trash. I lived as a woman with a guy for a year, and I had no trouble fooling the neighbors I was a girl. My lover thought he was straight because he was the aggressor in bed; now he's married to a sex change. Of course, I don't really look like a girl. I'm six-foot-two, but people see what they want to see."

He introduced me to a heavy, red-haired man in his forties who is a big-wig (literally as well as figuratively) in the Florida drag world. "The Miss Florida Pageant is terrific," he said in a voice as deep as Dietrich's. "It's the biggest pageant for drags in the country. Some 2,200 people come to it on a Monday night in May. The contestants make fabulous entrances—on live horses or flying in from the ceiling or with snakes or lions; they're sponsored by gay businesses (baths, bars). Last year Channel 4 on TV gave us four stars and said it was something for the entire family. The only difference between us and the Miss America Contest is Bert Parks. The contestants wear a bathing suit and an evening gown and show their talent. People in the audience wear tuxes and arrive in limos; they come from all over the country. The front row seats are reserved four years in advance. People pay ten dollars or $12.50 for a ticket." He reflected for a moment. "It's great because it shows straights what gays can do."

Drag was once a major gay pursuit throughout the country, and it still lingers on in pockets in unexpected places—the interlocking chain of Royal Courts up and down the West Coast, for instance. Show drags and contest drags, of course, are a very different breed from street drags. The show drags and especially contest drags are often white, middle-class and fairly conservative. On the West Coast several gay activists told me that the Royal Courts despise gay liberation and will not participate in parades or in any programs to benefit the gay community; members of the Royal Courts never wear drag in heterosexual public environments and are in general rather closety. This species of drag is still thriving in the South, and nowhere more so than in Miami. Street drags, by contrast, are something quite different. They always live in big cities and are more common in the North than the South, in the East than in the West. They are often working class (many of them black or Hispanic) and quite a few attempt to "pass" in public as real women, even as female prostitutes.

I have no theories, just a few thoughts, about why show drag is so popular in the South. Southerners are social beings,

and a rich and well-established social life has been built up
around the rituals of drag—in New Orleans the gay Krewes, in
Miami the contests, in small towns the drag shows at gay bars.
Most Southerners still live in small towns where gay society is
necessarily restricted and the straight world more oppressive, if
only by virtue of being omnipresent. Drag worn within the bar
or at private parties provides a sharp division between gay life
and straight; such a caesura is necessary to give adequate stress
to the specialness of a few stolen hours in a gay setting. Since
gay liberation has made so little headway in Southern towns (or
cities, for that matter), drag, camp and nelly behavior linger on
as the only available means of expressing a distinct identity:
"Look at how gay we are," the drags seem to be saying.

Drag also strikes its devotees as glamorous. Oppressed people
often dream of another world, one kinder, more tolerant, more
soignée. For many small-town Southerners the only image of
another world they receive is from television and the movies.
These gay boys in the South, usually isolated from "high" culture (ballet, theater and opera), grow up watching show business
extravaganzas on the tube and then re-creating them in the
privacy of their bedrooms. The "stars" are emblems of the imagination and of civility, and the most vibrant stars, as we know,
are women. Moreover, Southern women, if I may be forgiven a
bias, have always seemed to me more approachable, more interesting than their husbands. The women are the readers, the
dreamers, the church workers, the guardians of "culture." Gays,
as outsiders, are drawn toward these feminine embodiments of
warmth, fantasy and civilization.

Curiously, the show biz personalities that gay men usually
imitate are strong, passionate women—not the Debbie Reynoldses
but the Judy Garlands and Ethel Mermans. These imitated
women set up an odd ambiguity in their acts. By being performers they announce they are crowd-*pleasers*, inoffensive enter-
tainers; but by introducing so much pathos (in Garland's case)
or raucousness and "ballsiness" (in Merman's), they threaten to
break past the proscenium arch and to grab each member of the
audience by the throat. The form is safe, in other words, but the
content is aggressive. Drags, by adding yet another layer of
artifice, boost both sides of the message: the make-believe of the

form; and the hurt and anger of the content. The women gays choose to impersonate are powerful, independent and even rebellious figures; in the act of imitation this power is simultaneously reduced and heightened.

Late one morning I drove from Miami Beach to Coconut Grove, forty-five minutes on a freeway as fast and furious as those in Los Angeles. I met an aristocratic WASP for lunch, a man I'll call Bryce. In his early sixties, six-foot-four inches tall, with blue eyes and silver hair, he looked like Jefferson after the Presidency, though his manner was far less magisterial than his appearance. We grabbed a spinach salad at the Cocoplum on Main Highway, a chic little spot nestled among boutiques, many of them run by gays or for gays. In the restaurant we were seated by "Hattie," so named because she wears so many hats. Today, all four feet of her height was crowned by a black fur turban that tied under the chin, her face (so like Wanda Landowska's) painted with the skill and exactitude of an Old Master. Outside our window, seated on newspaper at the end of a short shopping mall, Draino, the local gay wino, holds forth. He swigs on a beer, talks to himself and wriggles his dirty toes in a patch of sunlight. When a bevy of elderly Miami Beach ladies attempts to enter the Cocoplum, Draino holds the door and makes such low, unsteady bows that he scares them off.

After lunch we go shopping. We stop in a de luxe kitchenware store, the Pampered Chef, and peruse several dowries' worth of enameled cast-iron French frying pans. Then we're off to the local craftsmen's exhibition hall (lots of ceramic tea sets, woven pillows, clever treatments of seashells and big pastel blue paintings in which six versions of the same woman's face melt from one phase of anguish into another—Sybil in troweled impasto).

Bryce has a real aptitude for village life. He likes visiting storeowners, going over local feuds and flurries, entertaining the same ten or fifteen friends ("The heavy jewlery set," as he calls his crowd of well-to-do older gay men). Like characters in an E. F. Benson novel, the gays of Coconut Grove are leisured and inquisitive, and the minor scandals of the town are fine grist for tiny mills.

After our shopping we drove to Bryce's house. He pointed out the houses of gays and laughingly told me that one could always spot them because they're invariably hidden behind a high fence or screen of plants. Bryce's mansion is concealed by a whole hedge of schefflera. The house is large and square, sitting in the midst of spacious grounds. It is built of local coral rock and Dade County pine, which is termite-proof. The front door, at the top of stairs, is a delicious mango shade. Up from the lawn soar giant palms—"I hate them," Bryce confesses, "great barber poles with just a few leaves at the very top." The cool, dim interior is English baronial, the sort of decor favored by steel magnates in the Twenties. The ceilings are beamed and in the living room a manor house fireplace takes up one wall. In the dining room stands a mahogany table for eight, the chairs' seats covered with petit point representing different sorts of seashell. Upstairs are three bedrooms; in Bryce's room the inside roof of his wood canopy bed is lined with mirrors. For a moment I look at a nineteenth-century photograph of Bryce's grandfather holding a pair of calipers and looking more like a romantic swain than an inventor; he is the source of the family fortune.

Back downstairs we sit on the screened-in back porch and sip something cold and cranberry. "Coral Gables and Coconut Grove are nice places for gays to live, especially older gays. The weather, the active social life and the casual ambience are all very pleasant. A gay group colonized this area shortly after World War II; many gays in the Air Force were down here for training and decided to stay. And of course Miami is still a big center for commercial aviation; the city's full of ball-bearing stewardesses." (When I looked blank, he explained he meant gay male stewards.) "This is not a place for ambitious young men. No one makes much money here except the decorators. I was working for the government and had myself transferred down here. Then my family died and I no longer had to work—and I decided I wouldn't."

Bryce showed me a picture of a handsome all-American boy. "I met Kieran when he was twenty-one and I was forty-two. We were lovers for five years and then we broke up; he wanted someone younger. But he was from a broken home and I wanted to hang on to him, so I adopted him. He's my son legally and will inherit my money. He lives right over there—" pointing through a scrim of trees—"in a smaller house of his own. He's an architect. We speak to each other every day on the phone, though we see each other only about once a week." Bryce talked some more about his relationship with Kieran and I could see that Bryce had done the "handsome thing" by Kieran—that thing more difficult to pull off than any other: giving someone money, especially if that someone is young and proud. Bryce had shrewdly attached no strings to the deal, certainly no sexual ties. It is not only more blessed to give, it is also more difficult—and giving requires of the benefactor a willingness to be abused by the recipient. "It's worked out fine," Bryce confided. "Kieran represents continuity in my life, a future, something I'm proud of. My friends are the other great pleasure. I can think of no lovelier moment than having a group of old friends in for a sit-down dinner on Christmas eve. We have the fire going, the air conditioning, greenery, red candles, red ribbons."

I asked him what he did with his time. "Oh, I work. Every Monday and Friday I make recordings of textbooks for blind students. It's interesting work; I've learned so much. Then there's the socializing. Once a year, in the summer, I have a large champagne party here in the garden, about eighty men. On Sundays we all go to Sewer Beach—that's a gay beach. After the beach we all come back here drunk and stagger around trying to play croquet, though the *current* tradition is playing pool (three of us have pool tables). We used to do a lot of boating, but two years ago I sold my twenty-five-foot sailboat; the bay's gotten too crowded. And we used to give fancy dinner parties for each other, but now the Candlelight Club has ruined social life. We all just go there; I can see six or eight of my friends there any evening. As for sex, I go to the baths three times a week; that's that. And I used to be active in the Metropolitan Community Church here, but now I've gotten out. It's been rather turbulent, five pastors in eight years. And during the anti-Anita campaign I was quite active in gay liberation."

I asked Bryce for his formula for happiness. "Money," he said, smiling. "Older gays with money seem to have a good time of it, though I suppose that must be true of straights, too. I'd hate to be an old pensioner."

"Armando" is a gay Cuban who has spent most of his life in Miami. When he was ten years old, in 1962, his family fled Cuba for the States. His father had grown up as a poor farmer; during the Depression he'd moved into town and started a grocery. Eventually, he had acquired rental property and a wholesale warehouse and store. His father supported Castro. "The tragedy of the revolution," Armando tells me, "is that it did not distinguish between the rich and the slowly emerging middle class. This middle class (my dad belonged to it) put Castro in power. Later, Dad lost everything under Castro and left the country."

A new thought causes Armando to smile—one of his few light moments; he is a very serious young man. "While I was a schoolchild I was tutored intensively in English. Then when we came to Miami—remember, it was our first plane flight, our first time off the island—my dad asked me to order coffee at the Royal Castle coffee shop. When the coffee arrived it was, of course, this weak and undrinkable American stuff. My dad was furious. He shouted at me, 'I paid for four years of tutoring and you can't even order *real* coffee!' "

Armando explained to me that in Miami there are two Cuban gay groups—those who are fairly open and adapted to American mores; and those who are older, heavily closeted and live with their families. "Don't forget that in the Cuban family the unmarried sons and daughters must stay at home with their parents. Moving out before marriage is a real scandal—it's almost as upsetting as coming out as a homosexual. Among Cubans it's all right for a son not to marry as long as he stays home and takes care of his mother; my father's business partner is fifty-two and still lives with his mother and that's considered admirable. When I left home, my dad begged me not to. He said, 'Look, if you want to mess around with girls, you can go to a motel, I'll pay for it, but stay here, your mother needs you.' "

Armando is by no means critical of Cuban mores. He and his lover (of Italian extraction) practice complete monogamy and fidelity. Armando thinks of promiscuity as a part of gay oppression, the classic furtiveness of closeted gays. He recognizes that his values resemble those of his parents. "I'm tired of hearing Anglos facilely dismiss Hispanics as machos off on a jealousy trip. I think jealousy, which appears to be nearly universal, must serve some function. I have problems with the casual gay life. In Miami Cuban gays know each other exclusively in a sexual context, but I don't like being a sex object in a relationship. My lover and I think that monogamy is at least a good way to get a relationship going. We're both jealous, we're both sexually compatible, we're both honest about sex fantasies we have about other men. We have our best sex after we go to the gym. We come home, all worked up over the gorgeous numbers we've seen, and we fall on each other. My lover was married for two years; she was the only woman he'd ever slept with and he was faithful to her while they were together. She died—now he's with me and he's faithful to me. It's really a matter of discipline. In this age of liberation many people have trouble with discipline, but I think it's essential—it's a way of *choosing* your life." After nearly a year of being together, Armando and his lover do seem to be very happy. If they are separated at a party they look uncomfortable until they're back within touching distance. The lover is jokier, more outgoing, less intense, but their compatibility is evident.

"My whole generation of Cubans in Miami has been under terrific strain, not just the gays," Armando continued. "Our parents never thought they'd remain in the States. They didn't want their kids to assimilate; they wanted to preserve Cuban culture intact. My sister is twenty-five but she still lives with our folks. My parents can't accept the American dating system—such late hours, so many different men, no supervision, no formal introductions to the family. Among Cuban gays you see many men who have completely rejected their people. They dress American, anglicize their names and dye their hair blond."

I asked Armando to describe how some of his Cuban friends have adapted to American gay life. "One of my closest friends lived with his family till a year ago. He didn't mind promiscuity at all, since his devotion to his parents left room only for casual sex. Now he's at college and he's worrying what will happen to him when his mother dies. He wonders if he'll be alone forever. He's never slept with a woman and the idea of marriage seems preposterous to him. He's intrigued by my lover and me; I think he may find a lover of his own eventually. I have a straight Cuban friend I've fooled around with. He's married. We did it in his car once. He told me he liked the idea I was so free. But now he never looks at me that way, and I've never seen him cruise other guys. He's very macho. Cuban culture regards *all* gay sex as a sin, though it's specially reprehensible if you play the 'woman's part.' It's a mistake, however, to confuse Cuban culture with Greek, let's say; in Greece the man who fucks a guy may be considered normal, but in Cuba any male-male contact is bad.

"Now another friend of mine is an older . . . queen, I guess you'd say. He lived away from Miami for a year, but he felt inadequate in the hip Anglo gay world and came back home. He also thinks it's immoral; he's still very religious. His religion is a sort of blend of Catholicism and voodoo. He's a devotee of St. Barbara. Now St. Barbara has two guises. In one she's just a nice lady who performs miracles; as a child I saw an immense statue of her in the south of Cuba, dressed in a velvet cloak and wearing human hair, her cloak covered with little tin amulets; a person who has a sore arm, say, gives the saint an amulet shaped like an arm. Her other guise is Santa Barbara Macho, in which she is mounted on a horse, dressed as a warrior and holding her sword up. My friend worships Santa Barbara Macho and puts in front of his little statue of her four fresh apples every day."

One afternoon I visited the offices of a gay male magazine in Miami famous for its photos of nude models. I spent some time with an editor, an elegant Cuban in his mid-thirties. He has full lips, so dark they're almost blue, and huge eyes ringed with lashes like the heart of a flycatcher. They're the most liquid eyes I've ever seen, which would give him a look of almost intrusive compassion did he not have a rigid, correct way of handling himself; he is very much the cultivated Spanish gentleman. Today he was wearing a brown checked jacket from Paris, the collar slightly turned up, a blue shirt and a dark brown satin tie, two thin gold rings on unexpected fingers. His nose is a bit out of joint—literally—which gives a lopsided masculine charm to an otherwise beautiful face. He has a precise, economical but relaxed way of moving, as though he had studied the Alexander technique for years.

Tomás, as I'll call him, has lined the walls of his office, from floor to ceiling, with photos, some of boys but others of contemporary paintings and designs. Across the hall were three people doing paste-ups; they would call back and forth to Tomás in Spanish. The atmosphere was hardworking but informal.

When I arrived a blond young man had just finished being inspected as a candidate for an upcoming centerfold. He was one of those people we might say are "pneumatic with youth," since their cushy, nubile bodies seem inflated by energy and vitality. He had pouty lips and shoulder-length hair. He was engaged in a whispered consultation with his manager, someone of the same age with hungry black eyes. They got up to leave and Tomás said to the model, "Get some sun, tone up, hold tight, we'll probably shoot Friday."

The next caller was a wiry, middle-aged man in a white sailor hat and giant blue and white Adidas. He had come to show his slides. As Tomás held them up to the light, the man muttered a running commentary: "This one is a gymnast, very shy, but if I could convince him to pose for you, would you want him?"

"Can you find him again?" Tomás asked.

The man was indignant. "Of course. I keep in touch with all my boys. Now, here's a very well-defined body. This guy is in Michigan, but he travels around."

Tomás paused for a moment over one slide. "This one is interesting, I like these older, hairier guys, but he flexes too much and his midriff is too thick." New slide. "Ah! This boy's the prettiest one, a wholesome, all-American face."

"Do you ever give photographic assignments?" the man asked.

"Not really," Tomás said. "But we're always interested in candid shots of hot men. If you catch them at a public event—a horse race, a baseball game, a rock concert—you don't need their okay. If it's a private setting, you need them to sign a permission slip. Unless, of course, you don't shoot their faces. I barge into tea rooms, locker rooms, jogging camps, the waterfront and just start snapping and hope I get something before I get chased out. I got some great shots of straight guys in a shower—but I had to run for my life."

When we were alone, Tomás told me that three-quarters of the men who pose for him are straight. "Most of them just wander in off the street. Eventually most good-looking kids filter through Florida. I never pay a model's way down here; it's not worth it. The models get just fifty dollars an hour. So maybe they make two or three hundred dollars from us; it's not really a career. *Gentleman's Quarterly* liked one of my models, but the guy didn't want to be bothered with New York; he'd rather loaf around in Miami and sniff coke."

I asked Tomás if he found his work fulfilling. "Absolutely. I work seven days a week and very long hours. My work is my life. I don't hang out with gays here in Miami. I see my family a lot. And I travel a lot for the magazine. Wherever I go I take pictures of hot men. I have very little sex. The photos *are* my sex life; I can work out all my fantasies. One month I can put a marine in girl's panties, the next I can show this perverse guy who's three feet tall with a foot-long dick, then I can turn around and give them elegance or raunchiness—whatever enters my head I can do. Otherwise I'd never live in Miami. There's no energy here. I never go to bars, I have just three friends. I work out with them at their home. The best thing in Florida is the weather; you can shoot almost every day."

The ethnic stereotype is that Hispanics are lazy, but in Miami Anglos have discovered, often to their irritation, that precisely the opposite is true: the Cubans are competitive and industrious. In the 1960s three-quarters of a million Cubans immigrated to Florida; now, with the American-Cuban détente, a new wave of Cubans is arriving in Miami. When a Miami newspaper columnist ran an article attributing the city's economic boom to the Cubans, he was showered with angry letters. One Anglo wrote, "I lost my contracting business due to the extreme competitiveness of Latins." Another wrote, "It's a damn shame you can't get a decent job in Miami unless you're bilingual. With 35,000 more Cubans coming, it will be near impossible."

"The Cubans are the only thing that makes this city work," a transplanted gay New Yorker told me excitedly. "I tried to build some condominium apartments, but the contractor's delays were so bad I pulled out. I'm used to the big city—God, do I miss it!" We were sitting in a white linen tent under shiny brass plantation fans. The Bloomingdale's tablecloth was held in place against the breeze by white plastic clamps.

I asked him why he'd moved to Miami.

"The good life. Look *around* you, for Chrissake!"

I did. Just beyond the tent a path of pebbles embedded in epoxy led to a large swimming pool and a guest house. Inside the main house I'd glimpsed the mirrored walls and ceiling of the dining room and, in the crowded living room, huge gaudy ceramic parrots on stands. Here in the tent the bamboo furniture was expensively upholstered.

"I sold out everything in the City" (New York City) "to move here, booming center of the South. Shit! I've been catering to the gay crowd, but they don't appreciate class. Now I'm opening a straight restaurant; I don't know any straight people except my mother. Should be fun."

With his feathered blond hair, his whiskey baritone and his nervous, heavy breathing, he seemed a mournful figure—the big-city operator far from home. While I sat with him he punched out half a dozen calls on his phone, shouted, argued and sweated, but his irritation with Florida's slow tempo only mounted. I studied his jewelry: gold I.D. bracelet, gold watch, "baroque" gold ring, gold necklace with a *cloisonné* anchor attached. He sighed, pouted, glistened, his eyes ringed with fatigue. His only consolation appeared to be his impertinent, cheerful Jamaican maid.

Downtown Miami at night seems surprisingly small-townish. The streets are empty except for a few old Cuban men drinking and shouting on a corner. The Double R, the leading gay bar, is inconspicuous and from the outside silent, dimly lit, virtually unmarked. It is a private club and the inner door is locked and manned by someone who checks out arrivals. I asked that man, a tall, lean dude, whether Anita Bryant had hurt the bar business. "No, you hear more about Anita outside Miami than here. At the Double R we're more interested in square dancing. Every Sunday, from six to eight, we have square dance instruction and from eight to nine we holler and carry on. Other bars are forming square dance groups; we've got four."

This Western bar (wagon wheel lamps, bare wood walls, a raised viewing platform behind a corral, sombreros painted on the john walls) was done up in high Christmas. A slowly revolving ceiling fan played havoc with the snowflakes, hundreds of scissored designs in white paper. Along two walls blind plastic windows had been frosted with spray paint. In one corner was a leather shop and in the back a cozy restaurant.

While I was in Miami I interviewed many people about the struggles at the voting booth against Anita Bryant. Oddly enough, most gay anger is not directed against Anita Bryant but against the gay leader, Bob Kunst. Kunst, a bearded man in his thirties, is a radical, and that doesn't go down well in Miami.

He has been variously described as an egotist and a loud-mouth publicity-seeker—and as a charmer. One of his enemies told me, "He always wears a beatific smile. He could charm the birds off the trees." One of his followers said, "Kunst is going to free us all; right now we're all still hidebound by convention." Kunst himself has asserted that much of the movement anti-pathy toward him is really disguised anti-Semitism, and indeed many of the epithets that have been hurled at him ("pushy," "abrasive," "vulgar") do sound like code-words for "Jewish."

During the first Dade County Gay Rights referendum, in the spring of 1977, Kunst ignored the Dade County Coalition for Human Rights, a moderate group, and started his own faction. A year after that disastrous defeat (gays garnered only 30 percent of the vote), Kunst announced that he was placing a new anti-discrimination ordinance on the November ballot. Most of the other gay leaders felt that to reopen these wounds so soon was extremely poor timing—and indeed Kunst and the ordinance once more went down in defeat. Commissioner Ruth Schack, who had supported the first ordinance, angrily announced, "It is clear that Bob Kunst represents no one, speaks for no one but his own warped, monstrous ego." To his credit, the second defeat was less overwhelming. And no one can deny that Kunst is militant and *way* out of the closet—which is by no means true of most gay Floridians.

Unfortunately, no one has stopped Anita. In 1979 she and her husband, Bob Green, published a new book, *At Any Cost*, in which they continue their attacks on gays, especially gay teachers, *even when they are closeted* (a new twist—in the past Bryant was opposed only to those who were out). Bryant and Green already operate a gay counseling service in Miami (designed to "cure" gays); in their book they propose a national toll-free hotline for counseling and referral and "intensive-treatment facilities" and "farm or ranch complexes for in-depth rehabilitation."

One Cuban who worked for the gay coalition told me that he felt gay leaders had made a mistake to ignore the Spanish-speaking population. "Out-of-state consultants from New York and San Francisco had decided in advance that Cubans don't vote and are best forgotten," I was told. "Before the election, while we were calling people to get out the vote, we were not permitted to phone people with Spanish surnames. The result was that gays lost 93 percent of the Cuban vote. But Anglos look down on closeted Cubans, and many Anglo gays are quite simply prejudiced against Hispanics."

Later I spoke to someone who had conducted a telephone survey of Miami *after* the election. "Unlike the gay pollsters, we did not have gays do the interviews. That's just elementary. Americans are so polite that they will not attack someone to his face. No, we hired older women to do the survey. What they discovered is that all but 10 percent of the Miami voters insisted they had never met a gay, and those who did say they knew gays could identify only obviously effeminate men. It's really, you see, a Catch-22 situation. Gays won't come out in Miami because the city is hostile to them; the city remains hostile because no one will come out."

One night I suddenly couldn't bear Miami another moment and hopped in my rented car and drove to Ft. Lauderdale. I checked into the Marlin Beach, the gay hotel "where the boys are." The hotel is a compound built around a swimming pool. By day the gay guests lounge by the pool or cross the highway and sun on the gay ocean beach. Around three in the afternoon a tea dance is held poolside; drinks are served by youths in shorts, the Poopettes. Inside is a bar, the Poop Deck Disco and a restaurant. In the basement is yet another dance floor, the Lower Deck Disco, and a soundproofed piano bar. Late at night, after the disco shuts down, the guests stand around the dark courtyard, rattle their ice and cruise each other. Everything is suddenly quiet and a bit sinister, as though this were a prison yard and those men the guards on patrol.

To emphasize this impression, the hotel can be entered only by the front door, which is closely watched. There are so many hungry young hustlers in Ft. Lauderdale that they must be kept out, lest they rob the rooms or roll the guests. Only if he is squired by a guest can a hustler gain admittance. The hotel seems a bit like a palace set down in a souk teeming with Arab boys.

Near the Marlin Beach are souvenir shops, bars, fast-food places, and here one observes kids, straight and gay, stumbling around on drugs—one limping, another on crutches, a third reeling against the wall. It really is like Tangier. The question doesn't arise as to who's gay or not; the kids are concerned not with getting laid but with getting high. If the one will lead to the other, fine; no questions asked. Ft. Lauderdale is a short, angry strip along the ocean, crawling with teens drugged or drunk or both. The two most common ages are sixteen and sixty—the latter buys the former. Beside me at dinner were two older men and a pretty but confused "boy." The oldest man in the group told Henny Youngman jokes and referred to himself coyly as "an older woman" while his companion cackled and the boy smiled and inexpertly tried to join in—but he didn't stand a chance. When I dine alone I frequently study straight couples; believe me, contrary to myth, the man is the one who does all the talking. And here was the new version of the man-woman game: the older men were powerful, talkative and ugly; the young man was submissive, silent and beautiful.

Outside, vulpine teens lurked around the door to the hotel looking for johns. They're kept at bay by a formidable bouncer—the guard of the seraglio protecting the harem, except it's our money, not our fading charms, that attracts the boys.

Outside, across the street, stage-struck palms hug the hot spots on the beach, waving their fronds toward us, perpetually saying farewell but never taking the plunge. Vans and pickup trucks and sports cars stop and start in congested traffic, everyone, straight and gay, cruising for drugs and thrills. In a shop window hang T-shirts proclaiming, "Rent a Kid Cheap," "I'm single and I love it," and "Arrive Stoned." This *is* the place to rent a kid cheap, though the kid may be skinny, haggard and nearly comatose when he arrives C.O.D. in your bed.

At the Poop Deck bar I strike up a conversation with a mild, bearded man in his late forties. He's a bit portly, has good white teeth and a sonorous voice. "I come down here six months every winter. I retired three years ago; I own three hotels up North. My lover is twenty-two. I met him six years ago in Vegas. He was vacationing there with his parents. I gave him my phone number. One night, after he'd returned with his family to Jersey, he called me and told me he wanted me. I said, 'I'll come get you,' and I did. I had a terrific row with his parents—his mother still won't speak to me."

"Did they press charges?"

"Oh, no, my lover was sixteen. What could they say?"

"Does your lover work?"

"He *better* not. No, I wouldn't want him working. We're *very* happy. We live in a condominium near here. Of course we both trick out, and if there's any friction we discuss it once a week on Wednesdays. He *shouts* at me." Warm, affectionate chuckle. "But we never go to bed angry. We work it out."

He told me that he had been married, but that his wife died young. They had three children, who are now in their twenties and married. "The kids have accepted my lover—they love him like a kid brother (they're all older than he is). I never thought I'd find someone else to love—but I have!" Without missing a beat he leaned fractionally closer. "See that little one over there? He just cruised me in the john and I asked him straight out if he was hustling and he said no. I might see him. I still fuck grls from time to time—it's better than (this sounds crude)—better than jerking off. But I find sex with boys much more passionate, much more emotional. Isn't this bartender hot?" He reached across the bar and grabbed the smiling bartender by the wrist. "Isn't he!"

"Very," I said.

"Well, I'm going to have him by the end of the summer—no, winter, whatever this is." He released the bartender. "I guess you'd say I'm an alcoholic. *Really*! I don't stumble but I do have wine in the morning, beer at noon, I drink all day every day."

I didn't know what I was expected to say. He found a new subject. "We don't have many friends down here. We spend most of our time together. He's off Christmas shopping now—how long does that take? If he left at noon, would he be home by now? It's nine."

"I suspect so."

"You don't know *him*."

In the lobby I saw a handsome young man and said hi. From there I went up to my room—and the next moment the young man was coughing discreetly outside my door. He told me that he was from Atlanta and had been down here for two months, just hanging out. I made general conversation—but no pass; suddenly he stood up and hastily took his leave. A few hours later I bumped into him at the Copa, a giant gay disco with several bars and an outdoor raw bar serving oysters, clams and shrimp. His eyes were swimming. "I'm on three Quaaludes," he whispered. "I wanted to hustle you, but when I saw I wasn't getting anywhere, I split." He smiled. "Wanta buy some 'ludes? They're pharmaceutical, just five bucks apiece. Or wanta go in with me and buy some cocaine for fifty? No? Would you lend me twenty dollars just till tomorrow morning, when I'll pay you back? Well, no harm in asking. Do you have a camera? Wanta take my picture for my portfolio? I'm getting ready for a modeling career in New York. Look at these cheekbones and lips."

"Yes," I said, "you do have nice fat lips."

"*Sensuous* lips," he said. "You know, some guy had the nerve to offer me just ten bucks. I told him to stuff it in his ear —or go buy a dirty straight boy. Filthy breeders."

"What?"

"That's what we call straights: breeders. Ugh."

I watched one couple on the dance floor as I sat on a gray carpeted cube. For a moment I thought they were straight, till I saw that the pretty barefoot figure in the French T-shirt and tailor-made pants was flat-chested and bore a tattoo on his *delicate* arms. But he had a woman's contained, down-played way of dancing in place in order to highlight the kung fu excesses of his partner. Neon stars ignited inside lucite receptacles and lit the white fake palms placed against dark gray walls.

Suddenly the music stopped and a drag beauty contest was announced. The contestants were all out for laughs, one fatter and more belligerent than the last. The most outrageous was a Divine clone, who lip-synched through "It Shoulda Been Me" as she threw her drink at the emcee and tore off her clothes.

In Ft. Lauderdale many gays make the assumption that all older men want adolescents and are willing to pay for them. I have hired hustlers all my life, but to be automatically expected to pay for sex depresses me. I suppose something in me responds to the commercial situation. The john buys the boy, and in that sense is in control, but within the encounter it is the john who humiliates himself before the hustler and "services" him. The slave (the john) owns the master (the hustler) and can give precise instructions as to how he wants to be dominated. Such a comprehensive program obviously has its appeal, but for me that appeal can be felt only when I believe I have alternatives, that at any moment I can enter an entirely different sort of drama—one, say, in which I figure as the pursued or the older friend or the bully or the child. Moreover, sex with hustlers can be intriguing if one senses that scoring plays a part in the hustler's erotic fantasies as well; when sex becomes simply an adjunct to obtaining drugs, however, it loses its allure. Vampirism (the john addicted to the hustler, the hustler addicted to drugs) doesn't appeal to me.

I have not, of course, described Ft. Lauderdale as it must seem to those gay men who live there; they, like people everywhere, lead varied lives not subject to generalization. But I have tried to single out the one feature that most strikes the tourist —that, indeed, exists *for* the tourist. One bright morning, before it clouded over, I lay on the beach, listening to the regular throb of the waves and the irregular squeals and hums of the traffic. I turned on my stomach, rested my chin on my hand and stared up someone's prone body—dramatic lesson in perspective. The huge bottoms of feet bracketed a major mound in blue satin (the crotch) topped by a maraschino cherry (the sunburned tip of the nose). The blue sky would have been a neutral background, a sheet of photographer's "seamless," except the sky was lit from within and figures placed against it were bounded by a firm, hard line. The figure I'm watching now is an exquisite sixteen-year-old frowning and applying oil to his body. The rest of us watch. It's a bit like Susannah and the Elders.

Key West is not yet Fire Island South. It's a real town that has a heterogenous population of 32,000 on an island about four miles long and two miles wide; it is also the southernmost point in the United States and enjoys some of the best weather in the country. Cuba is just ninety miles away.

I stayed with a friend in a Cuban cigar-maker's small cottage that was about a fifteen-minute bike ride from the center of town, Duval Street and Front Street. No one in my neighborhood was gay, at least as far as I could tell. Next door was a straight hippie commune—four little houses nestled behind a larger one in a paradisal garden. My host intends to create a similar compound. The other neighbors were Cuban families and retired Anglo couples.

Everything on the island can be reached by bicycle. At night, after you leave the bars, you ride home down quiet, deserted streets lined with nineteenth-century houses in a potpourri of styles—conch houses built by New England ship captains, Cuban houses, Bahamian houses—the diversity attesting to the town's complex history. Some of the houses are masked behind pierced veils of wood fretwork, many sparklingly restored, others almost audibly dilapidating into the rank soil. As you head toward the cemetery you begin a long, gentle ascent. An old Cuban woman peddles past on a cross street. Flowers and plants, their colors lost except where they blush faintly under blue lamplight, twine florid passagework around the four-square symmetry of human habitation. A pickup truck throbs at a stoplight; inside are straight guys in T-shirts putting beers away and joking. You glide past the cemetery, closed after dark, though you can see the raised, above-ground tombs through the staves of the fence, clumps of plastic flowers piled here and there on glittering slabs. A cool breeze flows over everything, fluttering your short sleeves and washing the island clean. On a corner three middle-aged Cuban men are sitting on chairs in front of a still-open but dimly lit *bodega*; they harangue the night away.

The next morning you drink your coffee and orange juice in the sunlight, blinking confusedly as you wait for them to energize you; the black and the gold liquids seem to be distillates of night and day. Then you peddle lazily to the gay beach. It's not very appealing—mostly pebbles and ratty palms. Some of the gay tourists, with their big-city pallor and muscles, are patrolling the cement pier. Few are in the water; the bottom is too shallow and mucky with seaweed. The wind is cold now, in early January, and many men have found refuge against a cement breakwater. The radios are tuned to a classical music program beamed from Havana.

The town seems to have attracted more gay couples as tourists than singles, some from the East Coast, most from the Midwest. You run into an exasperated friend from Philadelphia who mutters, "Damn couples! I can't get laid here and the beach is rotten. I'm heading back to Lauderdale, land of blond bunnies."

Since you're not alone, the possibilities for scoring interest you less. What you enjoy is the very pokiness of the town; as my mother would say, it's "downright trifling," it's so lazy. And the bicycle! It has restored you to the free, winged moments of adolescence when you were the Mercury of the silver spokes. In the afternoon you bike down to the harbor and trudge through a dull exhibition of just barely alive turtles, somnolent in dirty tanks. You consider and reject the notion of going out in a glass-bottom boat. Maybe tomorrow, if you find the energy, you might go snorkling; there's a gay swimming and snorkling cruise out to the reef.

But now it's cocktail time. In a restaurant that's 1940s modern, all curved walls, glass brick and asymmetrical bar, you work your way through a fruit punch and a bucket of a hundred small rock shrimp that you must peel yourself (the most ambitious chore of the day). As sunset approaches, the downtown traffic suddenly clots and coagulates. With the others you rush down to the stone pier. Hundreds of people have gathered there, all of them milling around carts hawking food, souvenirs and crafts. Standing in the transfixed audience of the sun king's *coucher* are hippies in their late thirties, a pale, elongated Parmigianino infant held against an earth mother's breast, her "old man" beside her skinny and feeble from brown rice, his straw hair tangled and woven with thongs and chipped beads. Sailboats returning to the harbor press sheets of cool linen across the sun's swollen, apoplectic face. Little kids play tag in and out of the crowds. Here and there are sunburned gays in cut-offs and guinea T-shirts. A bluegrass banjo has attracted a circle. Ten paces on, two white-faced mimes silently cavort under the sun's burning spot. The crowd has become so thick that there is scarcely room to stand. The sun touches the horizon and blazes a watery path toward us. Like a falling, molten coin, it hisses into the bay and vanishes—as everyone applauds. The applause dies away and everyone feels slightly foolish, touched by a mystery that dwarfs us all. Though the parked cars are soon gunning their motors, half an hour elapses before the lot is emptied.

After a leisurely dinner, nap, shower and change of clothes, you head out for the bars. First stop: Delmonico's. As though in a movie, you dissolve effortlessly off the street right onto the small dance floor, work up a sweat in ten tunes and drift out to the garden in back—an acre of winding paths, falling water and concealed leafy places for strange encounters. A couple of blocks down the street is the Monster, a disco and restaurant of several bars and levels, a place that *feels* like a grounded pleasure boat. On the roof you half-recline on cushions, let the beat of the music register in your bones as you puzzle out unfamiliar constellations in the sky. Propped against the railing, a young man in white leans into the wind and the night like a figurehead.

Over the smudged, decrepit outlines of the old Key West, gays are dropping a plastic overlay, the revised version—dozens of new boutiques and some thirty-five gay guest houses, hotels and motels, all opened since 1975. The true character of the old Key West is corrupt, lazy and honkytonk: it boasts of the longest run in the country of *Deep Throat* and *The Devil in Miss Jones*; several local officials have been implicated in the drug trade; straight bars overflow with drinkers and country and western tunes on any weekday, afternoon or evening. The new gay entrepreneurs, most of them Yankees, are alternately mystified and exasperated by the town's sun-stunned pace. Despite such drawbacks, the gay Key West Business Guild, which has 100 member firms, keeps planning activities for gay tourists—a dinner-dance cruise on a hired boat, a gay skating night every Tuesday (including a costume skating party on Halloween and a red-white-and-blue affair on the Fourth of July). Nor has the drowsy tempo kept the gay guest houses from being among the most professional in the country; indeed, Key West has more and better gay accommodations for tourists than any other resort. The Business Guild and the town council are even planning to improve the gay beach, since that's been something of a disappointment to visitors.

In the spring of 1979 there were a few incidents in which straights attacked gays; the most famous victim was Tennessee Williams, who insists his assailants were from out of town. The atmosphere has certainly not been helped by a Baptist minister, the Reverend Morris Wright, who has urged his congregation to take action against "female impersonators and queers."

The brouhaha has probably been overplayed. The Business Guild has hired two off-duty sheriff's deputies and a patrol car to cruise the streets; it has also retained a legal aide to protect gay tourists if they're arrested. The rate of violence is certainly lower than in any major city and it will die down once the gentrifying gays drive out the rednecks. Or *buy* them out. The real estate values are soaring in Key West even faster than in other parts of the nation. A two-room cottage that was worth $9,000 in 1975 is selling for $65,000 now, and most larger houses are going for well over $100,000.

On the way in from the airport to Memphis, one passes a remarkable billboard proclaiming. "Tennessee has *rescinded* its *ratification* of ERA," which means that the state has gone back on its pledge to provide equality for half the human race.

I stayed at the Holiday Inn—the flagship of all Holiday Inns. Jimmy Carter, I was told, had been a guest the preceding week during the midterm Democratic Convention. Nearby is the Holiday Inn University, where inn managers are trained. Many things in America that are speedy and standardized have begun or at least flourished in Memphis; as one gay Memphian told me proudly, "Memphis has everything you'd want in franchised food." Memphis can claim the first Admiral Benbow Inn, the first Downtowner Motel, the first Kress store and the first Dobbs House.

In December Memphis is cool and drizzly. My room overlooked the Mississippi, swollen and swift; all day and night commercial ships slid silently by. A gay couple in their twenties invited me to their apartment. They were a contrasting but oddly harmonious and complementary duo. One of them, "Carter," had cultivated a waspish, sour, cutting manner, but under the bitter coating was a sugar pill. He was the "character," the individualist, the holder of unpopular opinions; he was also, once you got to know him, the dreamer and the poet manqué. His lover, "A.J.," is a nonstop rattle-on who always sees the good side of people and who introduces even the mildest criticism by saying, "I shouldn't mention this, but. . . ." For him, the only sin is silence, but that sin he never allows to be committed in his presence. He is quick to agree even when assent is not appropriate. Whereas A.J.'s mood is relentlessly positive, Carter changes colors faster than a disco light show; within seconds he can go from crusty to ornery to tender to maudlin to pure *Passive*. But Carter is smart and enjoys a sociologist's perspective on himself as he switches from bitch to sad little boy. A.J. looks like a Polish angel with his straight, sealskin eyebrows, his Harpo blond hair, his big, straight nose and the purple slash of his mouth across his pale white face; he's tall, skinny and sexy—to the degree that anyone who talks so much can be sexy. Carter is softer, more refined, paunchy, prematurely balding and even prematurely deliquescing, as though eager to reach an age appropriate to his W. C. Fields' nastiness.

Carter greets me in a denim jumpsuit and instantly asks me, "Are people in New York still wearing jumpsuits? I got this one on sale; maybe that should have told me something." A.J., who is an interior designer, has done their apartment in what he calls the "eclectic" style, something he vastly favors but that Memphis is not yet "ready" for. The living room is a pleasant, subdued room with a tweed love seat, a glass coffee table on a brass stand, a brass lamp, black plastic chairs and coral wall-to-wall carpeting, a big fern in a straw basket and a rush broom tacked to the wall where someone else might have placed, say, a painting.

When I ask Carter for his impressions of Memphis he makes a face. "People here just stand around and gawk. No one makes a move. All the men here are femme. Every gay man in town at one time or another plans to make his fortune in drag. One of my best friends is a drag, but he's not convincing; he's too good-looking to be a girl. I'm the oddball in Memphis because I don't go to bars. I hate going out. We had twelve people here last week for hot buttered rum."

He launched into his history. "I was born and raised in Memphis. I'm from what's called a 'good' family; I went to the best college hereabouts. I minored in French and I once lived in France for three months. I can write in French, but now there's no use for it . . . I'm forgetting it. . . ." For some reason I think of one of Chekhov's three sisters, the one who is forgetting Italian and can no longer remember the word for "window." Carter sighs luxuriously; regret is not a forbidden emotion in the South.

"I came out when I was a junior in college. I met this fat, balding, bisexual 'switch-hitter'—that was his word, 'switch-hitter'—and he was my first experience." The gruesome humorist in Carter causes him to relish the recital of "fat, balding, bisexual switch-hitter"—the horror of so much realism tickles him, and I can see a laugh playing over his lips. Suddenly he is the languorous Southern lady again: "I hope you are not irritated by the smell of eucalyptus. I must have it in the room to relieve my sinuses. Memphis is very humid and it's hell on the sinuses. In the spring the valley moisture traps pollen in the air. In the summer it's a sticky hundred degrees and you want to melt. But at least there's very little pollution. That's an advantage, very little pollution. And we have wonderful drinking water, right from artesian wells. Have you tried our water? Want some?"

I decline the offer for the moment and ask him if the cult of leather and western has caught on in Memphis yet. "Oh, no, lots are in the closet here, but when they finally come out they're all femme. Actually, I like the drags better than the usual femmes because the drags at least are gutsy. The only problem is that the drags and the dykes fight with each other in the bars. All the dykes here are great big diesel dykes—fat, fighting, brawling—and all the guys are ultra-femme."

"What are you telling this man?" A.J. protests. "Don't listen to him. He has a warped view of everything."

"I do not," Carter says peevishly. For a moment he sinks into a pout. Then he brightens and says, "I always say what's on my mind. I'm not phony like everyone else. The other night I was at a piano bar and I sent the pianist a note telling him how terrible he was. We've been living in this apartment for two and a half years and we've run through the gamut of phonies. People who've turned on us. I don't know why. Because we're a couple? I'm not always hugging on A.J."

A.J., midway through Carter's speech, has started nodding like a Chinese doll and repeating some of Carter's words at random. "You're right, you're right—" and he heads off into an entirely new conversation.

But something Carter has said interests me. I ask Carter if he and A.J. know other couples. "Oh, no, we're the only gay couple we know. There aren't many gay couples in Memphis. Maybe in the upper crust, the pissy crowd—if there is one. If there are real rich gays, they're very discreet; no one knows them. As for our crowd, no one has a lover except us. In fact, people here seldom go to bed with each other. They scoot down to New Orleans for a wild weekend or they wait for strangers to come to town."

Discounting any possible exaggeration, I still recognize this phenomenon as a remnant of the old pre-liberation days. Since the level of self-hatred is so high among unliberated homosexuals, they can never be attracted to their gay friends or even acquaintances (straight friends are another story). In such a context, familiarity does breed contempt.

I ask A.J. about religion and gays in Memphis. "This is the middle of the Bible Belt. There's no gambling here. No racetrack. No baths. And as many churches as filling stations. There are no hard-core movie theaters, straight or gay, though we do have these dirty quarter movie places. It's mostly Baptist here. Luckily, Anita Bryant hasn't visited yet and there's no big anti-gay crusade yet."

Carter says sourly. "Memphis is just an overgrown country town. We'd like to get out. But how?" He sighs.

A.J. nods and smiles and continues in a new vein. "The cops here are all redneck. Lots of plainsclothesmen, who stage raids on the dirty bookstores and bars. If a guy comes up to you and says, 'I'm new in town. I've just been here for three months. Do you know any bisexual bars?'—well, you just *know* he's a cop. The cops can stop you if you've had just a beer or two and put you in jail for drunk while driving; they use that excuse to harass lots of gays."

Carter is playing heat now and fanning himself. "We had a gay rapist." The shocking line, dropped casually, is a familiar Southern device for initiating a new conversation (and returning the attention to oneself), though in most cases the introduction is followed by a story that is bland enough. In this case, however, the story is worthy of the opener. "He was called the Midtown Molester. (This is Midtown we're in, the gay section —we call it 'Homo Heights'). He raped four or five guys at gun-point. It just lasted a month; there were no murders. He turned out to be a teacher." One often hears the ignorant remark that "men can't be raped," and yet a rape center in Philadelphia has reported quite a few cases of raped men and psychotherapists are familiar with the phenomenon. I was in group therapy once with a guy who had been brutally raped as a teenager—his introduction to sex.

"Poor Memphis," Carter went on, now that he had taken focus again; he had shifted from scandal to lamentation. "There are so many strikes here. Last year we had a fireman's strike. Right from this window we could watch four or five fires break-ing out all over the city on an evening. There wasn't a lot of looting. Firemen set vacant buildings on fire, just to show how sorely they were to be missed. Then there was a police strike. *Then* a teacher's strike. For a hundred years Memphis has been trying to get it together, with no success. When people are told by their companies that they're being transferred to Memphis, their hearts just *sink*. When Martin Luther King was shot here,

Time magazine called Memphis a decaying river town. That hurt. It really hurt. But it's true, all true."

A friend of Carter's, "Luke," dropped in. He had brought a copy of *The Joy of Gay Sex* to be autographed. "This is my bible," he said. "You know, I'm so worried about these venereal diseases."

"Haven't you ever had one? Not even clap?" I asked. All three shook their heads.

"We had those little bugs once," Carter remarked. "Crabs? We caught them in Atlanta at a bath house. My, were we upset. We shaved off all our hair, even on our heads." A.J. nodded vigorously. I suggested that one application of A-200 would have done the trick, but they looked unconvinced.

Luke then confessed that he has been fucked only eight times in his life, the last time by a "straight" man. "Eight hours later I had the trots," he complained.

A.J. was nodding and mumbling, "Sure, sure, that'll happen, wears down the tread, hurts like hell, not good for you to get fucked, *you* fuck *him* the next time, he's got to learn to share." Obviously *The Joy of Gay Sex*, bible or no, had taught Luke nothing.

Luke told me that he worked for five dollars an hour checking and bagging in a supermarket. "I was in the manager's office but I cashed a con man's check—the con man was my lover for two weeks—so I was demoted back to the check-out counter. I'd never met a con man before; I'd just heard about them."

Luke said that he didn't like being gay. "They call it the gay life, but I think it's sad," he remarked. "During high school I had only two dates with girls. I wanted girls, but I was afraid to feel them up, afraid of rejection. Last weekend I spent with a girl. It was the first time I'd made it with a girl. It felt terrific. I've only been out for two years. In all that time I've only had sex with fifteen people, and those I've met through friends, certainly not at the bars. The bars are for socializing and dancing, period. In Overton Park there's some outdoors cruising. And of course the quarter movies. I love to have sex with straight men there. The real challenge is to get a straight man to suck *me*."

He told me he was twenty-two. He was a chubby young man on a strenuous diet who was working out religiously; by now he's probably a god. He was wearing glasses and a T-shirt with a panda on it ("It's a girl's T-shirt—but I *wanted* it"). "My family is Jewish," he said. "My mother's from here but my father is from the North. That's why I don't have a Southern accent—except when I play Scarlett O'Hara. I don't blame my parents for making me gay, though they were always urging me to go out on dates with girls, so I rebelled just to show them. One good thing: they always whipped me when I said, 'Nigger,' so today I have no prejudice against blacks. 'Course I wouldn't go to bed with one, but that's because they're all femme."

"Let's get out of here," Carter announced. We drove through the city to a party; everyone discussed his new car and its "options." We moved through midtown with its big white houses of two stories and green tile roofs, the mansions of the Twenties, set far back from the street. ("They say," Carter remarked, "that every third house is owned by a queer in this neighborhood. I believe it!") We passed through the gloomy downtown: a long, windswept, empty shopper's mall ("World's longest," Luke announced); the abandoned cotton warehouses beside the swift, historic, muddy, treacherous Mississippi; the boarded-up King Cotton Hotel; the boarded-up Beale Street; the newly renovated Orpheum Theater, fifty years old and the benefactor of an ongoing preservation campaign; no one in sight, not a single pedestrian.

Carter began to tell me about his aspirations. "I'm sick of my job. I'd like to be an airline steward. Now that would be glamorous. Can't you see me, A.J., in one of those uniforms? I'd fly to the ends of the earth. . . . I've been going to interviews for a job for the last seven years."

As we were parking, A.J. and Carter were able to tell who was at the party by the cars in the lot; they recognized them all, and I was reminded what a small town Memphis really must be. We were in a townhouse complex and the party was being given by five gay residents in the communal entertainment center, which they had reserved for the evening. The hosts had provided lots of cookies and cakes and an eggnog punch and a chemical log fitfully burning blue in the fireplace, but the guests were all expected to bring their own liquor. I was surprised to see no joints being passed around; Carter told me that

Memphis gays do smoke dope sometimes, but that heavier drugs have not caught on and that gays are less drug-oriented than young straights.

One of the hosts was a willowy boy with a thick hillbilly accent who wove his way from group to group until he leaned into us, proclaiming he was "smashed." He gave me a very flattering neck-to-knee inspection and said, "Hah, big boy." Then, with a hint of intention, he spilled his drink on his crotch and said to me, "Will you help me rub this thang?"

One topic was the midterm Democratic convention. A Houston newspaper had written that a visit to Memphis had revealed it was the most backward of all Southern cities. "Well, it is," someone conceded, "but what can we do? The governor of Tennessee is envious of Memphis and he won't do anything to help. And the big-wigs in the city won't fix up the downtown. Poor old Beale Street was supposed to be fixed up, but it's just a ghost town. And the city *is* 50 percent black, which *is* a problem."

Mention of the governor elicited comment on the fact that he had just received a $15,000 Lincoln from his cabinet members, despite the fact that he and his attorney general were allegedly implicated in a scheme to sell paroles to prisoners—or arrange for their escape—for $10,000 each.

I chatted with an extremely tall man of forty-eight who runs a diet center in Memphis. "Thank God for fast-food," he said. "The big obesity problem in Memphis is in the age group of twenty-three to thirty, since they're the ones who go to these fast-food joints. They've lost the art of cooking, and they're all in a rush."

I was introduced to a tall medical student who told me he regarded Memphis as "romantic." When I mentioned I'd met some Memphians who appeared to be discouraged, he said, "But I'll bet they're not natives. They're all from little farms and towns in Arkansas and Tennessee. I've got an aunt who lives in Dallas who's always lording it over us about how fabulous Dallas is, but I told her we had the first art museum in the South and the first community theater and we are a cultural and musical center." The student smiled a bit sheepishly as though at the absurdity of this claim. "I think Memphis must be revived by its gays. That's what happened in Atlanta; its renaissance is really due to its gays, and we should do the same. We've got everything here in Memphis; it's a legendary, romantic city, it really is."

Culturally, of course, Memphis is best known for Elvis Presley; a boulevard was named for him *before* he died. His mansion, Graceland, is a city shrine, its gates a representation in white metal of musical notes and the slouching performer with his guitar. All over town T-shirts are for sale that say, "Yours in eternity, Elvis." As your car emerges out of the flood and flurry of an automatic carwash and your window dries, you catch sight of a woman pulled up to the pump whom you flash on as His Greatest Fan: forty, harlequin glasses, three chins, hair in a dusty, lacquered dome. Memphis is still a big rock city. The Coliseum holds 12,000, the Liberty Bowl Memorial Stadium can accommodate 50,000, and both are frequently sold out to rock fans. The Rolling Stones have been through twice and Barry Manilow is always a favorite. Isaac Hayes and Charlie Rich are famous Memphis residents—perhaps the most famous, always taking into account the obese, drugged, gyrating figure of Elvis, still a living presence.

The city, somewhat unexpectedly, has a thriving theater scene. There are two excellent black companies, a resident professional playhouse on Overton Square (the trendy center of boutiques and chic restaurants), a repertory company in the restored Orpheum, and Theater Memphis, not to mention a dinner theater and various university productions.

The party was picking up. The chemical log even seemed to have taken on some color and zest. There was a lot of Southern whooping and alcoholic abandon. I was never neglected for a moment; that wonderful social tact, extinct in the rest of the country, seldom lets up in the South. "Superficial," as some may say, but out of such superficialities civilized life is quilted.

A fine young man, tall and about twenty-five, joined me. He told me that he had been brought up in the Church of Christ ("Much stricter than the Baptists," he hastened to add). His brother, who lives out West, is also gay. "And we think our sister is, too, though she won't talk about it. But she had a breakdown and was hospitalized when her woman roommate moved out.

Recently, during a family get-together, my brother and I were helping Mom in the kitchen and our sister was outside helping Dad repair his car. We got a fit of giggles. 'There's something for everyone in this family,' my brother said. Our parents have tacitly accepted we're gay, though they won't talk about it. We gave them *A Family Matter*, that book for the parents of gays, but they never said a word about it. When I proposed that my lover and I celebrate our anniversary when my folks were celebrating theirs, Mother just grew silent and the idea was dropped." I spent some time with this young man and his lover; it struck me that he had more self-respect, more buoyancy and confidence, than the other Memphians I'd met; he is also the only one of the lot to have come out with his family.

Carter had retreated to a corner by this point. He was eager for us to get on to another party, one being given by his upstairs neighbor. Here, too, there were plates of goodies, though the guests had brought their own bottles. The company was much smaller, no more than ten people grouped around a huge Christmas tree, each isolated by the booming rock music.

The host was a man in his forties with blond, shiny hair in very tight and extraordinarily regular curls (a wig or a permanent). He was in a brown jumpsuit. He told me that he drives a truck.

"I'm a member of the Metropolitan Community Church," he said, as we stood in the entranceway, slightly out of the roar of the music. "My mother was a Catholic, my father a Baptist, but I disagree with the Catholics on birth control and the Baptists on politics and money—they're always preaching from the pulpit, 'We've got to beat City Hall on this or that.' And of course I always felt rejected in both churches for being gay. Our church—it's really a mission; you need forty members for a church and we're just thirty—we have such a feeling of warmth and acceptance. I've been a member for three months. We meet every Sunday in the bridal chapel of a church. We sing a lot. The minister, who's a very strong woman, brings homosexuality into every sermon, but only as part of a larger surround. We're not very active in gay politics—maybe we should be. Maybe not."

He drew closer and lowered his voice. "About nine weeks ago I came to know Jesus Christ for the first time. It was during the service and suddenly I felt such peace and joy within me that I couldn't contain myself—I had to tell the others. They were so happy for me. It's been a long time since I've had someone, a lover, and I'm always worrying about that, but now I'm filled with calm because I know when it's the right time and the right person He will send me someone. If I go ahead and find someone on my own, it won't work out. We have an activity once a month —a picnic or a hayride. This month is was Christmas caroling."

The host introduced me to the only woman in the room. I had heard about her earlier from Carter; she was a great friend of his and spent many evenings with Carter and A.J. She was in her mid-thirties, single, a bit overweight but pretty, dressed in a floor-length rayon gown. She told me that she was reading a religious book about "the unhappy homosexual" and it was giving her lots of insights. Though she thinks homosexuality is a sin, she likes individual gay men. Back in her home town (population 500), her brother, who's converted from Methodism to Church of God, *hates* homosexuals with cross-eyed fury, as does her father, though her mother doesn't say much on the subject beyond remarking that it's "sad." Their little town has only one identifiable gay, who's also mentally retarded.

She complained that Memphis was not a city for straight singles. "It's a family town. Church and family. And it's been in an economic slump for ten years. The city fathers don't want it to grow. People are not proud to be from Memphis. Young people are all moving away."

Carter and A.J. were arguing. As they downed rum and Coke they became convinced they should leave Memphis. A.J. was saying, "Houston is my goal—that's where the money is."

Carter was holding out for New York. "You'll be a big interior designer there and I'll be a steward and travel the world out of Kennedy."

"What about Europe?" someone asked.

Luke couldn't resist remarking, "I feel sorry for the Europeans—everything destroyed and falling down and the people starving." Then he brightened and turned to our host "Bill." "Bill is like Europe—mostly decayed but still good in a few places."

The argument between Carter and A.J. was still going on.

The relative merits of Houston, Dallas, New York, Los Angeles, Atlanta were discussed and dismissed. For a few minutes New York seemed to be winning out; Carter painted it in the most seductive hues. They would have a glamorous apartment on Fifth Avenue, a fascinating, cosmopolitan circle, a "membership" at Studio 54. But then A.J. started worrying about giving up his car. If only the car didn't stand in the way, this whole dream could come true. Houston seemed suitably rich and automotive, though Carter feared it was all redneck. A few drinks later they both looked discouraged. "We'll never leave. It'll never happen." They were holding hands and I saw tears in Carter's eyes.

Through Carter and A.J. I met a black fashion designer of twenty-eight, thin and about six-foot-four. Edward, as I'll call him, had a red handkerchief in the right back pocket of his pants, short hair, clipped mustache, immense, elegant hands, a snowstorm for a smile, a slight scar by one eye. More remarkably, he had invented an accent for himself that is half Oxbridge and half black Tennessee. As a result, a sentence or two would be drawled in the most affected English manner—but then he'd give a characteristic Black English verb construction ("he knowed" or "she look") or double up with a big Southern hee-haw, a knee-slapping laugh. The way he spoke, however, was not jarring.

"I'm not accepted by blacks here," Edward said, smiling gently. "I'm too white-oriented they say. I deal very rarely with black gays; they go to bars in cliques—" here he switches into black dialect—"cliques are real *tahred*. . . ." Now he's Oxbridge again. "I have a gay black friend who plans to get married soon to please his parents. I rejected his advances and said, 'Why should I establish a relationship with you, when you won't introduce me to your family?' No, Southern blacks can't deal with me and Northern blacks can't deal with me. But foreign whites like me. I like them. I had an affair with a German last summer. I made the mistake—" peals of laughter—"of running up lots of bills on charge cards." Now black: "Them chahge cahds. . . ." English: "But I'm paying them off, and as soon as I do I'm heading for New York City. Maybe I'm running away from myself. *I love* clothes. I want to design women's clothes; women are *so* frivolous, their fashions change more quickly, more creativity, softer fabrics.

I just made a gray, double-breasted suit for a local woman. Beautiful, if I do say so—the suit, not the woman."

I asked him what he thought of gay liberation. He threw up his hands—a rather cataclysmic gesture, given their size. "Politics is horrid and gay politics is worse," he said. "I am not interested in the masses. I'm interested in my own survival. I have to deal with the double oppression of being black and gay. My secret is a strong individualism. *I like me* is my motto and my strength." The strength, however achieved, is undeniable. When we went together into an expensive, very white bar, the fashion designer was at once relaxed and lordly; from his great height he seemed to be reassuring the waitress that everything would be all right. He positively generated alpha waves. When I was with him the ordinary questions of race and virility-effeminacy did not arise; he transcended them, or held them in a solution of his own receipt. The *holding*, to be sure, was all his own doing, and it occurred to me to wonder what price in simple energy he was paying.

He turned to more general topics. "People talk about the black macho ethic. But I think it's more a question of inhibition. Blacks are more inhibited than whites."

I must have started at this remark; he laughed quietly and repeated his observation. "I'm serious. And why shouldn't that be true? Or are you thinking about savages in Africa? No, blacks are poor and religious and that means they're inhibited, straight and gay. Now, blacks will make exceptions for *rich* blacks. A rich black entertainer can be as outrageous as he likes, because blacks are concerned with wealth; money outweighs almost everything else."

He told me that he thought the race lines were hardening in the South. Among the whites the Ku Klux Klan was enjoying a new popularity, while among blacks a new militancy seemed to be in the air. "Certainly blacks are more unified than in the past, more separatist—though it's never a simple matter. In the gay world, the races seldom mix, although I've met several whites in Memphis who will go to bed only with blacks. I've noticed that those whites usually prefer effeminate blacks; that's a perpetuation of the old slave mentality. The butch white is so clearly in control of the effeminate black. Yankees have it all wrong; y'all imagine that whites in the South lust after big black bucks. They don't. Southern whites fall for docile, childlike, effeminate blacks." He then turned the talk to fashion, the dream world he found more congenial than this troubled sphere of race and sexuality.

New Orleanians used to call their city the "Big Easy," and the epithet suits the place. Subtropical, poor, bohemian, amoral, festive, the city is the most seductive spot in the South, one where all the ordinary rules are suspended. Not long ago a high official announced, "It's illegal to *give* bribes but not to *receive* them," and that can stand as a sample of the Alice-in-Wonderland reasoning that prevails over this sinful Catholic city, this glamorous hybrid, this blend of Spanish, French, black, Choctaw and Anglo cultures.

Poverty is the best preservative. Because New Orleans is so destitute, it has had to remain content with its Greek Revival mansions, its West Indies cottages, its Late Georgian and Creole houses, its French mansard roofs casting shade on Spanish wrought-iron balconies, its courtyards, loggias and cobblestone streets. Now the urge to restore, to embalm, has taken over and the Vieux Carré is safe. Today no one can tear down a building in the Quarter; more radically, if anyone tampers with a facade he cannot simply preserve it in its present state but must restore it to its original condition. Thus, if an arcade was plastered over in the mid-nineteenth century, the modern owner, if he or she is going to make any changes, must dig up the original plans and expose the arches that have been concealed for a hundred years.

This most charming of American cities is a jambalaya of sounds, sights and smells. Here are a few snapshots at random:

• Two flutes, a block away or next door, rapidly soar through a duet; a giant fly strumming against the screen on the window provides the continuo.

• An unshaved man in a cool, empty shop sits in the mid-morning (without a book, paper or any other occupation) beside a mound of cannoli under wax paper.

• An elderly woman with blue sunglasses sips iced tea under an umbrella on her second-story balcony, which is a wilderness of plants and flowers.

• Behind the locked metal gates guarding the imposing portiere of a mansion on Esplanade, plants in stone vases are dying of thirst. The marble steps are littered with stacks of unopened mail and the brand new Yellow Pages.

• An energetic, sweating Japanese TV crew is filming an octogenarian black jazz musician in front of Preservation Hall. The musician, sleepy and good-natured, smiles as he holds his big double bass. He looks longingly over his shoulder into the cool dimness of the jazz club. For some reason he strikes me as an ancient catfish hauled up from the muddy depths of the Mississippi.

• A young waitress in white blouse and black skirt, her hair up in a French twist, serves *café au lait* and a *beignet* at the Café du Monde. Then she stands by the door, leans over in a grand bow, hangs there and bounces—a dancer's relaxing technique. Her three gold necklaces catch the light.

• In an auto shop a man in his undershirt reaches over his belly to wind an invoice into an ancient Royal typewriter.

• Gas jets in glass lamps burn at midday, palely wavering beside a sign that reads, "Breakfast served 24 hours a day."

• Overheard in Jackson Square: "We're hill folk. He don't approve of us—he's Delta."

• A *grande dame* inspects photographs of nude men in a gallery and says heatedly to the proprietor, "Why, these men are unclothed. We are not in the Garden of Eden. God intended us to be *clothed*." The shopkeeper sips his Coke through a straw and murmurs, "Ah, yes, God the dressmaker."

• A high school girl with her grinning, skinny date at night on Bourbon Street tries to wheedle a free hot dog out of a black man standing beside his cart. "If you dew," she says, extending her frosted glass, "Ah'll give yew a tayste of mah Hurry-kyne." Hurricanes are the special drink of one of the popular bars in the Quarter.

• A former football star, now an alcoholic mess with a melon for a tummy, staggers past Lafitte's, addressing invisible people, a drink in his hand. "Hello, Miss Thing," he says, bow-

ing. "Love your hat," he tells another figment. My companion
says to me, "I see he's still *beveraging*. That's what we call him:
the Beveragette."

I spent a lot of time with George Dureau, a native of New
Orleans and the city's best-known painter and photographer. He
is *joli-laid*, forty-five, his face as prepossessing as I suspect Jove's
must be: jet-black hair to his shoulders, thick black mustaches
that flow into his black beard, powerful black nostrils from
which one expects to see steam escape and that rhyme with intense black eyes set in lidless Mongolian sockets above high
Mongolian cheekbones. If he were music, Sibelius would be the
composer. If an animal, a surprisingly graceful bear.

George lives on the second floor of an unrestored 1850
Greek Revival mansion on Esplanade, one of the streets that
bound the French Quarter. One pair of white columns is placed
directly above another. Inside, at the top of a flight of stairs,
giant hemp laundry baskets contain hundreds of rolled-up
sketches. In the bedroom is a four-poster bed and little else beside hundreds of plants, some healthy and others despairing, as
though the gardener were practicing cruel favoritism. "Oddly,"
George remarks, "the plants that are flourishing are those that
came to me in the worst condition. I'm good only at miracles."
In the adjoining studio strips of photos litter the floor, contact
sheets are thrown about, canvases are stacked everywhere—
dozens of canvases, a few tacked to the wall, and many hanging
stretchers. In another room, beside a great window that slides
open from the very floor, someone is asleep. In the cozy back
sitting room, arty disorder reigns: a couch groaning under pillows . . . a terra cotta bowl displaying three avocados lying on
their sides . . . a pineapple in lonely splendor in another dish
. . . a straw hat perched on the arm of a chair . . . french
windows thrown open to catch the night breeze . . . a single
dim lamp in the corner . . . a record of Fauré's *Dolly Suite*, the
most civilized, happy-sad music I know.

Many of the best paintings and most of the photographs are
portraits or studies of black men. I haven't met the subjects, but
the paintings *seem* to be strong likenesses; at least each face is
memorable, its individuality as unique as a snow crystal. The

technique itself, however, is often slapdash; Dureau gives the impression of working with a big, fast, wet brush, and the canvases often look like sketches. He lives with these hundreds of unfinished drawings and paintings and works on dozens at a time, in no hurry "to terminate the relationship," as he says.

By contrast, the photographs are studied, becalmed, classic. In one, a black man of twenty with a hurt, sensitive, angry face stands in the nude, offering his superb body more as an insult than as a gift. He has one arm that ends at the elbow and resembles a broken antique statue. We know the Greeks painted their statues; could the color have been black?

In another photo a serene black potentate, Assyrian head turned in profile, muscular torso turned toward us, stares out at his empire from under a high black turban, cresting above his forehead like the ultimate pompadour. "I kept wondering what sort of hair he had under that turban," George remarks. "Little corn rows? Or was it slicked back? Was he bald? I saw him everywhere in New Orleans, always in the most striking costumes he'd made himself—but he always had the turban on. One day, after he'd been posing for me, I said, 'Ali, my fiancé, what do you have under that turban?' 'Newspapers,' he said. 'My hair's kind of short—it breaks off. So I stuff in some crumpled newspapers, you know?'"

I asked George how he attracted his black models to his studio. "Well, I court people as friends and if they become models or lovers, so be it. The courtships are varied; I have a great number of black friends. They may visit me often or seldom. They frequently bring friends to meet the artist man 'who's different from other dudes, who don't seem like a white man,' who knows, sometimes, more about them than they know about themselves—or can say. I'm George the artist to them. They so respect the idea of an artist that they say it *art-tist*, the only time an *r* and a *t* ever get pronounced in New Orleans. If artist were the word for a grocer they'd say 'awness.'"

What sort of friendships have developed out of his art? "This casual but continuous salon has grown over the last fifteen or twenty years. Some of the relationships are paternal, some brotherly, some are respectfully formal, intellectual or artistic. Sexual relations sometimes develop, but I don't require that. Of course often I must pursue some wonderful or terrible-looking person I admire. I will drive around in my truck stopping to speak to someone or to offer a ride. I'm a bit of a calculating poseur. I keep a pile of impressive publicity and typical photographs at the ready on my car seat. When I explain that portraiture is my business, I usually hear, 'Yeah, I been thinking about takin' a picture.' Most everyone wants to be photographed or drawn by a sympathetic, receptive talent. My sample works demonstrate that I care a lot about my subjects. Although some people may be shy about sitting for a stranger, most would like to be talked into it. Often I receive a few phone calls and tolerate unkept appointments before the sitting finally takes place. I'm patient. I've been called 'The Good Shepherd' and 'The Hound of Heaven.' Having decided that a man has a message for posterity and that my talent is the vehicle, I will make it happen in two days or two years. I am diligent about these multitudinous courtships, perhaps because I have such good feelings about my unique worth and the nobility of my purpose."

And do his black friends ever resent him for being white? "I am a feverish worker—no effete snob—and a generous provider when I can be. Since my friends are often struggling or unemployable, I might strike them as privileged. And since I mix with many levels of society in my work I could seem grand. But as important to me as my androgyny (from tough to gentle) is my social mobility (from slave to king); I move from dishwasher and laundryman to artist and patriarch. Most of my black friends know I am a willing exile from the society that excludes them. My art has been born out of my egalitarian affections, and I've paid dearly for this."

Do these friendships spill over into sex? "I have always had many unions in the works, with different intensities and expectations. One night I was lying with a friend whom I've nicknamed Hercules Crip in front of the TV just relaxing and stroking. His is a stormy life and I am a good drydock. I am more comforting than threatening. He is a handsome and powerful man cut short by a jumble of birth defects: the confused fingers of his right hand, an abbreviated left leg—and his right leg is completely missing, leaving a neat and pleasant buttocks-stump full and round with a bit of a surgical tit that it was my friendly habit to tickle, provoking in him a childlike grin or giggle. This particular evening I felt a small bone or foot deep within at the hip socket. He turned and grinned at me, vacantly, expectantly. I asked, 'What is this little bone?' He said, somewhat reluctantly, 'That's what's left of a little bitty leg and foot that was hanging there when I was a kid. But it didn't do nothin' but get in the way, so they cut it off so I could wear my prosthesis.' I squeezed it gently and he gave me a broad grin and said, 'Man, you somethin'.' I said, 'Anybody else know about this bone, boy?' He said, 'No,' softly. 'Good,' I said, 'it's mine and it shall be called Little Footlet, Son of the Artist.' He cracked up, then we embraced, we wrestled and hopped about, we laughed ourselves to sleep. I had made friends with his painful past. I could reintroduce it to him as a harmless friend of mine. Sounds silly. Few people will look at a stump or hurt limb, much less speak of it or touch it. I think a wounded part needs a special welcome back into life. A stump is a lonely place where all that loneliness dwells."

One afternoon, as we were walking through the flea market down by the Mississippi near the old U.S. Mint (its fence staves patiently hammered and wrought by slave labor so long ago), George told me about his Mardi Gras costume. "I put some wadding under my upper lip to fill it out and flatten my nose. I colored my face and hands black. I put on rags and wrapped one arm around across my back and concealed it with a backpack. I put on a fake stump. Then I acted sort of drunk and mean, so that when folks saw me coming they'd say, 'Oh-oh, here's bad news.' Well, no one recognized me. I mean, no one even looked at me. They'd glimpse that stump and not only didn't they look at *it*, they didn't look at *me*. Reminds me of years back when I showed a painting of a black man to a Garden District matron and she said, 'Where? Painting? I don't see a painting.' "

As a local celebrity, George had been called on to "evaluate" the flea market. Someone was trying to evict the flea market and introduce something classier; the manager of the market—a middle-aged hippie in a long robe who looked like a minor Manchu official of the last century, all goatee and ruling-class stomach, dusty sandals and teeth stained with betel nut—had called George and others in to write comments on the various displays. We walked, forms in hand, past the tables laden with a deco lamp from someone's attic, a snuff box, tinted photos of scenic spots, antlers, a coat rack made out of a deer's hoof, sunbonnets, dolls with hoop skirts stretched over toilet paper, old-fashioned flat irons, horseshoes, Chinese figurines from the Fifties, sand poured in colored layers into bottles to form pictures of cactus on the desert and ships at sea, hot sweet potato pies (small and savory), big ropes of garlic, plastic amber beads. . . . There was no way to itemize our reactions, but we knew we liked it all, the profusion and the crowds and the milling. We liked snooping around ordinary people's hoarded or despised treasures. That's what we wrote.

We stopped in a restaurant for a drink and the blond waitress came up and said, "Is your name Dureau?" "Yes," said George, "is yours?" "I wish it was, then I'd paint like a Gawd. . . ." Wafted out by her admiration, we climbed into the truck and sped off for the Garden District. Block after block of columned mansions streamed by, one with a curved portico, another a late Greek Revival cottage, a third a massive Italianate house with a black wrought-iron balcony, still another a villa in the "Swiss Chalet" style of the 1860s, all set in spacious lawns and covered with flowers and shaded by old trees. "See that one," George remarked as we went past a mansion falling into disrepair. "When the neighbors got after them to fix it up, they said, 'We're too poor to paint and too proud to whitewash.' When they gave their daughter her debut, they had to hold it by candlelight in the house because the electricity had been turned off. And the next morning they had to steal the paper from the neighbor's steps to read all about the big event."

We had paused for this story. Another car approached us on the cross street and screeched to a halt. A nervous young lady flew out of her car and over to us. "George, George Dureau, am I glad to see you! I loved your big retrospective show. And I need your advice about my own painting." Still another woman had swarmed out of her house and approached us. "George Dureau, see this house, it's mine, I just bought it. Like it? I want to buy a painting." George said, "Then come by my studio." "May I!" she exclaimed, visibly thrilled. "May I *really*!"

Somehow we got disentangled and proceeded on our way. He conveyed me to the Faubourg Marigny ("We call it Fag-burg, since so many gays live here"). Some people say it was the first suburb in the States; it was built to receive the overflow from the original French Quarter.

George bids me farewell and I go to visit "Henry," a Southern man of letters who lives in Marigny. Henry stopped smoking three years ago after an asthma attack and gained 30 pounds, but his face is still thin and wistfully pretty. He has two poodles named after characters in Faulkner. The house, shaded against the heat of the day by louvered shutters, is tidy and crowded with things. "My friends say it looks like a little old lady's house," Henry remarks, laughing. He knows all about the figure he cuts. Today's he's steamed up over a strange missive he's received from the West Coast. A few weeks previously, a San Franciscan of forty and his new beau of twenty had visited for several days. The guests were appalled by the heavy drinking and the constant campiness. They, of course, were vegetarians and tee-totalers; while they meditated, did yoga, played the flute or jogged, Henry and his cronies threw back the Scotches and became morose or bitchy or maudlin. The horror of it all was that the twenty-year-old Californian found this Southern "decadence" fascinating and new and grew apart from his older, ascetic companion. By the end of the week the young man was carousing on his own and stumbling down Bourbon Street to pick up tricks at improbable hours, while his estranged friend meditated furiously or phoned his Gestalt therapist. When he was back home in San Francisco, his revenge was to write a thinly veiled "short story" about the disastrous week, type it up and send a copy to poor Henry. Strange notion of a bread-and-butter note. In the story the San Franciscan, naturally, is cast in a sympathetic light whereas Henry is portrayed as a drunk queen clutching tatters of Spanish moss and faded Southern grandeur about his adipose shoulders.

Henry and I sit in his narrow, modernized kitchen and eat three pounds of crawfish, spicy and succulent. In a trice I've learned how to snap off the neck and pry open the shell and suck out the claws. He tells me stories about Walker Percy and Eudora Welty, the two best writers living in the South today. But he's informative about many less famous Southern novelists I've never heard of, and I recognize that North and South are still two cultures.

Although New Orleans has long been an inspiration and a host to painters, novelists and poets, few stay here for long. Henry has a curious meteorological theory worthy of Goethe (or Gertrude Stein): "The humidity here is too oppressive for creative efforts." The owner of a bookstore tells me that New Orleans, like Venice, is a poetic city with prosaic citizens: "They don't read. They may have a sort of abstract respect for the arts, but they don't patronize them." There are other parallels between New Orleans and Venice—the good food, the commitment to tourism (and to Carnival), the opulence mixing easily with the poverty, the romantic past, the permissive brand of Catholicism, the reputation as a bordello, the confluence of several cultures. . . .

The attitude toward homosexuality in New Orleans is difficult to pinpoint. Henry tells me that within the Quarter homosexuality is quite free and accepted even by straights. Gay tourism is undeniably big business. I stayed in the Ursuline Guesthouse, a charming spot and one of the many small residences for gays in the Vieux Carré. There are at least two dozen gay bars, four baths (the Club Gemini is the best), a gay disco open twenty-four hours a day (picture boogying at ten in the morning on a Tuesday), gay restaurants—in fact the whole Quarter has a gay ambience.

Mardi Gras is largely a gay holiday and the drag contests are a central part of the festivities. Mardi Gras begins in December and continues until the first day of Lent, usually in late February. Throughout this period there are parties nearly every night. I chatted with a young man from an old Cajun family who told me that he belongs not to one of the official Krewes but to an informal circle of actors, writers and painters who give eight costume balls during the season. About three hundred people attend each function and dress according to the theme of the evening: Beauty and the Beast; black and white harlequin; the nineteenth-century circus performer; and so on. In this man's opinion, gay activism in New Orleans is social, not political. "Many prominent New Orleanians, even those who are married, are gay and they are eager to protect gays. Gay life is well integrated into the life of the city. Tourism, after all, is our second biggest industry after shipping. The people wouldn't understand protest marches, but they do respect the old, established role of gays in Mardi Gras. This whole city lives for Mardi Gras. In May people begin sewing their costumes for the next season. During the season itself all work stops in the city, people don't show up at their jobs. It's one long party. It's the way we do things." He told me all this as he sipped a Falstaff beer with salt on the metal lid ("It's a Cajun custom—great for getting fat and driving the blood pressure up").

Among the best known gay Krewes are Amon Ra, Olympus, Petronius and Armenius. At their balls spectacular entrances are made by the Reigning King and Queen as well as the Returning King and Queen. The Krewe Captain and Krewe Lieutenant are other coveted positions. The entertainment at these parties is elaborate and rehearsed for months—or so I've heard tell. I've never been to Mardi Gras in New Orleans, but a few years ago I was "dating" in New York a nice Cajun from New Orleans who was small, dark and intensely masculine. He had a low voice, a beard and a butch reticence. I was always plaguing him to show me snapshots from home (I knew he had volumes of these pictures) but he refused—until one night he relented. I couldn't understand why he had been so apprehensive.

Once I delved into the photo albums it all came clear. Page after page of color pictures showed him in women's costumes, all spectacular. He had been the Captain of a Krewe and one year the Queen. In one snapshot there would be seven men sewing sequins on his train, sprawled on the floor and stitching or sipping beers. In the next section I'd see the same slightly dumpy men done up as ladies at Versailles—each of them frozen in a spotlight and weighted under pounds of powdered hair and squeezed within flowing silk contraptions. My beau's train was forty feet long. As Reigning Queen I think he was Marie Antoinette; as Returning Queen he may have been Ondine (at least he looked subaqueous). It was obviously a full life, though not one easily explained in New York—or anywhere else outside New Orleans.

I gave a reading the last night I was in New Orleans and never have I had such a responsive audience, one that relished every Baroque touch in a prose that has struck several severe Yankee critics as nothing *but* touches. The eccentricity, the fleeting suggestions of humor, the grotesquerie—nothing was lost on these Southerners. I felt that years of their living for fancy-dress parties had prepared them for my admittedly *special* kind of fiction. At the reading I met three gay men who were not natives and who did not like New Orleans. "It's a corrupt place," one of them said. "All efforts go into Mardi Gras—which is silly. And the gays may be cute and fun, but they're not educated—no one is down here. The economy is in such bad shape that there's little room for personal advancement. It's the best of old-style gay life—queens, drag, dishing, parties, tricking. But it's very hard to have a serious conversation here or find a good job or meet a masculine gay man." This last complaint recalled a shrill cry that had risen spontaneously one night out of the crowd at Lafitte's: "Where have all the *men* gone?" The Gertrude Stein Society is the largest political gay group, but it numbers only two hundred members—far fewer than the social clubs and Krewes. This year for the first time the Gertrude Stein is hoping to run an openly gay candidate from the Quarter. "What's important to remember," said one of the Stein members, "is that gays are *tolerated* in New Orleans but they are never *respected*."

An engaging young man whom I'll call Yves drew me aside. He was twenty-four, had pale brown eyes, a nascent ginger mustache, brown hair, an intelligent, open expression and a subtly refined manner. I asked him about his keys on the right. "Oh, I'm right-handed," he said. After a moment he added, "I'm open to anything. I met this sadist from L.A. and he and his wife keep sending me Submit Cards, but I finally wrote back that I'm more interested in just dating and romance." He spent two years in New York and one in Paris. He hates the Northeast and is delighted to be back in New Orleans. He is recording the last of the French patois being spoken among Louisiana blacks. "Their Cajun bosses can no longer speak or understand French. The language died out pretty much during the Thirties when officials resolved that Louisiana must become a one-language, English-speaking state. The blacks were spared. They talk to each other in patois; it's very functional, since they can insult the white boss or say anything they like. It's a private language. The French government is interested in notating this quickly disappearing dialect."

I asked Yves about his own gay life in the city. "I grew up in the Garden District. My parents always had wild alcoholic parties. My uncle was gay and I can remember as a child going to visit him in his own sitting room during one of my parents' parties. There he'd be with his other gay friends, all aunties, and they'd be sitting there in dresses. No one raised an eyebrow. I didn't think of myself as gay. Or rather, I knew many men who were married *and* gay, and I thought I'd be like them. It's called an 'uptown marriage.' You live with your wife and children uptown and you keep a boy in the Quarter. In the last century the Creoles kept mistresses in the Quarter, and more than one kept a boy—it's a very old custom. I had a fiancée. She and I had grown up together. She'd given me her virginity and that was a very big deal. When I was seventeen I started sneaking off to Lafitte's. I'd take her home after dates and usually end up at the bar. One night she was drunk and suspicious and she followed me to the bar. At the door she demanded that the bouncer let her in: 'I've come to see my husband.' She and I started having a knock-down drag-out when we suddenly looked up and there, coming down the stairs from the bar above, was her *father*! She and I hadn't known about him and he hadn't known about me."

He smiled and shrugged. "That's a very New Orleans story. Now she's engaged to another man, but I saw *him* last night at Lafitte's and I grabbed him by the collar and told him I'd beat him bloody if he didn't *tell* her before marrying her."

I asked him where he lived. "In the little house behind my parents' place—it's called the *garçonnière*. It was given to me when I was eighteen; that's a New Orleans custom. The adults don't *want* to know about the private lives of their children."

In Atlanta I stayed with a pair of lovers, one white and one black, in a black neighborhood that is to some extent gay. Their house was in the southwest section of the city, an area that was built as a solidly middle-class neighborhood in the first decades of the century. The whites have all fled to the suburbs now and blacks have taken over. The houses are big and capacious, set in lawns planted with old-fashioned flowers—roses, hydrangeas. Shade trees arch over the streets. On a single block two houses, long since abandoned, will be falling down. Two others will be inhabited but badly in need of repair. The rest will be immaculately maintained and freshly painted. They sell for about $30,000 each. A few blocks away from where I stayed a developer has tarted up a small section; he's paved the sidewalks with brick, built high fences, put in new street lamps from which he has suspended white signs on which the house numbers are printed in black. The houses themselves he has crudely restored with eye-grabbing but inharmonious and out-of-scale bits of brightly-painted carved wood. The typical white Atlantan has never been in this area and will not know what I'm talking about. In fact, when I had dinner with some white friends in Atlanta, they were dying to know what black gays in Atlanta thought and did and how they lived; sadly, on the way to that dinner my new black friends begged me to tell them later all about white gay Atlanta. The two worlds are utterly separate.

This is not a simple matter of cultural isolation but of deliberate exclusion. The gay bars are owned and operated by whites and the policy is to keep blacks out. Whenever a black comes to the door of a bar he is asked to present *five* pieces of I.D.; should he pass that requirement, he would be told he must have his birth certificate or his passport. There are really only two or three bars where gay blacks can go and they are low-down, dangerous places, of no interest to the middle-class blacks I met.

One of my hosts was a black man who had been brought up in Boston and who'd lived in Atlanta for only a few years. I asked him to contrast the two cities. "In Boston all the blacks want a white lover; they're terrible social climbers. Here there's less mixing—you seldom see mixed couples—so blacks go with each other. Blacks here are much friendlier than back home; their social isolation, however, has made them very clannish."

A young black gay from Philadelphia told me that he had come to Atlanta for a week's vacation and fallen in love with the city. When he told his family he was moving to Atlanta, they held a virtual wake for him. They and their parents had lived in the North for fifty years and warned him that Southerners would lynch him. "But I've done so well on my job and I have such a nice place to live that now they're all talking of moving down here. Of course there are differences. The pace is slower, religion is much more important here, most of the black gays I know go to church on Sunday—there's absolutely nothing else to do on Sundays. There are fewer artistic activities, no street life downtown, and among blacks there's an extreme cliquishness. But all in all, no one ever wants to leave Atlanta. When people are transferred away, they all angle to come back. It commands more loyalty from its people than any city I've ever known."

The Philadelphian went on to isolate another difference—the reticence of Southern blacks. "In Philadelphia we all talk about what's on our minds. We confide everything. But not down here. It's as though people are less introspective."

A young black man from Alabama who now lives in Atlanta perked up at this comment. "But that's the South, white or black. Southern families have no communication. When I decided to go to college I told my mother *after* I'd registered and was ready to go—June, my senior year in high school. She said, 'You going right away? I thought you were going to work first.' I said, 'No, I'm going now.' She said, 'Mm-hmmn,' nothing more."

My host, whom I'll call Ted, had a sweet round face, almost motherly. It was the color of French roast coffee beans with just a touch of dark rose on the innermost surface of his lower lip. He had big ears and bits of gray in his medium-length wiry hair. You could tell he was from Boston. Though he'd picked up a bit of Southern lilt, he still dropped his R's. And he was more relaxed around whites than his other black friends. Since his lover was white, as a couple they socialized with many whites, both straight and gay.

His lover, "Anton," had been a professor in New England. One day he could no longer bear his life, despite his love for Ted (they'd already been together for nine years at that point). Anton simply disappeared. He sold his car and vanished without his clothes and with very little money. He made no attempt to contact his family or Ted or his friends. He took a bus to Atlanta only because no one would think to look for him there. He'd never been to Atlanta and knew no one in the city. He assumed a new name, invented a new past and entered a new career.

After six months he phoned Ted and invited him to visit him in Atlanta.

As Ted told me, "I didn't know what to expect. I just came for a week. But I was so charmed by a little African Methodist Episcopalian church that I decided to stay. It was built by whites for slaves before the Civil War, and it's still in a white neighborhood, a very fancy neighborhood. Anton and I visited it one afternoon and this marvelous formal black minister, very old, came out to see us; he reminded me of my grandfather and I decided to stay."

Ted was very religious. He had a patient, tender nature, completely free from rancor; I've called it "motherly," but in fact it was parental. He made no sweaty protestations of goodness. He exerted no visible effort, and yet his peaceable spirit seemed to set every place he went in order. Though he had taught school for years, he was now content to sell men's clothes. "It's interesting," he said. "Watching them. People come off on dress now, not sex. The whole thing is to get dressed up—the straights are much worse than the gays. The gay kids wear big baggy pants, little thin ties, unstructured jackets—a sort of modified Punk look. But the straight black teenagers will come in with *Gentleman's Quarterly* and buy eighty-dollar shoes. Layaway. Calvin Klein jeans. Forty-dollar Niké racing shoes. Busing has had an effect. Kids from poor neighborhoods are brought into a rich area; sometimes the only way they can compete is through clothes." He laughed his high sort of hee-hee laugh. The odd thing is that when Ted spoke you felt he was an up-to-date, educated Boston man. But when he laughed he sounded like black farmers I've known in the South—a high, sometimes falsetto laugh, shaken out of the body like coins from a piggy bank. And when he listened, you saw vestiges of the old black churchgoer. He'd nod and in a low voice murmur the last word someone said. Or he'd tilt his face back and lower his eyes, as though that was the best way to listen—to the preacher? To bask in that radiance?

Ted loved to cook for his friends, and the first night I was in town he turned out something elaborate and delicious. Two gay black friends came by. One of them, William, as I'll call him, was a successful community leader. He had the charisma of a preacher—and indeed he sometimes gave sermons at his church. When someone told William he should become a full-time minister, he said, "Now why do you say *that*?" with a smile that revealed he had this career very much in mind. He must be startling in the pulpit—towering, small-waisted and long-legged, skinny, his eyes behind glasses the color of amber held up to the light. He had an irrefutable way of releasing an elated smile at the end of a sentence, a smile that silenced all contradiction and hinted at Larger Mysteries. He would say, "We're all traveling the same highway but in different cars"—and give that smile. The subject of black drag queens came up and William mentioned that when he was a child his mother had told him to stay away from drags. "Don't pick up snakes," she had said. I asked him if he thought drags were snakes. He looked slightly pained and said, "Edmund, I don't judge *anyone*," and released his smile.

I believe it. He's very religious and meditates on the "Daily Word" and the Bible three times a day. Before we parted he gave me something to help me on my travels—a printed card called "Keep On The Beam" by Emmet Fox. The metaphor was flying on a radio beam; in this case the plane is you and the beam God's Presence: "You are off the beam the moment you are *angry* or *resentful* or *jealous* or *frightened* or *depressed*. . . ."

I asked him how he reconciled his homosexuality with his religion. He said, "Edmund, do you know that poem by Langston Hughes that goes something like, 'I sent God a letter marked Personal and he sent me back a letter marked Personal'? I see my sexual orientation as something between me and God; it's nobody else's business."

Does he ever mention his homosexuality to the straight community? "Sometimes," he said. "Depends. If I'm dealing with a young person who has the *maturity* to understand, I might try to teach him or her the beautiful side of gay life." He smiled. "But I see no reason to defend my life. No reason at all." He drew himself up in his chair. "But Atlanta is a very small town and you must be discreet. You can't help bumping into everyone here." When I asked him how he met sexual partners, everything became vague; I had penetrated too far beyond the altar railing. But then he relented and said, "You can meet people through parties and through friends. Since we don't have entrée to the bars, we entertain at home a lot. I sometimes go up to people and introduce myself. I might go up to someone in the Central City Park. . . . But it's mostly parties here. We're trying to start a Man-of-the-Month plan. One person a month in our group plans an outing to a restaurant or a play or a picnic somewhere. All he has to do is make the arrangements. The most exclusive black club here is the Atlanta Committee. They give a very important affair every Thanksgiving. They're part of a whole chain of such clubs in other cities."

Ted told me that he had few complaints about racism. "When integration came to Atlanta, the straight whites accepted the letter of the law . . . *scrupulously*," he said. "I've never heard a single insult or ever been refused service anywhere. But the blacks down here became so used to segregation that many of them are not daring. Often, when I go out to dinner with Anton, I'll be the only black in the restaurant. Once we were in a little Georgia town in a fancy restaurant and one by one all the black kitchen help—all five of them—came out to stare at the nigger eating with the white folks. Georgians observe desegregation very strictly. They may not like it, but they are punctilious. Once I did a photographic assignment that took me to a remote part of Georgia where I had to deal with a real redneck who catches frogs at night. I suspect he was a Klansman, but even he was polite and correct."

After dinner I asked the three blacks in the room whether they regarded black culture as anti-gay. "That's what they say," said William, the tall community worker. "But I wonder. I visited this one black church here in the city where a drag queen is very prominent. He wears full drag to church and is respected for his piety and his good works." The young man from Alabama said that he had known many drags to sing in church choirs, even to sit in the women's section and to sing in high soprano falsetto. "Many of them live their whole lives as women."

Ted said that he thought his straight neighbors knew he was gay and were indifferent to the question. "Even the Black Muslims. They're *supposed* to be against homosexuality, and so they are in theory, but I wonder. . . ." He laughed.

At various points during my stay with Ted and Anton a fourteen-year-old black boy, extremely shy, would zig-zag through the house like a dragonfly and whisper something to Ted before taking off. I was never introduced to him. When I asked Ted who he was, he said, "Oh, that's my play son."

"What?"

"I guess that's a Southern expression. My play son. He's a neighbor boy I'm helping to raise. When his parents can't buy him something, I pitch in. I pick him up after his job as a dishwasher at midnight and bring him home. I teach him things and take him places. I also have a play daughter. She's just fifteen and she got pregnant, so now I have a play granddaughter as well." Ted was so much a part of the community that he could assist others in raising their kids—a socially useful role for gays, I should think. So many childless gays want children. Too often in the white world, however, children are carefully screened from "perverts," the very men and women who have the money and leisure and interest to help them. And the gay ghettos isolate homosexuals from all contact with children.

Ted told me that his great-uncle had been gay. "He'd go down to Barbados when he was old and bring back these kids, fourteen and fifteen, and he and his wife would adopt them. They were always very beautiful! I don't know if he slept with them. I don't think so. Anyway, they turned out fine—poor orphans who wouldn't have had a chance otherwise."

We drank our coffee in Ted and Anton's living room. Three walls were painted mustard, a fourth a contrasting umber. Three tatty love seats were drawn around a narrow wood coffee table. On the walls were paintings by friends; above the fireplace hung a painting of a unicorn by Anton's mother's female lover. "Yes," said Anton, "Mother discovered late in life she's gay. Ted and I have spent several vacations with Mom and her friend."

On top of the upright piano were two pictures of Ted's mother. In one she was a young girl in a singing group. "I was very attached to my mother and my grandmother. After my grandmother died I developed all her symptoms. My mother died two years ago. Last week I was in the hospital with a suspected heart condition and I dreamed my mother was calling for me. But finally I thought, She's already gone to her glory. My play children need me here on earth."

A week after I left Atlanta Ted died of a heart attack while eating dinner with Anton. He was only forty-one. I keep wondering what will happen to Anton and to the play family.

My last day in Atlanta I spent with a prominent young white architect. We had lunch with an older married man who's gay and one of the social leaders of the city. The married man lives in the "chateau country" of Buckhead, an area of imposing mansions and velvety lawns. The look of this poor neighborhood is perhaps best exemplified by Swan House, the best known showplace in Buckhead: two tiers of forty steps each soaring up on either side of falling fountains toward a white facade pierced by two stories of eight windows across and crowned by a pediment where two antique statues frame an *oeil-de-boeuf* window—a conglomeration as reckless as my description.

As we drove down one block, the married man pointed out seven houses among the first ten we passed where the husbands, all married, are gay. "Oh, sure, their wives usually know, but what are they going to do? Get divorced and live in an *apartment*!? There are tons of forty-year-old divorcées on the market, all waiting. Better to grin and bear it and to throw yourself into the garden club or the junior league or the Driving Club. Besides, gay men make good daddies. My sons are very macho."

We dropped the married man off and took a tour of the city. First there was Disneyland—downtown, that is. Peachtree Center, with its miles of boutiques surrounding the seventy-story tower of Peachtree Plaza Hotel. This is a glassed-in world of vast atriums, crude, rough-cast concrete walls, exposed glass elevators that resemble Prince Matchabelli perfume bottles, noisy macaws in cages, deafening waterfalls, hanging gardens and a continuous, humming cascade of escalators. Sunlight filters down from distant skylights. We wandered into a magazine store that had one collection of maybe fifty journals dedicated to yachting and outdoor life and another rack equally large given over to decorating and homemaking: His and Hers. At the Omni International Complex (the sort of place Atlantans like to call a "megastructure") we drank coffee and looked down on the mammoth skating rink. Three white women and three black men, obviously a professional group of some sort, were rehearsing their act. In this one complex there are six movie theaters, the eight-acre World Congress Center, a 2,000-seat auditorium and a 17,000-seat arena, home of the Hawks and the Flames, not to mention scores of elegant restaurants and boutiques.

We toured the posh residential neighborhood where the architect had grown up and he showed me the houses on his block where those childhood playmates had lived who've turned out to be gay. "Nine men and two lesbians! One of the girls is running a trailer park in Florida (she's very butch) and the other is elegant and severe and she lives in Paris with an intellectual woman." We dropped in on one of his friends, who greeted us at the door in his boxer shorts and undershirt; he was on roller skates, wielding a mop. The rooms were carpetless, the dining room lined in tin-foil and lighted by a disco ball. In the sun room was a giant stuffed kapok hamburger. The windows were lined with wrapping paper on which shutters had been drawn. In the back yard was a blue construction paper "swimming pool." We giggled and had a drink and moved on. Our next visit was to a demented twenty-seven-year-old "writer" from Alabama who was holed up in a filthy basement apartment piled to the ceiling with books. "I support myself as a waiter. I love it—the *material* it provides," he said, knowingly. "I'm writing a novel about coming out *and* integration in the South *and* the phoniness of Alabama. I'm up to page 600. The hero is . . . well, based on me. I want the book to be out by the 1980 election; I think it might influence the outcome. My style is hypnotic. It's a simple story. It's full of my philosophy of life; I think of myself as the Philosopher of the Common Man."

My host lives above his office close to downtown. He is from Atlanta. He studied in New York and was tempted to remain there. "But I didn't want to be forty and living in a two-room apartment on Beekman. Here I have a nice life, five employees, a Buick, tons of friends. For nine years I had a lover who is fifteen years older than I. When I was in my twenties all our friends were in their forties and fifties. We had everything we wanted—a lake house, our own house in town. Southern gays, you must remember, are crazy about their *homes*; the queens near here had the Episcopalian bishop come in and *bless* their new house. But I was bored. Then I got hepatitis *twice* and I couldn't drink. Our crowd was based on drinking. I fell into a new grass-smoking younger crowd, and the grass opened up a sex and fantasy world for me. My lover and I broke up. I don't have a new lover. My work keeps me busy—and my family. Since my father's death I'm the man in the family, which is a big job."

I asked him what he does for kicks. "I live three blocks from the big local disco. Or I can go to After Dark, the dirty book-shop, get blown and be home in half an hour. I date several guys."

That evening the architect gave a dinner party for eight. The guests were lively, smart, handsome and successful. Com-pared to Florida or Memphis, Atlanta is certainly a benign place for gays. The city may not be thriving as it was in the Sixties, but it's much more civilized than that other Sunbelt boom town, Houston. Unlike Houston, Atlanta is fairly cool, hilly, leafy and zoned. It's also a lot safer for gays. In fact, Atlanta likes to think of itself as "The New York of the South," and in some ways that epithet is accurate—both cities are dynamic, both are fashion and convention centers, both are sophisticated.

The subject of the Gay Day parade came up. My host, the architect, said, "Isn't it a shame that only the freaks march? I've got this great idea—all of our friends should march, though of course we'd have to wear masks. But it would still make some kind of statement." The exact nature of that statement, I fear, may be more ambiguous than he thought; even in the modern South, gays still form a masked cadre.

NEW YORK CITY

Design for Living

In 1947, when I was seven, I rode the James Whitcomb Riley between Chicago and Cincinnati by myself, and on the club car I met a New Yorker—my first. I can't really summon up his image now beyond the sound of a strange accent and the look of an oddly tailored jacket (unpadded shoulders, cuffs which must have been cut slightly on the bias to expose the dazzling edge of shirt I remember). What I recall most vividly was my fascination. I studied him closely; he had an amusing way of treating me as another adult; he was the first grownup I'd met who didn't resemble all the others.

A few years later my father took me to New York. We had dinner at Asti's, a restaurant where customers and waiters sang arias from operas. (I remember the bill for the four of us was a hundred dollars—an astounding figure in those days.) With kamikaze bravado I introduced myself to Jerome Hines, the Metropolitan *basso*, who graciously invited us to sit in his box the next night and hear him sing the role of the high priest in *The Magic Flute*. What impressed me the most was the scene where the lovers

pass through fire and water; the illusionism of the water, a great
cataract plunging from the top of the stage, was uncanny, inex-
plicable, though I found the music itself a disappointment compared to the rapturous kitsch of Puccini, which I'd heard at the
Cincinnati summer opera in the zoo.

I attended the University of Michigan at Ann Arbor, which
attracted so many New Yorkers that the agricultural students
at Michigan State called our school "Jew U." (we called theirs
"Moo U."). I remember asking one of the New Yorkers the
main difference between the Midwest and Manhattan. "Out
here," he said, "you go into a clothes store, try on a suit, chit-chat,
finally ask how much it costs. If it's too much you say you'll be
back tomorrow. In New York you ask the price as you enter and
shout 'Two hundred *dollars!*' and storm out."

I moved to New York on July 19, 1962 in pursuit of someone
I later captured and lived with for five years. That first night he
took me to dinner at a gay restaurant in the Village. Washington
Square and the streets surrounding it were so filled with people
I was both frightened and exhilarated. And the very words together, "gay restaurant," struck me as a delightful impossibility.
I had heard of gay baths and been to gay bars, but a gay restaurant sounded unexpectedly civilized, as though there were
something to gay life beyond sex and cruising for sex.

Coming of age and establishing a gay identity in New York in
the Sixties—in my twenties—partook of the atmosphere of a rehearsal for an Anouilh fancy-dress comedy. The lavish costumes,
to be supplied later by the wardrobe mistress, were merely suggested by bits of satin and velvet worn over jeans. The elaborate
language and sophisticated attitudes of the characters were constantly being interrupted by the actors' questions to the director:
"Where am I now? What am I feeling? What's my next action?"
Job security and rising salaries financed our bold experiments
and permitted us to sneer at the "establishment," which we treated
with the same insolence and deference we felt for our parents. I
worked as a staff writer for Time, Inc., from 1962 to 1970, but I
never regarded myself as a company man. I rushed home from
work to my apartment on Macdougal Street, ate something and
promptly went to bed. At eleven I would rise, dress as a hippie
and head out for the bars. All the years I was at *Time* I never

spent an official evening with the boss, nor was I ever quizzed about my private life.

Out-of-towners have remarked on the "cruel impersonality" of New York office life, but the rigid distinction between work and play seems to us not cruel but benign. Employees, who may fraternize comfortably enough on the job, are not expected to have anything in common. Nor do they. The city is made up of so many different ethnic groups, each with its own pleasures, that they could never intermingle harmoniously off the job. This woman lives on Staten Island in an Orthodox Jewish community and keeps kosher. That man is an Ivy League blueblood and commutes an hour and a half to Bernardsville, New Jersey. The art director is an Italian from Queens, the copy chief a Puerto Rican from the Bronx, her assistant a Sikh from Riverdale. Cultural and geographic distances isolate fellow workers—surely an advantage to all but the lonely.

The huge numbers of people permit specialization. In other American cities one must compromise one's individuality in order to have a circle. In Houston the leather boy who likes opera is hard put to find friends devoted to both scenes. In Los Angeles the insomniac who plays chess and pursues teenagers might find few companions to embrace all these interests at once. In Seattle the collector of Judy Garland memorabilia who insists on a wrestling match before sex might feel misunderstood. Not so in New York. Every hybrid, no matter how unlikely, can elect his company. Recently a friend of mine who appeared in a play about Count Dracula encountered a series of dramatically pallid and formal stage-door johnnies. Eventually he discovered they all belonged to the same club of gay vampires. Once when I read a story to a New York gay group, I was approached afterwards by a young man who invited me to join *his* group. Since my story had shown two lesbians good-naturedly outwitting a gay man, the new acquaintance sensed I might be in accord with the goals of his organization. The members idolized lesbians. All their efforts were bent toward securing universal power for women. They themselves (all gay men) despised their own bodies and regarded an erection with horror. Ejaculation could be countenanced only if emitted by a *flaccid penis* (great emphasis, over and over, on those two words, as though they were a political slogan, as no doubt they were). Once women had perfected the mechanics of virgin birth, the men had pledged to commit suicide.

Not for New York is the simple dichotomy between pissy queens and fun-loving fags so common elsewhere. Money, status, hobbies, politics and obsessions sort themselves out in New York in bewilderingly original combinations. On Fire Island I once met a whole household of bearded he-men who had evolved a group predilection for *silent drag*. The first summer they were together they'd giggled on stoned evenings and donned bits of tatty finery. The second summer particular dresses had become associated with particular imaginary, though still vocal, women ("Tom, do you want to be Carol tonight?"). By the third summer, dozens of acid trips later, the women had become mute. Dinners could be disconcerting for someone's uninitiated trick. As he toyed with his mousse, his appetite suddenly gone, the housemembers would disappear one by one only to return as harrowingly silent vamps, sex kittens and *grandes dames*, kohled eyes burning out of rice-powdered faces or above fans suddenly snapped open. I ran into the entire bunch one misty dawn on a wooded path; they were all carrying lace parasols and nicely conducting their trains.

Such specialization can be a temptation toward destruction. Of course, short of suicide, we're never quite certain we have been destroyed . . . yet. Certainly, I have seen people whose obsessions have narrowed them to the point of extinction: the leather man who works in the Leather Loft and goes to leather bars and reads *Drummer*. The compulsive cruiser who leaves the dirty-movie theater to go to the dirty bookstore before hitting the Glory Hole. But for every such story I can think of three counter-examples. Take the leather man who works in a leather bar but used his tips to finance his own theater, where I once saw excellent productions of Joe Orton's *What the Butler Saw* and Brendan Behan's *The Quare Fellow*. The bartender-impresario-playwright, always clanking and creaking about, spent most of his time with his largely straight actors and actresses. Or take the S&M tapdancer who between his admittedly *recherché* engagements teaches dance or does secretarial work and hangs out with performers from Al Carmines's Judson Church.

New York permits homosexuals an unparalleled chance to assemble a mix-and-match life. If I lived in another city, I suspect I would belong to two quite different circles—one artistic, the other gay. Naturally these two groups might overlap, but only slightly. In New York most of my friends are gay men and women who are almost all in the arts. This sort of specialization need not promote madness. For one thing, even the category of gay artist is far from simple. I move in at least three entirely different groups of that description. One is young and active in gay politics. A second is in its fifties and groaning under the prizes it has accumulated.

The third group includes those poets and painters who live on in the lengthening shadow of a dead genius; they are his widows. Like him the men have high, sissy voices and the knack of injecting so much irony into their speech that they never know (or at least I never know) whether they're serious about anything. Their group style is alcoholic, noncompetitive, ambitious and hardworking—an odd, seemingly contradictory set of attributes. Their loyalty to each other is inviolable, at least when dealing with outsiders. Their parties are always mixed and the women are generally straight. Although quite a few people in this circle are famous, the tone at least pretends to be egali-tarian. As in most such groups, the painters are wealthy and the poets hard-up, but the economics of the marketplace mean little to them; their affection was established long before any of them had made a name. Heterosexuals and bisexuals mix freely with the gays—in fact, such distinctions would seem ludicrous to them. All the stars are in their fifties now, but children and the old participate in their gatherings with impunity—as does that most driven of New York species, the young man on the make. Late in the evening the children and the very old have toddled off to bed, the famous are drunk and drowsy; only the young men are still alert, avid for opportunity and recognition, testy about real or imagined slights.

The gay men in this clique are openly gay in society, but they refuse to be labeled gay writers or gay artists; such a designation they would see as limiting, irrelevant, even humili-ating. As one celebrated writer has told me, "I'm gay—God knows I make no secret of that—and I'm a poet, but I'm not a gay poet. What would that mean, anyway? Someone who writes about cocksucking? Or one who expresses the famous gay sensibility?"

The point is certainly defensible. Most people in the arts aspire toward the widest possible audience, or if it must be a coterie, than one based on taste and fellow feeling; sexuality is scarcely a guarantee of sympathetic response. My ideal reader, at least when I write fiction, is a cultivated heterosexual woman in her sixties who knows English perfectly but is not an American. Reaching her, despite our differences, is a project that for some reason excites my imagination; I picture her as the "interior paramour." Would I lose all hope of her buying my novels if they were quarantined in a Gay Lit section of the bookstore, as perhaps they already are?

For several years now the question of the gay sensibility—is there such a thing? and, if so, what is it?—has been discussed with little to show for the effort. Part of the problem, no doubt, lies in the word *sensibility*, since it suggests something very general (a cast of mind) and very rarefied (perhaps due to its original meaning of "sensitivity"). Can any of us identify a sensibility of any sort? Is there a black sensibility? A French sensibility? A feminine sensibility? My first reaction is to consider these three proposed sensibilities as racist, jingoist and sexist, as mystical attributes assigned to groups rather than individuals. But even if this fear could be set aside how would we define, say, the French sensibility? If we said it is precise and logical, we would exclude Rimbaud; if concise and chaste, we would rule out Proust; if frivolous and witty, we would lose Hugo—and so on.

In the case of gays, there have been various aesthetic vogues in the last hundred years that small cliques have adopted—a conscious, voluntary allegiance to a group style. A vogue or a movement is something much more circumscribed in history and in intent than the eternal, involuntary sensibility. Decadence, attracting such figures as Oscar Wilde and Ronald Firbank, was a movement characterized by exquisitely rendered surfaces, a concentration on detail rather than overall structure and the elevation of the doctrine of "art for art's sake." This was the "artificial paradise" to which the outcast artist could escape, an illusory world in which the values that condemned eccentric behavior could be temporarily suspended or reversed. No wonder that Wilde's unit of wit is the paradox. Jean Genet is the final and fullest avatar of this impulse.

In the Fifties and Sixties the prevailing gay taste was camp. It also reversed (or leveled) values, but it employed a different strategy. Rather than declaring that evil is good, that sin is saintliness, camp announced that the vulgar is amusing, that "failed glamour" (in Sontag's phrase) can become an ironic triumph with the collaboration of a sympathetic audience.

Both Decadence and camp can be read as thwarted manifestations of gay anger—thwarted because the gays who took up these styles seldom felt they had direct and legitimate grounds for protest against heterosexual oppression. As a result, the decadents embraced traditional values and merely inverted them; in Genet's novels cowardliness becomes courage, betrayal loyalty, effeminacy heroism, though we are constantly reminded that such victories are merely verbal.

Camp as a recuperation of oppression is more difficult to interpret than Decadence because it is more evasive, more defended, far more slippery. By declaring that bad art is good, tackiness tasteful, the camp vogue announces its dictatorial power—the power to switch all the minuses to pluses and vice versa. Not *all*, for the hierarchy of camp excellence is arbitrary and unsystematic, at points blurring distinctions (thereby equating, as Andrew Britton has remarked, the true merit of Von Sternberg's films with the inanities of Busby Berkeley's); at other points treating a genuine artist's work with maddening condescension (thereby ignoring Douglas Sirk's lush, melodramatic vision and extracting crude pleasure from the "period" absurdities of his dialogue); and at still other points jeeringly regarding the "enemy" (John Wayne, Anita Bryant) as comparable follies (thereby brushing aside the very real issues of art and politics and confusing Wayne, an often sensitive actor who offscreen made reactionary remarks, with Bryant, a talentless demagogue and therefore a much simpler case). Because camp is so arbitrary, it frightens the uninitiated or at least makes them uneasy. I would claim that the *function* of camp is to promote such uneasiness; it is a muted, irresponsible form of antagonism, one too silly to be held accountable, a safe way of subverting the system.

These, then, are two of several gay styles that can be analyzed in social and political terms, though such an analysis explains nothing of the idiosyncratic value of a Wilde or a Firbank or a Genet, three figures more interesting for their differences than their similarities.

Today the emergence of gay liberation has made the indirection of the past less necessary. No longer does the gay aesthete set himself up as a capricious and, above all, intimidating artificer and arbiter. The relatively greater frankness of expression has made even art itself less useful, less compelling to the majority of gays. We can now see that gay art was often a ghetto industry (the artist, rejected elsewhere, becomes the self-employed laborer) and a covert, circuitous vehicle for frustration. The new gay arts are flashier and simpler, more spontaneous, explicit, unmediated (I'm thinking of the *son et lumière* in the disco, the violent impact of the windows of Robert Currie and Victor Hugo, often so brashly hostile, the fluid grace of new women's fashions, the idealizing drawings of George Stavrinos). The new gay statements are unambiguous—the swoony mythology of *Dancer From the Dance* and the vitriolic satire of *Faggots*. Just as liberation has brought an end to the sly *doubles entendres* of gay talk, in the same way it has done away with some of the evasions of gay art. (That art at its best *should* be evasive and quirky is another question altogether.)

Liberation, of course, is only partial—and few gays achieve it until after they have experienced oppression. Gay art, therefore, retains traces of its original accent. Oppression can turn people into dreamers, make them stage mental plays of revenge, triumph or ecstatic reconciliation; it produces actors conscious of the exact nuance of feigned behavior. The grand, theatrical effect still seems to typify gay art. The apartment treated as a stage set—dramatically lit, designed to be taken in all at once and from the entrance—remains a gay apartment, whether the decor is high camp or high tech, cluttered comfort or austere emptiness. In literature I cannot imagine a gay writer imitating the gray and brown abnegations of Joseph Conrad or the patient, dogged grumbling of the late Céline. Gay taste is intriguing, ingratiating, effective.

Some people would argue that gay male artists can more readily encompass scenes of delicacy, prettiness, tenderness. This wider emotional and aesthetic range is not exclusively gay; Turgenev in the last century and Mauriac in ours, to choose just two names, were heterosexual men attuned to the feminine. And in the future gay male artists may lose this traditional advantage. For surely today the masculinization of gay life, at least on the two coasts, is nearly complete. Gay men not only look butch but they are increasingly thinking and acting butch as well. Paradoxically, the new brutalism could be the reigning gay sensibility of the moment, one directly opposed to the refinement of the past. It is only an impression, but my sense is that fewer and fewer young gay men in New York even socialize with women, straight or gay. Most of my older gay friends spend few all-male evenings but the younger ones seem less comfortable at mixed parties. They might have a woman friend from school or the office, but she is saved for the lunch *à deux* or the Sunday evening kitchen supper. To be sure, such male exclusiveness does not prevail in the more companionable worlds of theater, dance and fashion.

Tentatively, then, I would say the current gay taste emanating out of New York is theatrical, elaborate, strangely detailed, but it is moving toward greater simplicity and explicitness. This new tone is often embodied in what could be called the Pleasure Machine—the shiny, hard-edged formality of *A Chorus Line* or the synergism of the disco or the eerie metaphysical grandeur of Robert Wilson's operas or the tough flashiness of Felice Picano's thriller, *The Lure*. All of these works are taut, energetic, a total assault on the senses (and in Wilson's case on the ego).

Am I, then, saying there is a gay sensibility after all?

I think not. The word, as I pointed out, is too abstract, too vague and therefore potentially totalitarian; one can at least imagine a future in which gay critics would dismiss gay novels for not exhibiting enough gay sensibility. With its sociological ring, gay sensibility might further promote the bad and already prevalent habit of treating novels as probes sunk into the social terrain; people interested in the mores of hustlers and transvestites might imagine that by reading *Our Lady of the Flowers* they would learn something of actual life—an injustice to the book and a hilariously warped version of life. One is reminded of the review Genet received in the *Chicago Sun-Times*: "Of special interest to police officers, judges, psychiatrists and psychologists, lawmakers at every level. . . ," a line surely parodied by Nabokov in the phony introduction to *Lolita* by the fictional John Ray, Jr., Ph.D.: " 'Lolita' should make all of us—parents, socialworkers, educators—apply ourselves with still greater vigilance and vision to the task of bringing up a better generation in a safer world." Artistic fiction, as most people agree, is less useful in providing factual information (or even accurately recorded polemic) than popular fiction. We can expect, then, that the best gay fiction of the future will fit no one's preconceptions of gay reality and gay sensibility.

What we can discuss, given these caveats, is the gay *taste* of a given period—a taste cultivated (even by some heterosexuals) or rejected (even by many homosexuals). What we can detect is a resemblance among many gay works of art made at a particular moment—a resemblance partially intended and partially drawn without design from a shared experience of anger or alienation or secret, molten camaraderie.

Whatever our sensibility may be, New York gays are justifiably proud of their status as taste-makers for the rest of the country, at least the young and up-to-date segment of the population. Our clothes and haircuts and records and dance steps and decor—our restlessly evolving style—soon enough become theirs. This could be seen as the good side of New York gay volatility, the ceaseless renewal of everything. Now that gay life has become so commercialized our taste is disseminated with alarming rapidity, and the tyranny of instant obsolescence is fueled by the high octane of greed. All over the country I saw a replication of quite recent if not current New York styles.

Occupying the center is the great consolation of New York gays. In return for the costliness and inconvenience, the squalor and discomfort of our lives, we get to participate in whatever is the *latest*. We are never left out of anything; we know what's happening, especially since so many of us practice what Paul Valéry called the "delirious professions." As Valéry wrote, "This is the name I give to all those trades whose main tool is one's opinion of oneself, and whose raw material is the opinion others have of you." Although Valéry was writing eighty years ago of Paris, he anticipated the excruciating position of those gay (and straight) New York "creative people" who must be perpetually original in a "population of uniques." The cruel contradiction of such a position is that the creative "live for nothing but to have, and make durable, the illusion of being the only one—for superiority is only a solitude situated at the present limits of a species." The exigencies of the drive to originality can, as Valéry understood, promote a deep uncertainty about one's personal value. If one is a product, is it new enough? Perfect? One of a kind?

Paradoxically, New York's very sophistication has made it strangely immune to feminism and gay liberation. Unlike the citizens of other places who might resist an idea until they capitulate to it, New Yorkers pass on an idea without possessing it. After all, the city is the media capital of the country and through its hands moves all the hype fed to the rest of America. Yet New York is always the chef, never the diner. Being up on something is a way of dismissing it. To espouse any point of view is a danger—it might leave us stuck with last year's cause. Prized for their novelty alone, ideas, gimmicks, trends become equivalent, interchangeable; someone's Punk outfit is as much a claim on our attention as someone else's politics.

Sometimes I look at the battered exteriors of apartment buildings in New York and think how these sorry shells have housed such a long procession of styles. The money! The effort! One tenant mirrors everything, the next panels the walls, the third lines them with mylar, the fourth turns to *toile de Jouy*, the fifth to pegboard or handblocked rice paper. The expensive if often shoddy interiors installed only to be dismantled, the exterior left untouched as it turns yet another shade sootier—this transience seems a fitting emblem for the way we stay up-to-date without ever changing.

For what New Yorkers know is that only power and money

really count. Unlike other American cities, especially those west
of the Mississippi, New York is conspicuously, shockingly strat-
ified. On the Upper East Side, streets are choked with limousines; a few blocks north, tenement dwellers are cold and hungry.
In a midtown elevator, a sleek, tanned, cologned executive of
sixty stands beside a ragged delivery "boy" of the same age.
Only in New York do members of the so-called middle class
(or "educated labor," to use a more exact term) feel outnum-
bered. Though we may broadcast new attitudes to the "prov-
inces" (as we call America), we are not ourselves fooled by the
rhetoric. Hippie communality, inner awareness, the religion of
art, Oriental mysticism, feminism—these are all articles that have
over the years been packaged in New York and shipped out for
popular consumption, but they have not been bought here. If
they are borrowed for a moment, they are held not as convic-
tions but as fashions.

The terrible knowingness of New Yorkers makes them immune to the effects of any ethos—except success. This immunity
has left New York gays contemptuous of gay liberation, since it
is already an overly familiar "concept." "Oh, God, do shut up
about that awful tripe. Frankly, I'm not a joiner, but if I were,
I sure as hell wouldn't join that tiresomeness. I mean, why risk
your neck for ungrateful hairburners and strident ribbon clerks?
Have I told you about my visit to Naropa? There's this darling·
Tibetan, and *everyone* was there: Allen Ginsberg, Bill Merwin,
Bill Burroughs . . . now *that* is something I could join. The
ethereal peace . . . get out your calendar and let's set up a date,
not next week, that's out, nor the next, I'm booked solid." This
is the chic low-consciousness of the city.

There are so many different gay New Yorks that any project
to enumerate them would be a pathetic failure. And each of
these groups is so large, thriving and confident that it only
dimly suspects the existence of the others. There is the Sunday
brunch intellectual crowd that meets in Chelsea, the gay deaf
baseball team, the gay musicians at Juillard, the "New Algon-
quin Circle" that meets Thursday evenings at Julius in the
Village. . . . One of the crudest ways of describing the city
is by neighborhood, a method that at least has the virtue of

fixing the stereotypes so that they may be criticized and corrected.

According to gay folklore, the East Side Queen lives somewhere between Forty-second and Ninety-sixth Streets and between Fifth Avenue and the East River. His apartment can be a luxurious cooperative overlooking Central Park and the reservoir; for four large rooms he might spend $150,000 initially, plus a monthly maintenance of $1,000. Or he could live in a tacky studio in a modern highrise on Third Avenue, for which he might pay a rent of $600. Or he could have an old rent-controlled walk-up on Second Avenue, for which he spends $120 a month.

The cliché is that the East Side Queen is living beyond his means and is willing to eat nothing but bread and water to maintain his "image." He is Michael in *The Boys in the Band*, with a closet full of cashmere sweaters he's charged and can't afford. He attends the opera on Monday, the most "social" evening. He shares a summer house in East Hampton, and in conversation he says, "I haven't yet opened the house in the Hamptons for the season" to make the following false implications: I own the house; I live in it alone; it may be in South Hampton; it's very grand and requires a staff to "open" it; and/or I don't work and will be spending the entire summer there. He may be a fashion model—or merely a lawyer or advertising copywriter or department store employee who looks like a fashion model. He may be an interior designer (don't call him a decorator or he'll die). At least half his social life is devoted to Advancing His Career. He stacks magazines neatly on his coffee table, slightly overlapped so the names may be taken in instantly; *Realités*, *The New Yorker*, *Architectural Digest*, *Town & Country*, *L'Uomo Vogue* and *Art News*. He hides the *TV Guide* and *After Dark*. The best play he has *ever* seen is *Equus*; his favorite recent musical is *Sweeney Todd* ("Thank *God* for Stephen Sondheim").

He pretends not to know his way around Greenwich Village and when he makes his weekly forays into it he exclaims, "Such fun! I haven't been here in years." Paradoxically, he is proud of his ability to find El Faro on Horatio and Greenwich Streets, where he dines with other Eastsiders. He still believes in the tasteful one-night stand and buys unusual breads and preserves at Bloomie's on Friday to feed the discriminating trick on Saturday morning, along with real orange juice and *café filtre*. He speaks frequently of his Cuisinart and of Marcella Hazan's cookbooks. He is an Anglophile and admits to being a Tory. He regards Ingmar Bergman as the greatest film director and avoids movies made in America. He's been known to date naïve rich girls fifteen years his junior and more than once he's announced his engagement to a Mitzi or Fifi or Lulu. He is relieved that being a conservative in politics seems once again sensible and even intellectual. *Proustian* is his favorite adjective. He is from Ohio but has a new accent that sounds intermittently English. From his New York blueblood friends he has learned to say the *h* in "herb," to stress the last syllable of "elsewhere," the first syllable of "ballet" and to pronounce "anyway" as "ennuh-way." His father is a pleasant, retired Naval officer whom he refers to enigmatically as "the Commodore" and whom he has never introduced to his friends.

Most of the Upper West Side of Manhattan, once the fashionable district, now has a somewhat dowdy look. Black and Puerto Rican families mingle with old Jewish immigrants, welfare hotel residents and young professionals. On some summer evenings, Upper Broadway would strike the fastidious visitor as closer to his or her idea of Calcutta than New York. Since the state mental hospitals have dumped their patients on the streets, heavily tranquilized psychotics can be seen quietly gabbling to themselves on benches on the pedestrian island in the center of the avenue. On the sidewalks ancient denizens of nursing homes are inching along in their aluminum walkers.

The younger, educated element has traditionally been typed as intellectual and Jewish. Professors from Columbia live in genteel squalor in rambling, eight-room apartments with children and pets; at their parties they consume wine and cheese and discuss tenure and mortgages, for the West Side has many brownstones that a family of moderate means might at least dream of buying.

The gays are clustered in studios primarily in the West Sixties and Seventies in the blocks just off Central Park. There are three or four gay bars in the area that no one takes seriously but that might just render up a passable trick on a cold winter's day. West Side gays spend a fortune in cab fares returning from Village hot spots late at night. The streets throughout the Upper West Side are not always safe and the restaurants are perfunctory; nevertheless, devoted residents assure each other that the district is "coming up" (i.e., becoming more white and expensive) and, until that happy goal is achieved, they praise the area for its "ethnic diversity" ("I could sit at my window for hours looking at all the interesting types going into the kosher butcher shop, the bodega where you can buy statues of black saints and voodoo aphrodisiacs, the Korean fruit market, the Hungarian pastry shop").

The cliché West Side gay is in his late twenties, works as an airline steward or architectural assistant, gets stoned with seven or eight friends on Friday while eating Famous Amos chocolate chip cookies and watching old movies on television and, like most New Yorkers but with more urgency, wants a new apartment, a new job and a new lover.

After work he exercises at the Sixty-third Street YMCA, one of the cruisiest spots in Manhattan. He stays in on weeknights and dances in the Village on Saturday. He cites Lincoln Center as an attraction of his neighborhood and does attend the ballet whenever someone older and richer invites him. The real glory of the neighborhood is Central Park, and there he jogs in summer and ice skates in winter—and cruises the dangerous Rambles in all seasons. His taste in decor verges toward dour oak "antiques," brass bedsteads and steamer trunks for coffee tables. He has a half-share in a Fire Island house (every other weekend). He is in group therapy and is convinced he's making "progress."

The stereotyped gay resident of Brooklyn Heights has a lover. They have been together for three years and are faithful, if you don't count those quickies on the Promenade or in the subway john. They have two floors and the garden of a brownstone on a quiet, tree-lined street. One of the men is an accountant and the other the production director of a medical textbook firm. Their mania is decorating their quarters, which they are "doing" in Biedermeier antiques, discovered on weekend trips through New England. They attend church and one of them sings in the choir. The other is an ambitious chef who can come up with eight-course dinners for friends. They are saving for a house in New Hope and will soon own it; of all gay New Yorkers they are the only ones who know how to manage their money. Their friends in Manhattan can be lured across the river only with great difficulty and then only three times a year; the Manhattanites invariably praise the serenity of the Heights to their hosts yet privately condemn it as "suburban" and wonder why anyone so close to New York would choose to lead a life so peripheral.

Greenwich Village is the gay ghetto, though in a city where one out of every four men is homosexual the term doesn't mean much. The gay Villager can be a well-heeled executive who works midtown but lives in a floor-through on Tenth Street off Fifth Avenue because he likes the bohemianism, the intimacy and the casualness of the neighborhood. Or he can be an actor-waiter-singer-dancer-pusher-hustler in a dismal room in a tenement filled with Italian families; he was originally attracted to the Village when he arrived in New York ten years ago by its artistic associations; he stayed for the sex. This is the world of freelancers, those gay men who can arrange their hours to suit themselves, who piece together a day out of two hours clerking in a boutique, three hours researching a history of magic and eleven hours of loafing.

The Village is the epitome of gay sex the world over. Christopher Street, once the Boulevard of Broken Dreams, is the very site of our Bastille, the Stonewall (now a natural wood craftshop and a bagel eatery). Here gay liberation began in the summer of 1969, and here the most advanced experiments in homosexual life are still being conducted (one learns that most experiments fail). I used to have a very bright gay barber in the Village and I could always chart the latest development from his remarks. Seven years ago he was telling me that masculinity was in, five years ago that fidelity was out, four years ago that sexless intimacy and raunchy anonymity constituted the new ideal, three years ago that the Village was "tired." He now lives in San Francisco.

For me New York gay life in the Seventies came as a completely new beginning. In January 1970 I moved to Rome after having lived in the Village for eight years. When I returned ten months later to the States, an old friend met me at the airport, popped an "up" in my mouth and took me on a tour of the brand-new back room bars.

My friend took me to Christopher's End, where a go-go boy with a pretty body and bad skin stripped down to his jockey shorts and then peeled those off and tossed them at us. A burly man in the audience clambered up onto the dais and tried to fuck the performer but was, apparently, too drunk to get an erection. After a while we drifted into the back room, which was so dark I never received a sense of its dimensions, though I do remember standing on a platform and staring through the slowly revolving blades of a fan into a cubbyhole where one naked man was fucking another. A flickering candle illuminated them. It was never clear whether they were customers or hired entertainment; the fan did give them the look of actors in a silent movie. All this was new.

At another bar, called the Zoo or the Zodiac (both existed, I've just confused them), a go-go boy did so well with a white towel under black light that I waited around till he got off—at 8 A.M. In the daylight he turned out to be a bleach blond with chipped teeth who lived in remotest Brooklyn with the bouncer, a 300-pound man who had just lost 50 pounds. I was too polite to back out and was driven all the way to their apartment, which was decorated with a huge blackamoor lamp from Castro Convertible.

For the longest time everyone kept saying the Seventies hadn't started yet. There was no style for the decade, no flair, no slogans. The mistake we made was that we were all looking for something as startling as the Beatles, acid, Pop Art, hippies and radical politics. What actually set in was a painful and unexpected working out of the terms the Sixties had so blithely tossed off. Street cruising gave way to half-clothed quickies; recently I overheard someone saying, "It's been months since I've had sex in bed." Because back rooms exist, everyone can parade the streets, exchanging glances but not submitting to the uncertainty of negotiating terms ("Your place or mine?" "What are

you into?"); everyone knows that after all (or nothing) is said
and done, there's a free blow-job waiting for him at the
back of the Strap. Drugs, once billed as an aid to self-discovery
through heightened perception, became a way of injecting lust
into encounters at the baths. At the baths everyone seemed to
be lying face down on a cot beside a can of Crisco; fist-fucking,
as one French *savant* has pointed out, is our century's only
brand-new contribution to the sexual armamentarium. Everyone
wanted to be *used* in some way or another; the tensions, the assertiveness, the chutzpah of daytime New York turned over at
night and became exquisitely passive. Fantasy costumes (gauze
robes, beaded headache bands, mirrored vests) were replaced by
boots and beards, the only concession to the old androgyny being
a discreet gold earbob or ivory figa. Today nothing looks more
forlorn than the faded sign in a suburban barber shop that reads
"Unisex."

Indeed, the unisex of the Sixties has been supplanted by
heavy sex in the Seventies, and the urge toward fantasy has
come out of the clothes closet and entered the bedroom or back
room. The end to role-playing . . . well, it never happened.
Although many gay people in New York may be happily living
in other, less rigorous decades, the gay male couple inhabiting
the Seventies is composed of two men who love each other, share
the same friends and interests and fuck each other almost inad-
vertently once every six months during a particularly stoned,
impromptu three-way. The rest of the time they get laid with
strangers in a context that bears the stylistic marks and some of
the reality of S&M. Inflicting and receiving excruciating physical pain may still be something of a rarity, but the sex rap
whispered in a stranger's ear conjures up nothing but violence.
Or if not violence, at least domination. The other day someone
said to me, "Are you into fantasies? I *do* five." "Oh?" "Yes, five:
rookie-coach; older brother-younger brother; sailor-slut; slave-
master; and father-son." I picked older brother-younger brother,
though it kept lapsing into a pastoral fantasy of identical twins.

The temptation, of course, is to lament our lost innocence
but my Christian Science training as a child (it stopped when I
was very young, scarcely eight) has made me into a permanent

Pollyanna. What *good* came out of the Seventies? I kept wondering. All the better as a question now that we're into the Eighties.

Well, perhaps sex and sentiment *should* be separated. Isn't sex, shadowed as it always is by jealousy and ruled by caprice, a rather risky basis for a sustained, important relationship? Perhaps our marriages should be sexless or "white" as the French used to say. And then, perhaps violence or at least domination is the true subtext of all sex, straight or gay. Even Rosemary Rogers, the author of such Gothic potboilers as *The Wildest Heart* and *Sweet Savage Love*, is getting rich feeding her women readers tales of unrelenting S&M.

As for the jeans, cowboy shirts and workboots, they at least have the virtue of being cheap. The uniform conceals the rise of what strikes me as a whole class of gay indigents. Sometimes I have the impression that every fourth man on Christopher Street is out of work, but the poverty is hidden by the costume. Hidden, that is, when the subject is sex, as it invariably is on Sheridan Square after dark, after dawn and all through the day.

In other contexts—at art gallery openings, at the theater, in uptown restaurants—wherever the subject is status, then the jeans are shed and the look of wealth assumed by those who can afford it. These days it's a modified Punk look, a Cardin suit with the jacket's sleeves pushed up, worn over a kid's green and black horizontal-striped play shirt, the neck closed by a skinny red tie tucked in the third button down, round, purple granny glasses hiding the eyes, greased black hair, cowboy boots, an impudent slouch to carry it all off, a Rolls hovering at the curb. No doubt this look will have faded by the time you read my description.

Finally, the adoration of machismo is intermittent, interchangeable, between parentheses. Tonight's top is tomorrow's bottom. We're all more interested that the ritual be enacted than concerned about which particular role we assume. The sadist barking commands at his slave is, ten minutes after climax, thoughtfully drawing him a bubble bath. The slave has had an experience something like being inducted into a religious order (the fast, the wait through the night on cold stone, at daybreak the vision of heaven's anger and grace) and the master—well, for him it's a milder pleasure, the recognition that he's conducted someone safely to bliss and that he himself has gained the not-quite-solid but nonetheless soothing sense of being . . . well, more a man. For the sadist's authority can always be challenged; the slave's degradation can't be taken away from him. I've read that masochists are less mentally stable than sadists, but the opposite is my impression. To me the sadist always appears a bit gloomy, a bit preoccupied, aware that he's a target for ridicule yet to come. Since the masochist has already feasted on ridicule, he feels cleansed, sure of himself—the next morning the masochist sails out confidently to do his shopping, a bounce in his step.

The characteristic face in New York these days is seasoned, wry, weathered by drama and farce. Drugs, heavy sex and the ironic, highly concentrated experience (so like that of actors everywhere) of leading uneventful, homebodyish lives when not on stage for those two searing hours each night—this reality, or release from it, has humbled us all. It has broken the tyranny beauty used to hold over us. All the looks anyone needs can be bought at the gym and from the local pusher; the lisped shriek of "Miss Thing!" has faded into the passing, over-the-shoulder offer of "loose joints." And we do in fact seem looser, easier in the joints, and if we must lace ourselves nightly into chaps and rough up more men than seems quite coherent with our soft-spoken, gentle personalities, at least we no longer need to be relentlessly witty or elegant.

At the moment, the four leading sex centers in the Village are, in an ascending order of heavy action, Flamingo, the Anvil, the St. Mark's Baths and the Mine Shaft. For several years now Flamingo has been the most celebrated gay disco in town. It is housed in a warehouse building on a corner of Houston Street unfrequented at night. Only members and their guests are admitted; a year's membership costs seventy-five dollars and the waiting list is long. The disco is open on weekends alone, and closed during the Fire Island Season (mid-May through October).

Recently I was invited to the Black Party by a friend. We went dressed in the requisite color, which turned out to mean leather to most celebrants. As we entered the club at one in the morning (the doors had opened at midnight) I saw a room full of husky men, many of them shirtless, sipping beer or Coke and casually watching the entertainment: on raised trestles along one wall, hired musclemen garbed as centurions or deep sea divers or motorcyclists. They struck conventional body-building poses. In the other room a shirtless stud stood just inside a small chamber, a chemical toilet in the middle of the traffic flow; I wasn't sure whether he was a member or an entertainer, whether he was posing for fun or for hire. Everyone in the audience could have been put on professional display, since the crowd was extraordinarily muscular. The average age, I'd guess, was thirty-two; these are the members of the mandarinate who migrate to Fire Island Pines in the summer.

In the inner room people were dancing. "This place is all about touching," someone told me. "They kept fiddling with the design till they got it right, till everyone had to slip and slide against everyone else." The lightshow was adequate but not obtrusive; too much showbiz and glitz would not have seemed butch enough, I guess. The blending of the records, the estimation of the crowd's mood, the choice of music were superb—the most discerning I'd come across anywhere. Along one wall enthusiasts from the floor had leaped up onto a ledge and were grinding in dervish solitude. The mirrored panels were frosted over with condensed sweat. One after another all remaining shirts were peeled off. A stranger, face impassive, nosed up to us and soon was lending us his hanky soaked in ethyl chloride—a quick transit to the icy heart of a minor moon drifting around Saturn. Just as casually he stumbled off.

Like most people for whom sex is more a matter of fantasy than sensation, I am ordinarily squeamish about touching an alien body. I loathe crowds. But tonight the drugs and the music and the exhilaration had stripped me of all such scruples. We were packed in so tightly we were forced to slither across each other's wet bodies and arms; I felt my arm moving like a piston in synchrony against a stranger's—and I did not pull away. Freed of my shirt and my touchiness, I surrendered myself to the idea that I was just like everyone else. A body among bodies. Since my father's death I had been appalled by the physical; a face kissing mine would go transparent, revealing the deathshead within. But on that night, for the first time in months, I recovered my lost zest—and did so by giving up precious me, that fragile self better and worse than the rest. "It's real tribal here, isn't it?" my friend shouted in my ear. I nodded. I ducked out "early"—at dawn; he stayed on till ten in the morning in that room as black as jeweler's velvet. He went home with someone he'd just met but whom I've known for years. "It was *real* intimate," my friend reported. "We fucked for hours and sat around and talked about everything—he's hung up about his cock size, which is dumb, he's got a great cock. And we slept in each other's arms till evening, when I got up and hurried home to my lover, who never goes to discos because he can't do drugs."

The motto—the pride!—of such New Yorkers is to work hard and play hard. All week long they stay in or work out at the gym and put in long hours at their demanding jobs where they are, often enough, loners in a straight world. Friday night they have a quiet supper with friends, Saturday afternoon they perform their chores and clean house, Saturday night they boogie, Sunday they sleep. The exclusiveness of Flamingo, the pretty bodies, the parade of so much brawn and so many brains—this is the impressive emblem of their success. Like a royal audience, the reward is as much in being admitted as having attended.

These people are ambitious. In many other cities it is enough to be hot or fun, but in New York one must also be smart and successful. The success need not be monetary. The city recognizes as valid dozens of different scales of success—a poor but famous Hebrew scholar ranks as high as a rich but vulgar theatrical agent. For bookworms who move to New York from the Midwest, it comes as a curious reversal to learn that in the city knowledge (or at least a reputation for having it) can carry a distinct social cachet. Granted that New York is a numbers game, but into its calculations are figured not only dollars made, years lived, physical dimensions achieved, friends (or "contacts") accumulated but also books read, facts stored, awards won, degrees earned. "He's very smart," is said as a less ambiguous compliment in New York than in gay culture at large. Wisdom, of course, is less prized than savvy, but even so the city's emphasis on a wide general culture (and expertise in one or two areas) makes it a more suitable place for older gays than most other places. The man of sixty who collects art or buys antiquities or publishes books will never be without his coterie in New York.

There is a less benign side to this cult of success. It does leave out the average person. And the young man who has not yet chosen a career or made much professional headway can go into a panic. The dangerous double lure of New York is its insistence on success and its array of distractions. There are so many fascinating people to talk to in New York, and there always seem to be lots of people who are just having fun.

The discipline required of a New York gay is formidable. So many drugs, so many tricks, so many parties, so many idle but engrossing conversations are available that the strength needed to resort to them only selectively is great indeed. If perhaps half of the men at Flamingo are working hard and playing hard, the rest are layabouts—handymen, hustlers, drug dealers, would-be actors and models. In calling them "layabouts" I am not imposing my own judgment on them but subscribing to theirs. The life of pleasure has not gained the acceptance in New York that it has found in San Francisco. While New York workaholics are hovering over their desks late at night, in San Francisco the *dolce far niente* crowd is turning on.

For Flamingo members the appetite for success is omnivorous. Not only must one be on the way up at work, one must also produce good conversation, good food, good sex, attract the right friends, dance all night, jog three miles, press 200 pounds and have an opinion about Caballé's *pianissimo*. One must have the drive of a tycoon, the allure of a kept boy, the stamina of an athlete, the bonhomie of a man of the world. It is not a formula for happiness. No one can embody all or even most of these virtues, and the failure to do so can produce grave self-doubts. For a night, a summer, even a year one might finally have "gotten it all together" (a phrase constantly on people's lips), but the chance of keeping it there is remote. Anxiety lies under a society governed by comparison, by muted competition.

I add "muted" because it has often struck me that gay men lack the talent of straight men for *friendly competition*, with a stress on both words. Gay men can be competitive—and murderous. Or they can be friendly and collaborative. But they seem incapable for the most part of the amicable rivalry that characterizes so many close relationships between straight men. Possibly this deficiency (if it exists) could be traced to the isolation of so many gays when they were teenagers, since the joshing, teasing but sunny sort of competition I have in mind first occurs among straight males in adolescence. Gay men entertain toward one another a feeling at once simpler and more complex—simpler when they achieve a moment of perfect harmony, more complex when they must acknowledge a desire to best their friends. Such a desire is not the cheerful, guilt-free emotion it can be among the most balanced of straight men.

An apologist for gays could argue that there is never anything "cheerful" about competition among friends, and that gays avoid such deceit attests to their genuine solidarity, based on a recognition that competition is divisive and that gays must support, not undermine, each other. I admire the sentiment but doubt its applicability. I detect covert competition among gay men, and in certain New York circles the competition is so extensive—sexual, financial, intellectual, social—that it can be devastating.

To provide the energy and élan needed for so much striving, the Flamingo crowd relies on drugs—and often abuses them. The taste for hallucinogens in the late Sixties and early Seventies has now given way to a less fanciful appetite for ups and downs, mechanisms for regulating the energy flow.

One of my best friends fell victim to this way of life. He was gifted with a blond, blue-eyed beauty and a complexion so delicate that he suffered from a condition that might be called "epidermography" (if you write your name on his back the letters will rise as red welts a moment later). He has a firm, almost grave masculine dignity, a profile that recalls F. Scott Fitzgerald's, a serious *burrowing* sort of intelligence—and, intermittently, a bright silver streak of silliness, the sublime sort. Throughout his twenties he was hardworking and somewhat obscure. He held down a difficult job and obtained a graduate degree. Every moment of his time, every penny of his salary, was carefully budgeted. He had quite consciously decided not to accept the favors from others that his beauty invited. During this period he had two lovers, the second a boy whom he put through college.

When he turned thirty, however, everything changed. A new lover was flashier, more social, more determined to make it. My friend entered the Fire Island–Flamingo world. Although he'd risen fairly high in business by then, his salary of $30,000 was no longer adequate. Like a character in Balzac, he "ruined" himself for love. Each summer he took a larger and larger house on Fire Island, from which he was finally expelled for his riotous parties. He maintained a station wagon in the city—an unthinkable luxury. In the winter he rented a ski house in Vermont. He and his lover lived surrounded by decorative youths, as many as six or eight at a time, who had to be fed, drugged and entertained nightly. To pay for the festivities my friend fell deeper and deeper into debt. Though he and his lover had a combined income of $50,000 (and a rent of just $120 a month), they could never quite keep up. Their drug bill alone could run to hundreds of dollars a week. I recall being their guest on Fire Island for two days. We were conveyed there in a rented limousine in which we consumed angel dust, Quaaludes and champagne, listened to the latest tapes and grinned with chemical delight at the stalled traffic. With us we brought two hundred dollars' worth of food and the same investment in drugs (their treat)—a simple $500 weekend.

My friend, once so serious and aloof, developed a drug habit that was no longer just recreational. He never read, he was never alone; the entourage could always be found hanging out in his apartment. One would sit at a table, eat TV dinners or pizza, watch a soundless color TV and listen to disco through earphones—not *my* idea of a dinner party, six drugged men chewing under headsets. After a bit it would be time to pile into the station wagon and glide through the spotlit, empty Wall Street district, passing more joints and absorbing the relentless shocks of more disco. The effort of maintaining such a household would have defeated Baron Hulot.

My friend's remarks became cryptic, circular, mystical. He converted to Catholicism. He fled to a therapist in Boston one weekend. He rented apartments on the sly, unbeknownst to his lover, and visited them fitfully, always planning to escape to them permanently but never doing so. On alternate days he envisioned a total and wonderful change in their life together that never came. One friend, who'd smoked too much angel dust, burned his lover's house to the ground. A second, worried about his failing looks and business, killed himself. A third, a *discaire*, also died; "That's absolutely the last disco funeral I'll ever attend," my friend reported. "You do know, don't you, that they played all his greatest tapes at the funeral."

At last my friend cracked. He lost his job, despite his years of service to the firm. Soon afterwards he had a full-scale epileptic attack—the result of a sudden withdrawal from barbiturates and amphetamines after a particularly busy weekend with the gang in Provincetown. During the seizure he broke a few ribs.

In the hospital for two months, he began to sort things out. He has now started his own business. He attends A.A. meetings; in the Viillage there are several gay A.A. meetings, always packed, many of those attending quite young and often cross-addicted. Although his homelife has not changed, his prospects seem saner. After not going to Flamingo for months, he returned recently for a party. Few of his buddies had noticed his absence. Without drugs the disco struck him as no more amusing than a throbbing headache.

The Anvil is just as druggy, just as energetic, but in no other way does it resemble Flamingo. For five dollars at the door one gains access to two floors of amusement. On the main floor a burlesque runway slices into the room; here I watched a black transvestite, pure sleaze in torn stockings, dirty maribou and a red wig, lip-sync her way through one of those songs in which a woman wails the choruses and talks through verses of the girl-I've-had-me-some-troubles variety, all the while manipulating her fingers (she teaches the deaf by day). She was followed by a less successful bandit in cowboy drag and a black mask; during the finale he did have the wit to stop gunslinging and lariat-twirling long enough to peel his clothes off to reveal a good, firm body.

In the Anvil's more exuberant past naked go-go boys have pranced up and down the bars, fucked each other with chains, lit themselves on fire and performed aerial gymnastics on trapezes dropped from the ceiling. During this period elegant straight couples were known to drop by wearing evening clothes; reputedly, one Very Great Lady even pulled off her diamond rings

and had a go at fisting an obliging performer. Next to the burlesque ramp is a disco floor and in one corner a shadowy back
room.

The sexual action goes on in the basement. A second bar
hovers mauvely under black light never so bright as to interfere
with the incomparable fuck movies on continuous view; all the
filmed figurantes are well under twenty. Many of the customers
are also quite young. Especially about five in the morning on
weekends young men from Jersey float in from discos, at last
dissuaded of the theory that sex is a sublimated form of dancing.
In low-ceilinged, dark or dimly lit back rooms (or back grottoes,
since the rooms seem like cool, rocky caves), bodies ceasely con-
jugate.

One of my dear friends is a convinced but discreet chicken
hawk. He is my age but looks ten, no, fifteen years younger. His
erotic fantasy is to be a youth among youths, not a dirty old man
preying upon them; the dimness of the Anvil lends credibility
to this dream, for there he does look just a kid. His first affair
started when he was six; his lover was the neighbor boy, a more
plausible twelve. For several years this idyll went on, and nothing
since has equalled it or replaced it. In addition he is an artist and
he loves beauty with a connoisseur's eye. Who is more beautiful
than a young man of sixteen?

A great deal has been written about the havoc pederasty
may or may not wreak on the young, but little has been said
about the disorder it introduces into the life of the lover of boys.
My friend is terrified that he will end up haunting playgrounds
and endure arrest, conviction and imprisonment. Because he has
a strong, intelligent control on his impulses, he exercises them
only in safe ways. He buys pornography of pubescent lads, but
this vicarious taste for the *fruit vert* has recently been frustrated.
A highly publicized crusade against kiddy porn has routed
the enemy; the only models in magazines today are repulsive,
hairy, sagging, leering ancients of twenty-two. Regulation of
pornography excites indignation in my friend, who sees dirty
pictures as a way of harmlessly venting rather than feeding "antisocial" impulses. Because he can daydream over pictures of youths
he need not "violate" them. His next best choice is a weekly visit
to the Club Baths on Friday, which is buddy night. Two are ad-

mitted for the price of one, and the two are often college students attracted by the bargain rates. On Saturday he goes to the Anvil where many of the customers are if not infants at least on the right side of twenty-one (the side of the angels).

His third strategy is to have a lover—or rather two lovers. One of them he has been with for twelve years; their third roommate is a dynamic, funny, *boyish* businessman in his mid-twenties. In addition, all three trick out with strangers, though they have a rule against bringing anyone home. More conventional observers keep predicting that such a novel relationship will end in tragedy, but it is already several years old and flourishing.

The St. Marks Baths, in the East Village, has recently become another New York institution. After a horrifying fire destroyed the original Everard Baths and killed several of its patrons, the heavy-sex crowd was without a home. The St. Marks filled that need. In place of the Everard's rotting marble, gummy tiles and terminal pool, the St. Marks substituted an unobtrusive, quietly masculine decor. At the entrance there is a good diner. There is no television, and disco music is confined to the front office and a back lounge, on the theory that nothing should compete with or mask the sounds of sex. Since S&M is so popular at the St. Marks, its three upper floors of rooms and corridors sound like the galleys of a slave ship—muttered obscenities, a slap, a whack with a belt, heavy breathing and tussling, a moan, a cry. Compared to this audible (and usually simulated) pain, the noise at all other baths resembles that of a modern ocean liner at dawn.

The cues to rough stuff are also visual. The pegs for hanging clothes in the room have been exactly placed to be visible from the door; passersby can see an occupant's discarded uniform—leather, Western, humanoid—and divine from it his fantasies. Every light in every room is on a dimmer; if the light is further focused and shrouded with a towel, the torso and legs are lost in shadow and a spotlight is cast on the upturned ass or the half-erect cock.

Without clothes the body becomes a weak signal, though cock rings, tattoos and tit rings send out some sort of message. Customers, however, are more and more returning to clothes, or their legible suggestions—a jock strap or athletic socks or a leather vest or no shirt but jeans. A white towel has turned out to be too innocent to project menace and too standardized to express a specific desire—better nakedness, a loping walk, pendulous cock, dead cigar (the stubby spear jutting at an angle out of the round buckler of the face—the classic symbol for male).

As you lie on your pallet with the door closed, you overhear long sex raps, elaborate verbal fantasies: "You're asleep, wake up, see me standing over you, I'm a lumberjack, I've got a fuckin' *power* saw in my hand, I'm rubbin' my cock, you see the bulge of my cock, it's gettin' harder. . . ." "Yeah, it's gettin' hard." And so on—all said in tough-guy whispers, the voice husky, uninflected, insistent, a voice pressed like a glass to the wall of the psyche. Or, more usually, the rap is primitive, scattered, the disorganized responses of the laboratory animal decorticated by drugs: names, commands, affirmations. ("Suck . . . yeah . . . open that . . . cock . . . balls . . . take it, *take* it!")

The violence resides almost entirely in the language. One man licking another's Frye boots would be hilarious were the act not labeled "humiliation." Someone once remarked that in adolescence pornography is a substitute for sex, whereas in adulthood sex is a substitute for pornography; the S&M rap is the conflation of pornography and sex, an act of extraordinary condensation. So essential is language to sado-masochism that a fully satisfying leather scene could be the most humdrum sex accompanied by a really filthy soundtrack.

An Australian friend—slight, impish, energetic, smart—recently visited me for a week. He spent four hours at the St. Marks and couldn't get laid—until he made contact with a French tourist, equally at sea. "I suppose no one fancied me," the Australian told me. "They're all muscular and into S&M, and they're looking for their doubles. The few who did like me wanted me to . . . uh, *fist* them. Or they wanted to play their fantasy games. What *is* this fantasy business? It doesn't exist back home—at least I haven't encountered it. Actually, I find New York a bit disappointing. On the streets everyone cruises, but no one stops to make a pickup. I suspect that if I could stay up till five in the morning I might have some luck—but I'm exhausted by two. The main thing is that I have *romantic* fantasies, not sexual ones. I'm not looking for a lover, I'm just seeking a romantic interlude. I mean, I see a man working in a card shop and I daydream about staying behind till closing time and then, in that novel setting— well, I don't fantasize about who will do what to whom. My fantasies never get that far. But this probably doesn't make much sense to a New Yorker. If I said I wanted to be bound and gagged —*that* you'd understand. I had much more fun in Toronto."

This gay tendency toward fantasy puzzles me. It is one that is more advanced in New York and San Francisco than elsewhere in the States. In these two cities homosexuals enjoy the greatest freedom. Unlike other minority groups, homosexuals through liberation (or is it license?) are becoming more idiosyncratic and less assimilated to the general population. Gay men are turning more and more toward fantasy, promiscuity and at least the rhetoric (if not always the reality) of violence. I am not speaking of the majority of gays; they, like straights, want a lover, a house, a stable life. No, I'm discussing the most extreme and conspicuous exemplars of a style that the new permissiveness has made possible.

One explanation of this style would hold that homosexuality is inherently "neurotic" and that in a permissive atmosphere the neurosis is sending forth its most garish flowers. A second explanation might assert that the subjugation of gays has been so prolonged and punitive that it has left us deformed; in the aftermath we are expressing the rage and the impersonality and the panic we've absorbed from the dominant culture. Our violent sex is the sign of that rage, deflected from its true object (heterosexual repressiveness) and misdirected against ourselves. Our promiscuity is, according to this view, merely an extension of the furtiveness we were forced to resort to in the alien and hostile world of the past (the historic past and our individual past). By this interpretation we would consider the current notion of hot sex in New York to be a mere transition, a new recuperation of old oppression, and we would expect this period to be followed by a sweeter, calmer one in which romance and intimacy and sustained partnership between lovers would emerge again.

A far more radical view of the present is an analysis of the nature of desire itself; the disadvantage of this theory is that it is less easily discussed than the ones I've already touched on. According to this view (advanced by several French critics of capitalism and Freudianism, including Guy Hocquenghem, author of *Homosexual Desire*), we must not think of sexual desire as merely or even primarily a biological drive. Rather, it is a code (and ultimately a verbal code) in which social tensions are inscribed. Theoretically, there is no reason desire cannot be ambiguous, fertile, fragmented, ubiquitous, bisexual, but it is in the interests of capitalist society to control the libido, to disciplne erotic energy. In this light we might interpret the overheard fantasy sex at the baths as the cacophony of *decoding*, the simultaneous playback and erasure of our unconscious tapes. Two strangers meet. Their imaginations are stimulated by drugs, the division between fantasy and reality is weakened by the dimmed lights and the building's banishment of time, seasons, weather, everyday responsibilities (there is no view of the outside streets and the only clock is in the front office). The customers' inhibitions are lowered by the fiction that here, in this place and for the space of this encounter, they can act freely (that is, compulsively). The ordinary social restraints have been lifted, including the need to behave in accordance with one's already established social personality.

In this freedom one may speak in tongues. Indeed, the very verbalization of desire, the naming of body parts and sexual actions and the explicit enunciation of fantasies—this verbalization exposes what created our culture's particular vision of desire in the first place: words. Shame, submission, domination, expiation—these are feelings instilled in the animal child through language, just as the genitalia first became eroticized through giving them names—and then banning the mention of those names. Presumably we all, straight and gay alike, perceive sex through this scrim of language, but for most of us the words lie just below consciousness—and therefore remain potent, tireless; the tape continues to loop, undamaged, its fidelity perfect, past the magnetic head. We remain automata programmed by cultural information fed to us by our families but collected from the society at large.

But at the baths everything is new, different, disordered,

hastening toward entropy. Because the words are available, spoken, conscious, they lose their power. Although the scripts followed by the actors may be the oldest, most hidden, most reactionary we know, their very enunciation erases them.

And surely such an explanation accounts for many peripheral phenomena, including the rapidity with which the New York homosexual community changes as it works its way back and back through virulent and damaging desires. At this very moment S&M, still so widespread, is beginning to lose its appeal. What will replace it? Man-woman (i.e., daddy-mommy) sex? Mother-child sex? (A friend of mine recently picked up a man who quite efficiently produced out of his briefcase the necessary props and asked to have his bottom talced, diapered and spanked while he, the baby, sucked on a pacifier.)

This theory also explains the feeling that New York is "tired," for surely the erasure of tape after tape must produce apathy and panic—what will be left? Will we still be able to get it up after we've worked our way through all the cassettes? What lies beyond the programmed codes of culture?

Logically, it strikes me that those thinkers such as Roland Barthes who regard the individual merely as a locus through which the codes traverse should not be allowed to speak of anything *beyond* the codes. And yet in his cryptic and lyric recent writings Barthes seems to be holding out for something he calls the "body"—a utopian entity of desire, original, unconditioned, individual. Others, such as Gilles Deleuze and Hocquenghem, have suggested that we will become pure "desiring machines," capable of plugging into any other machine; this is the dream of polymorphous perversity and, not incidentally, the end of homosexuality as exclusive behavior: if desire floats free, no longer linked to social and economic forces, then it can and must attach itself indiscriminately to men and women, adults and children—to everyone, sequentially or all at once . . . or so the theory goes.

My own expectations are less exciting. Although I think the French have proposed an interesting and often useful vocabulary, I become uncomfortable when the individual is forgotten or subsumed under Large General Forces. Yes, sex may be at least in part inflected by politics, our fantasies may be at least in part a compendium of cultural myths, but the ways in which sex and fantasy ripen within the individual seem to me to vary so greatly that summaries become useless, even dangerous.

But if I were to venture my own generalizations, I would say that with the collapse of other social values (those of religion, patriotism, the family and so on), sex has been forced to take up the slack, to become our sole mode of transcendence and our only touchstone of authenticity. The cry for scorching, multiple orgasms, the drive toward impeccable and virtuoso performance, the belief that only in complete sexual compatibility lies true intimacy, the insistence that sex is the only mode for experiencing thrills, for achieving love, for assessing and demonstrating personal worth—all these projects are absurd. I can picture wiser people in the next century regarding our sexual mania as akin to the religious madness of the Middle Ages—a cooperative delusion. I feel that homosexuals, now identified as the element in our society most obsessed with sex, will in fact be the agents to cure the mania. Sex will be restored to its appropriate place as a pleasure, a communication, an appetite, an art; it will no longer pose as a religion, a reason for being. In our present isolation we have few ways beside sex to feel connected with one another; in the future there might be surer modes for achieving a sense of community.

I am immediately suspicious of my own messianic claims for homosexuals. In particular I fear that individual homosexuals living now can only suffer the anxieties rather than enjoy the rewards of our period. A visit to the Mine Shaft, for instance, presents a spectacle that could just as easily be labeled degradation as liberation.

The Mine Shaft is located on a dark corner in the West Village meatpacking district. In the morning this area is noisy with hissing air brakes and quick with butchers in bloody white aprons guiding dead animals out of refrigerated trucks into cold storage. Traveling hooks swing sides of beef across sidewalks. On cold days metal oil drums blaze with fire and the men warm their hands over the flames. At night the streets are deserted, the pavement slick with blood. Everything smells of lanolin.

Something of a dress code prevails at the Mine Shaft. A man outfitted in dress slacks and sandals or an alligator shirt might be turned away, while someone in muddy boots, torn jeans and a T-shirt stiff with come would be readily admitted. One ascends stairs and pays four dollars for two drinks at the door. Inside is a cloak room where some people check all their clothes, others just selected articles. Two bars and two pool tables and a juke box comprise the furnishings of the first room, where sex seldom takes place; this is where one works up his nerve, tanks up or momentarily recovers.

Through an archway is a large very dim room. Along one wall in doorless cubicles couples stand and carry on. Elsewhere slings are hung from the ceiling; men are suspended in these, feet up as in obstetrical stirrups, and submit to being fist-fucked. One flimsy wall in the center of the room is perforated with glory holes. Two staircases lead downstairs to still darker rooms, cold cement vaults. In one is a bathtub where naked men sit and wait to be pissed on. Roosting on a toilet, often enough, is another human pissoir.

One night I watched two middle-aged men, obviously lovers, enact their fantasy. One got down on all fours, naked except for his dog collar. A corner had been designated the dog house. The standing man was his master. The "dog," a truly vicious mutt, kept rushing out of the dog house to bite the leg of his master who, in turn, was forced to whip the slavering beast back into his quarters. After an hour of this exhausting "training," hound and human packed up and returned to the bar, where they drank beers and observed a game of pool with vacant, bored eyes.

On another occasion I watched a youngish sadist unpack his paraphernalia and proceed to lift the naked body of his ancient lover from the floor by thongs attached to the nipples and scrotum; the masochist never uttered a sound. Some evenings at the Mine Shaft are devoted to ass-eaters, others to fist-fuckers. The last time I visited the Mine Shaft I was standing in a crowd watching something unspeakable when the man standing beside me suddenly crashed forward on his face. I lifted him and hauled him out to the cloak room. He was bleeding profusely and was unconscious, though his pulse was discernible. A treacherous combination of booze and downs, I suppose. He was patched up, revived and sent off in a cab to the emergency room of St. Vincent's.

For most people the Mine Shaft is less destructive. Since it is a place, not a person, it is morally neutral. What it offers are the props of passion, an arena for experiment, a stimulating dimness. Many of the dramas enacted there are mild enough; some are creative. Sex therapists ascribe most sexual dysfunctions (impotence, delayed or premature ejaculation in men) to, among other causes, an inability to generate erotic fantasies; for that reason pornography of all sorts is often used to restore function. People have seen things at the Mine Shaft they would not dream of performing themselves, but the spectacle of such varied sexual scenarios can awaken their imaginations. One prominent sex therapist sends some of his patients to the baths; the Mine Shaft might serve as another stimulus.

It strikes me that a kind of hypocrisy is so prevalent as to be almost undetectable: the habit of castigating in print what one accepts, even enjoys, in life. I feel the temptation myself to pass judgment in this essay on those situations that I ramble through once a month without a thought. Is it because language belongs to the oppressor? I've already mentioned that sexual fantasy is primarily verbal. If so, then inhibition is just as verbal, and the words are ones we did not invent but must pay lip service to. Or when we write do we feel that we're legislators, setting guidelines for others that we would not follow ourselves? Or do we regard written language as more public, more ceremonial, than thought? Just as family men condemn the profanity on the stage that they use constantly in conversation, in the same way we may look to written language as an idealization rather than a reflection of ourselves.

The actual quality of a night at the Mine Shaft is hazier, less focused, more Brownian than any account of it might suggest. You see a friend at the bar and gossip with him for a few minutes. Then you enter the back rooms and wait for your eyes to adjust to the darkness. You touch, with your blind hand, something that feels like a—could it be? Yes, it is—a shoeshine stand. A man dressed as a cop is having his shoes polished. You approach someone but without the right degree of stoned, entranced conviction and with a doubt about his looks and likes; he picks up your hesitation and slips away. Someone stares at you through eyes burnt out of the white mask of his face. His intensity scares you off. In a corner something is developing. People gravitate toward it, as do you. The other men are too tall for you to see past them, but the spectator beside you gropes you, you him, and something about his timing, his body heat, even the tenor of his voice as he clears his throat and the line of his profile seen against the light awakens a response. Soon you're off in a corner, kissing. Someone shadowy sinks to his knees at your feet. Your new friend takes off his shirt then peels yours off—his is a healthy, firm body with an appealing bit of wobble at the waist, his neck scented—no, his hair—with the antique charm of Vitalis. You disengage yourselves from the man clawing at your crotches and return to the bar for a beer. He's a soldier from California, first time in New York. Long chat about his body-building ambitions, then a new round with him of half-clothed sex in the back room. He leaves. You see another friend you've lost touch with; he fills you in on his news. You both agree that the Mine Shaft is "tired" (failing to mention it's five in the morning and you've each come twice). No one will defend a place devoted to desire once the desire has been sated.

New York provides its citizens with unlimited sexual possibilities, much as any great city does. But what is unique to New York is the *cruising*. Everyone—man, woman and child—cruises, though this word, with its sexual connotations, may be misleading. What I'm singling out are the scanning eyes that lock for an instant, the cool and thorough appraisals of someone's person and apparel—the staring, in a word. On the street, at the checkout counter, in bank queues, between tables at restaurants, the staring is continuous, a civic habit. Part of it is, no doubt, simple nosiness. Part is sexual curiosity. Or sartorial envy. Where did he get a jacket cut like that? What has she done to her hair I might emulate? Would I look good in shoes like those?

But mostly the staring is an acknowledgment that New York life is theatrical. Richard Sennett in *The Fall of Public Man* declares that modern man is "an actor without a stage," that our misplaced notions of privacy and our singleminded devotion to intimacy have led us to ignore, even despise, the life of the streets, the nodding acquaintanceships with hundreds of people who are neither friends nor strangers. In New York, however, such a street life does exist, the stage is provided, a sense of being observed is given. When I return to New York I'm always struck by the excitement of being noticed and of noticing others. I am not a self-contained monad cycling through blind channels; rather, I am someone out to *farmi vivo*, as the Italians say, to "make myself alive" in a responsive and observing public.

But public life is only one of the city's attractions. Its greatest offering to gays is friendship. My mother used to urge me to marry someone so I wouldn't be alone. Since I lived alone she pictured me as lonely. What she had no way of understanding was how enveloping friendship can be in New York; for many people it has taken the place of love. Sex is casual, romance short-lived; the real continuity in many people's lives comes from their friends. Some advocates of friendship would argue that to receive sustenance from a dozen men and women is better than to pair off with just one other person, from whom one expects too much and receives too little. Better to enjoy romance in the form of successive "affairlets," each six months long, and to find true security in friendships that sometimes endure for decades. Country, small-town or suburban life may require that one have a lover; wherever gays are isolated or worked into the fabric of heterosexual society, they are happiest when they live with a lover. But in New York people pair off only because they want to and only so long as the relationship works; often enough it works because the two men share a professional interest.

Of course the rhetoric has not kept pace with the reality; at some point in the evening the friend in the midst of friends will piously sigh over that lover he's never been able to find. What he fails to admit is that a full-time, live-in lover would wreak havoc on his meticulously designed social arrangements, as balanced and as much in motion as a Calder mobile. Living with a lover over several years is also, paradoxically, a sort of farewell to romance. The most ardent, disrupting and exalting moment in any affair is the courtship; the aftermath calls for constant compromises, adjustments, discussions. The pleasures of a sustained love affair can be great—the intimacy, the "creatureliness," the security, the constant companionship, the sense of a shared destiny—but these are not the pleasures of romantic passion. The great romantics, I would contend, have no romances. They *begin* affairs, never complete them.

Perhaps I can clarify my point by saying that for many New Yorkers the conventional conflation of sex, romance and friendship into marriage has been exploded and the elements separated out. Sex is performed with strangers, romance is captured in brief affairs, friendship is assigned to friends. In this formula, one notices, the only stable element is friendship. The division is rather reminiscent of Freud's tripartite scheme of the id (sex), ego (friendship) and superego (romance). Whether compartmentalizing such functions is more or less workable than traditional marriage I have no idea; I do know that the division promotes passionate, durable friendships.

Visitors to the city have commented that New Yorkers, far from being friendly, are cold, even hostile. Naturally in any great city people will be suspicious of strangers. Besides, everyone is in a rush. But even at home New Yorkers can seem forbidding. New Yorkers are so *affairés* they carry date books in their hip pockets; they are also formal, more like Europeans than Americans. I mean to say New Yorkers seldom drop in on each other unless they are college students or recent arrivals. For the rest of us a date must be planned a week in advance.

If this surface can be penetrated, New Yorkers can be seen as attentive, loving friends—and the vehicle of this affection is the telephone. Only over the phone does anything get said; at dinner the tyranny of small-talk is relentless. Ceaselessly, day and night, friends check in with each other on the phone, and someone who cannot be seen in the flesh till a week from Tuesday can be heard twice a day every day.

In New York your friends need not like each other. You can belong to at least two quite different sets and still see mavericks who'd not fit into either group. One friend is a much older man (approaching seventy) who prepares exquisite suppers for you and with whom you discuss one subject only: love. He falls asleep when the conversation strays from that topic. In his apartment every light is screened by a silk shade hung with tassles; a dozen clocks in as many voices chime out the hour; family photos, some a hundred years old, crowd the top of a desk; artificial flames rotate within the useless fireplace; the needle lifts from an old Peggy Lee record and falls on an older Zarah Leander record. Deep into the night, concealed behind his dark glasses and his polished narrative style, he tells the rosary of past romances. . . . Another friend is met every Saturday afternoon at the Sheridan Square Gymnasium. While hoisting heavy metal you and he discuss cute boys, Virginia Woolf, sexual politics, new bars and innermost thoughts; it is a friendship free of all coercion and so full of affection that, out of nowhere, tears of gratitude and pleasure spring to your eyes at unpredictable moments. . . . Yet another friend, a literary critic and a balletomane, has heard (over the phone, of course) every detail of your life for the last ten years, as you've heard his. He lends you money, asks advice, gives counsel, deeply cares about whether you made it to the dentist or not—he is the witness (or auditor) of your life on the plane where it is lived, which often has more to do with money and the dentist than ideas and ideals. . . . Another friend serves as your conscience. She *does* live on the plane of ideas and hers are always undergoing the most strenuous testing; more moral and intellectual than you are, she gives you the benefit (sometimes the healing scourge) of her thoughts.

And there are the ex-lovers, that phalanx of men who remain true to you, even all these years later, after their fashion. . . . They are those rare friends with whom you can sit in utter silence, reading a book or looking out the window, the supreme intimacy. They always tell you how handsome you are, since they see you as you were ten, fifteen, twenty years ago. And there are the *new* friends, those men who take you off to undiscovered discos or give you a rather too detailed architectural tour of SoHo or who see you in a false but flattering light. Although New York gays can claim to be only slightly more liberal than the population at large, they do at least possess the foundation on which to build a saner view of things. That foundation is knowledge. I don't want to make too much of the democracy of gay life, but gay men undeniably are more likely than straights to reach across social and age barriers in search of sex. Sex leads to friendship, and friendship leads to the exchange of information. I have friends of every age and ethnic background; I feel that I am less insulated than my straight counterpart (I sometimes try to picture that poor hypothetical devil).

I also have straight friends. Heterosexual women in New York, especially those who have espoused some version of feminism, seem to be dealing with the same sort of questions gay men face. The things I talk about with the straight women I know include: how to maintain one's independence without armoring oneself against love; how to accept role-playing in the bedroom without falling into it in the rest of one's life; how to give their full due to friends and lovers alike; how to remain courageous as one drifts farther and farther away from convention. These are experiential matters, more easily solved in theory than in practice.

For me, the most attractive aspect of New York life is its large gay artistic community. If all the celebrated composers, painters and writers were to come out at once, the news would be startling even to gays in other cities who practice or follow the arts. This New York closetiness I find tiresome, but it does not prevent me from enjoying the company of gay artists. More so than any other American city, New York offers the gay man with artistic interests infinite possibilities of friendship. I should hasten to mention that the widespread heterosexual delusion that gays *control* the arts and the media is ridiculous. For decades few publishers issued serious gay fiction, and even now there are relatively few titles. In the mid-Sixties a gay novel of mine went to twenty-two New York publishers, only to be rejected by them all. Subsequently I met several closeted gay editors at various houses who told me they had turned down my book since to espouse it would be tantamount to their own coming out. Similarly, even today there are only a dozen male editors in New York who are willing to deal with gay fiction (there are quite a few more women).

The theater is worse. One hears a great deal about the gay takeover of Broadway, but where are the gay plays? Every other season two or three out of the eighty or so plays to open on Broadway might treat a gay subject. If gays do in fact constitute 10 percent of the population, this frequency scarcely corresponds with our numbers, especially considering the concentration of gays in New York. The odd thing is that at any given time there will be one or two gay off-Off-Broadway troupes, a gay art gallery, possibly a few performances of a gay dance company, a scattering of gay books—and this will be the entire "official" output of the New York gay community. What is seldom noticed is that at least a third of the so-called mainstream "heterosexual" art has also been created by gays. Although gays contribute largely to the city's (and country's) cultural life, the extent of this contribution is seldom noticed.

Fire Island is the chief gay resort for New Yorkers. Since so few of us own cars, it would be attractive for that reason alone; it can be reached by bus or train and ferry (all cars except a few service vehicles are banned from the island). More important, though Fire Island is only two hours away from Manhattan, it provides a dramatic contrast to the city. A sandbar just a mile wide that runs along the east coast of Long Island, Fire Island is usually at least 10 degrees cooler than the city in the summer. Its white sand beaches are among the widest and most beautiful in the country. Its houses are nestled in the dunes; many of the structures stand high on stilts. Raised wooden walkways lead from the harbor to the houses and criss-cross the interior. Much of the island is given over to wildlife preserves and at dawn or dusk one can encounter deer in one's backyard. Poison ivy, blueberry bushes, sassafras and wind-tormented trees form the ground covering; the ground itself is mostly sand. Birds chatter on eaves or telephone wires. The rumble of a child's wagon on the boardwalk (wagons are the means for conveying groceries home) can be heard blocks away.

There are two gay communities on the island and several more straight communities. Cherry Grove is the older of the gay communities; it dates back to the turn of the century but became primarily gay only after World War II. It sometimes seems a throwback to the gay life of the 1950s. Its houses are crowded close together and assigned campy names ("Thimk Pimk" or "The Time and the Place"). In the Grove one sees blacks and Puerto Ricans, a few drags, a few older queens in flowing caftans and one hears old-style dishing and Judy Garland records—all unthinkable in the Pines. Until ten years ago the Pines was still at least half straight; now it is almost entirely gay. A couple miles up the beach from the Grove, the Pines is considerably more glamorous and expensive. Its houses are not wedged tightly together. Many of them have been designed by fanciful architects and along the ocean one sees a house that resembles a roller coaster or a medieval keep or the Kodak pavilion at the World's Fair—nothing vulgar, mind you, just a hint of grotesquerie. Spacious sun decks behind high walls, swimming pools, weathered wood exteriors, high tech interiors, sliding glass doors, spotlights on dimmers—this is the look in the Pines.

The houses these days rent for the summer for anything from $10,000 to $20,000 and sell for as much as half a million. Since the periphery is national parkland, the community cannot grow outwards, yet every year more and more people hope to spend the season there. To meet the high rents, sometimes as many as ten men share a house—even more, if half-shares (every other weekend) are sold. Despite the prices, the place remains so attractive that gay men and lesbians from Europe and the West Coast flock to it for their holidays.

The people who pay nothing for their vacations and enjoy the island the most are the houseboys. Whereas most of the renters must work in the city, the houseboys are free to cavort, sun and socialize during the week, when the population thins out. These "boys," usually in their early twenties, must perform just a few chores (cleaning, laundry, laying in of groceries); the rest of the time they have no responsibilities. They are also paid nothing or very little beyond free room and board. On Friday afternoon the renters arrive. Boatload after boatload of tense, pale men in business suits pulls in. They bring with them the striving, the nervousness, the speediness of the city. Resenting the houseboy's tan and tranquillity, they snap at him. Someone gets on the phone and invites a dozen friends to cocktails. Someone else heads right for his room and collapses into a three-hour nap. Someone else plunges into the pool. Drinks are made and consumed. The shower never stops running. A dinner for ten is planned. Two members of the house are antisocial and broke; they resent the invasion and the expense of the dinner party (all expenses are shared) and sharp words are exchanged. An ugly mood takes over the house. One member wants silence, another insists on playing his Donna Summer record and getting everyone "up."

Friends drift in and out of the house. The night turns cool and people don flannel shirts or sweaters. The cocktail crowd comes and goes. The overly elaborate dinner is not put on the table until eleven-thirty. But no matter—by that time everyone has mellowed out. A remedy for raw nerves has been served to everyone. Each guest has consumed two blackbirds to get some energy. To dull the speed edge, he has swallowed a Tuinal. This is the foundation makeup for tonight's face. To provide a few highlights people smoke angel dust; now they're nicely stoned. Then to introduce a bit of glitter, to hallucinate, they do some acid. Now, to direct this head toward sex, a bit of MDA is thrown in. For that last touch of blush-on, that final glow, cocaine is snorted. The charred roast is scarcely touched. At one everyone hastens down to the Sandpiper to dance till four. Following the disco is a private party with just fifty friends. By dawn everyone is in a loving mood. A Mozart piano concerto is played on the stereo. People are passing Quaaludes and iced vodka or Tuinals and Scotch (it's not *comme il faut* to mix these combinations and do, say, Quaaludes and Scotch).

The drug crowd is just one part of Fire Island. In some houses the members may be homebodies who go to bed early and rise at dawn for bird-watching. In another a painter, who lives on the island for the entire summer, is quietly working on his deck and emerges only for groceries and midnight skirmishes. One house will be full of models who must get their sleep and watch their diets. Another is made up of weightlifters who spend their Saturdays pumping iron. One house is indefatigably social, another consecrated to sex. In some houses the shareholders scarcely know each other and have been assembled from advertisements; in others the members are old friends who've rented together for six or seven seasons.

In general, life on Fire Island is less sybaritic and more ascetic than rumor would have it. The schedule can be daunting. During the day one must put in one's hours on the beach, tanning, swimming and socializing. The foot traffic along the beach is constant; nods are exchanged; visits to the towels of friends are paid; house calls are made. In the afternoon the "meat rack" between the Grove and the Pines is active. In the hot sun men wind their way down sand paths between low trees and scrubby bushes to find impromptu sex. Then it's cocktail time and a long beauty rest. After the nap one arises, does the *grande toilette* and prepares dinner.

When the group around the table is congenial, those long,

long Fire Island dinners can be a delight. People become confiding, reflective, self-revealing in a way they never would in the city. Strange and exciting conjunctions of people are brought together: a famous elderly music critic exchanges views on rock with a nineteen-year-old redneck from Missouri, just arrived in town; an accountant tells everyone about his hitherto unmentioned years as a kept boy in Paris; an adept at yoga inspires the group to meet every morning with him to exercise; a journalist just back from India discusses Far Eastern politics; a Southerner, his accent long since erased, produces an unexpected sweet potato pie; a fatty from the Bronx discovers a shared passion for old trolleys and streetcars in another guest, a lean cowboy from Tucson. The evening stretches on and on.

The chores, the clothes, the expenses, the adjustment to group living all can make Fire Island rigorous. The much celebrated sexual free-for-all may be somewhat disappointing. Since the houses are so crowded, few people can invite a trick home. Moreover, the place is so observant and so gossipy (all tongues and eyes) that no one wants to be seen approaching a stranger and receiving a rejection. The solution is the bushes. After the disco shuts down scores of men file down the walkways into the dunes at the Grove end of the Pines. The starry sky, the cool night breeze, the salty tang in the air, the sight of bronzed bodies in white shirts and pants glimpsed through trees can be both poetic and arousing.

Perhaps the most overwhelming moment on Fire Island is the afternoon tea dance at the Botel. On two spacious decks the best-looking men in the city are assembled. In swim trunks or jeans or gauzy after-beach trousers or leather vests over bare torsos, everyone stands about and drinks and chats. There's a movie star. Over there is the owner of a disco and his clique. Here's my doctor talking to my lawyer. He's the model on the cover of that magazine. His friend is a European prince turned fashion designer. The money represented on the deck, if calculated in terms of dentistry, plastic surgery, gymnasium fees and clothes bills, not to mention the price of renting and maintaining a house, is formidable. Inside, on the dance floor, men are dancing in groups, blowing whistles, shouting with frenzy, eyeing everyone. Just beyond the deck is the harbor, where massive white yachts are moored. On their decks the crews (many of them older heterosexuals) are holding court.

For my part, as a person of average looks and average income, Fire Island has given me some of my greatest highs (sex on the deserted beach at dawn, instant intimacy with a stranger in a hammock on someone's deck in the afternoon), but it has always filled me with insecurity. As a spectacle of gay affluence and gay male beauty, however, it is unrivalled. That much is certain.

BOSTON AND WASHINGTON, D.C.

The Political Choice

As politically active gays work to secure the legal and economic rights of lesbians and homosexuals, a central disagreement has arisen, a question of principles as much as tactics. The majority believes that most gays are essentially like straights save for the seemingly disturbing but actually neutral and irrelevant matter of affectional preference. To this way of thinking, lesbians and gay men are like women and men everywhere and represent the same ethnic and socioeconomic diversity as heterosexuals. These leaders think that the function of gay liberation is to defuse fear and hatred of homosexuals through education and to secure legislation ending discrimination in housing and employment. Gay subculture, they might add, is merely defensive, a ghetto created by prejudice and likely to dissolve once gays are integrated into the mainstream.

The best way to bring about this assimilation is by working within the system—through electing officials sympathetic to gays, battling bigots in court cases, and educating the public at large by sensitive and liberal television programs, movies and books; more particularly, adolescents in school should be informed in sex education and civics classes about the range of human sexual expression and the need for tolerance. To overcome misleading stereotypes about gays, the public needs to learn that gay women can be feminine, gay men can be masculine, gays of both sexes can be religious, successful in business, dependable as members of the community, responsible as parents and so on. The image of gays as child molestors, as unstable employees, as atheists, as freaks given over to weird sex scenes (transvestism, leather, promiscuity) must be strenuously corrected, even at the price of disowning the more bizarre elements in the gay community.

Radical gays deplore almost everything about this approach. As a strategy, it is dangerously wrong, they feel. Politicians are always in need of an issue, a scandal, an enemy, and gays are a safe minority group to attack. Now that it has become so difficult for campaigning politicians to take stands on substantive matters, local and national office-seekers are all the more attracted to inflammatory "moral" issues (abortion, ERA, prayer in the classroom, homosexuality). Gays are especially vulnerable in this political climate. Obviously, the best way to attack gays is by scaring the public with lurid stories of gay "sex rings," orgies, pedophilia, sado-masochism, mass murder, drug addiction and so on. Gay radicals might say we are only as strong as our most exposed flank; once those in power begin to dragnet and prosecute gay "freaks," then the entire gay community, no matter how ordinary and respectable it might be, will quickly come under attack. It does no good to disown questionable elements in gay life; we must defend them.

So much for tactics. As for ideals, gay radicals have no desire to see gays normalized and turned into useful members of the system as it now exists. They believe that gays can serve as the vanguard of a liberation movement that might transform American society into something better, more humane, more equitable, less repressed. So far, so good. But at this point radicals part company with one another. Some are Marxists, who envision an alliance between gays and the working class; they feel that the oppression of gays and the proletariat makes them natural allies. Other radicals are feminists who consider homosexuality as a refiguring of traditional sex-linked role-playing; gays are explorers of the terrain of androgyny. Still other radicals are back-to-the-earth hippies or urban communitarians or anarchists. No matter what shade of ideology they may espouse, these lesbians and gay men are more concerned with working out a "correct'" position than with winning adherents. Most of them are distrustful of electoral politics and the machinery of conventional society. Many were New Leftists during the 1960s.

At the risk of oversimplifying, I would contend that Boston represents a center for gay radicalism and that Washington, D.C., is a stronghold for more conventional lesbian and homosexual politics. I would like to consider the two cities largely in that light.

Boston is a talk shop. On my travels I have met gays in various towns who have complained they have trouble meeting intelligent, educated homosexuals interested in political, artistic and social issues. I recommend they head for Boston.

I spent the sunny June afternoon I arrived with my hosts, a young professor at one of the city's many famous universities and his lover, a graduate student in English. They had met in Northern California and brought with them a lightheartedness, a capacity for stoned silliness, a reverence for the high culture of the East and extraordinary physical beauty. The professor was very excited; he had just unearthed a number of medieval poems in Latin written by monks to young boys. These poems had been ignored or suppressed for centuries, and only the diligence of German scholars had preserved the texts at all.

We sat on the Esplanade embankment and sunned and watched the small sailboats skimming up and down the Charles River, one of the boats skirting dangerously close to the massive stone pylons of a bridge before coming about just in time. The sight of tan flesh and wind-filled canvas in a city gave me a sense of delighted confusion and reminded me of San Francisco. The cities do have their similarities; they are both intimate and sophisticated—and both are very gay. The differences, of course, are more remarkable. Boston is brainy. Wherever you go you overhear serious conversation. It's also very old; the Boston Common, the oldest park in the country, was founded in 1634. And it is a city of the strongest social contrasts. It is solidly

Irish Catholic; someone I talked to in Boston dubbed it "Little Dublin." Its working-class Irish population cooperates with a Democratic machine that is the most dictatorial and corrupt in the nation, now that Mayor Daley of Chicago is dead. But another part of Boston is progressive; the senators from Massachusetts are the most liberal in the nation, and the state has a long tradition of progressivism. In the last century it led the struggles for free public education, temperance, pacifism, prison reform, abolition of slavery and the amelioration of the suffering of paupers, the deaf, the blind, the insane and the retarded.

In the summer Boston is a continuous street fair. The parks are crowded with *flâneurs*, musicians, athletes, necking couples. Beacon Hill—with its brick sidewalks and granite curbs, its patrician Federal houses and gas lamps—is overrun by tourists politely blinking as they read historic plaques celebrating a past they never knew they had, a past of conscience-wracked Puritans, Enlightenment legislators and philanthropic merchants. On Louisburg Square I looked everywhere for the tinted windowpanes I remembered from a childhood visit to Boston. At last I discovered two panes, one pale amethyst, the other purple; I was reminded that glass is a liquid that continues to flow (that's why it warps with age). Perhaps if I return after another hundred years those panes will be violet puddles on the cobblestones.

Down by Faneuil Hall in the evening old Italian couples "come out" for the evening to sit on benches and gossip and observe the passing show. Jugglers and mimes draw crowds, shoppers drift through boutiques, peddlers hawk heart-shaped mylar balloons, red on one side and silver on the other. At the nearby Union Oyster House customers sit around the semi-circular mahogany oyster bar before going upstairs to narrow wood booths for clam chowder and lobsters. In the last light of the evening brassy boys selling vegetables from carts whistle at passing women and girls and refer to their *juicy* tomatoes. Over in Cambridge at the subway stop a string quartet, hired by the transit authority, entertains waiting passengers with a bit of Alban Berg.

The three main gay neighborhoods are Beacon Hill, the Back Bay and the South End. In none is the concentration of gays sufficient to speak of a "ghetto," yet the boutiques and the restored houses in all three areas attest to a middle-class gay presence. My friends and I had dinner in such a house in the South End. We parked in a narrow, ancient square where the house-fronts formed a solid phalanx behind the luxuriance of mature trees. A stone stoop led up to the parlor floor—entrance hall, formal dining room and, overlooking a garden in the back, a big modern kitchen. The company that night included a gay psychologist, a psychiatrist, a translator and an administrator of special education. Everyone had prepared a dish; the theme was vaguely Near Eastern and we worked our way through a spicy soup, marinated lamb on skewers, a Greek salad and (for a native touch) homemade ice cream and cookies.

The conversation ranged freely over many subjects. Why are there so many gay deaf people? One theory: their deafness prevents them from being socialized into concealing their sexuality and so the natural incidence of homosexuality that would occur in any population becomes more evident. Is homosexuality an artificial invention of the Victorian era? Most of us agreed with the point that Michel Foucault makes that the Victorians (who invented the term *homosexuality*) threw a new emphasis on the condition by defining it. Were Masters and Johnson accurate in citing the high level of heterosexual fantasies among lesbians and gay men? The psychiatrist thought the findings were correct and added, "Straight people have quite a few gay fantasies as well." Should we gay men sleep with women? The consensus: Yes. Heterosexual sex is the last taboo of gay life.

Upstairs in the large sitting room, as we spread out on a polybrachial sectional couch, people talked about the failure of busing in Boston, the philosophy of Condillac and the phenomenon of feral children. It was heady stuff, but the talk was not designed to exclude anyone nor was the stage seized by anyone for grandstanding. Just easy talk among friends, with time out for jokes, refills of drinks, anecdotes. Everything, in fact, was personal—talk arose out of personal experience and was resolved there.

Washington, D.C., has as many educated people as Boston,

but in Washington everyone is a specialist (he's in cancer research, she's an Africanist, this one's a lobbyist for farmers, that one's the liaison in charge of Chinese affairs between the State Department and the Joint Chiefs of Staff), and the tacit agreement is to discuss nothing except local real estate (the latest prices fetched in Georgetown or the newest renovations on the Hill). The need for secrecy or the gulf between any two professional pursuits forbids an exchange of ideas. Academic life around the country often participates in this same disturbing feature of the capital—its nullity. Sophisticated women and men professors recognize they have nothing in common beyond the hazards of urban pioneering and the challenges of leading genteel but counter-cultural lives in a mass society (the search for bean curd and fresh pasta in a shopping center given over to canned peas and Wonder Bread, the difficulty of finding the right Montessori school for the kids, the necessity of starting a neighborhood recycling center in a nation committed to pollution and waste). Sure, everyone knows George is doing something "on" Milton and Helen is tackling Wittgenstein's ethics, but neither topic is proper for the dinner table. Bridge and gas prices and vacation plans are far more suitable.

Boston, on the other hand, has its own way of suppressing an exchange of ideas—especially about homosexuality. At Harvard, as at elite schools everywhere, today's undergraduates are too career-oriented to risk compromising their futures by allying themselves with such an unpopular cause as homosexual rights. Among the graduate students and gay faculty members, the oppression (to the degree it exists) is more subtle. Most people who take to Harvard discard the manner to which they were born and adopt the school's manner, which is beguilingly cosmopolitan—so attractive and compelling that it crowds out all others. It is a style that is unemphatic, intellectual, comprehending. As one Harvard man explained to me, "Coming out at Harvard was wonderful—painless, a big anti-climax. No one cared. If anything, I gained a certain cachet. There are so many upper-class WASPs at Harvard, and their greatest fear is that privilege has somehow robbed them of experience. They worry that they're not black, not poor, not gay, and they're eager to be let in on everything. But this acceptance, wonderful as it is, can be subtly undermining. A gay dance at Harvard is a farce. The way to make a gay dance a *Harvard* gay dance would be to invite lots of straight people. The point is: the Harvard manner is so alluring that no gay could ever abandon it for, say, a gay manner. I think it's important for a gay to be among gays for a period, maybe a year or two, maybe more—to lead a gay life. But no one at Harvard would want to do that. The other drawback about Harvard is that it's so passionless. The emphasis here is on *competence*.

"I remember a professor who came here from the University of Chicago; he tried to get his students to examine a passage from Plato and discuss whether it was *true* or not. Harvard students were confused. They could relate Plato to Christian thought or contrast him with Aristotle, they could discuss the liberal tradition and so on—but they didn't want to consider whether what Plato said was *true*. The emphasis here is on cornering the market on one branch of knowledge—but not on fighting for a cause or taking a stand. That's why Harvard turns out so many scholars but so few thinkers. This attitude defuses all political programs, including gay liberation. But it would be a mistake to dismiss Harvard. A gay man can find acceptance here; whether he can find self-acceptance is another question."

This complexity did not characterize a group I met that was not affiliated to Harvard or any other university. Through an acquaintance I spent an afternoon with a small circle of eight friends who have been getting together several times a week for the last five years to discuss gay issues. When *Dancer From the Dance* was published, they all read it and talked about it. When Dan White's sentence was handed down, they convened to share their sense of outrage. When an issue of *Christopher Street* comes out, they debate the merits of the stories and articles.

The friends, all men, are in their late twenties and early thirties. One is a psychotherapist, a second a nurse, a third a travel agent, a fourth a graduate student at M.I.T. They first met at a gay coffee house in the Charles Street Meeting House (the *Gay Community News* was also born there). That was five years ago. Since then they have been getting together at various coffee shops and bars; right now a gay bar in Cambridge is one of their haunts, primarily because the music is not so loud as to forbid conversation. Two affairs emerged from within the group, but both have peacefully died away, leaving no ripples behind. On Sundays the group plays volleyball in the park in Fenway (in the winter at a gym). In warm weather the friends also go mountain climbing or take bicycle trips or spend the weekend at a cabin on a pond in Plymouth. Last Halloween everyone donned drag for the first and only time; I was shown a before-and-after shot. In the first shot were the beards and the jeans and the boots; in the second were the beards and the gowns and the heels.

The group is considering buying a house in Fenway. "It's a great neighborhood," one of them tells me, "funky, faded, close to the center. People say it's dangerous, but it's not. We would *not* live communally. Some of us tried that with other gay groups in the early Seventies. There's still a lot of communal gay living in Boston—the Fort Hill Faggots on the edge of Roxbury, for instance. But we each have too strong a sense of individuality. Yet it would be nice to have a house together. We're not too happy about becoming middle-class gentrifying gays, however. We wouldn't want to evict poor families, the way gays have done in the South End. I live in the South End and all six of my gay neighbors voted for Ford. I couldn't *believe* it; I keep wondering if life has become too sweet on Waltham Street. One of my neighbors is a middle-class black gay man, who makes $30,000 working for Ma Bell and who's a Republican."

I asked the group if their friendships presented any problems. "Yes," the psychotherapist said. He was in his late thirties, older than the others—a handsome man with a powerful body and prematurely graying long hair. He was also one of the two native Bostonians in the crowd. "Friends are threatened if you have a lover. And friendship is fine—I can call up anyone and meet him whenever I want at a bar or coffee shop. Friends fill all my needs for intimacy—except at night. You still go home alone. I have a nesting instinct, I think, maybe because I'm getting older. But I wonder if I'll ever settle down as long as I get so much from my friends."

Communal living is one of the experiments among radical gays in the Boston area. I interviewed a gay writer of thirty-eight

who lives two hours away from Boston on a farm. Eight men
inhabit three houses and a cabin that they built themselves. Although they originally intended to share expenses, profits, chores
and meals, they've ended up by leading separate lives and maintaining separate bankbooks. In the group, one member is a
realtor, two are carpenters, another a textile designer, one a
writer, another a stone mason and yet another is working on
a CETA program to clear land for a cemetery. The houses are
in the woods and each is concealed from the others by a hill
and trees, though it's only a five-minute walk from one place
to another. The man I interviewed has an octagonal timber
frame house where he lives alone. His is the only house without
electricity. His radio is battery-powered, his refrigerator and
lamps run on gas.

I asked him to describe his typical day. "I get up at eight
in the morning and jog, then I have a bite of breakfast and do
my correspondence, which is always formidable. I write for a
newspaper in town; I get twenty-five dollars an article and I
usually do three a week. I also contribute to many gay peri-
odicals which, as you know, pay little or nothing. I listen to
'All Things Considered,' an excellent news program on National
Public Radio; it's an hour-and-a-half long and I tune in to it
every day. Once a week I drive to town, which is eight miles
away, and shop at the food coop. I might work in the garden—
mulch hay or haul up water in the truck. I take a lot of walks.
Once a week I go over to a neighbor's and watch TV. I'm
active in an anti-nuclear group and I serve on the local Board
of Health and the Conservation Commission."

I asked what his rural neighbors thought of the gay men
in their midst. "We haven't really made a point of our being
gay in the town, though we do nothing to hide it. I think that
we built our houses ourselves stands in our favor. Also that
we're not just summer or weekend people but rather live and
work in the community. There's an old New England tradition
of respect for privacy that still holds in the country if not in
the city; it's the 'good fences make good neighbors' philosophy.
I guess most folks around us see us more as hippies-who-live-
back-in-the-woods than as gays."

My informant has been active in gay politics in the Boston

area for some time, and I asked him about gay radicals. "There are a lot of groups—the Boston Lesbians and Gay Men Against the Right and the Lavender Resistance and many others. The goal for most is to inject gay consciousness into the Left, and Leftist consciousness into gay liberation. Problems keep cropping up—Cuba, for instance. Some gay Leftists think we should overlook Castro's repressive policies toward gays—the concentration camps. I don't. I can't support a regime that imprisons gays."

I asked him about his own views. "I feel a strong attachment to the Left. My parents were both communists and union organizers; I grew up on a chicken farm in the Catskills. But I feel no loyalty to the patriarchal socialist movement or to Marxist-Leninist orthodoxy. What I do still feel is an attachment to the Leftist tradition of fighting social and economic injustice. Beyond that, I reject the idea of the 'inevitability' of the revolution, the 'scientific' pretensions of Marxism, the lack of civil rights in the Soviet Union and the complete tyranny of that government. What interests me are the writings of women, gay men and ecologists. I've evolved away from the notion that a fully developed ideology can answer all questions. Take the current issue of pedophilia. There's no way to answer it without exploring it. We need information and time for deliberation. There are no clear answers—who would provide them? Feminists? Socialists? I'm also against the idea of a *vanguard* of politically 'correct' people destined to lead the masses in a violent struggle against oppressors; for me, the vanguard is *also* oppressive. I say I'm a socialist, but for me socialism means ending the exploitation of labor and the inequities between rich and poor. That's all."

His mention of pedophilia touched upon *the* most controversial issue in Boston gay circles. The subject became explosive in 1978 when a "sex ring" in the Boston suburb of Revere was exposed. On December 8, 1977, District Attorney Garrett Byrne, seeking reelection once again (he was eighty at the time), stirred up excitement by announcing that he had indicted twenty-four adult men for "raping" boys between the ages of eight and thirteen. Byrne also set up a special hotline, which outraged citizens were encouraged to phone anonymously in order to report the names of other gay men suspected of having sex with minors. The next day the Boston *Herald-American* published on the first page the names, addresses and places of employment of the accused men.

Members of Boston's radical gay paper, *Fag Rag*, immediately responded to the charges by forming a Boston/Boise Committee (named after the famous witch-hunt of gay men in Boise, Idaho, in 1955). Under pressure from the Committee, the D.A. discontinued the use of the hotline. The Committee then investigated the facts behind the D.A.'s allegations. As it turned out, most of the "boys" were not eight to thirteen, as originally announced, but rather thirteen to fifteen; since the indictments referred to sex acts that had in some cases happened several years earlier, quite a few of the boys were now in their twenties. Similarly, the charge of "rape" turned out to be a technicality. No one had accused the men of forcibly taking the boys in sex; rather, since the age of sexual consent in Massachusetts is sixteen, any adult who engages in sex with someone under that age is guilty of statutory rape. The penalty for this "crime" can be up to life in prison.

As information about the "sex ring" came to light, gays recognized that what had happened was that a number of adolescents had been hanging out at the house of a local gay man. There they had had sex with older men, sometimes for money and sometimes just for fun. None of the boys had initiated a complaint against the older men, though several were coerced by the police and clergymen into *saying* they were victims. As John Mitzel has written in *Alternate*, "As to the 'sex ring,' we found out that the police, priests and psychiatrists had combined to pressure the 13 youths to testify before the grand jury. This was particularly true of the State's main 'victim,' Gary. Gary, now 17, lived alone with his mother. Gary is gay and has been sexually active since before he was 12. After the police located him, he and his mother were visited *no less than 6 times* by their parish priest who urged him to cooperate with the authorities. Police showed nude pictures of Gary to his friends and neighbors and encouraged them to badger him. He and his mother (recipients of state social aid) were threatened with a cut-off of funds if he didn't testify. The mother was finally prodded to sign over custody of the youth to the police. Gary was then locked up in a youth detention facility and told that *if* he continued to refuse cooperation, then *he* would be indicted for 'sex crimes.' He relented and is now the 'victim' against four different men."

I talked to one of those four men. In 1955 he opened a martial arts school, where he was also an instructor. When he was indicted he was forced to sell the school in order to pay his lawyer bills; he is now selling his house as well. "Gary was just a friend of mine, a guy who'd come by my place for sex. I didn't know he was a hustler, I just knew him as a kid from Revere. But my side of the story hasn't been revealed. I'm now writing a book about it. Gary came to a meeting of the Boston/Boise Committee and kissed me. He said that he had been forced to squeal on me. It was a put-up job."

In the first of the Revere trials, a Boston psychiatrist, Dr. Donald Allen, was convicted on four counts of statutory rape of a fifteen-year-old and sentenced to five years on probation. Although Dr. Allen claimed that he had been doing "research" for a study of hustling, the jury preferred to believe his "victim," Gary. Most of the other cases have simply fizzled. Twenty-four men were originally indicted, but only twenty were actually arrested (the remaining four either didn't exist or eluded the police). Of those twenty, one turned state's witness, a few cases were dropped and eleven pleaded guilty to one count (statutory rape)—which led to a sentence of unsupervised probation. One man, however, whose case was unrelated to the Revere "ring," had already spent twenty years in the Sexually Dangerous Ward of Bridgewater State Hospital (subject of Fred Wiseman's film, *Titticut Follies*). When he was released he returned to his old boy scout troop and allegedly started blowing the kids again—and was shipped back to Bridgewater.

By politicizing the trial, the Boston/Boise Committee kept it from being the usual legal sham. The accused, rather than routinely pleading guilty to all charges against them, decided to plea-bargain. The public was forced to reconsider its attitudes toward sex between men and adolescents. And the District Attorney's office, after overreaching itself, seems unlikely to pursue other gay sex scandals in the Boston area. A great deal of credit goes to the Committee and especially to John Mitzel, whose crisp accounts in the gay press of the trial and the issues kept the gay community informed and alerted (I am indebted to those stories for my own summary).

Ancillary to the trial were several other dramas. In March 1978 more than 100 men were arrested in the Boston Public Library by cops who picked up anyone who "looked" gay. The police had obviously decided to step up the offensive, for surely if there are two areas of gay life likely to outrage the straight community they are sex with minors and sex in public places. The gays of Boston immediately responded with a mass rally in front of the library.

On April 5, 1978, Gore Vidal spoke at the Arlington Street Church in a benefit for the Boston/Boise Committee. In the audience were Massachusetts Superior Court Chief Justice Robert M. Bonin and his wife. The next day Bonin was suspended from his duties for attending the speech. The State Senate passed a Bill of Address removing Bonin from office—but before the Governor could sign it, Bonin resigned.

To add to the madness Anita Bryant arrived on the scene. She was booked into the Hynes War Memorial Auditorium, but of its 5,000 seats only seventy-eight were sold (many of those tickets were bought by gays who intended to disrupt her concert). Anita had planned to sing on behalf of a Rightist Senatorial candidate, Howard Phillips—but the fundraiser had to be cancelled.

Within the gay community itself, the Revere trials created a deep split. On the one side were those "respectable" gays, led by the conservative Gay Business Association and lesbian legislator Elaine Noble; they disowned the Revere defendants and urged gays not to demonstrate against Anita Bryant. On the other side were the militant gays who took a spirited stand against Bryant and the witch-hunt; they were led by the Boston/Boise Committee and other radicals.

A lasting result of the Committee's activities was its sponsorship of a one-day conference on the issue of man-boy love.

The conference, held on December 2, 1978, was the first of its kind in the United States (in England, Germany and Scandinavia pedophile organizations have existed for a number of years). A second conference on the subject was held in the spring of 1979 in New York City. A permanent organization, the North American Man/Boy Love Association, has been formed.

Gay Leftists in the United States and abroad have been debating the issue of gay pederasty and pedophilia with considerable energy. *Pederasty* is defined by my dictionary as "anal intercourse esp. with a boy as the passive partner," and *pedophilia* as "paraphilia [unusual sexual practices] in which children are the preferred sexual object." England's Paedophile Information Exchange defines pedophilia as "sexual love directed towards children . . . usually somewhere in the 8-15 range." I have also heard mention of *ephebephilia*, or love of youths in the sixteen-to-nineteen-year-old range.

Three crucial questions have emerged in these discussions: the meaning of consent; the age of the youngster; and the danger of exploitation. Those who oppose pedophilia argue that the "consent" or seeming cooperation of an eight-year-old is meaningless. The child may be too frightened or ashamed or confused to object to sexual advances from an adult. And if the child dislikes those advances, he may be afraid to voice his complaints. Those who defend pedophilia reply that children are capable, from infancy on, of showing reluctance. As the Paedophile Information Exchange puts it, "If the child seems puzzled and hesitant, rather than relaxed and cheerful, he [the adult] should assume he hasn't [the child's consent]." As for the question of age, many gay theorists contend that the age of consent should be lowered to fourteen. The age of consent is an anomaly in Massachusetts, for instance. A boy may marry at fourteen and a girl at twelve, both may receive contraceptives and girls may seek abortions without parental consent—but no one under sixteen can legally give sexual consent and all forms of sexual activity with someone under sixteen are classified as rape.

Lowering the age of consent to fourteen or even twelve seems consonant with at least one large segment of public opinion. In Sweden fifteen is the age of consent, for gays as well as straights (the age for gay teens used to be eighteen). If we imagine specific cases, some people would not object to sex between a fourteen-year-old and a twelve-year-old, nor to sex between a seventeen-year-old and a fourteen-year-old. In other words, a two- or three-year age difference between the partners seems fairly acceptable to many people. But when the difference is twenty or thirty years or more (a twelve-year-old boy, say, and a fifty-year-old man), then objections arise. And when the younger partner is pre-pubic, then most people object to the alliance, no matter how old the older partner may be.

These objections are related to the third issue, the question of exploitation. Critics of pedophilia contend that children are easily manipulated by adults—through threats, through actual force, through verbal coercion, through money. A kid who wants extra spending money might be lured into sex by an unscrupulous adult—and "ruined." An expert in child psychiatry has told me that pedophilia can later cause the child to view sex with icy detachment. When I pressed him to explain, the psychiatrist admitted he based this opinion on one case alone, a young man who, when he was twelve, had been forced to be his father's sexual partner. Incest, I should think, introduces problems of its own, distinct from the problems of having sex at an early age.

Champions of pedophilia (and many other people) argue that children are already exploited by adults in our society—they are bullied by their parents, kept in financial and legal subjugation, frequently battered. And they have little legal recourse in attempting to escape punitive adults. The child labor laws make it impossible for them to gain financial independence. They can't vote, they can't drink, they can't run away, they can't enter certain movie theaters, they can't refuse to go to school, they can't disobey curfew laws—and they can't determine their own sexual needs and preferences. Pedophiles find it ironic that our society should be so worked up over the issue of sexual exploitation of children and so unconcerned with all other (and possibly more damaging) forms of exploitation. If anything, the pedophiles argue, sex may be the one way in which children can win serious consideration from adults and function with them on an equal plane; if a child is your lover, you will treat him with respect.

Among gays, feminists have been the most vocal in denouncing pedophilia. They equate the sexual exploitation of boys with the sexual abuse of girls and women. The use of the word "rape" to define the "crimes" in the Revere trials caused some feminists to imagine that the youngsters *had* been abused. In my own discussions with women, both straight and gay, I've noticed that the picture they have in mind is usually of a boy, eyes streaming with tears and face buried in a pillow, being buggered by a cruel rapist. I have suggested that the *actual* image may more often be of a skinny fourteen-year-old standing above a balding man and ordering him to suck it (in most of the Revere cases the older men were accused of performing fellatio on teenage boys). But women persist in seeing the boy as a stand-in for a girl and the older man as a counterpart to the heterosexual rapist. When teenage boys (if not pre-pubic boys) are involved, the adult is more often the "passive" partner—and the boy, if he has any street smarts at all, knows that he can bring down the law on the man's head if things do not go exactly as he wants. Moreover, the "boy" of fourteen or fifteen is often physically stronger than his older partner; indeed, tough teenage hustlers frequently beat and rob older johns. I'm not denying that some older men do rape smaller, weaker boys, but the incidence is not nearly as high as many people think.

At this point I should mention one obvious fact—all the statistics show that most rapists and "child molestors" are heterosexual men.

I am not in the business of recommending guidelines for sex with youngsters; I simply haven't gathered enough information about the various issues involved. But one proposal that sounds reasonable to me would be to lower the age of consent to twelve for boys and girls, regardless of whether the sex involved is straight or gay and regardless of the age of the older partner. I do not think prostitution should be legally curbed. Prostitution is a practice that involves the consent of both buyer and bought; it should be the domain of private morality and not of legal regulation. True rape (as opposed to statutory

rape in which no coercion has occurred) should be subject to
the most stringent punishment, no matter what the age or gender
of the two partners.

But still the question of sex with children remains. In order
to gather more information about it, I interviewed a man in
Boston who has a lover of twelve (he met him when the boy
was nine). The man was thirty-six, dressed in faded denims, his
face as innocent and mournful as Petrouchka's. His voice was
breathy and light, his manner anxious and almost humble. He
himself seemed as naïve as a child and had a child's lack of
guile. I didn't want to know his name; in fact I never learned it.

As we sat in a gloomy hotel bar in the long afternoon, we
kept our voices lowered, and we both looked around frequently
before making a remark. This sort of covertness recalled for me
the hushed, guilty tones in which homosexuality itself used to
be discussed in the 1950s. I felt strongly attracted to him. When
he spoke of his lover he opened his hands, palms up, in his
lap, as though it were his strongest case, as for him it must be.
His skin was winter white except under his large, open blue
eyes where there were dark smudges. His hair was flaxen and
long and it curled only at the ends, a last moment rebellion in
something otherwise obedient.

I asked him how he'd met his lover. "At the beach. He was
there with his mother. He came over to me and started talking.
You see, the kids must make all the moves. I wouldn't know
how to initiate a friendship with a child. But children do respond to an interest in them—I think they can *feel* the love and
fascination. So, he started coming over to my house."

"Does his mother know?" I asked.

"She knows as much as she wants to. She knows that he was
cranky before and had trouble in his schoolwork and that now
he's calmer and getting good grades. She *could* know more if
she asked her son, but I don't think she wants to know the
specifics. She knows we're friends; what she sees is positive."

"Did your friend take the sexual initiative with you?"

"Absolutely. I've been into kids since I was twenty-two, and
in every case the kids were the aggressors. But that's a sort of
sadness for me. I happen to be turned on by sissy boys, but like

most pedophiles I'm scared of them. An effeminate boy blows your cover. People suspect something's going on. The kid himself is often too passive to make a move, and the parents are already worried about him and guard him carefully. So I end up with all-American, butchy little straight boys."

"Straight?"

"Yes. Although I can fall in love only with a child, I think I could stay faithful to him as he grew older. But my ex-lovers, all of whom I'm still in touch with, are straight. One is a d.j., another a pre-med student, another a chef's apprentice—and all are straight, though one considers himself bisexual. The strange thing is that a sissy boy is the one who really needs and wants an older man to love him and take care of him, but the culture makes that impossible."

He asked me if I was turned off by what he was telling me. I had the impression that if at any moment I were to shrink back in horror, he would accept that verdict as just. I have mentioned he was humble, for surely it was humility that made him say to me now, "You're objective, you're not involved in this man-boy love movement—does it strike you as warped?"

I told him my own experiences. I had been a sissy boy, constantly hankering after the affection of an adult man (anyone over seventeen—a soldier, say—seemed adult). When I was nine the neighbor of some Texas relatives had kissed me on the lips—but I had assumed the lust was all on my side, and I felt ashamed of my longings. Three years later my camp counselor had drawn me aside one afternoon and shown me his "art" photos of naked men on the beach. Now, of course, I recognize he was studying my responses in order to plan his own, but I kept mine as neutral as possible, for again I assumed that for him the photos were art and that they excited only me. When I was thirteen I did sleep with an adult Indian in Acapulco and at fifteen I had a brief affair with a man in his forties, whose children were older than I. This man I'd seen on a park bench by the lake in Chicago; he was dressed in coat and tie, studying architectural plans just before a meeting. He gave me no signals but, suddenly bold, I sat down beside him, chatted him up, followed him to his car. At last he smiled and said, "What do you want from me?" I was always trying to seduce men but they feared me as jail-bait.

"Yes," said Petrouchka, "A kid has to work very hard to get a man. My current friend wanted to make love right away—'have some fun,' as he said, but I put it off for three weeks."

"What do you two do in bed?" I asked.

"Usually a kid wants to do everything for the first month or so, then it settles down into a pattern. My friend likes to suck my balls while I jerk off. He likes to feel that rhythm of my hand, and he likes to see the come on my stomach and to rub it into my skin. It's very important to talk about sex to kids. You should talk everything out before you do anything. I've asked my former lovers, now that they've grown up, to tell me what I did that was right and what was wrong. My last lover told me that he didn't like getting fucked. 'Why didn't you *tell* me?' I asked. 'Because you liked it so much—I wanted to please you.' That's the problem; kids want to please you."

"Were you," I asked, "very disappointed when your friend went through puberty?"

"Not at all. He's much more independent now. I don't see him so often. I'm moving to Europe—" he broke off and rubbed his forehead. "This stuff scares the shit out of me. I'm not a psychopath. I couldn't take imprisonment. I'd—I'd just die. The guy who got me into this scene has been in prison for ten years. He was given drug therapy and shock therapy. He's out now, but he's a vegetable. I'm thinking of becoming celibate again. For years I was celibate; now I'm going to go back to it. I might work with kids, hang around them, but I've got to give up sex with them."

"Have you had any bad experiences?"

"When I was younger. One or two kids weren't enough for me. I'd get involved with the whole neighborhood. I was living in a small town, a great place for kids. The funny thing was that I was beat up twice by teenagers, each time by guys whom I'd *rejected* when they were kids. Sometimes I think grownups who hate gays are the ones who were turned down. Now I'm older and I've calmed down; one boy is more than enough for me." I was reminded of the passage in *Lolita* that disturbs me the most: Humbert Humbert, now in full possession of Lolita, sits in a parked car with her, masturbating, while he looks at *other* little girls leaving school. His singular love for Lolita I could accept; that he needed other children struck me as perverse. I was willing to let Petrouchka have his one lover, but I rebelled against the army of boys.

I mentioned *Lolita* to him and he said, "Of course most pedophiles are attracted to little girls as well. I am."

"Yes?"

"Sure. Most pedophiles are married men and have children of their own. You could say they are attracted to adult women and children of both sexes—that's very common."

"Are you never attracted to adult men?"

"I've been to bed with even quite old men, but more as a favor to them than as a pleasure of my own. I *feel* the attraction but—I guess I'm screwed up."

"Would you have wished to have lived with other desires?"

"Yes! The energy this takes up! Sometimes I've felt I was losing my mind. I could have accomplished so much more if I hadn't been cursed—or if society had been different."

"Sometimes," I said, "I think gay radicals have made a mistake to take up the cause of pedophiles. There's been so much about pedophilia in the radical press—*Fag Rag*'s special supplement; the *Body Politic*'s 'Men Loving Boys Loving Men.' There's no way this society is ever going to accept man-boy love. And it's not as though there are very many boy-lovers. . . ." I was aware of the cruelty of what I was saying.

"You're right," he conceded. "If it was just a matter of tactics, gays should tar and feather pedophiles. But it isn't logical, it's a matter of humanity, of sympathy." Admirable and heartfelt as his statement was, it must have struck him as too forceful, not humble enough, since now he asked, "Why do you think people hate pedophilia so much? Mind you, I hate *violence* to kids. But real love for kids, why is that so bad?"

No answer, or rather too many, came to mind. A book by Philippe Ariès, *Centuries of Childhood*, had suggested that childhood as a distinct, innocent stage in life had been invented in the early eighteenth century by the emerging bourgeoisie. Before that children had worn adult clothes, played adult games, attended school with adults, tossed off ribald jokes, preached sermons and gained fame as Greek and Hebrew scholars. The invention of childhood paralleled the creation of suburbs. No longer did the rich man and his family live in the city, rubbing shoulders with the poor. Resentment between the classes had made proximity dangerous. Now the father went off to town to do battle, but he kept his family in a sheltered retreat. The more unscrupulous the father became in his business dealings, the more he attributed innocence to his children and virtue to his wife. Could it be that the more we sense our adult lives, even our adult sex lives, are "depraved," the more we insist on the angelic purity of our children? Does the pedophile threaten this dichotomy, introduce our sinfulness even into the secret garden, force us to recognize how melancholy and "fallen" our lives have turned out to be?

Or is the hatred of pedophilia linked to the incest taboo? In canvassing my friends about pedophilia, I find they all mention incest early on, though no one seems to know how to develop the idea. One mentions that the function of the incest taboo is to keep the family relationships free of sex, since sex might lead to favoritism and jealousy and violence—a threat to domestic tranquillity. But if the taboo is so strong it must be repressing an urge equally potent. The pedophile, in other words, makes manifest the latent desire to have sex with one's own children, and he must be punished as relentlessly as we extirpate forbidden desires from within ourselves.

When I was a child and wanted an older lover, he was envisioned as a savior, someone who would free me from the tyranny of my parents, who would *value* me. I mentioned this to Petrouchka and he said, "Sure, when a kid's in bed with you, he knows he's your peer. You need him, he can make you happy, and he exults in his power." This triumphant child I saw as so different from the ordinary American kid, described so well by the African narrator in John Updike's *The Coup*: "Frank Jr. was a furtive, semi-obese child of fourteen . . . whose complexion showed the ravages of sleeping alone, night after night, in an overheated room with teddy bears, felt pennants, and dotted Swiss curtains. The smile he grudged me displayed a barbarous, no doubt painful tooth-armor of silver and steel. His limp dank handshake savored of masturbatory rites. . . . I thought, Here is the inheritor of capitalism and imperialism, of the Crusades and the spinning jenny."

By this point Petrouchka and I had left the bar and walked to his car. We stood on a windy street and shook hands farewell. I said to him, "People say that each of us thinks of himself forever as being one particular age. I don't think it has anything to do with 'maturity.' It's just a matter of an image you have of yourself. What age do you think of yourself as being?"

"Nine," he said. He smiled. "Not always. I can be an older man, attracted to older men. To you, for instance."

"I'm very attracted to you as well," I said. "While you were talking, I kept wishing I'd met you when I was nine and you the age you are now."

He laughed for the first time. "I had the same thought, the very same."

The political tone in Washington would eschew all discussion of man-boy love as politically disastrous. Gay leaders in the capital would say that such a discussion plays right into the hands of homophobes. After all, Anita Bryant's organization was named "Save Our Children," and fear of child molestors motivates much of the hatred of homosexuals across the nation. In particular, the myth that openly gay teachers might molest their students or infect them with an unsavory respect for the gay lifestyle has been used successfully as an argument for rescinding pro-gay ordinances in several cities. Since in fact gays are no more likely than straights to molest children, why should we have to espouse or even discuss such an unpopular cause?

The literature put out by the Gay Rights National Lobby in Washington captures the sensible, practical tone of political gays in the capital. A pamphlet called "A Look At Gay Teachers" shows on the cover a lesbian instructor (mid-thirties, white, attractive, her hair neither short nor long) pushing a child on a swing (the child is white, about five or six and not identifiable as either a boy or girl). The copy is in the form of questions and answers. To the question, "But won't Gay teachers molest the children?" the answer is given: "No. Almost all authorities, including the American Psychiatric Association and the National Institute of Mental Health, agree that Gay people are no more likely to molest children than are heterosexuals. Of course, any teacher who attempts to molest a child should be removed immediately. . . ."

To the question, "Won't the presence of Gay teachers cause the students to be Gay?" the pamphlet's answer is: "Sexuality is not like a political ideology that can be taught. The leading experts in the country, such as Dr. John Money of Johns Hopkins, agree that sexual orientation is determined by age 3 or 4 and will not change significantly thereafter." When a gay teacher is asked if he would advocate his homosexuality in class, he responds: " 'No. It's totally inappropriate to advocate personal matters in the classroom, whether they be religion, political philosophy, or sexuality. . . . We don't preach homosexuality to our students—we teach the subject matter of our classes—English, history, math or whatever. . . . Gay teachers aren't much different from any others.' "

Politics is the art of the possible, and Washington's gay leaders, many of them experienced in local and federal government, can gauge with professional acumen what will go down and what won't. Nor are their goals and slogans merely expedient hypocrisies; they would insist that most gay people *are* ordinary folks whose views and aspirations should not be misrepresented and jeopardized by the weird beliefs of a few gay eccentrics.

I interviewed Steve Endean, our first gay lobbyist in Washington, a well-spoken young man from Minneapolis who was active in the unsuccessful campaign to preserve the gay rights ordinance in St. Paul. He assumed his Washington position in the fall of 1978. "The movement," he said, "needs patterned, mature, planned programs—not just rage and marches. That energy is good—but it needs to be harnessed. Otherwise, when the anger subsides, it turns out nothing has been accomplished."

I asked him to describe his goals. "I work to defeat bills aimed against gays and lesbians. There's a new lobby called

'Christian Voice' that claims 100,000 members and that is strongly anti-gay. They are currently sending out five million letters to Christians, urging them to write Congresspeople on issues such as gay rights. In their first mailing they say, 'I am rushing you this urgent letter because the children in your neighborhood are in danger' and 'How would you feel if tomorrow your child . . . was taught by a practicing homosexual?' "

As to the positive programs he was launching, Endean told me, "A federal gay civil rights bill is obviously our long-range goal. I view this as an extended campaign. Within the next ten years I think we'll get *serious* consideration for it. The way we've already been able to build support simply amazes other public interest groups. Right now we have about fifty co-sponsors of the bill in Congress. Most of them are urban, progressive and Democratic (only three are Republicans). Seven of the freshmen are co-sponsors—which indicates that acceptance of homosexuality is a generational matter and that time is on our side. Beyond getting co-sponsors, I'm briefing Congresspeople and softening up conservatives (by appealing to the right to privacy for gays and everyone else) and I'm trying to line up liberals across the board. We're also linking up with other public interest groups—Americans for Democratic Action, the American Civil Liberties Union, a group of progressive nuns and so on; all these groups have pro-gay positions but they could be more active."

What about appealing to the gay community itself? "Well, that's our biggest job. We need to build a constituent network so we know how to reach gay rights supporters across the country. We need to know the community, religious and political leaders who support us. We need to be able to alert gays and their friends everywhere in order to tell them when to write their representatives in Congress. We need documentation of cases of discrimination against gay people in employment and housing. That's essential for demonstrating the *need* for legislation. In Minnesota we did not build up a constituent network—and that's why we weren't able to get a pro-gay bill passed in the state legislature. You have to remember that the fundamentalists who are opposed to us have a great deal of fervor—and an excellent church network. Generally speaking, liberal causes depend on truth and justice to see them through, whereas conservatives rely on letters from voters—and those letters are what count in the end."

What are Endean's immediate objectives? "We want a gay rights plank to be discussed at the 1980 Democratic convention. We have a real shot at getting the plank adopted, but in any event a debate would be aired on prime-time TV and the plank would be put on the agenda of future business for all progressives. We already have fifty delegates pledged to support us; most of them are women and feminists. On the state level we're working for civil rights legislation and the repeal of sodomy laws. We are *not* trying to legalize gay marriage or gay adoption—those are issues that would alienate most of our straight friends and arouse a storm of bad publicity. We're also compiling a list of Congresspeople and other elected officials who've supported gay rights—and been reelected. We want to show officials that favoring gay rights is not a kiss of death at the polls. We need to show people in power that gays really do suffer from discrimination and are an oppressed minority; Ted Kennedy, for instance, thinks of gays as rich and oppressive, because that's the kind of gays he happens to know. I'm sure he'll come around; he's progressive in all other areas. We've begun to make some inroads with union leaders as well."

I felt confidence in Steve Endean. He's relaxed, well-informed, friendly, practical. Though he's mastering the complexities of Washington politics, he does not seem overly impressed with the allure of power. He's a reasonable man with a solid liberal background in gay politics, a Midwestern, middle-class guy, personable but not gorgeous, outspoken but not rude, dedicated but not humorless.*

I asked Endean what he thought of the man-boy love ques-

---

* *Regular membership in the Gay Rights National Lobby costs $20.00; organizational membership is $25.00. Mail contributions to Gay Rights National Lobby, 1606 17th Street, N.W., Washington, D.C. 20009.*

tion. He smiled. "That's the politics of self-indulgence. Our movement cannot survive the boy-love issue. It's not a question of who's right, it's a matter of political naïveté. New York and San Francisco seem to have a monopoly on craziness and naïveté. Whereas D.C. activists, by pursuing a more moderate line, have been wonderfully successful. They have real clout in this city. Gay liberation needs middle-class gays. It's important to make gay liberation a chic cause among young gay professionals—they're the ones with the money and the energy and the influence. Let me give you an example. In Minneapolis there was a group of young professional gay guys who got together to play volleyball. There are about fifty of them and they call themselves the 'Little Sisters of Lasalle.' Now most gay lib types would trash them for their sexist name and their closetiness, but they got interested in gay rights and backed it with a lot of money. We need more of that."

I asked him what he thought of Washington. "I haven't seen that much of it. I work anywhere from sixty to 120 hours a week. But it seems to be a good city for gays. Of course there are problems here. The papers, the *Post* and the *Star*, need to report gay issues more fairly. The bars here card blacks—which is horrible. There is discrimination; when I was applying for an apartment, I was turned down three times after I mentioned I worked for the Gay Rights National Lobby. The percentage of gays on Capitol Hill is very high—probably a quarter of all the employees there. There's no organized network among them. Most of them are afraid for their jobs. As you know, congressional staffs are not protected by any of the usual civil rights laws. An openly gay staff person is seen as a liability. Gays on the Hill cannot advocate gay rights, but they could give information to gay groups. There's one senatorial assistant on the Hill who's out—but the other gays won't speak to him. There's one person in Congress who may come out sometime in the next three years. But the paranoia up there is incredible."

I asked Endean if he feared a gay backlash from the New Right. "We've got to keep after them, but I think things are in our favor. The New Right hasn't been effective in mustering support for its social issues except in its campaign against abortion. And it can't seem to get its candidates elected. Anita's candidate for governor in Florida, for instance, came in fourth. If we can just hold on, things have got to improve."

They've already improved in the country's capital. Life around the gay ghetto, centered on Dupont Circle, is dulcet. On a spring evening the streets are crowded with strollers and cruisers. Washington is a city of readers, and the bookstores are always busy. One has a restaurant in the back, and you can sit outside under an umbrella, sip wine, snack on paté and watch the joggers huffing past or women in saris ambling by with their children. Gay eyes are quick and knowing around Dupont Circle; three hairdressers lounging in the doorway of their shop take you in as you walk past. At the Lambda Rising gay bookstore women and men are browsing downstairs, while upstairs a gay poet is giving a reading. The sidewalks are clean, the buildings are low, the shops are fashionable, the overheard bits of conversation are up-to-date (the latest movie, the latest cheese store, the latest play at Kennedy Center).

One night I attended a meeting of a gay discussion group. Tonight's meeting was being held in what most Americans would consider a modest house but that in crowded Washington, where real estate is higher than anywhere else in the country, counts as luxury quarters—a two-story, two-bedroom family home. About fifteen men sat on the floor in the living room and discussed the new gay fiction. I met a druggist, a policy planner for a government agency, a medical researcher, a fundraiser for educational organizations. Most of the men in the room were in their thirties or forties. All were white and the average income, I suspect, was about $35,000. Most of them attended Ivy League schools, are at home anywhere in the world, and speak several languages.

The attitude of those straight and gay bureaucrats I've met toward the American people alternates between contempt (the poor dumb bunnies) and solemnity (we are, after all, public servants). The official functions of the city are subject to close national scrutiny, whereas the private lives of its citizens are exempt from all comment—unless one of those lives breaks into notoriety. This double standard promotes a strangely split urban personality: the same people who are cavalier, urbane, knowing at home become correct, folksy and obtuse on the Hill. And no matter how sophisticated one may be among intimates, on the job one is "hard-hitting," "clean-cut," a "straight-shooter." Whereas in England the ruling class still affects a giddiness, an air of amateur bumbling and confusion, in the United States the élite poses for its portrait as a banker from Akron.

Someone from New York visiting Washington feels like a poor relation. Indeed, Washington has become the financial center of the country and, after its years as a sleepy Southern town, has at last become the imperial city its founders envisioned. Take the subway (called the Metro). Escalators longer than those anywhere but in Moscow carry passengers into the station where computers swallow coins and return magnetized fare cards that, when inserted in turnstiles, give admittance to a vast, corbeled vault. The long, high, majestic ceiling seems more suited to a chancery or church—and in fact choirs have tested the acoustics and found them excellent. Blocks lining the platform light up as the train approaches—the only warning, since the wheels are silent. The cars themselves are clean, air-conditioned, well-lit and monitored by closed-circuit televisions with which a guard can spot mischief.

The village of Alexandria, Virginia, is typical of the capital's posh outlying suburbs. Its eighteenth-century federal houses are clustered close together, and most of them have been restored. The poor families who lived there till recently have been bought out or dispossessed and dispersed into decaying and more remote suburbs, where they have less chance to see one another, pool their grievances—or to protest. An old factory near the river has been converted into a dovecote of boutiques. Restaurants retain the homely features of the past and charge the prices of the future. One residential block is cobbled with the original stones. New buildings, ponderously large, have been decked out in red brick and white trim, an obeisance to the materials if not the pleasing proportions of Georgian architecture. So many gays cruise in the bushes outside town that local bird-watchers have complained—for ecological, not moral reasons.

In Washington itself the city's dual personality (official respectability and private self-indulgence) is evident everywhere. Tourists—those average citizens who strike the cosmopolitan Washingtonians as faintly oafish—file through the many museums and respectfully touch the icons, the Washington and Lincoln and Jefferson monuments, which in the winter appear as yellowish in the snow as teeth wreathed in shaving cream, but in the summer look as white as salt-licks, nourishing to cows but not to sleek carnivores. For the bovine these lawns are barbered, these streets are scoured, these facades are floodlit. The locals, however, pay no attention. They are too busy shopping in the cute little places that have been excavated out of the old barge house beside the Georgetown canal or fleeing in limousines to their horse farms in rural Virginia or catching up on reports of Asian starvation in the cool study of the simple Victorian house just bought for $400,000. When the steamy summer descends they head north for Nantucket or Maine and leave the city to the docile herbivores they rule.

I had dinner with a designer in Georgetown at the Aux Fruits de Mer, a noisy, crowded French restaurant, the former site of a gay bar. My companion said, "I avoid the GSers. You know, the civil servants. They're all given a Government Service rating. They're bland, unimaginative—don't rock the boat is their motto. You know, the sort of guy who collects stamps or builds model planes. There's a very clear pecking order. You can look up your new lover's GS rating—it's a matter of public record—and find out his salary. People here are not like New Yorkers; they don't want to be superstars. In fact, they have some contempt for stars and only grudging respect for big media personalities. Here what people want is not celebrity but power. What they *call* power, though it only amounts to influence. You're powerful in Washington if you can call up the FBI and have them rush some files over to you, or if you can get some senator's office to treat you with respect. Access to information. Matters of protocol. Deference at parties."

Georgetown, like all eighteenth-century towns, is congested, concentrated—a snooper's delight. Its houses are tiny; I overheard a Southern woman tourist telling her companion, "You

wouldn't catch *me* living in one of these iddy-biddy doll houses!"
On warm nights gays hang out on the corner of Thirtieth and
Dunbarton, a few doors down from Kissinger's old house and a
block from Harriman's, where they cruise straight Secret Service
men attending some great personage who might be at home or
visiting a party. I went to such a party. The host was a lobbyist;
he was busy defeating legislation that might cause the cost of his
product to rise. To perform this chore he was spending large
sums from the company's war chest. Tonight he was entertaining the wife of a White House big-wig.

The dual nature of Washington was very much in evidence.
The host, a campy thing who could metamorphose in a second
into a clean-cut young man, drew me aside and said, "I'm *dying*
to marry a rich dyke—you know any?" Someone who had been
elected "gay bartender of the year" was serving—but all the
couples dancing in the double drawing-room were men with
women. Someone estimated that all the men were gay as were
half the women, but to the eyes of the wife of the Great Man
the gathering must have appeared conventional enough.

From Georgetown I was whirred off to Lost and Found,
the gay disco of the moment, a big place with several bars, including one in a Western motif, and a room where Sunday
brunch is served—all set down in a deserted warehouse district.
Everyone seemed happy, civilized, WASP. The prevailing look
in Washington is preppie: Lacoste shirts, ironed jeans, loafers.
For more elegant gatherings clothes can be bought at Britches
on Wisconsin in Georgetown: the slender watches from Switzer-
land, the tweed jackets, the cashmere sweaters. If every woman
in Georgetown tries to look as though she's just stepped out of
a Breck ad, the men attempt to appear as though they've just
come from the Hunt Cup in Baltimore. "I love Washington,"
a friend of mine who recently moved there from Philadelphia
told me. "In Philadelphia most guys in a gay bar are high-school
graduates if that (except for a tiny élite of gay aristocrats); here
they all have college degrees. They're young, they're well paid.
Of course it's a company town and everyone has to be minimally
discreet, but you must also remember that Washington has the
biggest gay population, percentage-wise, in the country. Whites

are only 26 percent of the population in D.C. right now, but by the end of the century we'll be 50 percent. The prices of houses are doubling every other year. The blacks are being forced out." He seemed happy with this development.

I spent a morning with an important black gay activist. He was a magnetic, handsome, big man, a former football player with a warm, thoughtful manner. The more I talked to him, the more I realized he stood where many diverse paths transect the issue of homosexuality. His voice was low, modulated, educated; just beneath his accent I detected an island lilt, the heritage of his father, a doctor from the West Indies. I asked him to tell me his background.

"I was reared in the South—first in South Carolina, then in Virginia. I was active in football and wrestling. After high school I joined the Marine Corps, where I had a white lover, an Episcopalian chaplain. I then attended a black college in Virginia, where again I went out for contact sports. While in college I fell in love with a man, whom I've been with for the last sixteen years. I've *also* been married for twelve years. I didn't tell my wife at first that I was gay. My lover also married, and he has a child. I had no political consciousness, but when I moved to Minneapolis I met a gay with a high consciousness— and I came out. My first political involvement was with Integrity, the gay Episcopalian organization. Now I'm an agnostic; I have problems with Christianity, which I see as a white man's institution and oppressive to both blacks and gays."

How does his life stand now? "It's very complicated," he said, laughing. "I have a new lover, and he's also married. My former lover has now taken up with my wife and become *her* lover. My wife has evolved her own consciousness; she no longer wants to be called my 'wife' but my 'lover,' and that seems right." As we were talking, the phone rang; it was a call from his new lover's wife. They had an intimate, friendly, joking conversation about how to get the lover out of his passing bad mood.

I felt out of my depth. I asked him how he described himself. "As a gay activist living a bisexual lifestyle with a strong preference for men. That's if you must have a label; I'd prefer to be seen as a sexual being, period. I feel I have a very rich life, but sometimes I get overextended."

And how had his situation found expression in his politics? "Many ways. I'm active in GAMMA, the Gay Married Men's Association. We have a hundred members here in D.C. My wife is a member of another group, GAMMA Wives. I have three children, so I'm a member of the National Network of Gay Fathers. People talk a lot about lesbian mothers but never about gay fathers. We have our own concerns. I'm a masculist, dedicated to men's rights. No alimony. Right to child custody for men. Freedom from role stereotypes. I believe that my brand of masculism is fully compatible with the women's movement. I am not anti-straight nor am I anti-white. Eventually there must be a liberation of straights in this country. I used to think bisexuality was a cop-out, but now I see I have double needs. I need diversity. I thrive on it."

How does he feel about living in Washington? "This is a city that forces the issues of blackness and gayness to come together. In some cities I can be black but not gay (that's true down South). In others, such as San Francisco, I can be gay, but when I lived there I got out of touch with my blackness. In D.C. both whites and blacks must deal with race, and whether straight or gay they must deal with sexual orientation. There are just too many blacks and too many gays to ignore either issue."

How does the heterosexual black community view gays? "Many blacks have trouble recognizing it's a legitimate civil rights issue. Some straight blacks think that gay blacks are reprehensible for not having children; it's a sort of genocide threat. Other straight blacks think that the issue of homosexuality is taking energy and attention away from the drive for black equality. The United States is both a sexist and racist society, and that has affected blacks as well. But blacks, at least, are more sensitive to civil rights issues than are most whites, and that should lead eventually to a coalition of blacks and gays. It's happened right here in Washington; our black mayor, Marion Berry, was put in office by just such a coalition. In Philadelphia a black and gay coalition is also forming."

And how do white gays see blacks and black gays in particular? "For a long time I thought gays were less racist. But now I see I was wrong. Both issues must be dealt with simultaneously—homosexuality and race. That's why we've organized the National Coalitions of Black Gays. When I worked for a social service agency I was told it was inappropriate to discuss lesbian and gay issues at work. At black political meetings I was told I was out of order in talking about gays. At gay meetings, I was told it was out of order to discuss blacks. I need to have a place where I'll never be out of order."

What actions are black gays considering? "Well, we've had a White House conference on Third World gays—that was held on June 5, 1979—only the second time a gay delegation has been officially received there. We're planning a National Third World Lesbian-Gay Conference, which will include Native Americans, Hispanics, blacks and Asians. Third World gay men must deal with their double oppression; Third World lesbians have a triple oppression to work out."

I asked him to describe black gay life in Washington. "There are three groups. One is élitist, cliquish, a closed circle in which status is important; you can enter it only if you have the right contacts. These gays have good jobs, they went to good schools, they belonged to the right fraternities, they own their own houses and have expensive cars. At the opposite end of the spectrum are the street people, those who circulate among the bars, baths, the porno movie theaters, the tea rooms. Many of them are unemployed and many are quite campy. Then a third group floats between the hierarchy and the street. They go to ritzy parties *and* hang out on the block. They have the highest political consciousness."

Have members of the local chapter of National Coalitions of Black Gays come out? "No. Some people criticize us for being so closeted. But you must look at the profile of visible gays. What do they have in common that allows them to come out? Most are living away from home and have no family and straight peer pressure. And most of them have achieved their professional goals and are comfortable economically. Now in D.C. most black gays were born and brought up here, and most are still struggling to achieve job security. The unemployment rate among blacks in D.C. is very high. In our group, most of the members are not willing to be identified. Those who are out and active are from some other city and financially comfortable."

I asked him if he had come out with his family. "My father is dead now. But when I was twenty-one I went to him and told him I was a bisexual and very upset about it. He said, 'Relax. So am I.' I was astounded. 'Of course,' he said, 'didn't you realize that my best friend, who's always lived with us, is also my lover?' I found out that my mother was also comfortable with my dad's lover. My four brothers and five sisters have all been supportive of my gayness. My father was the best role model I could have had. He may have been stern, but he advocated taking a stand for what you believe in. He was a doctor. After I came out to him, he gave me information about gay health matters and information about gay sex. He was a great man."

The leader of gay politics in Washington is Dr. Franklin Kameny. He lives in a pleasant rented house rather far from the center of the city. Although the garden is well tended and the house from outside seems the usual tidy red brick home, inside everything is chaos. In his office newspapers, legal books, letters and brochures are piled high on every available surface; some of them are yellowing with age. When he speaks, one has the impression that he is not aware of his sympathetic listener but that he is addressing a hostile Congress or the Supreme Court or the American people. His speech is as rapid-fire as Walter Winchell's used to be. When he pauses, he sings his *uhh* on a piercing high note, as do the Cantonese. His eyes graze one's own only at the ends of phrases. His diction is formal, even elocutionary; he punches key words and trills his *r*'s. All in all, he seems extremely shy, a retiring astronomer whom history forced into leadership. Indeed, he tells me that when he had to give a three-minute speech in high school he spent two weeks of paralyzing fear in anticipation—but that now and for the last fifteen years he has given at least 150 lectures a year. He has a slight stoop, gray eyebrows, no sense of fashion—and he projects more feistiness than I've seen in any other gay leader.

"Washington is the most comfortable city in the world for gays," he shouts. "This is utopia. The police are no problem, we have a strong gay rights law, the local candidates come to us begging for endorsement; this year our gay pride day is a *week*, not a day, and it's a street fair, not a march, and we're celebrating what we *have* rather than agitating for denied rights. '*Keep Gay Rights*' is our slogan. In May 1972 the school board voted not to discriminate against hiring openly gay teachers. In November 1973 the Human Rights bill was passed. And in March 1979 the city council passed a bill to exclude all future referenda on gay rights. Gay rights here are secure forever.

"My central focus has been federal government policies toward gays. I was fired in December 1957 by the government for being gay (I was a Ph.D. astronomer). Well, I don't like to lose my battles. I was the first to fight such dismissals. In 1961 I carried my case to the Supreme Court, which rejected it. That fall I founded the Washington Mattachine Society, one of the five or six gay organizations in the country at the time. In 1965 I led a demonstration—four years before Stonewall. I've learned to work with cunning and cajolery, hounding and harassment, patience and persistence. It was an eighteen-year crusade, but in July 1975 the Civil Services Commission policy was changed at last. Gays can no longer be dismissed from government jobs for their sexual orientation. I'm not talking of Congressional jobs of course—they're exempt from all civil rights laws. The Department of Defense has capitulated to me. Three of the last four presidents of the Gay Activist Alliance in Washington have worked for the government. The current G.A.A. president works in the Library of Congress. My new targets are the CIA and the FBI—they're holdouts, as is the State Department."

Dr. Kameny is currently representing John Calzada, a file clerk who was fired from the FBI with a note that read: "This action is being taken in view of your homosexuality which in turn has led to your commission of homosexual acts in the State of Virginia where such acts are considered a felony. . . ." Calzada lives in Arlington. The dismissal immediately touched off reactions within the agency and without. Fellow employees have called Calzada to pledge their moral support. Although the FBI has eased some of its up-tight policies since the death of J. Edgar Hoover, it still reportedly frowns on interracial marriages and couples who live together without marrying. Anti-gay policies are only part of the agency's general failure to keep up with the times. Outside the agency, Representative Ted Weiss, a Democrat from New York, called the dismissal "an outrageous example of discrimination and bigotry," and a spokesman for the Justice Department (which holds jurisdiction over the FBI) declared that there is "no rule or policy that disqualifies a person from the Department because he or she may be homosexual."

I asked Dr. Kameny if he is a lawyer. "No," he said. "I am, however, *the* authority on the federal government and gays and I've often served as counsel.

"I'm from New York originally, though I've lived in Washington for twenty-three years. My father was an electrical engineer. My mother is eighty-three and active in the Parents of Gays organization. When I was in my middle teens I gained complete faith in the validity of my own intellectual processes. I decided that if the world and I differ, I'm right and it's wrong and I have no intention of backing down. Sears Roebuck and I have the same phone number except for one digit; when I kept receiving their calls, I wrote them and suggested they change *their* number. That's the sort of person I am. I went to Harvard where I became active in black civil rights and the American Civil Liberties Union. I came out in 1954 when I was twenty-nine. I experienced no guilt—I knew I was right. I regretted I'd wasted fifteen good years, but made up for lost time with *zest* and *vigor!* In 1971 I ran for Congress as an openly gay representative. I was one of six candidates. There were three major candidates and three minor ones—I received more votes than the other two minor candidates. Of course I had no expectation of winning; I just wanted to politicize the gay community. Running the campaign was the most arduous experience of my life, and I will run again only if I have a reasonable chance of winning. I support myself by rearranging my bills. I lecture, I do paralegal work and I receive occasional contributions and donations. The last twenty years have been fulfilling and more exciting than all my expectations—but I'm impoverished. I've paid my dues. The world owes me more than I owe it. I've put in for a new job in Washington."

I asked him what he thought of gay politics in New York and San Francisco. "I watch those cities with horrified fascination as more and more atrocities build up. New Yorkers know how to attack other gays, but they have no feel for the realities of politics, they resist unity. All ideology and rhetoric and no practical sense. In New York and San Francisco gays *exult* in divisiveness."

And how is Washington different? "We understand that politics is a matter of power economics. The currency is *votes* and you must prove you have a constituency. You build up a credit line—a large number of registered gay voters, gays as poll-watchers at every precinct. If politicians know that gays are turning out, then gays keep their credit line open. If you can show you have a machine, you get what you want. Then, at crucial moments, you call in your credits, but *wisely*. We never show divisiveness in public. We get together and work out our differences privately and in advance. When we speak to the mayor we do so with one voice. If a politician hears two conflicting signals from the gay community, he ignores the community."

What is his program for gays across the country? "I have a four-point program. First, get gay rights ordinances and laws passed everywhere; they let gay people function openly. Second, stage attacks on the sodomy laws. Recently twenty-two states have repealed their sodomy laws (in Massachusetts and D.C. they are about to be reconsidered). The old sodomy laws are not directed against the actors—straight or gay—but against the acts. They forbid all oral sex or anal sex, whether the partners are straight or gay, married or single. Twenty-one states still have such laws. Recently there's been a new trend—passing sodomy laws directed against gays alone. Seven states have passed such laws in the last few years. They must be repealed. Third, gay candidates must run for office—but only *good* candidates. It's useless to run gay incompetents. And finally, there must be increased education of the public through positive media portrayals of gays and through religious organizations and schools. I think gay liberation must be kept as a single cause. It may overlap with feminism, but the two causes are not congruent. An *ad hoc* coalition, however, is entirely in order. Like feminists, I bitterly resent sexism, but in its guise as homophobia, and I will always battle homophobia conceptually, ideologically and functionally."

Once the official interview was concluded, Dr. Kameny became milder. He called me a cab and stood outside with me as I waited for it. He pointed out his low license plate number. "There are only 1,250 low numbers in the District. Three gay leaders have them—it's silly but important symbolically. Symbols count."

By overdramatizing the differences between Boston and Washington (there are of course radicals and moderates in both cities), I have created an antithesis—but may it not be a false one?

Undoubtedly the two groups have different pictures of how they'd like the future to be. The radicals would call for a thorough change of national (and international) institutions and ways of living. The moderates would want gays to swim into the mainstream. Whereas the radical goal is to transform society, the moderate goal is to enter it.

Are these goals incompatible? Yes, of course.

But at this moment, at least, I see no reason the two groups can't work together. The freedoms the moderates want can all be defined negatively—an *absence* of bias against gays, an *end* to job and housing discrimination, a *discarding* of the negative stereotypes of the past. These aims cannot in themselves be unacceptable to radicals, save to those Marxists who believe that ameliorations and halfway measures can only dampen revolutionary fires (better naked suffering than masked discontent).

Temperamentally, of course, the two factions are at odds. Radicals would rather clarify a theory than win an election. Nor will radicals put their fiery dishes on the back burner as we wait for simpler fare to be prepared. Tactically, radicals favor anger and confrontation, and will not conceal differences they may have with other gays; moderates, by contrast, favor persuasion, politicking and a united front.

Nevertheless, I think a hierarchy of goals might be established. The negative freedoms of the moderates seem worth winning, no matter what further transformations of society one might want to engineer. A basic platform of civil rights should command the allegiance of all gays and their progressive friends. But perhaps, as usual, I'm being overly optimistic.

EPILOGUE

Self-Criticism

At the end of gay consciousness-raising sessions (and Maoist meetings), each participant briefly criticizes himself or herself, and so shall I at the end of my book.

The most maddening fault that runs through these pages, I feel, is a peculiar alternation between socialism and snobbism. The chapters are presented roughly in the order I wrote them, and in the course of the writing I detect a lessening of the snobbism and a surer (or at least tighter) grasp on socialism. Writing the book radicalized me. But there seems to be no way to reconcile these two warring tendencies. Logically they shouldn't appear in the same book—or person. But both, I fear, are part of my character, and in relaying my impressions I exposed this disturbing contradiction.

Snobbism, of course, was partly a prophylactic against the unfamiliar. I had lived in New York since 1962 with the exception of ten months in Rome and less time than that in San Francisco. I have never owned a car or a television and before this trip I'd never seen a shopping mall. My tastes and values were far from those of most Americans, even most gay Americans. Many of the places I wrote about I was visiting for the first time and in several cities I knew no one in advance. Though traveling sounds glamorous, I found it arduous and alienating. Listening to other people and seldom talking is frustrating for someone as opinionated as I am. Eating alone and sleeping in rented rooms can be depressing. And I was often insecure, especially about my looks. As I approached my fortieth birthday I feared I'd lost the physical attractiveness that might have made me more welcome even five years earlier in Gay America—which must count as a sorry comment on the prejudice against age I've absorbed and that other gays radiate. Because of the fear of the new and the disruption of my sense of confidence, I sometimes responded with a disdain I now regret.

My brand of socialism I should explain. It is perhaps more a sympathy than a program. In analyzing the behavior of individuals or groups, I'm more inclined to seek sociological rather than psychological causes. Of those causes, economic ones seem to me the most powerful, though they seldom come unclothed by ideology. I am by nature more inclined to side with the poor and with the Third World, though paradoxically I'm more at home with rich whites. I do not defend the Soviet Union, China or any other existing "communist" regime that denies civil liberties and eschews democracy. Nor do I subscribe to the "scientific" pretensions of Marxism, to its belief in the inevitable triumph of the proletariat nor to its analysis of all conflicts as rooted in class. Like the Leftist I interviewed in Boston, I distrust a revolutionary élite that presumes to speak for the rest of us and, like him, I'm interested in witnessing an end to racism, sexism, the exploitation of workers and other social inequities so long as the means for eradicating them are consonant with nonviolence and democracy.

In short, no socialist model worthy of imitation exists. The Left has been betrayed by Marxist theory and totalitarian practice, much as psychiatry has been subverted by Freudian orthodoxy and totalitarian practice. The decent society one might long for would be as respectful of individual difference as it would be solicitous of collective welfare. Such a vision is still in the process of being formed, or being imagined, and feminism and gay liberation, which demand a rethinking of private life and its connections to politics, can be one locus in which that transformation occurs. Gay life—rich, messy, promiscuous—will never please an ideologue; it's too untidy, too linked to the unpredictable vagaries of anarchic desire. But what gay life does offer is some *give* in the social machine. If Americans, those least political of all social animals, must doubt the sexual given, then that skepticism may shift to other aspects of our national life. In the most radical gay cities, New York, Boston and San Francisco, such a shift is already beginning to take place.

I criticize my book for concentrating on gay men in big cities and for ignoring lesbians as well as small-town or rural life. The exclusion of lesbians was largely practical. Lesbians are so nearly invisible in America (one way in which they are oppressed) that they would have been difficult for me to find had I not ventured into lesbian bars, where men seldom have entrée. Political lesbians, moreover, might have resisted and resented with some justice my attempts to speak for them. The two worlds do come together, however, in smaller towns, but those I did not visit. I never had either the time or the money to penetrate the necessarily more closeted gay life of small towns. Working on a limited budget and even borrowing money to complete my travels, I found it simpler to head for big cities during those short periods I could spare from my duties as a teacher. Understandable as my strategy might be, it has given a strangely lopsided view of American gay life.

The book has many other faults. It scants older men and married men, it says nothing of gay Asians or gay Jews, it largely overlooks gay working-class men. Worse, it gives highly colored but doubtlessly distorted views of the cities I write about. My only justification is to point to my method: these are travel notes in which I recorded my impressions.

The value of the book, I hope, lies in its bearing news from one quarter to another (from Seattle to New York, say) or from one group to another (from Atlanta blacks to Atlanta whites, for instance). I hope it will enable gays and straights to imagine other lives. That was what writing the book did for me.